It's Time to Clean Your Windows

Designing GUIs That Work

It's Time to Clean Your Windows

Designing GUIs That Work

Wilbert O. Galitz

A Wiley–QED Publication

John Wiley & Sons, Inc.

New York • Chichester • Brisbane • Toronto • Singapore

ISBN 0 471-60668-5

For my grandchildren, Mitchell, Barry, and Deirdra Galitz, Malta, Illinois, and Lauren and Scott Roepel, Owasso, Oklahoma. They cannot imagine a world without computers.

Contents

Foreword

In information systems, today's only certainty is that there will be at some point yet another paradigm shift, technological, organizational, or functional. Client/server computing, open systems, disbursed databases, new application development tools, and workstations are among the new wave of innovation. Hardly has the dust settled than another paradigm shift becomes the driving force that is going to solve all our information problems. It reminds me of the government with its ever-growing need for new taxes that will be used to solve the same problems we were supposed to have solved with the last tax increase. The more things change, the less they change, as someone once said. I guess we are good at learning new technologies but not very good at applying them effectively.

Management is looking for new technologies to improve the bottom line. End-users are demanding the latest workstation and GUI solutions to sometimes poorly defined problems. How you deal with this is important to your career because you are to blame when the system doesn't give the users what they "asked for," or the screens are not "user friendly." Let's face it—it's your fault if you don't know how to design a screen properly.

Just because you are a good systems designer or programmer, it doesn't mean you know anything about designing effective, readable GUI screens. User friendly means much more than cute icons around the border of a screen. It means making the system easy to use, and because the screen is the user interface, a properly designed screen translates to a more effective system. Happy users make your job easier.

This book will show you how to do that. Look at Figure P.1a. It's awful! It represents the bad old block mode days of the 70's where screens were comprised of entry fields, had little alignment, no groupings, incomprehensible captions, unintelligible and condemning error messages, and a command field to tax one's memory.

Figure P.1.a.

```
TDX95210              ACME RENTAL COMPANY              10/11/78 10:25

NAME                             TEL          RO
_____    _____    _____

PUD      RD      C    RT         MPD
_____   _____  __   _____   __







ENTRY ERROR XX4656289960.997

COMMAND===>
```

Figure P.1.b.

```
                    THE CAR RENTAL COMPANY
RENTER >>      Name:        _____
               Telephone:   (___) ___ ____

LOCATION >>    Office:      _____
               Pick-up Date:  __ __ __
               Return Date:   __ __ __

AUTOMOBILE >>  Class:        __        (PR,ST,FU,MD,CO,SC)
               Rate:         _____
               Miles Per Day: ___

The maximum allowed miles per day is 150.
               Enter   F1=Help   F3=Exit   F12=Cancel
```

Now look at Figure P.1b. It represents good design of the 80's as suggested in Bill's book *Handbook of Screen Design*. Alignment, columnization, groupings, headings, comprehensible messages, and function key listings to remind users of choices. Still only entry fields, however.

The next screen, Figure P.1c, represents graphical screen design of the 90's. Borders around groupings and pushbuttons to designate commands. Entry fields are supplemented with other kinds of controls, including drop-down combination boxes, spin boxes, etc.

Figure P.1.c.

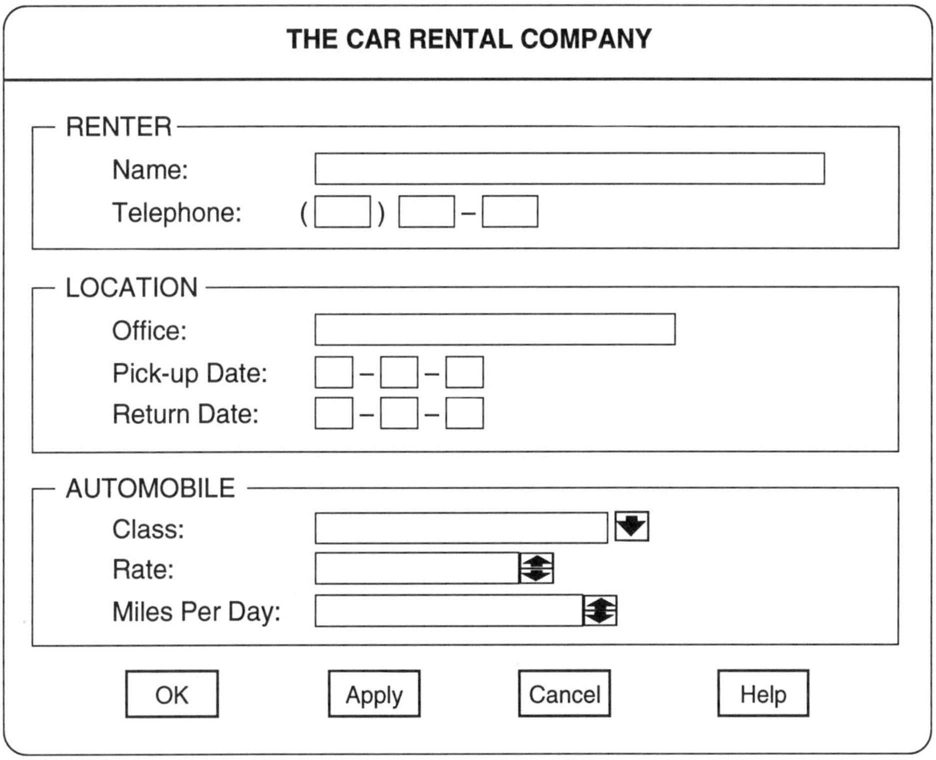

Now look at Figure P.2a. It doesn't look too bad until you look at Figure P.2b.

Figure P.3a is an actual screen from Microsoft Windows. What could possibly be improved? Well, look at screen P.3b and it will be evident to you.

If you don't see the improvements in the designs that Bill Galitz did, then you must read this book because your success depends on it. There is a lot to learn about screen design. This is what this book is about. Bill Galitz shows you how to design user-friendly and effective GUI. It's not hard, but if you don't get the guidance you need, you will always be one step behind the technology. GUI is here to stay, and the success of many systems will depend on how well the screens are designed. Bill has done a masterful job in providing a practical guide to optimal screen design. You will learn how to test for good design, how the human eye picks up information, hardware and software considerations, field alignments, and the use of color.

Figure P.2.a.

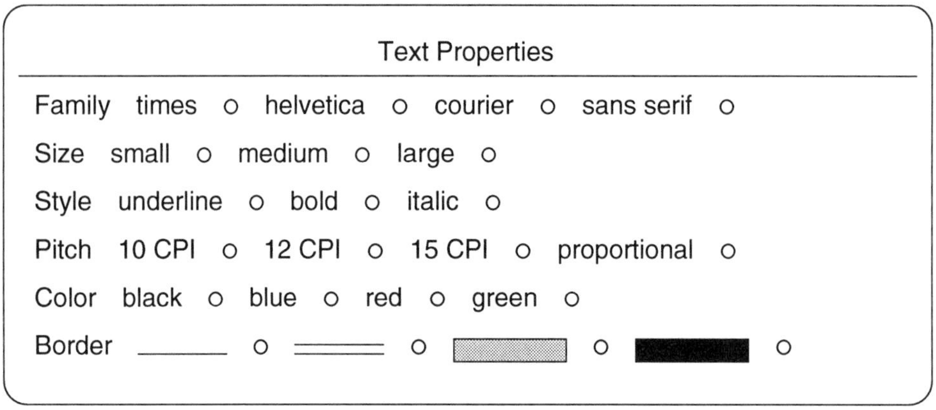

Text Properties

Family   times   ○   helvetica   ○   courier   ○   sans serif   ○

Size   small   ○   medium   ○   large   ○

Style   underline   ○   bold   ○   italic   ○

Pitch   10 CPI   ○   12 CPI   ○   15 CPI   ○   proportional   ○

Color   black   ○   blue   ○   red   ○   green   ○

Border _____ ○ ===== ○ ▨▨▨▨ ○ ████ ○

Figure P.2.b.

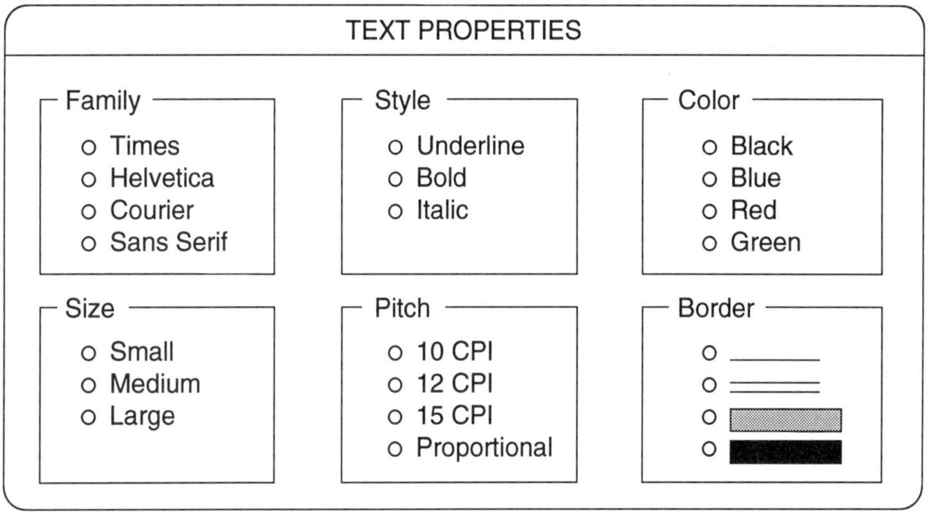

TEXT PROPERTIES

Family
- o Times
- o Helvetica
- o Courier
- o Sans Serif

Style
- o Underline
- o Bold
- o Italic

Color
- o Black
- o Blue
- o Red
- o Green

Size
- o Small
- o Medium
- o Large

Pitch
- o 10 CPI
- o 12 CPI
- o 15 CPI
- o Proportional

Border
- o ———
- o ═══
- o � (shaded bar)
- o ▉ (black bar)

Figure P.3.a.

| PIF Editor | |

Program Filename: [   ]

Window Title: [   ]

Optional Parameters: [   ]

Start-up Directory: [   ]

Video Memory: o Text   o Low Graphics   o High Graphics

Memory Requirements: KB Required [   ]   KB Desired [   ]

EMS Memory: KB Required [   ]   KB Limit [   ]

XMS Memory: KB Required [   ]   KB Limit [   ]

Display Usage: o Full Screen   Execution: o Background
                 o Windowed   o Exclusive

☐ Close Window on Exit

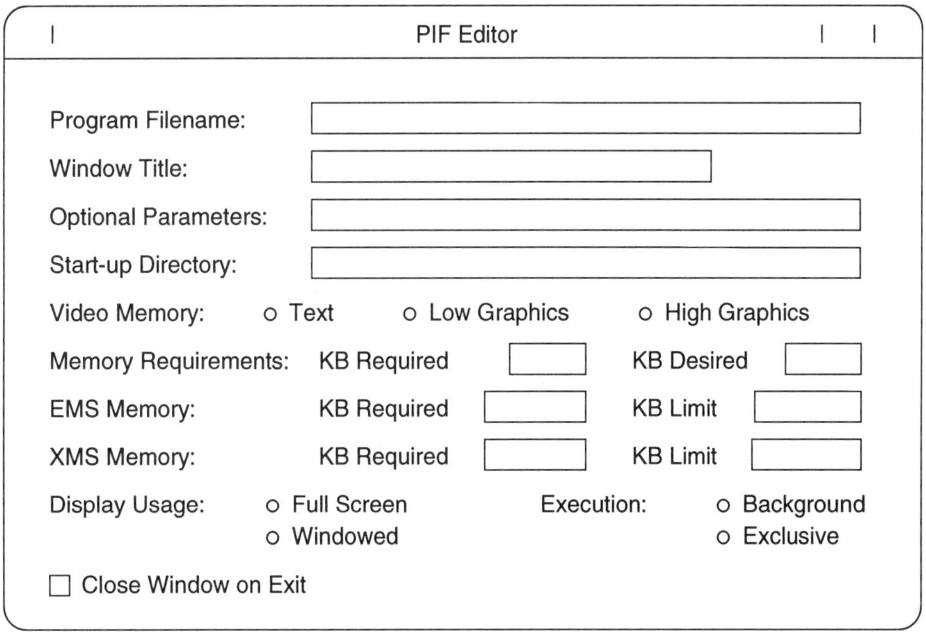

Figure P.3.b.

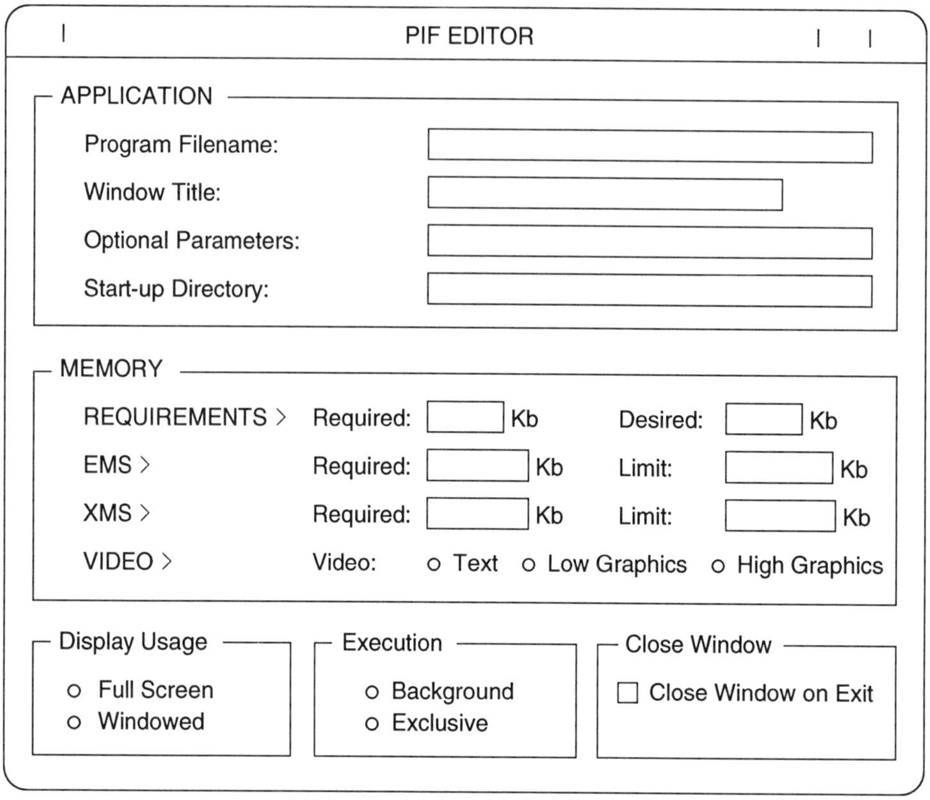

```
┌──────────────────────────────────────────────────────────────────┐
│  |                        PIF EDITOR                      |    |   │
├──────────────────────────────────────────────────────────────────┤
│  ┌─ APPLICATION ──────────────────────────────────────────────┐  │
│  │                                                             │  │
│  │    Program Filename:    [                              ]    │  │
│  │                                                             │  │
│  │    Window Title:        [                          ]        │  │
│  │                                                             │  │
│  │    Optional Parameters: [                              ]    │  │
│  │                                                             │  │
│  │    Start-up Directory:  [                              ]    │  │
│  │                                                             │  │
│  └─────────────────────────────────────────────────────────────┘ │
│                                                                    │
│  ┌─ MEMORY ───────────────────────────────────────────────────┐  │
│  │  REQUIREMENTS >   Required: [     ] Kb   Desired: [     ] Kb │  │
│  │  EMS >            Required: [     ] Kb   Limit:   [     ] Kb │  │
│  │  XMS >            Required: [     ] Kb   Limit:   [     ] Kb │  │
│  │  VIDEO >          Video:   o Text  o Low Graphics  o High Graphics │
│  └─────────────────────────────────────────────────────────────┘ │
│                                                                    │
│  ┌─ Display Usage ──┐ ┌─ Execution ──┐ ┌─ Close Window ────────┐ │
│  │  o Full Screen   │ │  o Background │ │ ☐ Close Window on Exit │ │
│  │  o Windowed      │ │  o Exclusive  │ │                        │ │
│  └──────────────────┘ └──────────────┘ └────────────────────────┘ │
└──────────────────────────────────────────────────────────────────┘
```

Here's an opportunity to learn how to "Clean your Windows." Remember, it's your fault when the system doesn't work as well as it should. You'll find that this book will help you become a much more effective designer.

Edwin F. Kerr, Vice President
Wiley–QED Publishing Program

Preface

This book is about designing good screens for a graphical system. It is the logical follow-on to my *Screen Design Handbook* first published by QED Information Sciences, Inc. in 1980, and now in its fourth edition.

Is good design important? It certainly is! Ask the users in the studies described in Chapter 1 whose productivity improved 25–40% as a result of well-designed screens.

What comprises good design? To be truly effective, good screen design requires an understanding of many things. Included are the characteristics of people; how we see, understand, and think. It also includes how information must be visually presented to enhance human acceptance and comprehension, and how physical actions must flow to minimize the potential for fatigue and injury. Good design must also consider the capabilities and limitations of the hardware and software of the human-computer interface.

Will graphics automatically assure good design? The style guides now available from many software providers are seen to solve many of the screen design problems that have existed for years, including much more user-centered design and application consistency. That they cannot is evidenced by the focus today on prototypes and usability testing. In reality, because of much greater design complexity, the opportunities for poor design are also increased.

What does this book do? This book addresses screen design from the user's perspective, spelling out hundreds of principles of good design in a clear and concise manner. It blends the results of screen design research, knowledge concerning people, knowledge about the hardware and software capabilities of the interface, and my practical experience which now spans 25 years in display-based systems.

How are the guidelines organized and presented? This book is both a reference book and a text book. A set of related principles are first presented in checklist form. Each checklist is then followed by much more detailed explanatory text. The text also contains many examples of poor and good design. The examples themselves are generic and illustrative in nature, not intending to reflect any one graphical product or system. In view of the ever-changing graphical landscape, this seems the most practical approach.

This book also serves as a companion text to my workshop on graphical screen design. Readers seeking more information concerning materials in the text, or who might wish to contribute additional information for future editions, may contact me at:

Wilbert O. Galitz, Inc.
P.O. Box 310
St. Helena Island, South Carolina 29920
(803) 525-0944

1

Introduction

As the twentieth century draws to a close and the computer industry matures, awareness that the human-computer interface is a key element in design is finally occurring. This awakening has been caused by a variety of factors. The combined voices of frustrated users, fed up with complicated procedures and incomprehensible screens, have finally become overwhelming. Examples of good design, when they did occur, have been presented as vivid proof that good design is possible. Technology, as it leaps forward, has eliminated many of the barriers to good screen design (such as slow response times) and unleashed a variety of new display and interaction techniques wrapped into a package called the Graphical User Interface, or as it is commonly called, GUI or "gooey."

POPULARITY OF GRAPHICS

Graphics has indeed revolutionized screen design and the user interface. A graphical screen bears scant resemblance to its text-based colleagues. Whereas a traditional screen maintains a one-dimensional, text-oriented, form-like quality, graphic screens can assume a three-dimensional look. Information can "float" in windows, small rectangular boxes seeming to rise above the background plane. Windows can also float above other windows. Information can appear, and disappear, as needed, and in some cases text can be replaced by symbols representing objects or actions. These symbols are commonly referred to as "icons."

Screen navigation and commands can be executed through menu bars and pull-downs. Menus may "pop-up." In the screen body, selection fields such as radio buttons, check boxes, list boxes, and palettes coexist with the reliable old entry field. More sophisticated entry fields with attached or drop-down menus of alternatives are also available. Screen objects and actions may be selected through use of pointing mechanisms such as the mouse or joystick instead of the traditional keyboard.

Increased computer power and the vast improvement in the display enable the user's actions to be reacted to quickly, dynamically, and meaningfully. This new interface is often characterized as representing one's "desktop" with scattered notes, papers, and objects such as files, trays, and trash cans arrayed around the screen.

Graphic presentation of information utilizes a person's information processing capabilities much more effectively than other presentation methods. Properly used, it minimizes the necessity for perceptual and mental recoding and reduces short-term memory loads. It also permits faster information transfer between computer and user by permitting more visual comparisons of amounts, trends, or relationships; more compact representation of information; and simplification of the perception of structure. Graphics can also add appeal or charm to the screen interface and permit greater customization to create a unique corporate style.

CONSTRAINTS IN GRAPHICAL SCREEN DESIGN

The benefits of a graphical system may be tempered by several possible problems. One or all may impact the effectiveness and usability of the system. These include the following:

Greater Design Complexity. The elements and techniques available to the graphical screen designer far outnumber those that have been at the disposal of the text-based screen designer. This can easily be seen by comparing the typical but nonexhaustive listings in Table 1.1. This "more" may not necessarily be better, unless it is carefully, thoughtfully, consistently, and simply applied. Since graphics are most often applied with color, the advantages and problems of color must also be considered. With graphics, the skill of the designer is increasingly challenged.

Lack of Experimentally Derived Design Guidelines. The graphical interface is burdened today by a lack of experimentally derived design guidelines. More designer interest has existed in solving technical rather than usability issues, so few studies that might aid making design decisions exist. It is also difficult to develop studies evaluating design alternatives because of increased GUI complexity. Too many variables that must be controlled make meaningful cause-and-effect relationships difficult to uncover. Consequently, there is little understanding of how most design aspects relate to productivity and satisfaction.

Inconsistencies in Technique and Terminology. Many technique, terminology, and "look and feel" differences exist between various graphical system providers. These inconsistencies occur because of both copyright and legal implications as well as product differentiation considerations. The result, how-

Table1.1.   A representative listing of typical textual and graphical screen elements and techniques.

Textual Screens	*Graphical Screens*
Title	Title
Screen ID	Screen ID
Headings	Menu Bars
Captions	Pull-Downs
Entry/Data Fields	Pop-Up Menus
Function Key Listings	Buttons
Command Fields	Window Style
Messages	Direct Manipulation
Blinking	Indirect Manipulation
Scrolling	Scrolling
High/Low Intensity	Headings
Upper/Mixed-Case Characters	Captions
Normal/Reverse Video	Entry/Data Fields
Underlining	Radio Buttons
	Check Boxes
	Value Sets
	List Boxes
	Spin Lists
	Attached Menu Boxes
	Drop-Down Menu Boxes
	Messages
	Mice
	Icons
	High/Low Intensity
	Highlighting/Lowlighting
	Upper/Mixed-Case Characters
	Multiple-Character Styles
	Multiple-Character Sizes
	Normal/Reverse Video
	Thin/Thick/Double Rulings
	Foreground Colors
	Background Colors
	Color Lightness Differences
	Proportion
	Oval Shapes
	Rectangular Shapes
	Scalloped Corners
	Beveled Edges
	Drop Shadows
	Shrinking/Growing
	Motion

ever, is that learning for both designers and users is much more difficult than it should be.

Hardware Constraints. Good design also requires hardware of adequate power, processing speed, screen resolution, and graphic capability. Any insufficiencies in these areas will prevent a graphic system's full potential from being realized.

Human Constraints. Human limitations may also exist in terms of one's capability of dealing with the increased complexity of the graphical interface. The variety of visual displays and motor skills required may still challenge all but the most sophisticated users. Correctly double-clicking a mouse, for example, is difficult for some people.

Application Considerations. Graphics may not be the best alternative in all situations. Some studies have found textual presentation of information (Shneiderman, 1977, 1982A; Stern, 1984) or tabular display of information (Tufte, 1983) superior to graphics. So, it is the content of the graphic that is critical to its usefulness. The wrong presentation or a cluttered presentation may actually lead to greater confusion, not less.

WHAT COMPRISES GOOD GRAPHICAL SCREEN DESIGN?

To be truly effective, good graphical screen design requires an understanding of many things. Included are the characteristics of people, including how we see, understand, and think. It also includes how information must be visually presented to enhance human comprehension and how physical actions must flow to minimize the potential for fatigue and injury. Good design must also consider the capabilities and limitations of the hardware and software at the human-computer interface.

THE BENEFITS OF GOOD DESIGN

At best, a poorly designed screen can exact a toll in human productivity, as illustrated in Figure 1.1.

Based on an actual system requiring processing of 4.8 million screens per year, an analysis established that if poor clarity forced screen users to spend 1 extra second per screen, almost 1 additional person-year would be required to process all screens. A 20-second degradation in screen processing time would cost an additional 14 person-years.

At its worst, a poorly designed screen can create an impression that understanding it will require more time than one can afford to commit, or that it is too complex to understand at all. Those who have the luxury of doing so (managers and professionals) may refuse to use it, and the objectives of the system for which it was designed will never be achieved.

Figure 1.1. Impact of inefficient screen design on processing time.

Additional Seconds Required per Screen in Seconds	Additional Person-Years Required to Process 4.8 Million Screens per Year
1	.7
5	3.6
10	7.1
20	14.2

The benefits of a well-designed screen have been under experimental scrutiny. Dunsmore (1982) attempted to improve screen clarity and readability by making screens less crowded. Separate items, which had been combined on the same display line to conserve space, were placed on separate lines instead. The result: Screen users were about 20 percent more productive with the less-crowded version. Keister and Gallaway (1983) reformatted a series of screens following many of the same concepts to be described in this handbook. The result: Screen users of the modified screens completed transactions in 25 percent less time and with 25 percent fewer errors than those who used the original screens.

Tullis (1981) has reported how reformatting inquiry screens following good design principles reduced decision-making time by about 40 percent, resulting in a savings of 79 person-years in the affected system. In a second study comparing 500 screens (Tullis, 1983), it was found that the time to extract information from displays of airline or lodging information was 128 percent faster for the best format than for the worst. Other recent studies have also shown that the proper formatting of information on screens does have a significant positive effect on performance (Mann and Schnetzler, 1986; Pulat and Nwankwo, 1987).

Screen design may also be contributing to the visual fatigue reported by some system users. Dainoff et al. (1986) have estimated that as many as 45 percent of all users may be victims of a CRT-induced visual fatigue. Matthews et al. (1989) report that in a study requiring extended CRT viewing, 60 percent of subjects reported eye-focusing problems and 40 percent reported pain in the eye area.

TEXT PURPOSE AND OBJECTIVES

The purpose of this text is to assist a designer in developing an effective graphical screen interface between a program and its intended users. It is intended as a ready reference source for all graphical screen design. Its specific objectives are to enable the reader to do the following:

- Describe the considerations that must be applied to the graphical screen design process.

- Describe the rationale and rules for an effective screen design methodology.
- Identify the components of graphical screens, including windows, menus, and controls.
- Design and organize graphical screens to encourage the fastest and most accurate execution of screen features.
- Choose screen colors and design screen icons.
- Perform the Graphical User Interface design process, including interface development and testing.

SCOPE

The materials in this book, although far from exhaustive, represent an attempt to identify, collect, and/or deduce and ultimately document a useful set of guidelines for screen design. This handbook is the most complete and thorough reference source available to the screen designer today. The guidelines have been culled from a variety of sources:

- Known human factors and psychological principles.
- Analysis of the results of experimental studies in the behavioral disciplines.
- Available guideline documents for people/machine interfaces.
- Informal studies conducted by the author.
- The author's experience.

Although the validity of some guidelines cannot be absolutely guaranteed, as a whole they will provide a solid foundation for most screen design activities, at least until experimental evidence is available to prove, disprove, or modify them.

These guidelines will not answer every design problem that may be encountered. Application-specific requirements and guideline incompatibilities will never free the designer from performing design tradeoffs. It is hoped, however, that these guidelines will promote "wiser" decisions than have been possible in the past.

OVERVIEW

Chapter 2 begins with a brief history of the human-computer interface and a survey of some current graphical systems. It then describes direct manipulation, the fundamental concept on which a graphical system is based. The chapter concludes by describing the characteristics that graphical systems possess. Chapter 3 presents the principles of graphical user interface design, consistency, directness, responsiveness, and so forth.

Chapter 4 provides an overview of the graphical screen design process. Twelve steps to successful design, each to be detailed in succeeding chapters, are introduced. The first step, understand the user, is addressed in Chapter 5.

Chapter 6 reviews three of the four important general considerations in screen design, the needs and capabilities of people, hardware, and software. The fourth, application considerations, is outlined in Chapter 7.

Windows, including components, types, and selection and manipulation guidelines are presented in Chapter 8. Chapter 9 describes the kind of graphical menus available. Design guidelines are detailed and guidance presented for selecting the right kind of menu for the task. Chapter 10 surveys the various device-based controls in existence, including the mouse, trackball, joystick, and keyboard. Guidelines for choosing the proper control for the user and task are described. Screen-based controls such as radio buttons, fixed list boxes, spin boxes, and entry fields are described in detail in Chapter 11. The proper usage of each kind of control is given and guidance presented for choosing the proper control for the user and task.

Chapter 12 describes how to organize and lay out windows in a meaningful and efficient manner. Important topics include groupings, alignment, and balance. How to use color efficiently is presented in Chapter 13, and Chapter 14 describes icons, including how to select and design them. Chapter 15 presents guidelines for several other screen components, including messages, feedback, and guidance and assistance. Chapter 16, the final chapter, outlines testing, the last step in the screen design process. Topics addressed include prototypes, the system test, and the ongoing screen evaluation process.

A FINAL WORD

While this text contains much to aid the screen designer, there may be shortcomings in its organization, content, or clarity. Readers having comments or suggestions concerning screen design, or the design process, are urged to communicate them to the author so they may be incorporated into subsequent editions. It is only by working together that we can provide an efficient and effective product.

2

Characteristics of the Graphical User Interface

A BRIEF HISTORY OF THE HUMAN-COMPUTER INTERFACE

The need for people to communicate with each other has existed since we first walked upon this planet. The lowest and most common level of communication modes we share are movements and gestures. Movements and gestures are language-independent, that is, they permit people who do not speak the same language to deal with one another.

The next level, in terms of universality and complexity, is spoken language. Most people can speak one language, some two or more. A spoken language is a very efficient mode of communication if both parties to the communication understand it.

At the third level of complexity is written language. While most people speak, not all can write. But for those who can, writing is still nowhere near as efficient a means of communication.

In modern times, we have the typewriter, another step upward in complexity. Significantly fewer people type than write, yet a practiced typist can find typing faster and more efficient than handwriting. (The unskilled may not find this the case.) Spoken language is still more efficient than typing, regardless of typing skill level.

Through its first few decades, a computer's ability to deal with a human communication was inversely related to what was easy for the user to do. The computer preferred a rigid, typed input; the user reacted slowly using this device and with varying degrees of skill. The human-computer dialogue reflected the computer's preferences, consisting of one or a combination of styles referred to as "Command Language," "Question and Answer," "Menu Selection," "Function Key Selection," and "Form Fill-In." For more details on these types of screens, see Galitz (1992).

Finally, late in the 1970s, another alternative surfaced. Research at

Table 2.1.   Chronological history of Graphical User Interfaces.

1980	• Pioneered at the Xerox Palo Alto Research Center.
	• First marketed as the Xerox STAR.
	— Introduced pointing, selection, and mouse.
1984	• Popularized by Apple.
	• Apple developed and marketed Lisa and Macintosh.
	— Macintosh first mass-marketed successful system.
1985	• Microsoft Windows 1.0 released.
1987	• X Window System becomes widely available.
	• IBM's System Application Architecture released.
	— Including Common User Access (CUA).
	• IBM's Presentation Manager released.
	— Intended as graphics operating system replacement for DOS.
1988	• NeXT's NeXTStep released.
	— First to simulate 3-dimensional screen.
1989	• UNIX-based GUIs released.
	— Open Look, by AT&T and Sun Microsystems.
	— Innovative appearance to avoid legal challenges.
	— Motif, for the Open Software Foundation by DEC and Hewlett-Packard.
	— Appearance and behavior based on Presentation Manager.
	• Microsoft Windows 3.0 released.
1992	• OS/2 Workplace Shell released.
	• Microsoft Windows 3.1 released.

Xerox's Palo Alto Research Center provided an alternative to the typewriter, an interface using a form of gesturing. This system, the Xerox STAR, introduced the mouse and pointing and selecting as the primary human-computer communication method. Xerox was never able to market the STAR successfully, but the concept was quickly picked up by Apple and Macintosh. Released in 1984, it was the first mass-market and successful system. A new concept was born, revolutionizing the human-computer interface. A chronological history of GUIs through the 1980s is found in Table 2.1.

SOME CURRENT GRAPHICAL SYSTEMS

In the last decade a number of graphic systems have been introduced and are available in the the marketplace. In the discussion that follows, an occasional reference will be made to some of them. These systems are briefly introduced in the following paragraphs. The reader in need of detailed information concerning their design and operation is referred to their design documentation. Another source of information is Marcus (1992), who provides a comparative evaluation of the operational characteristics of several of those listed.

Macintosh. Introduced in 1984 by Apple, it was the first mass-marketed, widely accepted graphic system providing the interaction style referred to as direct manipulation. Its success is attributed to its consistent and user-oriented interface. Its simplicity makes it easy to learn but limits the flexibility available to the expert user. Over 8,000 applications exist.

NeXTStep. Introduced in 1988 by NeXT, it was the first to present a simulated three-dimensional appearance for its components. Like the Macintosh, its simplicity and user-oriented interface is oriented toward inexperienced and nontechnical users. It provides a very good set of end-user customization tools.

OPEN LOOK. OPEN LOOK was developed as the standard operating environment for UNIX System V.4 by AT&T and Sun Microsystems. Providing more functionality than Macintosh or NeXTStep, it provides more power and flexibility for the expert user at the cost of increased learning requirements for the inexperienced user. It possesses many innovative appearance and behavioral characteristics in order to avoid potential legal challenges, and it also provides an excellent functional specification and style guide. OPEN LOOK is used by Sun Microsystems workstations and over 30 applications exist.

DECwindows. An interface for workstation software, it was announced in 1987. One of its goals was to achieve a consistent interface across operating systems, including VMS and UNIX, and across different input and screen configurations. A resulting product for achieving consistency is the XUI (X User Interface) style guide and toolkit.

OSF/Motif. A window-manager and user interface toolkit, it was developed by Digital Equipment Corporation and Hewlett-Packard for the Open Software Foundation (OSF). Its appearance and behavior are based upon OS/2 Presentation Manager. Customization is encouraged, and some stylistic guidance is provided through a style guide (Open Software Foundation, 1991). Like NeXTStep, it presents a simulated three-dimensional appearance. Over 100 applications exist for UNIX-based workstations.

Microsoft Windows. Created in 1985 as a graphics-oriented alternative to MS-DOS, it opened the door to graphics-oriented software on the PC. Initially limited by the design characteristics of DOS, it has recently been enhanced. The user interface is relatively easy for inexperienced users, and its extensive use of keyboard equivalents is intended to ease the transition for experienced DOS users. Over 1,200 applications exist.

OS/2 Presentation Manager. Developed jointly by Microsoft and IBM in 1987, it was intended as the graphics operating system replacement for MS-DOS.

OS/2 Workplace Shell. Developed by IBM when Microsoft and IBM dissolved their business relationship, OS/2 Workplace Shell is the GUI for OS/2 2.0 and beyond.

THE CONCEPT OF DIRECT MANIPULATION

The term used to describe the style of interaction for these new graphical systems was first used by Shneiderman (1982). He called them "direct manipulation" systems, suggesting they possess the following characteristics:

The system is portrayed as an extension of the real world. It is assumed that the system user is already familiar with the objects and actions in his or her environment of interest. The system replicates them and portrays them on a different medium, the screen. The user has the power to access and modify these objects, among which are windows. The user is allowed to work in a familiar environment and in a familiar way, focusing on the data, not the application and tools. The physical organization of the system, which may be unfamiliar, is hidden and not a distraction.

Continuous visibility of objects and actions. Like one's desktop and office, objects are continuously visible. Reminders of actions to be performed are also obvious, labelled buttons replacing complex syntax and command names. Cursor action and motion occurs in physically obvious and intuitively natural ways. Nelson (1980) described this as "virtual reality," a representation of reality that can be manipulated. Hatfield (1981) is credited with calling it "WYSIWYG" (what you see is what you get). Rutkowski (1982) described it as "transparency," where one's intellect is applied to the task, not the tool. Hutchins et al. (1986) consider it direct involvement with the world of objects rather than communicating with an intermediary.

One problem in direct manipulation, however, is that there is no direct analogy in the desktop world for all windowing operations. A piece of paper on one's desk maintains a constant size, never shrinking or growing. Windows can do both. Solving this problem requires embedding a control panel, a familiar concept to most people, in the window's border. This control panel is manipulated, not the window itself.

Actions are rapid and incremental with visible display of results. Since tactile feedback is not yet possible (as would occur with one's hand), the results of actions are immediately displayed on the screen in their new and current form. Auditory feedback may also be provided. The impact of a previous action is quickly seen and the evolution of tasks is effortless.

Incremental actions are easily reversible. Actions, if not correct or not desired, can be easily undone.

Earlier Direct Manipulation Systems.

Using the above definition, the concept of direct manipulation actually preceded graphical systems. The earliest full screen text editors possessed similar characteristics. Screens of text resembling a piece of paper on one's desk could be created (extension of real world) and then reviewed in their entirety (continuous visibility). Editing or restructuring could be easily accomplished (through rapid incremental actions) and the results immediately seen. Actions could be reversed when necessary.

It took the advent of graphical systems to crystallize the concept, however.

Indirect manipulation. In practice, direct manipulation of all screen objects and actions may not be feasible to implement because of the following:

- The operation may be difficult to conceptualize.
- The graphics capability of the system is limited.
- The amount of space available for manipulation controls in the window border may be limited.
- It may be difficult for users to learn and remember all the icons and actions.

When this occurs, "indirect manipulation" is often provided. Indirect manipulation substitutes words and text, such as pull-down or pop-up menus, for symbols, and substitutes typing for pointing. Many window systems are a combination of both kinds of manipulation. A menu may be accessed by pointing at a menu icon and selecting it. The menu itself, however, is a textual list of operations. When an operation is selected from the list, by pointing or typing, the system executes it as a command.

Which style of interaction—direct manipulation, indirect manipulation, or a combination of both—is best, under what conditions, and for whom remains an unanswered question.

GRAPHICAL SYSTEMS: ADVANTAGES AND DISADVANTAGES

Graphical systems burst upon the office with great promise. The simplified interface they present is thought to reduce the memory requirements imposed on the user, making more effective use of one's information processing capabilities and dramatically reducing system learning requirements. For many users they have done all these things.

The success of graphical systems has been attributed to a host of factors. The following are commonly referenced in literature and endorsed by their advocates as advantages of these systems.

Faster recognition. Symbols have been found to be recognized faster and more accurately than text (Ellis and Dewar, 1979). The graphical attributes of icons such as shape and color are very useful for quickly classifying objects, elements, or text by some common property (Gittens, 1986). An example of a good classification scheme that speeds up recognition is icons developed for indicating the kind of message presented to the viewer by the system. The text of an informational message is preceded by a small letter *i* in a circle, the text for action messages by a stop sign.

Faster learning. A graphical, pictorial representation has been found to aid learning (Polya, 1957). Symbols can also be easily learned (Walker et al., 1965).

Faster use and problem solving. Visual or spatial representation of information has been found to be easier to retain and manipulate (Wertheimer, 1959) and leads to faster and more successful problem solving (Carroll et al., 1980). Symbols have also been found to be effective in conveying simple instructions (Dickey and Schneider, 1971).

Easier remembering. Because of greater simplicity, it is easier for casual users to retain operational concepts.

More natural. Graphic representations of objects are thought to be more "natural" and closer to innate human capabilities. In humans, actions and visual skills emerged before languages. Lodding (1983) suggests symbolic displays are more natural and advantageous because the human mind has a powerful image memory.

Exploits visual / spatial cues. Spatial relationships are usually found to be understood more quickly than verbal representations. Heckel (1984) suggests that thinking visually is better than thinking logically.

Fosters more concrete thinking. Displayed objects are directly in the high-level task domain. There is no need mentally to decompose tasks into multiple commands with complex syntactic form (Shneiderman, 1982). Abstract thinking is therefore minimized.

Provides context. Displayed objects are visible providing current context.

Fewer errors. More concrete thinking affords fewer opportunities for errors. Reversibility of actions reduces error rates because it is always possible to undo the last step. Error messages are rarely needed.

Increased feeling of control. The user initiates actions and feels in control. This increases user confidence and hastens system mastery.

Immediate feedback. The results of actions furthering user goals can be seen immediately. Learning is quickened. If response is not in the desired direction, the direction can be quickly changed.

Predictable system responses. Predictable system responses also speed learning.

Easily reversible actions. The user has more control. This ability to reverse unwanted actions also increases user confidence and hastens system mastery.

Less anxiety concerning use. Hesitant or new users feel less anxiety when using the system because it is so easily comprehended, easy to control, has predictable responses, and can reverse actions.

More attractive. Direct-manipulation systems are more entertaining, more clever, and more appealing. This is especially important for the cautious or skeptical user.

May consume less space. Icons may take up less space than the equivalent in words. More information can be packed in a given area of the screen.

Replaces "national" languages. Language-based systems are seldom universally applicable. Language translations frequently cause problems in a text-based system. Icons possess much more universality than text and are much more easily comprehended worldwide.

Easily augmented with text displays. Where iconic design limitations exist, direct-manipulation systems can easily be augmented with text displays. The reverse is not true.

Low typing requirements. Pointing and selection controls such as the mouse or trackball eliminate the need for typing skills.

Smooth transition from command language system. Moving from a command language to direct-manipulation has been found to be easy. The reverse is not true (Tombaugh et al., 1989).

The body of positive research, hypotheses, and comment concerning graphical systems is now being challenged by some studies, findings, and opinions that graphical representation and interaction may not necessarily always be better and, in some cases, may be poorer than textual or alphanumeric displays. Some feel that as graphical systems become increasingly sophisticated and continue to expand, interfaces have become increasingly more complex, sometimes arcane, and even bizarre (Baecker et al., 1991). Among the disadvantages put forth are these:

Limited power. Direct manipulation systems are more difficult to design. For more complex applications this can be a severe restriction. Poor design can undermine acceptance.

Working domain is the present. Direct-manipulation systems, while providing context, also require the user to work in the "present." Hulteen (1989), in a parody of "WYSIWYG," suggests, "What you see is all you get." Walker (1989) argues that language takes you out of the here and now and the visually present. Language, she continues, makes it easier to find things.

Not always familiar. Icons may not be as familiar as words or numbers. We have been exposed to words and numbers for a long time. Remington and Williams (1986) found that numeric symbols elicited faster responses than graphic symbols in a visual search task. Cairney and Sless (1982) and Zwaga and Boersema (1983) found some current or proposed symbols were not very effective. Hair (1991) had to modify a new system during testing by replacing iconic representations with a textual outline format. The users, lawyers, were unfamiliar with icons and preferred a more familiar format.

Learning still necessary. The first time one encounters many graphical systems, what to do is not immediately obvious. Meanings of many words and icons may not be known. It is not often possible to guess their meanings, especially the more arbitrary "symbols." A learning and remembering requirement is imposed on many users. A text-based system can easily be structured to incorporate a set of clear instructions: (1) Do this, (2) Now do this, and so on.

Human comprehension limitations. The number of different icons that can be introduced is restricted due to human comprehension limitations. Studies continually find that the number of different symbols a person can differentiate and deal with is much more limited that text. (See Figure 14.2.) Gittens (1986) argues it will be difficult to find or develop and use icons dealing with the large number of computer system concepts and command parameters that exist. Kolers (1969) notes that claims for the easy understanding of pictograms are exaggerated, and that recognizing icons requires much perceptual learning, abstracting ability, and intelligence.

Design limitations. The number of symbols that can be clearly produced using today's technology is limited. A body of recognizable symbols must be produced that are equally legible and equally recognizable using differing technologies. This is extremely difficult today.

Few "tested" icons exist. Icons, as with typefaces, must appear in different sizes, weights, and styles. As with text, an entire "font" of clearly recognizable symbols must be developed. It is not simply a question of developing an icon and simply enlarging or reducing it. Changed size can differentially affect symbol line widths, open areas, and so forth, dramatically affecting its recognizability. Typeface design for words and text is literally the product of 300 years of experimentation and studies. Icons must be researched, designed, tested, and then introduced into the marketplace. Marcus (1984) says the consequences of poor, or improper, design will be confusion and lower productivity for users.

Inefficient for touch typists. For an experienced touch typist, the keyboard is a very fast and powerful device. Moving a mouse or some other pointing mechanism may be slower.

Inefficient for expert users. Inefficiencies develop when there are more objects and actions than can fit on the screen. Concatenation for a command language is impossible.

Not always preferred style of interaction. Not all users prefer an iconic interface. Brems and Whitten (1987), in comparing commands illustrated by icons, icons with text, or text-only, found that users preferred alternatives with textual captions.

Not always fastest style of interaction. Stern (1984) found that graphic instructions on an automated bank teller machine were inferior to textual instructions.

Increased chances of clutter and confusion. A graphical system does not guarantee elimination of clutter on a screen. The converse is true; the chance for clutter is increased, thereby increasing the chance of possibility of confusion. How much screen clutter one can deal with is open to speculation.

May consume more screen space. Not all applications will consume less screen space. A listing of names and telephone numbers in a textual format will be more efficient than a card file.

Some Studies and a Conclusion

Walker (1989) points out that most of the benefits of one interaction style versus another are anecdotal. This has made the debate between advocates of graphical and other styles of interaction more religious than scientific. This is certainly true for many of the arguments. In the last several years, however, there have been a handful of studies comparing alternative interaction styles. It is useful to summarize what they have found.

One of the first studies was undertaken by Whiteside et al. (1985). They compared the usability characteristics of seven systems, including direct-manipulation, menu, and command language styles of interaction. They found that user performance did not depend on the type of system. There were large differences in learnability and usability between all. How well the system was designed was the best indicator of success, not the style of interaction.

Brems and Whitten (1987) evaluated a family of seven commands for user preferences. The alternative design styles were commands described by icons only, icons with textual captions, and textual captions only. While the meanings of the icons were easily learned, textual captions were preferred to uncaptioned icons. Learning, they concluded, was not a good indicator of preference.

Frese et al. (1987) compared learning and performance for direct-manipulation and command-based word processing systems. While no differences existed after the first experimental session, the direct-manipulation system user's performance became increasingly superior as the study progressed (and task complexity increased). It appeared that the direct-manipulation system facilitated the learning process as task complexity increased.

Shneiderman and Margono (1987) compared some simple file manipulation tasks using a graphical system (Macintosh) and a command language system (DOS). The graphical system was found best in learnability, performance time, and subjective ratings. Two other studies have also found graphical systems superior to command language styles for some kinds of tasks (Karat, 1987; Guastello et al., 1989).

The conclusion, based upon what research and experience have shown, is that the different interface styles have different strengths and weaknesses. Some concepts and tasks are very hard to convey symbolically and do not seem to be suited for a graphical system. Other concepts and tasks, however, may be well suited. Which tasks are best suited for which styles still needs much study.

The following has also become clear:

- The design of an interface and not its interaction style is the best determinant of ease of use.
- User preferences must be considered in choosing an interaction style.
- The success of a graphical system depends on the skills of its designers in following established principles of usability.

CHARACTERISTICS OF THE GRAPHICAL USER INTERFACE

A graphical system possesses a set of defining concepts. Included are sophisticated visual presentation, pick and click interaction, a restricted set of interface options, visualization, object-orientation, extensive utilization of a person's recognition memory, and concurrent performance of functions.

Sophisticated visual presentation. Visual presentation is the visual aspect of the interface. It is what people see on the screen. The sophistication of a graphical system permits displaying lines, including drawings and icons. It also permits display of a variety of character fonts, including different sizes and styles. The display of 16 million or more colors is possible on some screens. Graphics also permits animation and the presentation of photographs and motion video.

The meaningful interface elements visually presented to the user in a graphical system include windows (primary, secondary, or dialog boxes), menus (menu bar, pull-down, pop-up, cascading), icons to represent objects such as programs or files, assorted screen-based controls (entry fields, selection lists, combination boxes, settings, scroll bars and buttons), and a mouse pointer and cursor. The objective is to reflect visually on the screen the real world of the user as realistically, meaningfully, simply, and clearly as possible.

Pick and click interaction. Elements of a graphical screen upon which some action is to be performed must first be identified. The motor activity required of a person to identify this element for a proposed action is commonly referred to as "pick," the signal to perform an action as "click." The primary mechanism for performing this "pick and click" is most often the mouse and its buttons. The mouse pointer is moved by the user to the relevant element (pick) and the action signalled (click). The secondary mechanism for performing these actions is the keyboard. Most systems permit pick and click to be performed using it as well.

Restricted set of interface options. The array of alternatives available to the user is what is presented on the screen or what may be retrieved through what is presented on the screen, nothing less, nothing more. This concept fostered the acronym "WYSIWYG."

Visualization. Visualization is a cognitive process that allows people to understand information that is difficult to perceive, because it is either too voluminous or too abstract. It involves changing an entity's representation to reveal gradually the structure and/or function of the underlying system or process.

Visualization is facilitated by presenting specialized graphic portrayals. The best visualization method for an activity depends on what people are trying to learn from the data. The goal is not necessarily to reproduce a realistic graphical image but one that conveys the most relevant information.

Effective visualizations can facilitate mental insights, increase productivity, and foster faster and more accurate use of data.

Object-oriented. A graphical system consists of objects and actions. *Objects* are what people see on the screen. They are manipulated as a single unit. A well-designed system keeps users focused on objects, not on how to carry out actions. Objects can be composed of *sub-objects*. For example, an object may be a document. The document's sub-objects may be a paragraph, sentence, word, or letter.

Objects also have *properties*. Properties are the unique characteristics of an object. Properties help to describe an object and can be changed by users. Examples of properties are text styles (such as normal or italics), font sizes (such as 12 or 18 points), or window background colors (such as black or blue).

In addition to objects, applications present one other type of information called *actions*. People take actions on objects. Actions may manipulate objects in specific ways (commands) or modify the properties of objects (property or attribute specification).

Commands are actions that manipulate objects in ways described by their command label. They are executed immediately when selected. Once executed, they cease to be relevant. Examples of commands are opening a document, printing a document, closing a window, or quitting an application.

Property/attribute specification actions establish or modify the attributes or properties of objects. When selected, they remain in effect until deselected. Examples include selecting cascaded windows to be displayed or a font style.

The following is a typical *property/attribute specification sequence:*

1. The user selects an object.
   — Several words of text are selected.
2. The user then selects an action to apply to that object.
   —The action BOLD is chosen.
3. The selected words are made bold and will remain bold until selected and changed again.

A series of actions may be performed on a selected object. Performing a series of actions on an object also permits and encourages system learning through exploration.

Use of recognition memory. Continuous visibility of objects and actions encourages use of a person's more powerful recognition memory. The "out of sight, out of mind" problem is eliminated.

Concurrent performance of functions. Graphic systems may do two or more things at one time. Multiple programs may run simultaneously. When a system is not busy on a primary task, it may process background tasks (cooperative multitasking). When applications are running as truly separate tasks, the system may divide the processing power into time slices and allocate portions to each application (preemptive multitasking).

Data may also be transferred between programs. It may be temporarily stored on a "clipboard" for later transfer or be automatically swapped between programs.

3

Principles of Graphical User Interface Design

A graphical computer, the most powerful tool in the array of office equipment, must be an extension of the worker. This means the system and its software must reflect a person's capabilities and respond to his or her specific needs. It should be useful, accomplishing some business objective faster and more efficiently than did the previously used method or tool. It must also be easy to learn, for people want to do, not learn to do. Finally, the system must be easy and fun to use, evoking a sense of pleasure and accomplishment, not tedium and frustration.

The graphical interface itself should serve as both a connector and a separator: a connector in that it ties the user to the power of the computer, and a separator in that it minimizes the possibility of the participants damaging one another. While the damage the user inflicts on the computer tends to be physical (a frustrated pounding of the keyboard), the damage caused by the computer is more psychological (a threat to one's self-esteem).

Throughout the human-computer interface's history, various researchers and writers have attempted to define a set of general principles of interface design. As the popularity of the graphical user interface has escalated, the principles have been framed within its context.

What follows is a compilation of these principles. They reflect not only what we know today, but what we think we know today. Many are based on research, others on the collective thinking of behaviorists working with the graphical user interface. These principles will continue to evolve, expand, and be refined as our experience with GUI's increases. We will begin with the first set of published principles, those for the Xerox STAR.

PRINCIPLES FOR THE XEROX STAR

The design of the STAR was guided by a set of principles that evolved over its lengthy development process (Smith et al., 1982; Verplank, 1988). These principles established the foundation for graphical interfaces.

The illusion of manipulable objects. Displayed objects that are selectable and manipulable must be created. A design challenge is to invent a set of displayable objects that are represented meaningfully and appropriately for the intended application. It must be clear that these objects can be selected and how to select them. When they are selected should also be obvious, as should be clear that the selected object will be the focus of the next action. Verplank calls this "graphics with handles on it." Standalone icons easily fulfilled this requirement. The handles for windows were placed in the borders (window-specific commands, pop-up menus, scrolling, etc.).

Visual order and viewer focus. Attention must be drawn, at the proper time, to the important and relevant elements of the display. Effective visual contrast between various components of the screen is used to achieve this goal (STAR was monochromatic so color was not used). Animation is also used to draw attention, as is sound. Feedback must also be provided to the user. Since the cursor is often the focus of viewer attention, it is a useful mechanism for providing this feedback (by changing shapes).

Revealed structure. The distance between one's intention and the effect must be minimized. Most often, the distance between intention and effect is lengthened as system power increases. The relationship between intention and effect must be tightened and made as apparent as possible to the user. The underlying structure is often revealed during the selection process.

Consistency. Consistency aids learning. Consistency is provided in such areas as element location, grammar, font shapes, styles, and sizes, selection indicators, and contrast and emphasis techniques.

Appropriate effect or emotional impact. The interface must provide the appropriate emotional effect for the product and its market. Is it a corporate, professional, and secure business system? Should it reflect the fantasy, wizardry, and bad puns of computer games?

A match with the medium. The interface must also reflect the capabilities of the device on which it will be displayed. Quality of screen images will be greatly impacted by a device's resolution and color-generation capabilities.

THE GENERAL PRINCIPLES

The design goals in creating a graphical user interface are described below. These principles are general characteristics of the interface, and they apply to all aspects. Specific guidelines on how to implement many of these goals will be presented in succeeding chapters. The compilation is presented alphabetically and the ordering is not intended to imply degree of importance. They are derived from the various principles described in Galitz (1992), IBM (1991), Mayhew (1992), Microsoft (1992), Open Software Foundation (1991), and Verplank (1988).

Aesthetically Pleasing

- Provide visual appeal by following presentation and graphic design principles:
  — Providing meaningful contrast between screen elements.
  — Creating groupings.
  — Aligning screen elements and groups.
  — Providing three-dimensional representation.
  — Using color effectively and simply.

A design aesthetic, or visually pleasing composition, is attractive to the eye. It draws attention subliminally, conveying a message clearly and quickly. A lack of visually pleasing composition is disorienting, obscures the intent and meaning, slows one down, and confuses.

Visual appeal is provided by following the presentation and graphic design principles to be discussed, including providing meaningful contrast between screen elements, creating spatial groupings, aligning screen elements, providing three-dimensional representation, and using color effectively. Good design combines power, functionality, and simplicity with a pleasing appearance.

Clarity

- The interface should be visually, conceptually, and linguistically clear, including:
  — Visual elements.
  — Functions.
  — Metaphors.
  — Words and text.

The interface must be clear in visual appearance, concept, and wording. Visual elements should be understandable, relating to the user's real-world concepts and functions. Metaphors, or analogies, should be realistic and simple. Interface words and text should be simple, unambiguous, and free of computer jargon.

Compatibility

- Provide compatibility with the following:
  - — The user.
  - — The task and job.
  - — The product.
- Adopt the user's perspective.

User compatibility. Design must be compatible with the needs of the user. Effective design starts with understanding the user's needs and adopting the user's point of view. One very common error among designers is to assume that users are all alike. A glance around the office should quickly put this assumption to rest. Another common error is to assume that all users think, feel and behave exactly like the developer. Studies have proven otherwise. Users have quite different needs, aspirations and attitudes than developers. A system reflecting only the knowledge and attitudes of its designers cannot be successful.

Know the user is *the* fundamental principle in interface design. User compatibility can only happen if understanding truly occurs.

Task and job compatibility. The organization of a system should match the tasks the user must accomplish to perform the job. The structure and flow of applications should permit easy transition between tasks. The user must never be forced to navigate between applications to complete routine daily tasks.

Product compatibility. The intended user of a new system is often the user of other systems or earlier version of the new system. Habits, expectations and a level of knowledge have been established and will be brought to bear when learning the new system. If these habits, expectations and knowledge cannot be applied to the new system, confusion results and learning requirements are greatly increased. While compatibility across products must always be considered in relation to improving interfaces, making new systems compatible with existing systems will take advantage of what users already know and reduce the necessity for new learning.

Comprehensibility

- A system should be easily learned and understood. A person should know the following:
  - — What to look at.
  - — What to do.
  - — When to do it.
  - — Why to do it.
  - — How to do it.
- The flow of actions, responses, visual presentations, and information should be in a sensible order that is easy to recollect and place in context.

A system should be intuitive and understandable, flowing in a comprehensible and meaningful order. The steps to complete a task should be obvious. Reading and digesting long explanations should never be necessary.

Configurability

- Permit easy configuration and reconfiguration of settings.
  - Enhances a sense of control.
  - Encourages an active role in understanding.
  - Allows for personal preferences.

Easy configuration and reconfiguration of a system enhances a sense of control, encourages an active role in understanding, and allows for personal preferences. Some users will prefer to reconfigure a system to better meet their preferences. Other users will not, accepting what is given. Still others will experiment with reconfiguration and then give up, running out of patience or time. For these latter groups of users a good default configuration must be provided. This default configuration must be easily established.

Consistency

- A system should look, act, and operate the same throughout.
  - Similar components should:
    - Have a similar look.
    - Have similar uses.
    - Operate similarly.
  - The same action should always yield the same result.
  - The function of elements should not change.
  - The position of standard elements should not change.

Design consistency is the common thread that runs throughout these guidelines. It is the cardinal rule of all design activities. Consistency is important because it can reduce requirements for human learning by allowing skills learned in one situation to be transferred to another like it. While any new automated system must impose some learning requirements on its users, it should avoid encumbering productive learning with nonproductive, unnecessary activity.

In addition to increased learning requirements, variety in design has a number of other prerequisites and by-products, including:

- More specialization by system users.
- Greater demand for higher skills.
- More preparation time and less production time.
- More frequent changes in procedures.

- More error-tolerant systems (because errors are more likely).
- More kinds of documentation.
- More time to find information in documents.
- More unlearning and learning when systems are changed.
- More demands on supervisors and managers.
- More things to do wrong.

Inconsistencies in design are caused by differences in people—several designers might each design the same system differently. Inconsistencies also occur when design activities are pressured by time constraints. All too often the solutions in those cases are exceptions that the user must learn to handle.

Users, however, perceive a system as a single entity. To them, it should look, act, and feel similarly throughout. Excess learning requirements become a barrier to their achieving and maintaining high performance and can ultimately influence user acceptance of the system.

Can consistency make a big difference? One study found that user thinking time nearly doubled when the position of screen elements, such as titles and field captions, was varied on a series of menu screens (Teitelbaum and Granda, 1983).

Standards and guidelines. Design consistency is achieved by developing and applying design standards or guidelines. In the late 1980s the computer industry and other organizations finally awakened to their need, and a flurry of guideline documents have recently been developed and are continuing to appear. These guidelines specify the appearance and behavior of the user interface. They describe the windows, menus, and various controls available, including what they look like and how they work. They also provide some guidance on when to use the various components.

Examples of industry-produced guidelines include Apple's *Human Interface Guidelines: The Apple Desktop Interface* (1987), Digital Equipment Corporation's *XUI Style Guide* (1988), IBM's *System Application Architecture Common User Access (SAA-CUA)* (1987, 1989a, 1989b, 1991), Sun Microsystem's *OPEN LOOK Graphical User Interface Application Style Guidelines* (1990), Open Software Foundation's *OSF/MOTIF Style Guide* (1991), and Microsoft's *The Windows Interface* (1992).

Organizations working on guidelines or standards include the International Standards Organization (ISO) (Brooke et al., 1990; Billingsley, 1991), the American National Standards Institute (ANSI) (Billingsley, 1991), and the Human Factors Society (Billingsley, 1991).

Control

- The user *must* control the interaction.
  - — Actions should result from explicit user requests.
  - — Actions should be performed quickly.
  - — Actions should be capable of interruption or termination.
  - — The user should never be interrupted for errors.

- The context maintained must be from the perspective of the user.
- The means to achieve goals should be flexible, compatible with the user's skills, experiences, habits, and preferences.
- Avoid modes since they constrain the actions available to the user.
- Permit the user to customize aspects of the interface.
  — A proper set of defaults must always be provided, however.

Control is feeling in charge, feeling that the system is responding to your actions. Feeling that you are being controlled by a machine is demoralizing and frustrating. The interface should present a toollike appearance. Control is achieved when a person, working at one's own pace, is able to determine what to do and how to do it. Simple, predictable, consistent, flexible, configurable, and passive interfaces provide control. Lack of control is signalled by unavailable systems, long delays in system responses, surprising system actions, tedious and long procedures that cannot be circumvented, difficulties in obtaining necessary information, and the inability to achieve the desired results.

In general, avoid modes since they restrict the actions available to the user at any given time. If modes must be used, they should be visually obvious (for example, a changed mouse pointer shape), easy to learn, and easy to remove.

The feeling of control has been found to be an excellent mitigator of the work stress associated with many automated systems (Gardell, 1979; Johansson et al., 1978; Karasek, 1979; Karasek et al., 1981; and Frankenhaeuser, 1979).

Directness

- Provide direct and intuitive ways to accomplish tasks.

Tasks should be performed directly and intuitively. Directness is provided by the object-action sequence of direct manipulation systems. Tasks are performed by directly selecting an object, then selecting an action to be performed.

Efficiency

- Minimize eye, hand, and other control movements.
- Transitions between various system controls should flow easily and freely.

Eye and hand movements must not be wasted. One's attention must be captured by relevant elements of the screen when needed. Sequential eye movements between screen elements should be predictable, obvious, and short. Manual transitions between various system controls should also be as short as possible. Avoid frequent transitions between input devices such as the keyboard and mouse.

Familiarity

- Employ familiar concepts and use a language that is familiar to the user.
- Keep the interface natural, mimicking the user's behavior patterns.
- Use real-world metaphors.

Incorporate concepts, terminology, work flows, and spatial arrangements already familiar to the user into the interface. Operations should mimic one's behavior patterns; dialogs should mimic one's thought processes and vocabulary.

Flexibility

- A system must be sensitive to the differing needs of its users, enabling a level and type of performance based upon one's:
  — Knowledge and skills.
  — Experience.
  — Personal preference.
  — Habits.
  — The conditions at that moment.

Flexibility is the system's capability to respond to individual differences in people. People should be able to interact with a system in terms of their own particular needs, including knowledge, experience, and personal preference. Flexibility is accomplished by providing multiple ways to access application functions and perform tasks. It is also accomplished through permitting configurability. Another benefit of flexibility is that it contributes to increased user control.

Flexibility is not without dangers. Highly flexible systems can confuse inexperienced users, causing them to make more errors. For this reason, flexibility appears desirable only for experienced expert users. The novice user should not be exposed to system flexibility at the start, but only as experience is gained. The concept of "progressive disclosure," to be discussed in the simplicity guideline to follow, is also applicable here.

Another problem with flexibility is that it may not always be used, people preferring to continue doing things in the way they first learned. A variety of factors may account for this, including an unwillingness to invest in additional learning, or, perhaps, new ways may just not be obvious. The former problem may be addressed by making the new ways as easy and safe to learn as possible, the latter by including in training and reference materials not only information about how to do things, but when they are likely to be useful.

Forgiving

- Tolerate and forgive common and unavoidable human errors.
- Prevent errors from occurring whenever possible.

- Protect against possible catastrophic errors.
- When an error does occur, provide constructive messages.

It is often said that "to err is human." The corollary to that statement, at least in computer systems, might be " . . . to forgive good design." People will make mistakes; a system should tolerate those that are common and unavoidable.

People like to explore and learn by trial and error. A system oversensitive to erroneous input will discourage user exploring and trying new things. Learning will be inhibited, and people will be overcautious, working slowly and carefully to avoid mistakes. Productivity will then suffer. A fear of making a mistake and not being able to recover from it is a primary contributor to fear of dealing with computers.

Prevent errors from occurring by anticipating where mistakes may occur and designing to prevent them. Permit people to review, change, and undo actions whenever necessary. Make it very difficult to perform actions that can have tragic results. When errors do occur, present clear instructions on how to correct them.

Predictability

- The natural progression of each task should be capable of being antici-
pated.
  — Provide distinct and recognizable screen elements.
  — Provide cues to the result of an action to be performed.
- All expectations should be fulfilled uniformly and completely.

Tasks, displays, and movement through a system should be capable of being anticipated as a result of the user's previous knowledge or experience. Current operations should provide clues as to what will come next. Anticipation, or predictability, reduces mistakes and enables tasks to be completed more quickly. All expectations possessed by the user should be fulfilled uniformly and completely. Predictability is greatly enhanced by design consistency.

Recovery

A system should permit:

- Commands or actions to be abolished or reversed.
- Immediate return to a certain point if difficulties arise.

People should be able to retract an action by issuing what Miller and Thomas (1977) call an *undo* command. Knowing they can withdraw a command reduces much of the distress of new users, who often worry about doing something wrong. The return point could be the previous screen, a recent closure point, or the beginning of some predetermined period, such as back 10 screens or some number of minutes. Reversing or abolishing an action is analogous to using an eraser to eliminate a pencil mark on a piece of paper.

The goal, as Martin (1973) says, is stability—returning easily to the right track when a wrong track has been taken. Recovery should be obvious, automatic, and easy and natural to perform. In short, it should be hard to get into deep water or go too far astray. Easy recovery from an action greatly facilitates learning by trial and error and exploration. If an action is not reversible, and its consequences are critical, it should be made difficult to accomplish.

Responsiveness

- The system must rapidly respond to the user's requests.
- Provide immediate acknowledgement for all user actions:
  — Visual.
  — Textual.
  — Auditory.

A user request must be responded to quickly. Knowledge of results, or feedback, is a necessary learning ingredient. It shapes human performance and instills confidence. All requests to the system must be acknowledged in some way. Feedback may be visual, the change in the shape of the mouse pointer, or textual, taking the form of a message. It may also be auditory, consisting of a unique sound or tone.

Never leave the screen blank for more than a moment, as the user may think the system has failed. If a request requires an unusually long processing time, or one that is longer than customary, provide an interim "in-progress" message. Also provide some unique form of communication if a user action results in a problem or possible problem.

Substantial or more informative feedback is most important for the casual or new system user. Expert users are often content to receive more modest feedback.

Simplicity

- Provide as simple an interface as possible.
- Five ways to provide simplicity:
  — Use progressive disclosure, hiding things until they are needed.
    — Present common and necessary functions first.
    — Prominently feature important functions.
    — Hide more sophisticated and less frequently used functions.
  — Provide defaults.

— Minimize screen alignment points.
— Make common actions simple at the expense of uncommon actions made harder.
— Provide uniformity and consistency.

Simplicity is the opposite of complexity. Complexity is a measure of the number of choices available at any point in the human-computer interaction. A great deal of functionality and power is usually associated with high complexity. Complexity most often overwhelms and confuses new and casual users of systems. Complex systems are often not fully used, or used ineffectively, because a person may follow known but more cumbersome methods instead of easier but undiscovered or unfamiliar methods.

A system lacking complexity may have a different set of faults. It may be tedious to use or not accomplish much. It is better, however, to provide less functionality that will get effectively used than to provide too much functionality yielding an interface hopelessly complex and extremely difficult to use.

Complexity, then, is a two-edged sword. To effectively solve problems it must exist, but it must not be apparent so the system may be effectively used by a person. The goal, then, is to provide a complex system but mask the complexity through a simple interface. There are several ways to minimize this complexity.

Progressive disclosure. Introduce system components gradually so the full complexity of the system is not visible at first encounter. Teach basic fundamentals first. Then, slowly introduce advanced or more sophisticated functions. This is called the layered, or spiral approach to learning. Such an approach was taken by Carroll and Carrithers (1984) who called it the "Training-Wheels System." They found that by disabling portions of the system that were not needed and that could lead to errors and confusion, improved system learning efficiency was achieved.

Provide defaults. Providing defaults is another form of system layering. When a system is first presented, provide a set of defaults for all system-configurable items. The new user will not be burdened with these decisions and can concentrate on the basic fundamentals first. Defaults can later be changed, if desired, as experience increases.

Minimize screen alignment points. A larger number of alignment points of elements displayed on a screen are associated with greater screen visual complexity. Minimizing these alignment points minimizes screen complexity. This concept will be discussed more fully later.

Make common actions simple. Make common actions within a system easier to accomplish than uncommon actions. Greater overall system efficiency results.

Provide uniformity and consistency. Inconsistency is a foolish form of complexity. It forces a person to learn that things that appear different are not really different.

Transparency

- Permit the user to focus on the task or job, without concern for the mechanics of the interface.
  — Workings, and reminders of workings, inside the computer should be invisible to the user.

Do not force the user to think about the technical details of the application. One's thoughts must be directed to the application, not communication. Reminders of the mechanics of the interface occur through use of technical jargon, heavy use of codes, and presentation of computer concepts and representations.

Trade-offs

- Final design will be based on a series of trade-offs balancing often conflicting design principles.
- People requirements always take precedence over technical requirements.

Design guidelines often cover a great deal of territory and often conflict with one another or with technical requirements. In such conflicts the designer must weigh the alternatives and reach a decision based on trade-offs concerning accuracy, time, cost, and ease of use. Making these trade-offs intelligently requires a thorough understanding of the user and all design considerations. The ultimate solution will be a blend of experimental data, good judgment, and the important user needs.

This leads to a second cardinal rule of graphical system development: *Human requirements always take precedence over technical requirements.* It may be easier for the designer to write a program or build a device that neglects user ease, but final system judgment will always come down to one simple fact. How well does the system meet the needs of the user?

4

The Graphical User Interface Screen Design Process—Overview

The remaining 12 chapters in this book are organized in the order of the design steps typically followed in creating a graphical system and screens. This organization enables all the screen design activities to be addressed easily, clearly, and sequentially. This organization into nonoverlapping linear tasks does not mean to imply, however, that the actual design process will fall into such neat categories, one step finishing and only then the next step starting. In reality, some steps will often overlap one another and design iterations will cause occasional movements backward as well as forward.

With this caution in mind, succeeding chapters address graphical screen design, and its associated activities in the following step-by-step manner.

STEP 1—UNDERSTAND THE USER (CHAPTER 5)

- Understand the human characteristics important to design.
- Identify the user's level of knowledge and experience.
- Identify the characteristics of the user's tasks and job.
- Identify the user's psychological characteristics.
- Identify the user's physical characteristics.

To begin, an understanding of the most important system part, the user, must be obtained. Understanding users and what they do is a critical and often difficult and undervalued process. Step 1 in the design process involves identifying user characteristics and understanding how they impact design.

STEP 2—UNDERSTAND THE SCREEN DESIGN CONSIDERATIONS (CHAPTER 6)

Human

- Apply the test for good design.
- Organize screen elements clearly and meaningfully.
- Present information distinctively.
- Present information simply and meaningfully.

Hardware

- Provide compatibility with the system's hardware capabilities.

Software

- Use provided toolkits and style guides.
- Effectively use various display features.

A well-designed screen must reflect the needs and capabilities of its users, be developed within the physical constraints imposed by the hardware on which it is displayed, and effectively utilize the capabilities of its controlling software. Step 2 involves understanding the capabilities of, and limitations imposed, by people, hardware, and software in designing screens. It presents a series of general design principles for presenting information to people.

STEP 3—UNDERSTAND THE APPLICATION (CHAPTER 7)

- Perform a business definition and requirements analysis.
- Determine basic application functions.
- Describe current activities through task analysis.
- Develop a conceptual model of the system.
- Establish design standards or style guides.
- Establish system usability design goals.
- Define the kinds of training and documentation needed.

A system must achieve the business objectives for which it is designed. To do so requires an understanding of the application. This is accomplished by determining basic application functions, describing user activities through task analysis, and developing a conceptual model of the system. Step 3 addresses these and other related application-specific activities.

STEP 4—DECIDE ON WINDOWS (CHAPTER 8)

- Organize window system functions.
- Determine the style or styles of windows to be presented.
- Divide the tasks into a series of windows.

Graphical screen design will consist of a series of windows. Step 4 involves understanding how windows are used and selecting the proper kinds for the tasks. The elements of windows are described, and the purpose and proper usage of various types of windows are detailed.

STEP 5—DETERMINE MENUS (CHAPTER 9)

- Understand the principles of menu design.
- Establish kinds of menus needed to perform the tasks.
- Determine what system-provided default menu items are available and use them, if applicable.
- Determine what critical functions are not represented by the default items.
  — Add any new required menu items.
  — Design new commands as necessary.
- Design menus using established design guidelines.

Graphical systems are heavily menu oriented. Menus are used to designate commands, properties that apply to an object, documents, and windows. To accomplish these goals, a graphical system presents a variety of menu styles to choose from. Step 5 involves understanding how menus are used and selecting the proper kinds for the tasks. The principles of menu design are described, and the purpose and proper usage of various menu types are detailed.

STEP 6—DETERMINE DEVICE-BASED CONTROLS (CHAPTER 10)

- Identify the characteristics and capabilities of the various device-based controls.
- Select the proper controls for the task.

Device-based controls are the mechanisms through which people communicate their desires to the system. In addition to the keyboard, a graphical system might offer the user a mouse, trackball, joystick, graphic tablet, touch screen, light pen, or some other similar device. Step 6 consists of identifying the characteristics and capabilities of these various control mechanisms and providing the proper ones for users and their tasks.

STEP 7—DETERMINE SCREEN-BASED CONTROLS (CHAPTER 11)

- Identify the characteristics and capabilities of the various screen-based controls.
- Select the proper controls for the task.

Screen-based controls are the elements of screens that permit the user to interact with data. The screen designer is presented an array of controls to choose from—entry fields, selection fields, combination fields, and settings. Selecting the right control for the task is often difficult, but proper selection is critical to system success. Step 7 consists of identifying the characteristics and capabilities of these various screen-based controls and providing the proper ones for users and their tasks.

STEP 8—ORGANIZE AND LAY OUT WINDOWS (CHAPTER 12)

- Identify other important window components.
- Arrange controls to encourage quick and accurate information comprehension and control execution.

After determining what screen-based controls are needed, they must next be presented clearly and meaningfully in the work area of the window. Proper presentation and organization will encourage quick and accurate information comprehension and the fastest possible execution of display features. Step 8 involves identifying all necessary screen components and then laying out screens elements and controls in the most effective manner possible.

STEP 9—CHOOSE THE PROPER COLORS FOR ALL SCREEN ELEMENTS (CHAPTER 13)

- Identify the advantages and uses of color.
- Understand possible problems and cautions.
- Understand human vision and how it handles color.
- Identify effective foreground/background colors.
- Identify colors and color combinations to avoid.

Color, if used properly, can emphasize the logical organization of a screen, facilitate the discrimination of screen components, accentuate differences, and make displays more interesting. If used improperly, color can be distracting and cause visual fatigue, impairing a system's usability. Step 9 involves understanding color and how to use it effectively on a screen.

STEP 10—CHOOSE WINDOW ICONS (CHAPTER 14)

- Determine what graphic images best represent the application.
- Determine what relevant default icons are available and use them.
- Create icons for images not represented by defaults through following established icon design guidelines.
- Organize icons meaningfully on a screen.

Graphic screens often contain icons, pictures to represent displayed objects or actions. Step 10 involves understanding what kinds of icons exist, what influences their usability, and how to design them in a meaningful and recognizable way.

STEP 11—PROVIDE THE PROPER MESSAGES, FEEDBACK, AND GUIDANCE (CHAPTER 15)

- Provide the proper words, messages, and text.
- Provide the proper feedback.
- Provide guidance and assistance as needed.

Effective messages, feedback, and guidance and assistance are also necessary elements of good design. Step 11 involves defining and presenting these elements in a timely manner and properly.

STEP 12—TEST AND REFINE THE SCREENS AS NECESSARY (CHAPTER 16)

- Develop a prototype.
- Test the prototype.
- Modify the prototype as required.
- Test the system.
- Evaluate the working system.

The design of graphical screens is a complicated process. A host of factors must be considered and numerous tradeoffs made. Indeed, the design of some screens may be based on skimpy data and reflect the most "educated guess" possible. Also, the implications for some design decisions may not be fully appreciated until the results can be seen. Waiting until after a system has been implemented to uncover any deficiencies and make any design changes can be aggravating, costly, and time consuming. To minimize these kinds of problems screens must be tested and refined *before* they are implemented. Step 12 involves testing the system by creating, evaluating, and modifying prototypes in an iterative manner. It also involves conducting a system test and an evaluation of the working system.

5

User Considerations

The journey into the world of graphical screen design and the screen design process must begin with an understanding of the system user, the most important part of any computer system, whose needs the systems are built to serve. Understanding users and what they do is a difficult and undervalued process but extremely important because of the gap in skills and attitudes existing between system users and developers.

STEP 1

- Understand the human characteristics important in design.
- Identify the user's level of knowledge and experience.
- Identify the characteristics of the user's tasks and jobs.
- Identify the user's psychological characteristics.
- Identify the user's physical characteristics.

We will begin by looking at some characteristics of past computer systems that have caused people trouble and the effect they have.

WHY PEOPLE HAVE TROUBLE WITH COMPUTER SYSTEMS

Although system design and its behavioral implications have come under intense scrutiny in recent years, as we have seen, this has not always been the case. Historically, the design of computer systems has been the responsibility of programmers, systems analysts, and system designers, many of whom possess extensive technical knowledge but little behavioral training. Design decisions have thus rested mostly on the designers' intuition and wealth of specialized knowledge, and consequently, poorly designed interfaces often go unrecognized.

The intuition of designers or of anyone else, no matter how good or bad they may be at what they do, is error-prone. It is too shallow a foundation on which to base design decisions. Specialized knowledge lulls one into a false sense of security. It enables one to interpret and deal with complex or ambiguous situations on the basis of context cues not visible to users, as well as knowledge of the computer system they do not possess. The result is a perfectly usable system to its designers but one the office worker is unable or unwilling to face up to and master.

What has made a system complex in the eyes of its user? Listed below are five contributing factors.

Use of jargon. Systems often talk in a strange language. Words alien to the office environment or used in different contexts, such as *filespec*, *abend*, *segment*, and *boot* proliferate. Learning to use a system often requires learning a new language.

Non-obvious design. Complex or novel design elements are not obvious or intuitive, but they must nevertheless be mastered. Operations may have prerequisite conditions that must be satisfied before they can be accomplished, or outcomes may not always be immediate, obvious, or visible. The overall framework of the system may be invisible, with the effect that results cannot always be related to the actions that accomplish them.

Fine distinctions. Different actions may accomplish the same thing, depending upon when they are performed, or different things may result from the same action. Often these distinctions are minute and difficult to keep track of. Critical distinctions are not made at the appropriate time, or distinctions having no real consequence are made instead, as illustrated by the user who insisted that problems were caused by pressing the ENTER key "in the wrong way" (Carroll et al.).

Disparity in problem-solving strategies. People learn best by doing. They have trouble following directions and do not always read instructions before taking an action. Human problem solving can best be characterized as "error-correcting" or "trial and error," whereby a tentative solution is formulated based on the available evidence and then tried. This tentative solution often has a low chance of success, but the results are used to modify one's next attempt and so increase the chances of success. Most computers, however, have enforced an "error-preventing" strategy, which assumes that a person will not take an action until a high degree of confidence exists in its success. The result is that people often head down wrong paths or get entangled in situations difficult if not impossible to get out of (Reed, 1982).

Design inconsistency. The same action may have different names: for example, "save" and "keep," "write" and "list." Or the same result may be described differently: for example, "not legal" and "not valid." The result is that system learning becomes an exercise in rote memorization. Meaningful or conceptual learning becomes very difficult.

RESPONSES TO POOR DESIGN

Unfortunately, people remember the one thing that went wrong, not the many that go right, so problems achieve an abnormal level of importance. Errors are a symptom of problems. The magnitude of errors in a computer-based system has been found to be as high as 46 percent for commands, tasks, or transaction (Barber, 1979; Card et al., 1980; and Ledgard et al., 1980).

Errors, and other problems that befuddle, lead to a variety of psychological and physical user responses. Some psychological responses are listed below (Foley and Wallace, 1974).

Confusion. Detail overwhelms the perceived structure. Meaningful patterns are difficult to ascertain, and the conceptual model or underlying framework cannot be established.

Panic. Panic may be introduced by unexpectedly long delays during times of severe or unusual pressure. The chief causes are unavailable systems and long response times.

Boredom. Boredom results from improper computer pacing (slow response times) and overly simplistic jobs.

Frustration. An inability to easily convey one's intentions to the computer causes frustration, which is heightened if an unexpected response cannot be undone or if what really took place cannot be determined. Inflexible and unforgiving systems are a major source of frustration.

These psychological responses diminish user effectiveness because they are severe blocks to concentration. Thoughts irrelevant to the task at hand are forced to attention and necessary concentration is impossible. The result, in addition to higher error rates, is poor performance, anxiety, and job dissatisfaction. Further, these psychological responses frequently lead to, or are accompanied by, the following physical responses (Eason, 1979; Stewart, 1976).

Abandonment of the system. The system is rejected and other information sources are relied upon. These sources must be available, and the user must have the discretion to perform the rejection. This is a common reaction of managerial and professional personnel. One study (Hiltz, 1984) found the system abandonment rate to be 40 percent.

Incomplete use of the system. Only a portion of the system's capabilities are used, usually those operations that are easiest to perform or that provide the most benefits. Historically, this has been the most common reaction to most systems.

Indirect use of the system. An intermediary is placed between the would-be user and the computer. Again, since this requires high status and discretion, it is another typical response of managers.

Modification of the task. The task is changed to match the capabilities of the system. This is a prevalent reaction when the tools are rigid and the problem is unstructured, as in scientific problem solving.

Compensatory activity. Additional actions are performed to compensate for system inadequacies. A common example is the manual reformatting of information to match the structure required by the computer. This is a reaction common to workers whose discretion is limited, such as clerical personnel.

Misuse of the system. The rules are bent to shortcut operational difficulties. This requires significant knowledge of the system and may affect system integrity.

Direct programming. The system is reprogrammed by its user to meet specific needs. This is a typical response of the sophisticated worker.

UNDERSTANDING USERS AND THEIR TASKS

While we would like to think the system user sits idly at his desk anxiously awaiting the arrival of the computer system and the salvation it will afford, the truth is mostly the opposite. The user in today's office is usually overworked, fatigued, and continually interrupted. Documentation tends not to be read and problems are not well understood, and little is known about what information is available to meet one's needs. Moreover, the user's skills have been greatly overestimated by the system designer, who is often isolated psychologically and physically from the user's situation. Unlike the user, the designer is capable of resolving most system problems and ambiguities through application of experience and background and technical knowledge. Yet often the designer cannot really believe that anyone is incapable of using the system created.

The user, while being subjected to the everyday pressures of the office, is probably technologically unsophisticated, computer illiterate, and possibly even antagonistic. He wants to spend time using a system, not learning to use it. His objective is simply to get some work done.

UNDERSTANDING THE USER

- *Understand the human characteristics important in design:*
  - *— Perception.*
  - *— Memory.*
  - *— Visual acuity.*
  - *— Learning.*
  - *— Skill.*
  - *— Individual differences.*

- Identify the user's level of knowledge and experience.
- Identify the characteristics of the user's tasks and job.
- Identify the user's psychological characteristics.
- Identify the user's physical characteristics.

HUMAN CHARACTERISTICS

A person is a complex organism with a variety of attributes that have an important influence on screen design. Of particular importance are perception, memory, visual acuity, learning, skill, and individual differences.

Perception

Perception is our awareness and understanding of the elements of our environment through physical sensation of our various senses. It is influenced, in part, by achieved experience. We classify stimuli based on models stored in our memories and in this way achieve understanding. Comparing the accumulated knowledge of the child with that of an adult in interpreting the world is a vivid example of the role of experience in perception. Perception is also influenced by expectancies. Proofreading errors are a perceptual expectancy error; we see not how a word is spelled but how we *expect* to see it spelled. Context, environment, and surroundings also influence individual perception. For example, two drawn lines of the same length may look the same length or a different length depending on the angle of adjacent lines or what other people have said about the size of the lines.

The human sensing mechanisms are bombarded by many stimuli, some of which are important and some of which are not. Important stimuli are called *signals*; those that are not important are called *noise*. Signals are more quickly comprehended if they are easily distinguishable from noise in the sensory environment. Noise interferes with the perception of signals to the extent that they are similar to one another. Noise can even mask a critical signal. For example, imagine a hidden word puzzle where meaningful words are buried in a large block matrix of alphabetic characters. The signals, alphabetic characters constituting meaningful words, are masked by the matrix of meaningless letters.

Stimuli may also assume the quality of signals in one situation and that of noise in another. Just as things may be important in one context and unimportant in another. Imagine, for example, walking on a downtown sidewalk in a large city and hearing a train whistle in the distance. Then imagine walking down a train track and hearing the same whistle in the distance. On the sidewalk the train whistle may not even be perceived, but walking down the train track, it will most certainly be heard loud and clear.

Other perceptual characteristics include the following:

Proximity. The eye and mind see objects as belonging together if they are near each other in space.

Similarity. The eye and mind see objects as belonging together if they share a common visual property, such as color, size, shape, brightness, or orientation.

Matching patterns. We respond similarly to the same shape in different sizes. The letters of the alphabet, for example, possess the same meaning, regardless of physical size.

Closure. Perception is synthetic; it establishes meaningful wholes. If something does not quite close itself, such as a circle, square, triangle, or word, we see it closed anyway.

Balance. We desire stabilization or equilibrium in our viewing environment. Vertical, horizontal, and right angles are the most visually satisfying and easiest to look at.

The human perceptual mechanism has significant implications in the screen design process.

Memory

Memory is not one of the most developed of human attributes. Short-term memory is highly susceptible to the interference of such distracting tasks as thinking, reciting, or listening, which are constantly erasing and overwriting it. Remembering a telephone number long enough to complete the dialing operation taxes the memory of many people. The short-term memory limit is generally viewed as 7 ± 2 "chunks" of information (Miller, 1956), and knowledge and experience govern the size and complexity of chunks that can be recalled. To illustrate, most native English-speaking people would find recalling seven English words much easier than recalling seven Russian words. Short-term memory is thought to last 15 to 30 seconds. Unlike short-term memory, with its distinct limitations, long-term memory is thought to be unlimited. An important memory consideration, with significant implications for screen design, is the difference in ability to recognize or recall words. The human active vocabulary (words that can be recalled) typically ranges between 2,000 and 3,000 words. Passive vocabulary (words that can be recognized) typically numbers about 100,000. Our powers of recognition are much greater than our powers of recall.

Visual Acuity

The capacity of the eye to resolve details is called visual acuity. It is the phenomenon that results in an object becoming more distinct as we turn our eyes toward it and rapidly loses distinctness as we turn our eyes away—that is, as the visual angle from the point of fixation increases. It has been shown that relative visual acuity is approximately halved at a distance of 2.5 degrees from the point of eye fixation (Bouma, 1970). Therefore, a 5-degree diameter circle centered around an eye "fixation" character on a display has been recommended as the area "near" that character (Tullis, 1983) or the maximum length for a displayed word (Danchak, 1976).

If one assumes that the average viewing distance of a display screen is 19 inches (475 mm), the size of the area on the screen of optimum visual acuity is 1.67 inches (41.8 mm). Assuming "average" character sizes and character and line spacings, the number of characters on a screen falling within this visual acuity circle is 88, with 15 characters being contained on the widest line, and 7 rows being consumed, as illustrated below.

```
        3213123
      54321212345
     6543211123456
    765432101234567
     6543211123456
      54321212345
        3213123
```

The eye's sensitivity increases for those characters closest to the fixation point (the "0") and decreases for those characters at the extreme edges of the circle (a 50/50 chance exists for getting these characters correctly identified). This may be presumed to be a visual "chunk" of a screen.

Learning

The human ability to learn is important—it clearly differentiates people from machines. A design developed to minimize human learning time can accelerate human performance. Given enough time, of course, people can improve their performance in almost any task. Most people can be taught to walk a tightrope, but a designer should not incorporate a tightrope into his design if a walkway is feasible.

Evidence derived from studies of computer system learning parallels that found in studies of learning in other areas. Users prefer to be active (Carroll et al., 1984), to explore (Robert, 1986) and to use a trial and error approach (Hiltz and Kerr, 1986). There is also evidence that users are very sensitive to even minor changes in the user interface, and that such changes may lead to problems in transferring from one system to another (Karat, 1986). Moreover, just the "perception" of having to learn huge amounts of information is enough to keep some people from using a system (Nielson et al., 1986).

Learning can be enhanced if it:

- Allows skills acquired in one situation to be used in another somewhat like it (design consistency accomplishes this).
- Provides complete and prompt feedback.
- Is phased, that is, it requires a person to know only the information needed at that stage of the learning process.

Skill

The goal of human performance is to perform skillfully. To do so requires linking inputs and outputs into a sequence of action. The essence of skill is performance of actions in the correct time sequence with adequate precision. It is characterized by consistency and economy of effort. Economy of effort is achieved by establishing a work pace that represents optimum efficiency. It is accomplished by increasing mastery of the system through such things as progressive learning of shortcuts, increased speed, and easier access to information or data.

Skills are hierarchical in nature, and many basic skills may be integrated to form increasingly complex ones. Lower-order skills tend to become routine and may drop out of consciousness. Screen design must permit development of more skillful performance.

Individual Differences

A complicating but very advantageous human characteristic is that we all differ—in looks, feelings, motor abilities, intellectual abilities, learning abilities and speeds, and so on. In a keyboard data entry task, for example, the best operators will probably be twice as fast as the poorest and make 10 times fewer errors.

Individual differences complicate design because the design must permit people with widely varying characteristics to satisfactorily and comfortably learn the task or job. In the past this has usually resulted in bringing designs down to the level of lowest abilities or selecting people with the minimum skills necessary to perform a job. But office technology now offers the possibility of tailoring jobs to the specific needs of people with varying and changing learning or skill levels. Screen design must permit this to occur.

The above characteristics are general qualities we all possess. There are also a host of other human considerations by which people may vary greatly. These are important and must also be identified in the screen design process. The following listings of these characteristics are derived from Mayhew (1992) and are summarized in Table 5.1.

UNDERSTANDING THE USER

- Understand the human characteristics important in design.
- *Identify the user's level of knowledge and experience.*
  - *— Computer literacy.*
  - *— System experience.*
  - *— Application experience.*
  - *— Task experience.*
  - *— Other systems use.*
  - *— Education.*
  - *— Reading level.*
  - *— Typing skill.*
  - *— Native language.*
- Identify the characteristics of the user's tasks and job.
- Identify the user's psychological characteristics.
- Identify the user's physical characteristics.

Table 5.1. Important user/task characteristics.

Knowledge/Experience	
Computer Literacy	Highly technical or experienced, moderate computer experience, or none.
System Experience	High, moderate, or low knowledge of a particular system and its methods of interaction.
Application Experience	High, moderate, or low knowledge of similar systems.
Task Experience	Level of knowledge of job and job tasks.
Other Systems Use	Frequent or infrequent use of other systems in doing job.
Education	High school, college, or advanced degree.
Reading Level	Less than 5th grade, 5th–12th, more than 12th grade.
Typing Skill	Expert (135 WPM), skilled (90 WPM), good (55 WPM), average (40 WPM), or "hunt and peck" (10 WPM).
Native Language	English, another, or several.

Job/Task	
Type of System Use	Mandatory or discretionary use of the system.
Frequency of Use	Continual, frequent, occasional, or once-in-a-lifetime use of system.
Turnover Rate	High, moderate, or low turnover rate for job holders.
Task Importance	High, moderate, or low importance of the task being performed.
Task Structure	Repetitiveness or predictability of tasks being automated, high, moderate, or low.
Primary Training	Extensive or formal training, self-training through manuals, or no training.
Job Category	Executive, manager, professional, secretary, clerk.

Psychological Characteristics	
Attitude	Positive, neutral, or negative feeling toward job or system.
Motivation	Low, moderate, or high due to interest or fear.
Cognitive Style	Verbal or spatial, analytic or intuitive, concrete or abstract.

Physical Characteristics	
Age	Young, middle aged, or elderly.
Gender	Male or female.
Handedness	Left, right, or ambidextrous.
Physical Handicaps	Blind, defective vision, deafness, motor handicap.

—Derived from Mayhew, 1992.

Knowledge and Experience

The knowledge possessed by a user, and experiences undergone, shapes the design of the interface in many ways. The following kinds of knowledge and experiences should be identified.

Computer literacy. Are the users highly technical such as programmers or experienced data entry clerks? Do they have moderate computer experience or none at all? Will they be familiar with computer concepts and terms, the keyboard and its keys, and a mouse or other input mechanisms?

System experience. Are users already familiar with the interaction requirements of the new system? Have they worked on a system with the same interface? Have they been exposed to a similar interface or will it be new?

At one time or another, various schemes have been proposed to classify the different and sometimes changing characteristics of people as they become more experienced using a system. Words to describe the new, relatively new, or infrequent user have included *naive, casual, inexperienced,* or *novice*. At the other end of the experience continuum lie terms such as *experienced, full-time,* or *expert*. The words themselves are less important than the behavioral characteristics they imply. Experience to date is uncovering some basic differences in feelings of ease of use based upon proficiency level. What is easy for the new user is not perceived as easy for the "old hand," and vice versa.

For consistency in our discussion, the term "novice" will be used for the new user; the term "expert," for the most proficient.

Novice users have been found to:

- Depend on system features that assist recognition memory: menus, prompting information, and instructional and help screens.
- Need restricted vocabularies, simple tasks, small numbers of possibilities, and very informative feedback.
- View practice as an aid to moving up to expert status.

Whereas, experts:

- Rely upon free recall.
- Expect rapid performance.
- Need less informative feedback.
- Seek efficiency by bypassing novice memory aids, reducing keystrokes, chunking and summarizing information, and introducing new vocabularies.

In actuality, the user population of most systems is spread out along the continuum anchored by these two extremes. And, equally important, the behavior of any one user at different times may be closer to one extreme or the other. A person may be very proficient—an expert—in one aspect of a system and ignorant—a novice—in other aspects at the same time (Draper, 1985).

Exactly how experts and novices actually differ from one another in terms of knowledge, problem-solving behavior, and other human characteristics has been the subject of some research in recent years. To summarize some of the findings (Mayer, 1988; Ortega, 1989):

Experts possess the following traits:

- They possess an integrated conceptual model of a system.
- They possess knowledge that is ordered more abstractly and more procedurally.
- They organize information more meaningfully, orient it toward their task.
- They structure information into more categories.
- They are better at making inferences and relating new knowledge to their objectives and goals.
- They pay less attention to low-level details.
- They pay less attention to surface features of a system.

Novices exhibit these characteristics:

- They possess a fragmented conceptual model of a system.
- They organize information less meaningfully, orient it toward surface features of the system.
- They structure information into fewer categories.
- They have difficulty in generating inferences and relating new knowledge to their objectives and goals.
- They pay more attention to low-level details.
- They pay more attention to surface features of the system.

A well-designed system, therefore, must support at the same time novice and expert behavior, as well as all levels of behavior in between.

Application experience. Have users worked with a similar application (e.g., word processing, airline reservation, etc.)? Are they familiar with the basic application terms? Or does little or no application experience exist?

Task experience. Are users experienced with the task being automated? If it is an insurance claim system, do users have experience with paying claims? If it is a banking system, do users have experience in similar banking applications? Or do users possess little or no knowledge of the tasks the system will be performing?

Other systems use. Will the user be using other systems while using the new system? If so, they will bring certain habits and expectancies. The more compatibility between systems, the lower the learning requirements for the new system and the higher the productivity using all systems.

Education. What is the general educational level of users? Do they generally have high school degrees, college degrees, or advanced degrees? Are the degrees in specialized areas related to new system use?

Reading level. If the interface is verbal, the vocabulary and grammatical structure must be at a level that is easily understood by the users. Reading level can often be inferred from one's education level.

Typing skill. Is the user a competent typist or of the "hunt and peck" variety? Are they familiar with the standard keyboard layout or other newer layouts? A competent typist may prefer to interact with the system exclusively through the keyboard whereas the unskilled may prefer the mouse.

Native language. Do the users speak English, another language, or several other languages? Will the screens have to be in English or in some other language? Other languages often impose different screen layout requirements. Will icons be meaningful for all the user cultures?

Most of these kinds of user knowledge and experience are independent of one another so many different profiles are possible. It is also useful to look ahead, assessing whether future users will possess the same qualities.

UNDERSTANDING THE USER

- Understand the human characteristics important in design.
- Identify the user's level of knowledge and experience.
- *Identify the characteristics of the user's tasks and jobs:*
  - *— Type of use, mandatory or discretionary.*
  - *— Frequency of use.*
  - *— Turnover rate.*
  - *— Task importance.*
  - *— Task structure.*
  - *— Primary training.*
  - *— Job category.*
- Identify the user's psychological characteristics.
- Identify the user's physical characteristics.

Tasks and Jobs

The user's job and the kinds and duration of tasks to be performed are also important in design. The following should be determined:

Mandatory or discretionary use. Users of the earliest computer systems were mandatory or nondiscretionary. That is, they required the computer to perform a task that, for all practical purposes, could be performed no other way. Characteristics of nondiscretionary use can be summarized as follows:

- The computer is used as part of employment.
- Time and effort in learning to use the computer are willingly invested.
- High motivation is often used to overcome low usability characteristics.
- The user may possess a technical background.
- The job may consist of a single task or function.

The nondiscretionary user must learn to live comfortably with a computer, for there is really no other choice. Examples of nondiscretionary use today include a flight reservations clerk booking seats, an insurance company employee entering data into the computer so a policy can be issued, and a programmer writing and debugging a program. The toll exacted by a poorly designed system in nondiscretionary use is measured primarily by productivity—for example, speed and errors—and poor customer satisfaction with the product of the system.

In recent years, as computers have become more common in the office, the discretionary user has become exposed to the benefits, and costs, of technology. He is much more self-directed than the nondiscretionary user—not being told how to work but being evaluated on the results of his efforts. For him, it is not the means but the results that are most important. In short, this user has never been told how to work in the past and refuses to be told so now. This newer kind of user is the office executive, manager, or other professional, whose computer use is completely discretionary. Common characteristics of the discretionary user are as follows:

- Utilization of the system is not necessary.
- Job can be performed without the system.
- Will not invest extra effort to use the system.
- Technical details are of no interest to user.
- Does not show high motivation to use the system.
- Is easily disenchanted.
- Voluntary use must be encouraged.
- Is a multifunction knowledge worker.
- Is from a heterogeneous culture.
- Did not expect to use system.
- Career path did not prepare him or her for system use.

Quite simply, this discretionary user often judges a system on the basis of expected effort versus results to be gained. If the benefits are seen to exceed the effort, the system will be used. If the effort is expected to exceed the benefits, it will not be used. Just the perception of a great effort to achieve minimal results is often enough to completely discourage system use, leading to system rejection, a common discretionary reaction.

Today, discretionary users also include the general population who are increasingly being asked to interact with a computer in their everyday lives. Examples of this kind of interaction include library information systems and bank automated teller machines (ATMs). This kind of user, or potential user, exhibits certain characteristics that vary. Citibank (1989) in studying users of ATMs identified five categories. Each group was about equal in size, encompassing about 20 percent of the general population. The groups, and their characteristics, are the following:

- People who understand technology and like it. They will use it under any and all circumstances.
- People who understand technology and like it. But they will only use it if the benefits are clear.
- People who understand technology but do not like it. They will only use it if the benefits are overwhelming.
- People who do not understand anything technical. They might use it if it is very easy.
- People who will never use technology of any kind.

Again, clear and obvious benefits and ease of learning use dominate these usage categories.

Frequency of use. Is system use a continual, frequent, occasional, or once-in-a-lifetime experience? Frequency of use affects both learning and memory. People who spend a lot of time using a system are usually willing to spend more time learning how to use it in seeking efficiency of operation. They will also more easily remember how to do things. Occasional or infrequent users prefer ease of learning and remembering, often at the expense of operational efficiency.

Task importance. How important is the task to the user? People are usually willing to spend more time learning applications supporting important and key job tasks as efficiency in operation is again sought. For less important tasks, ease of learning and remembering are preferred, as extensive learning time and effort will not be tolerated.

Task structure. How structured is the task being performed, is it repetitive and predictable or not so? In general, the less structure, the more flexibility should exist in the interface. Highly structured tasks require highly structured interfaces.

Turnover rate. Is the turnover rate for the job high, moderate, or low? Jobs with high turnover rates would not be good candidates for systems requiring a great deal of training and learning. With low turnover rates, a greater training expense can be justified. With jobs possessing high turnover rates, it is always useful to determine why. Perhaps the new system can restructure monotonous jobs, creating more challenge and thereby reducing the turnover rate.

Primary training. Will the system training be extensive and formal, self-training from manuals, or will training be impossible? With less training, the requirement for system ease of use increases.

Job category. Is the user an executive, manager, professional, secretary, or clerk? While job titles have no direct bearing on design per se, they do enable one to predict some job characteristics when little else is known about the user. For example, executives and managers are most often discretionary users while clerks are most often mandatory. Secretaries usually have typing skills and both secretaries and clerks usually have higher turnover rates than executives and managers.

UNDERSTANDING THE USER

- Understand the human characteristics important in design.
- Identify the user's level of knowledge and experience.
- Identify the characteristics of the user's tasks and jobs.
- *Identify the user's psychological characteristics:*
  — *Attitude.*
  — *Motivation.*
  — *Cognitive style.*
- Identify the user's physical characteristics.

Psychological Characteristics

A person's psychological characteristics also affect one's performance of tasks requiring motor, cognitive, or perceptual skills.

Attitude and motivation. Is the user's attitude toward the system positive, neutral, or negative? Is motivation high, moderate, or low? While all these feelings are not caused by, and cannot be controlled by, the designer, a positive attitude and motivation allows the user to concentrate on the productivity qualities of the system. Poor feelings, however, can be addressed by designing a system to provide more power, challenge, and interest for the user with the goal of increasing job satisfaction.

Cognitive style. People differ in how they think about and solve problems. Some people are better at verbal thinking, working more effectively with words and equations. Others are better at spatial reasoning—manipulating symbols, pictures, and images. Some people are analytic thinkers, systematically analyzing the facets of a problem. Others are intuitive, relying on rules of thumb, hunches, and educated guesses. Some people are more concrete in their thinking, others more abstract. This is speculative, but the verbal, analytic, concrete thinker might prefer a textual style of interface. The spatial, intuitive, abstract thinker might feel more at home using a multimedia graphical interface.

UNDERSTANDING THE USER

- Understand the human characteristics important in design.
- Identify the user's level of knowledge and experience.
- Identify the characteristics of the user's tasks and jobs.
- Identify the user's psychological characteristics.
- *Identify the user's physical characteristics:*
  - *— Age.*
  - *— Gender.*
  - *— Handedness.*
  - *— Physical handicaps.*

Physical Characteristics

The physical characteristics of people can also affect their performance with a system.

Age. Are the users young, middle aged, or elderly? Older people may not have the manual dexterity to accurately operate many input devices. A double-click on a mouse, for example, is more difficult to perform as dexterity declines.

Gender. A user's sex may have an impact on both motor and cognitive performance. Women are not as strong as men so moving heavy displays or controls may be more difficult. Women also have smaller hands than men so controls designed for the hand size of one may not be used as effectively by the other. Significantly more men are color blind than women, so women may perform better on tasks and screens using color coding.

Handedness. A user's handedness, left or right, can affect ease of use of an input mechanism depending on whether it has been optimized for one or the other hand.

Physical handicaps. Blindness, defective vision, colorblindness, deafness, and motor handicaps can affect a performance on a system if it was not designed with these handicaps in mind.

METHODS FOR GAINING UNDERSTANDING OF USERS

- Visit customer locations, particularly if they are unfamiliar to you, to gain an understanding of the work environment.
- Talk with users about their problems, difficulties, wishes, and what works well now. Establish direct contact, avoid relying on intermediaries.
- Observe users working to see the tasks, difficulties, and problems.
- Videotape users working to illustrate and study problems and difficulties.
- Learn about the work organization where the system will be installed.
- Have users think aloud as they work to uncover details that may not otherwise be solicited.
- Try the job yourself. It may expose difficulties that are not known, or expressed, by users.
- Prepare surveys and questionnaires to obtain a larger sample of user opinions.
- Establish testable behavioral target goals to give management a measure for what progress has been made and what is still required.

Gould (1988) suggests using the above techniques to gain an understanding of users and their tasks. It is also very helpful to involve the user in the design process. Involving the user in design from the beginning provides a direct source to the extensive knowledge he or she possesses. It also allows the designer to confront the user's resistance to change. People dislike change for a variety of reasons, among them fear of the unknown and lack of identification. Involvement in design removes the unknown and gives the user a stake in the system, or an identification with it. One caution, however: User involvement in design should be based on job or task knowledge, not status or position.

In conclusion, this chapter has addressed one of the most important principles in interface and screen design. Simply summarized, it is this: *Know the user*.

6

General Screen Design Considerations

A well-designed screen accomplishes the following:

- Reflects the needs and capabilities of its users.
- Is developed within the physical constraints imposed by the hardware on which it is displayed.
- Effectively utilizes the capabilities of its controlling software.
- Achieves the business objectives of the system for which it is designed.

STEP 2

- Identify the considerations important in screen design.

  Human considerations

  — Apply the test for good design.
  — Organize screen elements clearly and meaningfully.
  — Present information distinctively.
  — Present information simply and meaningfully.

  Hardware considerations

  — Design must be compatible with the hardware capabilities of the system.

  Software considerations

  — Utilize the toolkits and style guides provided by many graphical systems.
  — Effectively use the various display features.

What follows is a compilation of general screen design guidelines for the graphical user interface. It begins with a series of considerations dealing with the user and concludes with those addressing hardware and software.

HUMAN CONSIDERATIONS IN SCREEN DESIGN

Use of a screen, and a system, is affected by a variety of factors. Included are how much information is presented on a screen, how a screen is organized, the language used on the screen, the distinctiveness of the screen's components, and providing the proper kind of feedback.

What are people looking for in the design of screens? One organization asked a group of screen users and got the following responses:

- An orderly, clean, clutter-free appearance.
- An obvious indication of what is being shown and what should be done with it.
- Expected information located where it *should* be.
- A clear indication of what relates to what, including options, captions, data, and so forth.
- Plain, simple English.
- A simple way of finding out what is in a system and how to get it out.
- A clear indication of when an action can make a permanent change in the data or system.

The desired direction is toward simplicity, clarity, and understandability—qualities lacking in many of today's screens.

The Test for a Good Design

- Can all screen elements be identified by cues other than by reading the words that make them up?

A simple test for good screen design does exist. A screen that passes this test will have surmounted the first obstacle to effectiveness.

The test. Can all screen elements (field captions, data, title, headings, types of controls, etc.) be identified without reading the words that make them up? That is, can a component of a screen be identified through cues independent of its content? If this is so, a person's attention can quickly be drawn to the part of the screen that is relevant at that moment. People often look at a screen for a particular reason, perhaps to locate a piece of information such as a customer name, to identify the name of the screen, or to find an instructional or error message. The signal at that moment is that element of interest on the screen. The noise is everything else on the screen. Cues independent of context that differentiate the components of the screen will reduce visual search times and minimize confusion.

Try this test on the front page of your morning newspaper. Where is the headline? A story heading? The weather report? How did you find them? The headline was identified probably by its visually large and bold type size; story headings, again by a type size visually different than other page components; the weather report, probably by its location (bottom right? top left?). Imagine finding the headline on the front page of the newspaper if the same type size and style was used for all components and their positions changed from day to day.

Unfortunately, many of today's screens cannot pass this simple test and are unnecessarily difficult to use. All the tools available to the creator of the newspaper's front page are not yet available to the screen designer. An effective solution can be achieved, however, with the equipment at hand. It simply involves the thoughtful application of the display techniques that exist, consistent locations, and the proper use of "white space."

ORGANIZING SCREEN ELEMENTS CLEARLY AND MEANINGFULLY

Visual clarity is achieved when the display elements are organized and presented in meaningful and understandable ways. Clarity is influenced by a multitude of factors. Important are consistency in element location, a visually pleasing composition, and a logical and sequential ordering. Also important are the presentation of the proper amount of information, groupings, and alignment of screen items. What must be avoided is visual clutter created by indistinct elements and random and confusing patterns.

Consistent Location of Elements

- Provide consistency in locations for screen elements.
  - Reserve specific areas of the screen for certain kinds of information.
  - Maintain these locations consistently on all screens.

Reserving specific areas of the screen for specific screen elements will aid people in memorizing their locations. A screen item may then always be quickly found. People do tend to have good memory locations. The graphical system products and style guides have established consistent locations for most screen elements.

The screen designer must be careful to provide consistent locations for application items found on more than one screen. These include such things as key fields, prompts, and headings. Inconsistent placement may confuse, and will slow down, the user.

Upper-Left Starting Point

- Provide an obvious starting point in the screen's upper-left corner.

Eyeball fixation studies indicate that in looking at displays of information, usually one's eyes move first to the upper-left center of the display, then quickly move through the display in a clockwise direction.

Streveler and Wasserman (1984) found that visual targets located in the upper-left quadrant of a screen were found fastest and those located in the lower right quadrant took longest to find.

Provide an obvious starting point in the upper-left corner of the screen. This is near where visual scanning begins and will permit a left-to-right, top-to-bottom reading as is common in Western cultures.

Visually Pleasing Composition

- Provide visually pleasing composition:
  — Balance.
  — Regularity.
  — Symmetry.
  — Predictability.
  — Economy.
  — Sequentiality.
  — Unity.
  — Proportion.
  — Simplicity.
  — Groupings.

Eyeball fixation studies also indicate that during the scanning of a display in a clockwise direction, people are influenced by the symmetrical balance and weight of the titles, graphics, and text of the display. The human perceptual mechanism seeks order and meaning and tries to impose structure when confronted with uncertainty. Whether a screen has meaningful and evident form or is cluttered and unclear is, therefore, immediately discerned. A cluttered or unclear screen requires that some effort be expended in learning and understanding what is presented. The screen user who must deal with the display is forced to spend time to learn and understand. The screen user who has an option concerning whether the screen will or will not be used may reject it at this point if the perceived effort is greater than the perceived gain.

Meaningfulness and evident form are significantly enhanced by a display that is pleasing to one's eye.

A design aesthetic, or visually pleasing composition, is attractive to the eye. It draws attention subliminally conveying a message clearly and quickly. A lack of visually pleasing composition is disorienting, obscures the intent and meaning, slows one down, and confuses.

The notion of what is artistic has evolved throughout history. Graphic design experts have, through perceptual research, derived a number of principles for what comprises a visually pleasing appearance (Taylor, 1960; Dondis, 1973). These include balance, regularity, symmetry, predictability, economy, sequentiality, unity, proportion, simplicity, and groupings. Keep in mind that this discussion of visually pleasing composition does not focus on the words on the screen, but on the perception of structure created by such concepts as spacing, intensities, and color. It is as if the screen is viewed through "squinted eyes," causing the words themselves to become a blur.

Balance

- Create screen balance by providing an equal weight of screen elements, left and right, top and bottom.

Balance, illustrated in Figure 6.1, is a stabilization or equilibrium, a midway center of suspension. The design elements have an equal weight, left to right, top to bottom. The opposite of balance is instability, the design elements seemingly ready to topple over. Our discomfort with instability, or imbalance, is reflected every time we straighten a picture hanging askew on the wall.

Dark colors, unusual shapes, and larger objects are "heavier," whereas light colors, regular shapes, and small objects are "lighter." Balance on a screen is accomplished through centering the display itself, maintaining an equal weighting of components on each side of the horizontal and vertical axis, and centering titles and illustrations.

Regularity

- Create screen regularity by establishing standard and consistently spaced horizontal and vertical alignment points.

Regularity, illustrated in Figure 6.2, is a uniformity of elements based on some principle or plan. Regularity in screen design is achieved by establishing standard and consistently spaced column and row starting points for display fields. The opposite, irregularity, exists when no such plan or principle is apparent.

Symmetry

- Create symmetry by replicating elements left and right of the screen center line.

Symmetry, illustrated in Figure 6.3, is axial duplication: A unit on one side of the center line is exactly replicated on the other side. This exact replication also creates balance, but the difference is that balance can be achieved without symmetry. Symmetry's opposite is asymmetry.

Predictability

- Create predictability by being consistent and following conventional orders or arrangements.

Figure 6.1.   Balance (vs. instability).

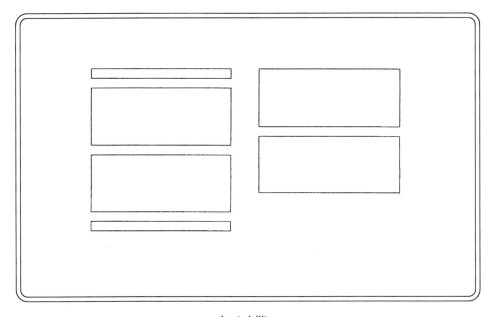

Balance

Instability

Figure 6.2.   Regularity (vs. irregularity).

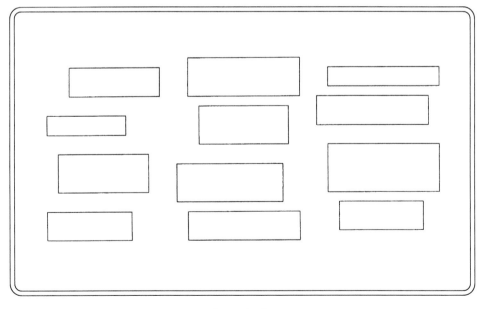

Regularity

Irregularity

Figure 6.3.   Symmetry (vs. asymmetry).

Symmetry

Asymmetry

Predictability, illustrated in Figure 6.4, suggests a highly conventional order or plan. Viewing one display enables one to predict how another display will look. Viewing part of a display enables one to predict how the remainder of the display will look. The opposite of predictability—spontaneity—suggests no plan and thus an inability to predict the structure of the remainder of a display or the structure of other displays. In screen design predictability is enhanced through design consistency.

Economy

- Provide economy by using as few styles, display techniques, and colors to get the message across as possible.

Economy, illustrated in Figure 6.5, is the frugal and judicious use of display elements to get the message across as simply as possible. The opposite is intricacy, the use of many elements just because they exist. Intricacy is ornamentation, which often detracts from clarity. Economy in screen design means mobilizing just enough display elements and techniques to communicate the desired message, and no more. The use of color in screens often violates this principle, with displays sometimes taking on the appearance of Christmas trees.

Sequentiality

- Provide sequentiality by arranging elements to guide the eye through the screen in an obvious, logical, rhythmic, and efficient manner.

Sequentiality, illustrated in Figure 6.6, is a plan of presentation to guide the eye through the screen in a logical, rhythmic order, with the most important information significantly placed. The opposite of sequentiality is randomness, where a flow cannot be detected. The eye tends to move from highly saturated colors to unsaturated colors, from dark to light areas, from big to little objects, and from unusual to usual shapes.

Unity

- Create unity by:
    - Using similar sizes, shapes, or colors for related information.
    - Leaving smaller space between elements of a screen than the space left at the margins.

Unity, illustrated in Figure 6.7, is coherence, a totality of elements that is visually all one piece. With unity, the elements seem to belong together, to dovetail so completely that they are seen as one thing. The opposite of unity is fragmentation, each piece retaining its own character. In screen design similar

Figure 6.4.   Predictability (vs. spontaneity).

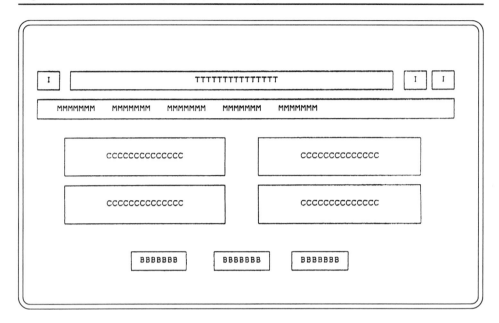

Predictability

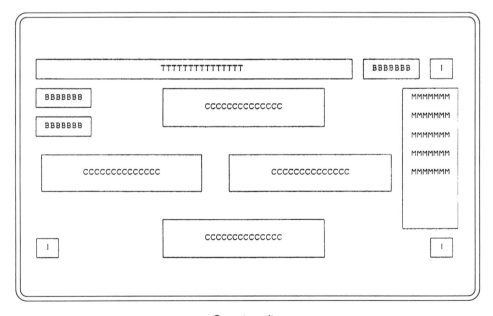

Spontaneity

Figure 6.5. Economy (vs. intricacy).

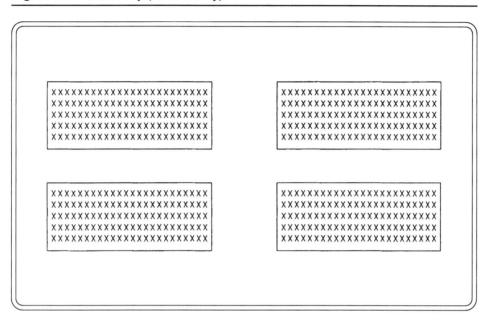

Economy

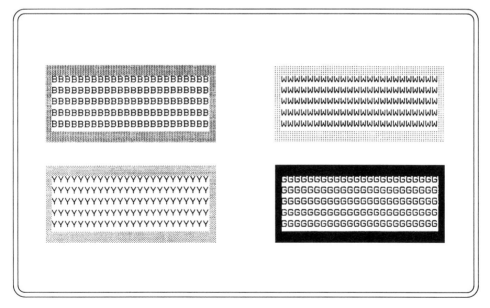

Intricacy

Figure 6.6.   Sequentiality (vs. randomness).

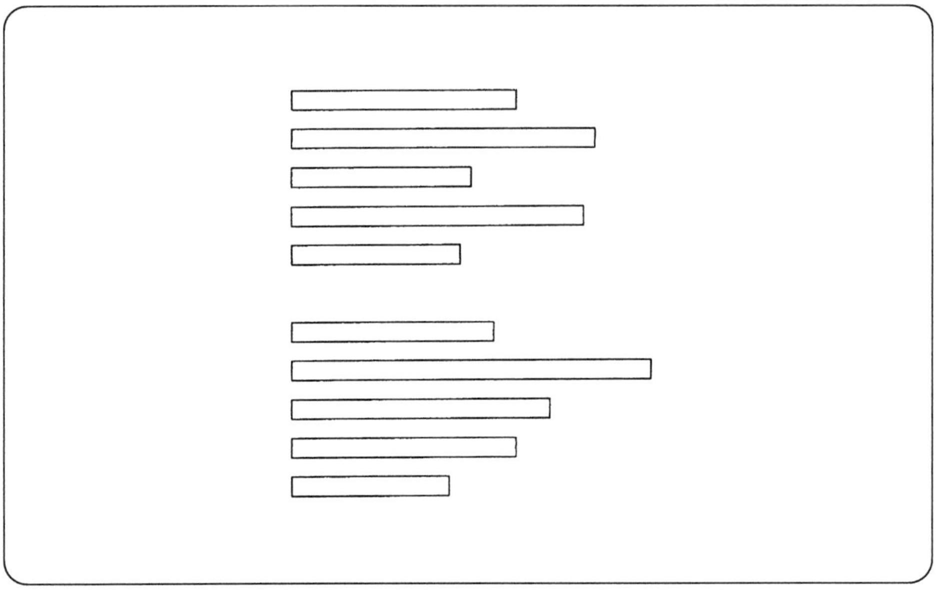

Sequentiality

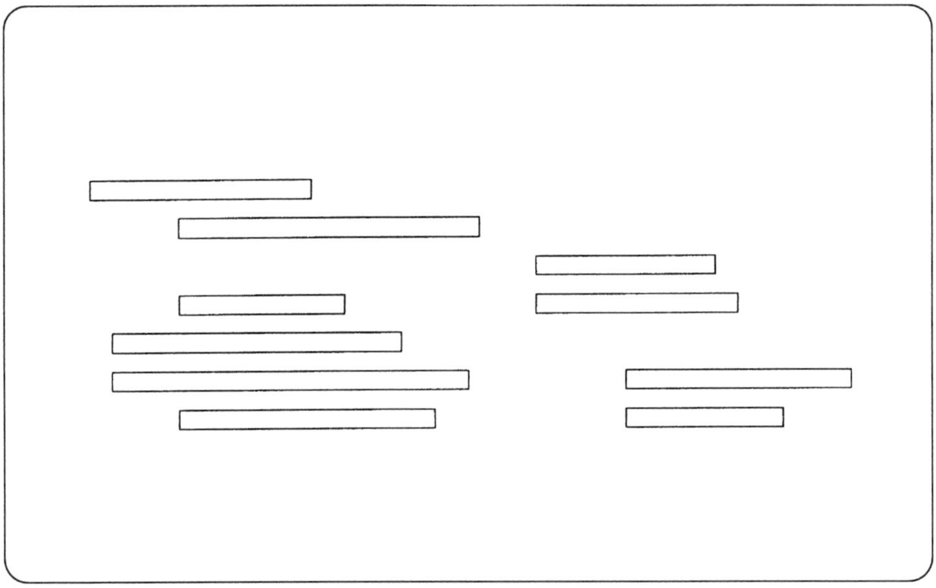

Randomness

Figure 6.7. Unity (vs. fragmentation).

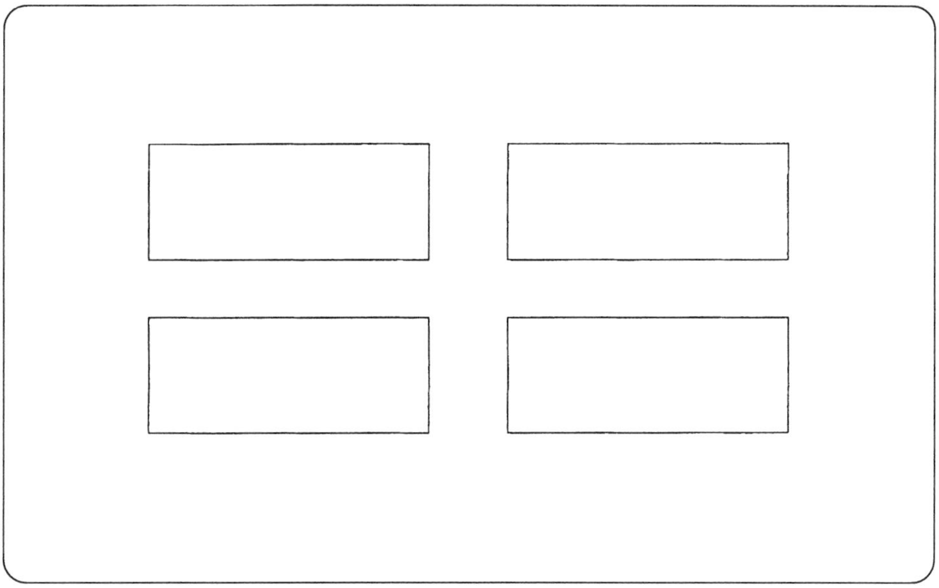

Unity

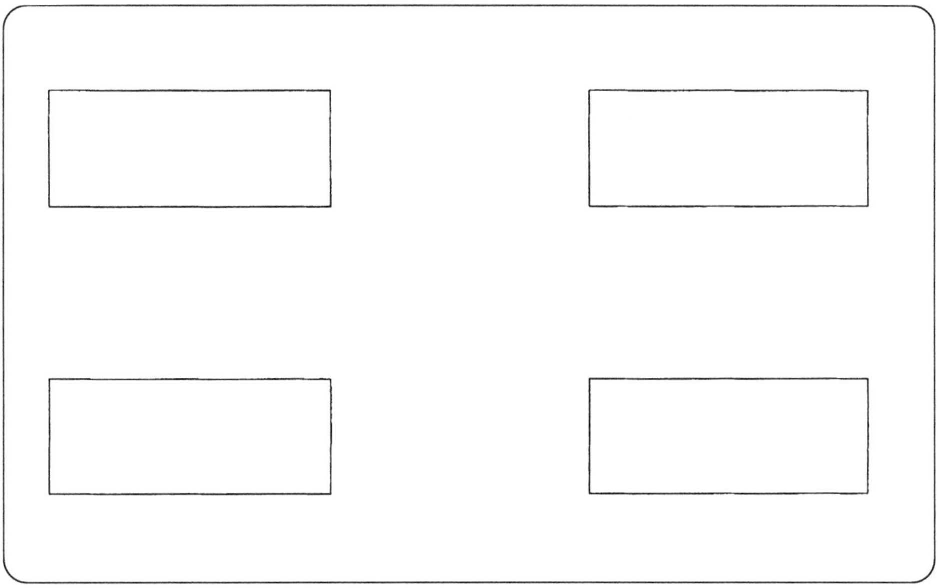

Fragmentation

sizes, shapes, and colors promote unity, as does "white space"—borders at the display boundary.

Proportion

- Create windows and groupings of data or text with aesthetically pleasing proportions.

Down through the ages, people and cultures have had preferred proportional relationships. What constitutes beauty in one culture is not necessarily considered the same by another culture, but some proportional shapes have stood the test of time and are found in abundance today.

Marcus (1992) describes the following shapes, illustrated in Figure 6.8, as aesthetically pleasing.

Square (1:1). The simplest of proportions, it has an attention-getting quality and suggests stability and permanence. When rotated it becomes a dynamic diamond, expressing movement and tension.

Square root of two (1:1.414). A divisible rectangle yielding two pleasing proportional shapes. When divided equally in two along its length, the two smaller shapes that result are also each a square root of two rectangles. This property only occurs with this proportion and is often used in book design. An open book has the same outside proportion as the individual pages within it. The square root of two has been adopted as a standard paper size in many countries of the world (the United States excluded).

Golden rectangle (1:1.618). An old (fifth century B.C.) proportion is the golden rectangle. Early Greek architecture used this proportion, and a mathematical relationship exists between this number and growth patterns in plant and animal life. This "divine division of a line" results when a line is divided such that the smaller part is to the greater part as the greater part is to the whole. The golden rectangle also has another unique property. A square created from part of the rectangle leaves a remaining area with sides also in the golden rectangle proportion.

Square root of three (1:1.732). Used less frequently than the other proportions, its narrowness gives it a distinctive shape.

Double square (1:2). Frequently seen in Japan, the tatami mat used for floor covering usually comes in this proportion. Rectangles more elongated than this one have shapes whose distinctiveness are more difficult to sense.

While these pleasing shapes have passed the test of time, not everything we encounter conforms to these principles. The American letter paper size has a ratio of 1:1.29, a typical American television screen a ratio of 1:1.33, and CRT screens typically have ratios in the range of about 1:1.33 to 1:1.50.

Figure 6.8. Pleasing proportions.

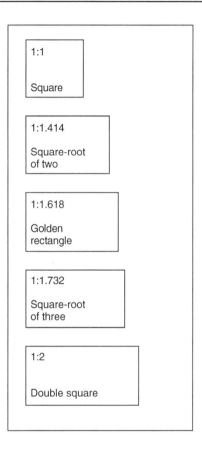

In screen design, aesthetically pleasing proportions should be considered for major components of the screen, including windows and groups of data or text.

Simplicity (Complexity)

- Optimize the number of elements on a screen, within limits of clarity.
- Minimize the alignment points, especially horizontal or columnar.

Simplicity, illustrated in Figure 6.9, is directness and singleness of form, a combination of elements that results in ease in comprehending the meaning of a pattern. The opposite pole on the continuum is complexity. The scale created may also be considered a scale of complexity, with extreme complexity at one end and minimal complexity at the other.

Figure 6.9   Simplicity (vs. complexity).

- A directness and singleness of form.
- Based upon knowledge of location of some elements, the location of others should be predictable.
- Complexity is a combination of elements that results in difficulties in establishing meaning in the pattern.

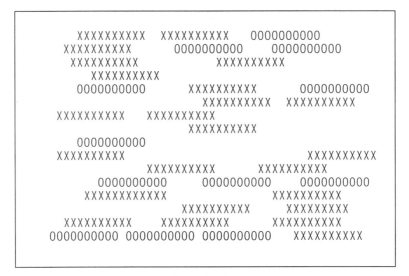

Simplicity

Complexity

Tullis (1983) has derived a measure of screen complexity based on the work of Bonsiepe (1968), who proposed a method of measuring the complexity of typographically designed pages through the application of information theory (Shannon and Weaver, 1949). This measure involves the following steps:

1. Draw a rectangle around each field on the screen, including captions, data, title, etc.
2. Count the number of fields and horizontal alignment points (the number of columns in which a field, inscribed by a rectangle, starts).
3. Count the number of fields and vertical alignment points (the number of rows in which a field, inscribed by a rectangle, starts).

This has been done for the text-based screens illustrated in Figures 6.10 and 6.11. These screens are examples from the earlier study by Tullis (1981) described in the introduction. They are an original inquiry screen (Figure 6.10) from the screens whose mean search time was 8.3 seconds, and a redesigned screen (Figure 6.11) from the screens whose mean search time was 5.0 seconds. A complexity calculation using information-theory for each screen is as follows:

- Figure 6.10 (original):
  — 22 fields with 6 horizontal (column) alignment points = 41 bits
  — 22 fields with 20 vertical (row) alignment points = 93 bits
  — Overall complexity = 134 bits
- Figure 6.11 (redesigned):
  — 18 fields with 7 horizontal (column) alignment points = 43 bits
  — 18 fields with 8 vertical (row) alignment points = 53 bits
  — Overall complexity = 96 bits

The redesigned screen is thus about 28 percent simpler than the original screen.

An easier method of calculation, yielding similar results, is to count the following: (1) the number of fields on the screen, (2) the number of horizontal (column) alignment points, and (3) the number of vertical (row) alignment points. The sums for the original and redesigned screens are

- Figure 6.10 (original):
  22 fields
  6   horizontal (column) alignment points
  20 vertical (row) alignment points
  48 = complexity
- Figure 6.11 (redesigned):
  18 fields
  7   horizontal (column) alignment points
  8   vertical (row) alignment points
  33 = complexity

By this calculation the redesigned screen is about 31 percent simpler than the original screen.

Figure 6.10. Original screen, from Tullis (1981), with title, captions, and data inscribed by rectangles.

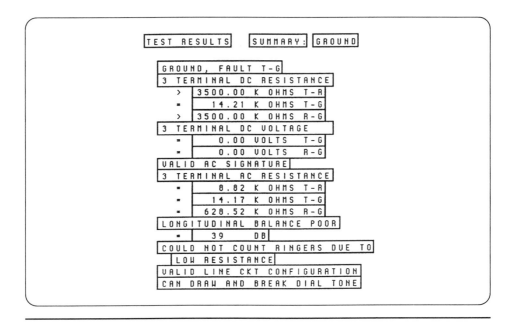

Figure 6.11. Redesigned screen, from Tullis (1981), with title, captions, and data inscribed by rectangles.

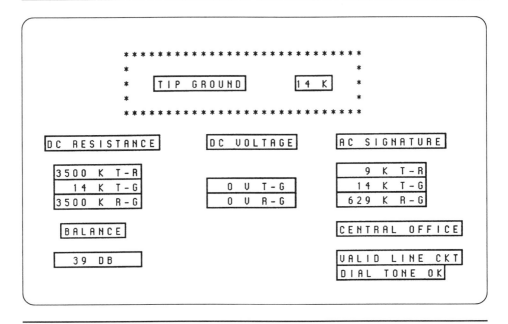

Complexity. By both calculations the redesigned screen has a lower complexity measure than the original screen. In the Tullis (1981) study, the redesigned and faster-to-use screens had lower complexity measures. This leads to the following complexity guidelines:

- Optimize the number of elements on a screen, within limits of clarity.
- Minimize the alignment points, especially horizontal or columnar.

Obviously, the way to minimize screen complexity is to reduce the number of fields displayed. Fewer fields will yield lower complexity measures. This is unrealistic, however, since ultimate simplicity means nothing is there, which obviously does not accomplish very much. Indeed, Vitz (1966) has found that people have subjective preferences for the right amount of information, and too little is as bad as too much. The practical answer, then, is to optimize the amount of information displayed, within limits of clarity. What is optimum must be considered in light of guidelines to follow, so a final judgment must be postponed.

What can be done, however, is to minimize alignment points, most importantly horizontal or columnar alignment points. Fewer alignment points will have a strong positive influence on the complexity calculation. Tullis (1983) has also found, in a follow-up study of some other screens, that fewer alignment points were among the strongest influences creating positive viewer feelings of visually pleasing composition.

Groupings

- Provide functional groupings of associated elements.
- Create spatial groupings as closely as possible to 5 degrees of visual angle.
  - 1.67 inches in diameter or about 6 to 7 lines of text, 12 to 14 characters in width.
- Visually reinforce groupings:
  - Provide adequate separation between groupings through liberal use of white space.
  - Provide line borders around groups.

Grouping elements on a screen aids in establishing structure and meaningful form. In addition to providing aesthetic appeal, grouping has been found to aid recall (Card, 1982) and result in a faster screen search (Dodson and Shields, 1978; Haubner and Neumann, 1986; Tullis, 1983, Triesman, 1982).

The perceptual principles of proximity, closure, similarity, and matching patterns foster visual groupings. But the search for a more objective definition of what constitutes a group has gone on for years. Tullis, in his 1981 study, described an objective method for establishing groups, based on the work of Zahn (1971) using the Gestalt psychologists' law of proximity. For Tullis, (1981) screens shown in Figures 6.12 and 6.13:

1. Compute the mean distance between each character and its nearest neighbor. Use a character distance of 1 between characters adjacent horizontally and 2 between characters adjacent vertically (between rows).
2. Multiply the mean distance derived by 2.
3. Connect with a line any character pair that is closer than the distance established in step 2.

This has been done for these inquiry screens, as illustrated in Figures 6.12 and 6.13.

- Figure 6.12 (original):
  — Mean distance between characters = 1.05.
  — Twice mean distance = 2.10.
  — A line is drawn between characters 1 or 2 apart, not 3 or more.
  — Resulting number of groups = 3.
- Figure 6.13 (redesigned):
  — Mean distance between characters = 1.09.
  — Twice mean distance = 2.18.
  — A line is drawn between characters 1 or 2 apart, not 3 or more.
  — Resulting number of groups = 13.

Figure 6.12. Original screen, from Tullis (1981), with grouping indicated.

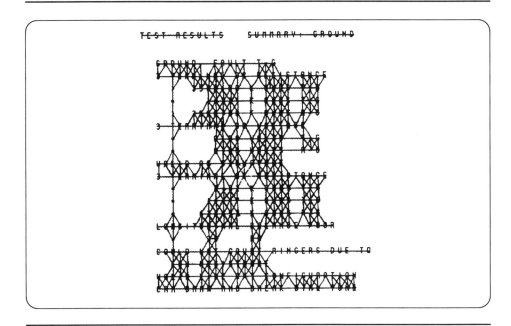

Figure 6.13. Redesigned screen, from Tullis (1981), with grouping indicated.

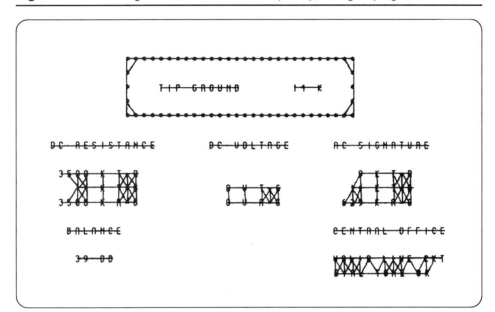

A simplification of this formula involves doing the following. Connect with a line all characters on the screen separated by no more than one space horizontally and no blank lines vertically. Groupings will become immediately obvious.

Another grouping measure was calculated by Tullis: the average size of each screen's group. The average size of the 3 groups in the original screen is 13.3 degrees, whereas the 13 groups on the redesigned screen average 5.2 degrees. The redesigned screen group size, interestingly, closely matches the 5-degree visual acuity screen chunk described in Chapter 5. It seems that groups 5 degrees or less in size can be scanned with one eye fixation per group. Therefore, screens with these size groupings can be searched faster. Groupings larger than 5 degrees require more eye fixations per grouping, slowing down screen scanning time. So, in addition to complexity, the Tullis redesigned screens differ from the original screens by some grouping measures. The more effective redesigned screens have a greater number of smaller size groups.

Tullis, in his 1983 follow-up study, also found that groupings were the strongest determinant of a screen's visual search time. If the size of a group on a screen increased, or the number of groups increased, search time also increased. Number and size of groups have an opposite relationship, however; if the number increases, size usually decreases. If the size increases, number usually decreases. What proves to be most effective is a middle-ground solution—a medium number of medium-sized groups.

Based upon this and other research, the grouping guidelines described above are presented.

Functional, semantic groups are those that make sense to the user. Related information should be displayed together. A logical place to "break" a screen is between functional groups of information, but a massive grouping of information should be broken up into smaller groups. The most reasonable point is every five rows. A six- or seven-row grouping may be displayed without a break, if necessary, but do not exceed seven rows.

The 11-to 15-character width limitation must take into consideration the data to be displayed. Confining data to this width makes no sense if it thus suffers a reduction in legibility. Legibility and comprehension are most important.

To give unity to a display, the space between groups should be less than that of the margins. Fortunately, most cathode ray tubes have a fairly wide built-in margin. The most common and obvious way to achieve spacing is through white or blank space, but there are other ways. Alternatives include contrasting display features such as differing intensity levels, image reversals (white characters on a black background versus black characters on a white background), borders and color. Spacing, however, appears to be stronger than color. Two studies (Haubner and Benz, 1983; Haubner and Neumann, 1986) found that adequate spacing, not color, is a more important determinant of ease of use for uncluttered, highly structured inquiry screens.

Perceptual Principles and Functional Grouping

- Use visual organization to create functional groupings.
  - — Proximity: 000   000   000
  - — Similarity: AAABBBCCC
  - — Closure: [ ]   [ ]   [ ]
  - — Matching patterns: >>   < >
- Combine visual organization principles in logical ways.
  - — Proximity and similarity: AAA   BBB   CCC
  - — Proximity and closure: [ ]   [ ]   [ ]
  - — Matching patterns and closure: ( )   < >   { }
  - — Proximity and ordering: 1234   1   5
                                              2   6
                                    5678   3   7
                                              4   8
- Avoid visual organization principles that conflict.
  - — Proximity opposing similarity: AAA   ABB   BBC   CCC
  - — Proximity opposing closure:] [   ] [   ] [
  - — Proximity opposing ordering: 1357   1   2
                                              3   4
                                    2468   5   6
                                              6   8

Perceptual principles can be used to aid screen functional groupings.

Use visual organization to create functional grouping. The most common perceptual principle used in screen design to aid visual groupings has been the proximity principle. The incorporation of adequate spacing between groups of related elements enhances the "togetherness" of each grouping. Space should always be considered a design component of a screen. The objective should never be to get rid of it.

The similarity principle can be used to call attention to various groupings through displaying them in a different intensity, font style, or color. The closure and matching patterns principles involve using lines, borders, and unique symbols to identify and relate common information.

Combine visual organization principles in logical ways. Visual organization principles can be combined to enhance groupings. Proximity, being a very strong perceptual principle, can guide the eye through an array of information to be scanned in a particular direction. Scanning direction can also be made obvious through similarity (color, intensity, etc.) or matching patterns (lines or borders).

Avoid visual organization principles that conflict. Principles may not always be compatible, however. When incompatibilities are encountered by the viewer, confusion results. In the examples above, proximity destroys similarity, proximity overwhelms closure, and proximity overwhelms logical ordering.

Grouping Using Borders and Backgrounds

- Consider incorporating line borders for relating groups of related information.
  — Broken lines using standard keyboard keys.

- -

= =

  — Solid lines.

  — Do not exceed three line thicknesses or two line styles on a screen, however.

- Consider incorporating a screened background for related information.
  - The background should not have the "emphasis" of the screen component that should be attended to. Consider about a 25 percent gray screening.
  - Reserve higher contrast or "emphasized" shades for screen components to which attention should be drawn.
- Consider incorporating a different color background for related information.

Line borders can greatly enhance groupings of information and direct the viewer's eye in the required direction of information scanning. Thacker (1987) found that displayed information with a border around it was reported to be easier to read, better in appearance, and preferable. On simple alphanumeric terminals, a row of dashes (– – –) or equal signs (= = =) can create a horizontal line. Vertical lines can be established using keys displaying solid (|) or broken (¦) lines. Avoid using asterisks for lines as they are too heavy visually. On a graphics terminal, solid lines can easily be created. Avoid too much use of lines, or too many kinds of lines, however, as they can cause visual clutter.

Amount of Information

- Present the proper amount of information for the task.
  - Too little is inefficient.
  - Too much is confusing.
- Present all information necessary for performing an action or making a decision on one screen, whenever possible.
  - People should not have to remember things from one screen to the next.
- Restrict screen or window density levels to no more than about 30 percent.

Presenting too much information on a screen is confusing; there will be greater competition among a screen's components for a person's attention. Visual search times will be longer and meaningful structure will be more difficult to perceive. Presenting too little information is inefficient and may tax a person's memory limitations.

In general, present all information necessary for performing an action or making a decision on one screen. This will require careful analysis of the user's tasks. One objective measure of "how much" should go on a screen has been developed: "density."

Density An objective measure of "how much" is density. Density, by definition, is a calculation of the proportion of display character positions in the screen, or an area of the screen containing something.

Density is clearly related to complexity since both measure "how much is there." Complexity looks at fields, density at characters, so they should rise and fall together.

In general, studies show that increasing the density of a display increases the time and errors in finding information (Callan et al., 1977; Dodson and Shields, 1978; Treisman, 1982). There are two types of density to be calculated on a screen; overall and local.

Overall density is a measure of the percentage of character positions on the entire screen containing data. Danchak (1976) stated that density (loading, as he called it) should not exceed 25 percent. Reporting the results of a qualitative judgment of "good" screens, he found their density was on the order of 15 percent. Tullis, in his 1981 study, reported that the density of screens from an up and running successful system ranged from 0.9 to 27.9 percent, with a mean of 14.2 percent. Using this and other research data, he concluded that the common upper-density limit appears to be on the order of 25 percent.

Thacker (1987) compared screens with densities of 14 percent, 29 percent, and 43 percent. Response time increased significantly as screen density increased. He found, however, that the time increase between 14 percent and 29 percent was much smaller than the time increase between 29 percent and 43 percent. He also found increased error rates with greater density, the 43 percent density screens showing significantly more errors.

Local density is a measure of how "tightly packed" the screen is. A measure of local density, derived by Tullis, is the percentage of characters in the 88-character visual acuity circle described in Chapter 5, modified by the weighting factors illustrated below.

```
      012222210
     0123445443210
    023456777654320
    1235679+9765321
    023456777654320
     0123445443210
      012222210
```

For every character on the screen, a local density is calculated using the above weighting factors, and then an average for all characters on the screen is established.

Figures 6.14 and 6.15 are the original and redesigned screens from the 1981 Tullis study. Density measures for these screens are:

- Figure 6.14 (original):
  — Overall density = 17.9 percent.
  — Local density = 58.0 percent.
- Figure 6.15 (redesigned):
  — Overall density = 10.8 percent.
  — Local density = 35.6 percent.

In both cases, the more effective redesigned screen had lower density measures. In his 1983 follow-up study, Tullis found a lower local density to be the most important characteristic, creating a positive "visually pleasing" feeling.

Figure 6.14. Original screen, from Tullis (1981).

```
          TEST RESULTS    SUMMARY: GROUND

          GROUND, FAULT T-G
          3 TERMINAL DC RESISTANCE
             >  3500.00 K OHMS T-R
             =    14.21 K OHMS T-G
             >  3500.00 K OHMS R-G
          3 TERMINAL DC VOLTAGE
             =     0.00 VOLTS  T-G
             =     0.00 VOLTS  R-G
          VALID RC SIGNATURE
          3 TERMINAL RC RESISTANCE
             =     8.82 K OHMS T-R
             =    14.17 K OHMS T-G
             =   628.52 K OHMS R-G
          LONGITUDINAL BALANCE POOR
             =    39    DB
          COULD NOT COUNT RINGERS DUE TO
             LOW RESISTANCE
          VALID LINE CKT CONFIGURATION
          CAN DRAW AND BREAK DIAL TONE
```

Figure 6.15. Redesigned screen, from Tullis (1981).

```
     *********************************
     *                               *
     *     TIP GROUND       14 K     *
     *                               *
     *********************************

  DC RESISTANCE        DC VOLTAGE        AC SIGNATURE

  3500 K T-R                              9 K T-R
    14 K T-G           0 V T-G           14 K T-G
  3500 K R-G           0 V R-G          629 K R-G

    BALANCE                             CENTRAL OFFICE

    39 DB                               VALID LINE CKT
                                        DIAL TONE OK
```

The research does suggest some density guidelines for screens. Maintain overall density levels no higher than about 30 percent. This upper overall density recommendation should be interpreted with extreme care. Density, by itself, does not affect whether or not what is displayed "makes sense." This is a completely different question. Density can always be reduced through substituting abbreviations for whole words. The cost of low density may be illegibility and poorer comprehension. Indeed, poorly designed screens have been redesigned to achieve greater clarity and have actually ended up with higher density measures than the original versions. How it all "hangs together" can never be divorced from how much is there.

Meaningful Ordering

- Provide an ordering of elements that:
  - Is logical and sequential.
  - Is rhythmic, guiding a person's eye through the display.
  - Encourages natural movement sequences.
  - Minimizes cursor and eye movement distances.
- Locate the most important and most frequently used elements or controls to the top left.
- Maintain a top-to-bottom, left-to-right flow.
- When groups of related information must be broken and displayed on separate screens, provide breaks at logical or natural points in the information flow.

The arrangement of screen items should appear logical and sensible to the user. Common ordering schemes are the following:

Conventional. Through convention and custom, some ordering schemes have evolved for certain elements. Examples are days of the week, months of the year, and one's name and address. These elements should be ordered in the customary way.

Sequence of use. Sequence of use grouping involves arranging information items in the order in which they are commonly received or transmitted, or in natural groups. An address, for example, is normally given by street, city, state, and zip code. Another example of natural grouping is the league standings of football teams, appearing in order of best to worst records.

Frequency of use. Frequency of use is a design technique based on the principle that information items used most frequently should be grouped at the beginning, the second most frequently used items grouped next, and so forth.

Function. Function involves grouping information items according to their purpose. All items pertaining to insurance coverages, for example, may be placed in one location. Such grouping also allow convenient group identification for the user.

Importance. Importance grouping is based on the information's importance to the task being performed. Important items are placed in the most prominent positions.

General to specific. If some data elements are more general than others, the general elements should precede the specific elements. This will usually occur when there is a hierarchical relationship among data elements.

Screen design normally reflects a combination of these techniques. Information may be organized functionally but, within each function, individual items may be arranged by sequence or importance. Numerous permutations are possible.

The direction of movement between screen items should be obvious, consistent, and rhythmic. The eye, or cursors, should not be forced or caused to wander long distances about the display seeking the next item. The eye can be guided through the screen with lines formed through use of white space and display elements. More complex movements may require the aid of display contrasts. Sequence of use can be made more obvious through the incorporation of borders around groupings of related information or screen controls. Borders provide visual cues concerning the arrangement of screen elements as the eye will tend to stay within a border to complete a task. Aligning elements will also minimize screen scanning and navigation movements. In establishing eye movement through a screen, also consider that the eye tends to move:

- From dark areas to light areas.
- From big objects to little objects.
- From unusual shapes to common shapes.
- From highly saturated colors to unsaturated colors.

These techniques can be used initially to focus a person's attention to one area of the screen and then direct it elsewhere.

Locate the most important or frequently used screen controls to the top left of the screen where initial attention is usually directed. This will also reduce the overall number of eye and manual control movements needed to work with a screen.

Maintain a top-to-bottom, left to right flow through the screen. This is contrary to the typical, text-based screen cursor movement direction that proceeds left to right, top to bottom. This top-to-bottom orientation is recommended for information entry for the following reasons:

- Eye movements between items will be shorter.
- Control cursor movements between items will be shorter.
- Groupings are more obvious perceptually.
- When one's eye moves away from the screen and then back, it returns to about the same place it left, even if it is seeking the next item in a sequence (a visual "anchor point" remains).

Top-to-bottom orientation is also recommended for presenting displays of information that must be scanned, as will be described shortly.

Distinctiveness

Elements of screen must be distinct, clearly distinguished from one another. Distinctiveness can be enhanced in a number of ways.

Separation and Contrast

- Individual screen controls, and groups of controls, must be perceptually distinct.
  — Screen controls:
    — Should not touch a window border.
    — Should not touch each other.
  — Field and group borders:
    — Should not touch a window border.
    — Should not touch each other.
  — Buttons:
    — Should not touch a window border.
    — Should not touch each other.
  — A button label should not touch the button border.
  — Adjacent screen elements must be displayed in colors or shades of sufficient contrast with one another.

All screen elements must be perceptually distinct. Distinctiveness is achieved by providing adequate separation between adjacent elements and screen boundaries and providing adequate separation between components of an element. Colors or shades used for adjacent screen elements must also contrast well with one another. Guidelines for color and shading are described in Chapter 13.

Conveying Depth of Levels

The spatial composition of a graphics screen, and currently important screen elements, can be emphasized by making them appear to be closer to the viewer. Techniques to accomplish this include overlapping, drop shadows, highlighting and lowlighting, growing and shrinking, and beveled edges (Marcus, 1992).

Overlapping, Shadows, Highlighting, Growing, and Beveled Edges

---

Overlapping
- Fully display windows where viewer attention must be directed.
- Partially hide windows not currently the focus of attention.

Drop Shadows

- Include a heavier shaded line along the bottom and right side of a pull-down or window where viewer attention must be directed.

Highlighting and Lowlighting

- Highlight windows where viewer attention must be directed.
- Lowlight windows not currently the focus of attention.

Shrinking and Growing

- Enlarge windows where viewer attention must be directed.
- Shrink windows not currently the focus of attention.

Beveled Edges

- Create beveled edges for action bar choices, buttons, windows, or icons.

Overlapping. Fully display the window or screen element of current relevance and partially hide beneath it other screen windows or elements, as illustrated in Figure 6.16. The completeness or continuity of outline of the relevant element will make it appear nearer than those partially covered.

Figure 6.16. Overlapping screen elements.

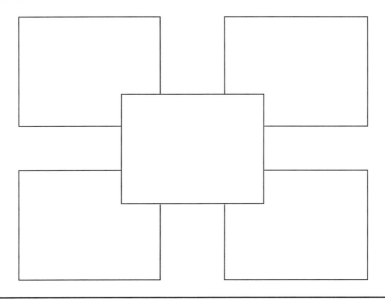

Figure 6.17. Drop shadow.

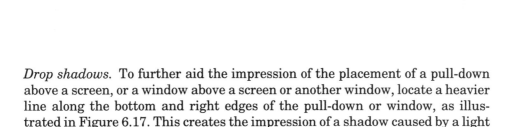

Drop shadows. To further aid the impression of the placement of a pull-down above a screen, or a window above a screen or another window, locate a heavier line along the bottom and right edges of the pull-down or window, as illustrated in Figure 6.17. This creates the impression of a shadow caused by a light source in the upper-left corner of the screen, reinforcing the nearness of the important element. The light source should always appear to be upper left, the shadow lower right.

Highlighting and lowlighting. Highlighted or brighter screen elements appear to come forward while lowlighted or less bright elements recede. Attention will be directed to the highlighted element.

Shrinking and growing. Important elements can be made to grow in size while less important elements remain small or shrink. An icon, for example, should expand to a window when it is selected. The movement, as it expands, will focus attention upon it.

Beveled edges. A beveled edge (non-right-angle lines to the screen element borders) will also give the impression of depth. With beveled edges, windows, buttons, and action bar choices will appear to arise from the screen, as illustrated in Figure 6.18. To strengthen the three-dimensional aspect of the screen element, give it a drop shadow by shading the bottom and right sides with either a tone of gray or a darker shade of the basic screen color.

Figure 6.18. Beveled edges.

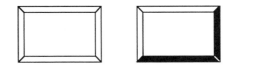

Other Ways To Convey Depth

Texture Change

- Display nonapplicable elements in a less dense texture.
- Display applicable elements in a more dense texture.

Color

- Display applicable elements in a saturated color.
- Display nonapplicable elements in a hazy, less saturated color.

Size Change

- Display applicable elements larger.
- Display nonapplicable elements smaller.

Clarity Change

- Display applicable elements clearly.
- Display nonapplicable elements fuzzy or blurred.

Vertical Location

- Display applicable elements in the lower part of the screen.
- Display nonapplicable elements in the upper part of the screen.

Spacing Change

- Display applicable elements widely spaced.
- Display nonapplicable elements narrowly spaced.

Receding Lines

- Display parallel lines receding to a vanishing point.

Motion Differences

- Move close objects at a faster rate.
- Move distant objects at a slower rate.

Other ways to establish the perception of depth on a screen, and to call attention to more important screen windows or elements, include the following (Hall, 1982 in Marcus, 1992). Often two or more of these techniques are combined.

Texture change. Increased density of an object implies a further distance. Increase the density of nonapplicable screen elements, display currently relevant elements less densely.

Color change. Objects farther away appear hazy and less saturated. Increase haziness as screen element importance diminishes; display currently relevant elements more vividly.

Size change. Objects farther away appear smaller. Decrease the size of nonapplicable screen elements; display currently relevant elements larger.

Clarity change. Objects not at the eye's focus distance appear fuzzy or blurred. Display nonapplicable elements blurred and currently relevant screen elements clear.

Vertical location. The horizon appears higher, objects up close lower. Present currently applicable screen elements at the bottom of the screen, nonapplicable elements at the screen's top.

Spacing change. Faraway objects appear more closely spaced, closer objects more widely spaced. Display nonapplicable elements more closely spaced, currently applicable screen elements more widely spaced.

Receding lines. Parallel lines receding to a vanishing point imply depth.

Motion change. Objects moving at uniform speeds appear slower the farther away they are.

Presenting Information Simply and Meaningfully

Following are guidelines for presenting information on screens. The fundamental goals are clarity and simplicity in form, comprehensibility in content, and pleasantness in tone.

General

- Present information in a directly usable form. Do not require reference to documentation, translations, transpositions, interpolations, etc.
- Use contrasting display features (different intensities and character sizes, underlining, reverse images, etc.) to call attention to:
  — Different screen components.
  — Items being operated upon.
  — Urgent items.
- Make visual appearance and procedural usage consistent.

Screen information should be presented in a directly usable form. Reference to documentation for interpretation should never be required. Contrasting display features should be used to call attention to different screen components, items being operated upon, or urgent items. Features chosen should aid in screen component identification so that attention may be quickly and accurately focused. Some recommended uses of display features are found in the following section on software considerations. Display methods chosen should always be consistent in visual appearance and procedural usage.

Upper- and Mixed-Case Font

- Use mixed case for:
  — Text.
  — Messages.
  — Menu descriptions.
  — Button descriptions.
  — Screen ID.
- Use upper case or capitalization for:
  — Title.
  — Section headings.
- Use either upper or lower case for:
  — Subsection headings.
  — Captions.
  — Data.
  — Competition aids.

The screen designer often has the choice of whether to display screen components in mixed-case or upper-case letters. Upper case means all capital letters. Mixed case usually implies a predominance of lower-case letters with occasional capitalization as needed (initial letter of first word, acronyms, abbreviations, proper nouns, etc.).

The research on textual material is clear. For example, Tinker (1955), in a study of reading from hard-copy materials, found that mixed-case text is read significantly faster than upper-case text. Rehe (1974) found a 13 percent advantage in reading speed for mixed-case text. Moskel et al. (1984) found even larger advantages of mixed-case text compared to upper case in comprehension and reading of screen materials. The advantage of mixed-case text is that it gives a word a more distinctive shape. Upper-case letters are all the same height; lower-case letters have different heights. These differences aid comprehension.

The research on screen captions, however, leans in another direction. Vartabedian (1974) established that screens with captions containing upper-case characters are searched faster than those using mixed-case characters. Williams (1988) found identical results with menu choice descriptions.

Why this difference? The materials finding superiority for mixed case appear to be of a longer textual-style nature. The caption materials appear to be single words or short phrases. It may be that the superiority of mixed case does not exhibit itself until text of an extended nature is read. Why short upper-case captions were actually superior to mixed case is unknown. In light of this research, the following is recommended.

Use mixed case for text, messages, menu bar actions, and pull-downs, pushbuttons, and the screen identifier. Text and messages in mixed case reflect the years of research on readability. The menu bar in mixed case will provide contrast with the nearby upper-case title.

Buttons in mixed case will provide case compatibility with the component of similar function, the menu bar. The screen ID in mixed case will deemphasize it slightly in relation to the screen title.

Use upper case for the title and section headings. Both will be emphasized, but not overly so.

The remainder of the screen elements may be displayed either way. Short captions in upper case may have some advantages according to the research. Displaying them in mixed case, however, will aid differentiating them from section headings. Longer, more narrative-style captions would probably benefit from mixed case. Function key descriptions and the command field in mixed case provide usage compatibility with the similar menu bar and pushbuttons. Function key descriptions and the command field in upper case, however, provide better differentiation with adjacent messages.

IBM's SAA CUA Design Guides present everything in mixed case. That this is an extrapolation of the textual reading research to all written words can only be assumed. What the guide seems to forget, however, is that the myriad of printed materials we see entirely in mixed case also benefits from different type sizes, styles, and boldnesses. Some screens do not yet have all the capabilities. There are also strict limits on how many different sizes, styles, and boldnesses may be used on one screen. Screen component visual differentiation is aided by using some capitalization, and research does not discount using it.

Typefaces—Styles and Sizes

Variations in typeface, weight, and size can be used to emphasize the structural relationship of graphical screen components. These variations should be limited, however, since too many display methods leads to clutter and the impression of confusion.

Typeface

- Use simple, readable fonts such as Times Roman or Helvetica.

Style

- Use no more than two styles of the same family.
- Use no more than two weights, regular and bold.

Size

- Use no more than three sizes.

Consistency

- Establish a consistent hierarchy and convention for using typefaces, styles, and sizes.

Figure 6.19.   The Times family of type.

Times Roman
Times Italic
Times Bold
Times Bold Italic
Times Outline
Times Shadow

Typeface. Visually simple, readable fonts are needed for clarity on screens. Ornate fonts should be avoided because they reduce legibility. Generally, sans serif typefaces are recommended (serifs are the small cross strokes that appear on the arms of some letters) if the type is less than 8 points in size or if the display environment is less than ideal. The serifs can wash out under these conditions. Types with serifs, it is felt, provide better links between letters in a word, provide a horizontal guideline for the eye, and help in distinguishing one letter from another. Helvetica is a sans serif typeface, while Times Roman is characterized by very small serifs.

Style. A typeface exists in a family of styles designed to complement one another, creating unity in design. Styles include italics, outlines, and shadows, and different weights, regular and bold. An example of a family is that of Times illustrated in Figure 6.19.

Never use more than two styles at one time. A regular type and its italics is a good combination. Also, restrict a type to two weights, regular and bold for example.

Similar typefaces are grouped into what are called races. One kind of race is called *roman*, which contains the Times typeface illustrated as well as the Bookman, Schoolbook, and Palatino typefaces. A second race is *sans serif*, where the typefaces Helvetica and Avant Garde reside. Another race is named Old English. An effective design can almost always be achieved by staying within one typeface race.

If it is necessary to mix typeface families on a screen, Lichty (1989) recommends the following:

- Never mix families within the same race. Typographic noise is created.
- Assign a separate purpose to each family. A sans serif typeface for the title and headings and a roman typeface for the body is a good combination.
- Allow one family to dominate.

For a much more detailed discussion of typefaces, see Lichty.

Sizes. Type sizes are described by points, the distance between the top of a letter's ascender and the bottom of its descender. One point equals $\frac{1}{72}$ inch. Variations in type sizes should also be minimized, no more than three being the maximum to be displayed at one time on a screen.

Consistency. Apply typeface, style, and size conventions in a consistent manner to all screen components. This will aid screen learning and improve screen readability.

Comparing paper to screen reading. Printing technology has been evolving for several centuries. Factors such as type size and style, character and line spacings, and column and margin widths have been the focus of research for a good part of that time. The product of this research is highly readable and attractive printed materials. Conversely, CRT-based characters are a relatively new innovation, with many technical limitations. The result is a displayed character that often lacks the high quality a paper medium can provide. This disparity in quality has resulted in performance differences when paper and screen reading of materials have been compared. Various researchers have found slower screen reading speeds, as much as 40 percent (Gould and Grischkowsky, 1984; Kruk and Muter, 1984; Muter et al., 1982; and Wright and Lickorish, 1983), and more errors (Gould and Grischkowsky, 1984; and Wright and Lickorish, 1983).

More recent research indicates that as display resolution improves, the reading speed differences can be reduced, if not entirely eliminated (Harpster et al., 1989). For extended reading, hard-copy display of material still has significant advantages, however.

Captions

- Identify controls with captions or labels.
- Fully spell out in a meaningful language to the user.
- Display in normal intensity.
- Use an upper-case or mixed-case font.
- When using mixed-case captions, capitalize the first letter of each significant word.
- Choose distinct captions that can be easily distinguished from other captions. Minimal differences (one letter or word) cause confusion.

Identify controls with captions. All screen data fields should be identified by captions. The context in which data is found in the world at large provides cues as to the data's meaning. A number on a telephone dial is readily identifiable as a telephone number; the number on a metal plate affixed to the back of an automobile is readily identified as a license number. The same data displayed on a screen, being out of context, may not be readily identifiable.

There are, however, some exceptions to this rule on inquiry screens. The structure of the data itself in some cases may be enough to identify its meaning. The most obvious example is name, street, city, state, and zip code. Date may be another possibility. Elimination of these common captions will serve further to clean up inquiry screens. Before eliminating them, however, it should be determined that all screen users will be able to identify these fields all the time.

Structure and size. Captions on inquiry screens, while supporting the data itself, must still clearly and concisely describe the information displayed. They are important for inexperienced screen users and for identifying similar-looking data or infrequently used data. As such, they should be fully spelled out in the natural language of the user. In general, abbreviations and contractions should not be used. To achieve the alignment recommendations to be discussed shortly, an occasional abbreviation or contraction may be necessary, but choose those that are common in the everyday language of the application or those that are meaningful and easily learned.

Significant word capitalization. When mixed-case field captions are used, capitalize the first letter of each significant word. A caption is not a sentence but the name for an area into which information will be keyed. This makes it a proper noun. When a caption is phrased as a question, then it is a sentence, and only its initial letter should be capitalized. Never begin a caption or sentence with a lower-case letter. A capital letter makes it easier for the eye to identify the start of each caption.

Unfortunately, SAA CUA does not follow the significant word capitalization principle of only using a capital letter for the initial letter of the caption.

Distinctiveness. Captions that are similar often repeat the same word or words over and over again. This increases the potential for confusion, adds to density, and often adds to screen clutter. A better solution is to incorporate the common words into headings, subheadings, or group identifiers.

Control Captions/Data Fields

- Differentiate captions from field data by using:
  - Contrasting features, such as different intensities, separating columns, boxes, etc.:

```
    Sex:  FEMALE
Relation:  DAUGHTER
```

— Consistent physical relationships:

```
    Sex:  FEMALE
Relation:  DAUGHTER
```

- For single data fields, place the caption to left of the data field:

```
Producer:  770117
```

- For columnar-oriented data, place the caption above the data fields:

```
Producers
770117
589136
642210
```

- Separate captions from data fields by at least one blank space:

```
City:  CHICAGO
```

Captions must be complete, clear, easy to identify, and distinguishable from other captions and data fields.

Differentiate captions from data. Captions and data should be visually distinguishable in some manner so that they do not have to be read in context to determine which is which. A common failing of many screens is that the captions and data have the same appearance and blend into one another when the screen is filled. This makes differentiation difficult and increases caption and field data search time. Methods to accomplish differentiation include using contrasting display features and consistent positional relationships.

For single data fields, place the caption to the left of the data field and separate the two with a colon(:). This author recommends the colon as the symbol to separate single captions and data fields oriented horizontally, or left to right. The colon is unobtrusive, does not physically resemble a letter or number, and is grammatically meaningful, "a punctuation mark used chiefly to direct attention to matter that follows" (Webster).

Since the recommended entry area for an entry control will be a box, adequately distinguishing the caption from the entry field itself, the inclusion of a colon may seem redundant. However, display/inquiry screens are most effective if the data displayed is not presented in a box, making a colon to distinguish caption from data necessary. Including a colon after all captions, therefore, will provide consistency across all screens. Figure 6.20 (starting on page 101) illustrates common caption-data field relationship problems and the recommended solution for displaying both entry fields and display/inquiry fields.

For columnar-oriented data, place the caption above the data fields. Captions should be placed above a stack of data fields that are repeated. Using horizontal caption formats for single fields and a columnar caption orientation for repeating fields will also provide better discrimination between single and repeating fields. The single-field caption will always precede the data, and captions for repeating columnar fields will always be above the top data field.

Control Caption/Data Field Justification

---

1. First Approach

- Left-justify both captions and data fields.
- Leave one space between the longest caption and the data field column.

```
DIVISION:      [              ]
DEPARTMENT:x   [          ]
    TITLE:     [               ]
```

2. Second Approach

- Left-justify data fields and right-justify captions to data fields.
- Leave one space between each.

```
   DIVISION:x [           ]
DEPARTMENT:   [        ]
     TITLE:   [             ]
```

Justification of single captions and data fields can be accomplished in several ways. These include:

A. Left-justifying captions; data field immediately follows caption.

```
BUILDING: [          ]
   FLOOR: [     ]
    ROOM: [      ]
```

B. Left-justifying captions; left-justified data fields; colon (:) associated with captions.

```
BUILDING: [          ]
FLOOR:    [    ]
ROOM:     [      ]
```

C. Left-justifying captions; left-justifying data fields; colon (:) associated with data field.

```
BUILDING : [          ]
FLOOR    : [    ]
ROOM     : [      ]
```

D. Right-justifying captions; left-justifying data fields.

```
BUILDING: [          ]
   FLOOR: [    ]
    ROOM: [      ]
```

Alternatives A and C are not recommended. Alternative A, left-justified aligned captions with data fields immediately following, results in poor alignment of data fields and increases the screen's complexity. It is more difficult to find data when searching data fields. Alternative C, while structurally sound, associates the colon (:) primarily with the data field. The strongest association of the colon should be with the caption.

The two most desirable alternatives are B and D. Alternative B, left-justified captions and data fields, is the first approach illustrated in these guidelines. Alternative D, right-justified captions and left-justified data fields, is the second approach illustrated in these guidelines.

Left-justified captions and data (B). A disadvantage to this approach is that the caption beginning point is usually farther from the entry field than the right-justified caption approach. A large mix in caption sizes can cause some captions to be far removed from their corresponding data field, greatly increasing eye movements between the two and possibly making it difficult to accurately tie caption to data field. Tying the caption to the data field by a line of dots (. . . . .) solves the association problem but adds a great deal of noise to the screen. This does not solve the eye movement problem. Eye movement inefficiencies can be addressed by abbreviating the longer captions. The cost is reduced caption clarity.

An advantage to this approach is that section headings using location positioning as the key element in their identification do stand out nicely from the crisp left-justified captions.

Right-justified captions and left-justified entry fields (D). A disadvantage here is that section headings using location positioning as the identification element do not stand out as well. They tend to get lost in the ragged left edge of the captions.

Advantages are that captions are always positioned close to their related data fields, thereby minimizing eye movements between the two, and that the screen takes on a more balanced look.

There is no universal agreement as to which is the better approach. Experimental studies have not provided any answers.

Examples to follow in this and succeeding chapters reflect both styles. This is done to enable the reader to see and evaluate each. Whichever method chosen, however, should be consistently followed in a system's screen design.

Special Symbols

- Consider special symbols for emphasis.
- Separate symbols from words by a space.

Special symbols. Special symbols should be considered to emphasize or call attention to elements on a screen. An error message, for example, can be preceded by an icon, or the "greater than" sign can be used to direct attention (AMOUNT >>). Symbols should be separated from words by one space.

Display/Inquiry Screens

Display/Inquiry screens are used to display the results of an inquiry request or the contents of computer files. Their design objective is human ease in locating data or information. Thus, they should be developed to optimize human scanning. Scanning is made easier if eye movements are minimized, required eye movement direction is obvious, and a consistent pattern is followed.

Screen Organization

- Only display information necessary to perform actions, make decisions, or answer questions.
- Group information in a logical or orderly manner, with the most frequently requested information in the upper left corner.
- For multiscreen transactions, locate most frequently requested information on the earliest screens.
- Do not pack the screen. Use spaces and lines to balance the screen perceptually.
- Columnize, maintaining a top-to-bottom, left-to-right scanning orientation.

Information contained on an inquiry screen should only be what is relevant. Forcing a user to wade through volumes of data is time consuming, costly, and error prone. Unfortunately, relevance is most often situation specific. A relevant item one time a screen is displayed may be irrelevant another time it is recalled.

Display/Inquiry screen organization should be logical, orderly, and meaningful. When information is structured in a manner that is consistent with a person's organizational view of a topic, more information is comprehended (Kintish, 1978).

Finding information on an inquiry screen can be speeded by a number of factors. First, if information is never used, do not display it. Limit a transaction or screen to what is necessary to perform actions, make decisions, or answer questions.

Second, for multiple-screen transactions, locate the most frequently sought information on the earliest transaction screens and the most frequently sought information on a screen in the upper left-hand corner.

Third, to aid in locating any particular item, provide easily scanned and identifiable groupings of information and, within each group, easily scanned and identifiable data fields. This is done through columnization with a top-to-bottom, left-to-right orientation. This means permitting the eye to move down a column from top to bottom, then moving to another column located to the right and again moving from top to bottom. This also means, if the situation warrants it, permitting the eye to move easily left to right across the top of columns to the proper column, before beginning the vertical scanning movement.

Top-to-bottom scanning will minimize eye movements through the screen and enable human perceptual powers to be utilized to their fullest. Inquiry screens are often visually scanned not through the captions but through the data fields themselves. A search for a customer name in a display of information often involves looking for a combination of characters that resembles the picture of a name that we have stored in our memory. The search task is to find a long string of alphabetic characters with one or two gaps (first name, middle initial, last name, perhaps). A date search might have the user seeking a numeric code broken by slashes. Other kinds of information also have recognizable patterns and shapes. Field captions usually play a minor role in the process, being necessary only to differentiate similar looking data fields. This leads to two key requirements in the design of design/inquiry screens: Call attention to data fields, and make the structural differences between data fields as obvious as possible. Differences are most noticeable in a columnar field structure, since it is easier to compare data fields when one is above the other.

Data Fields

- Provide visual emphasis to the data fields.
- Display directly usable information:
  — Fully spell out all codes.
  — Include natural splits or predefined breaks in displaying data.

```
338302286              072179                     162152

338-30-2286          07/21/79                  16:21:52
```

- Display data in mixed-case or upper-case.
  - Display data strings of five or more numbers or alphanumeric characters with no natural breaks in groups of three or four characters with a blank between each group.

```
  K349612094                                 K349 612 094
```

- Left-justify text and alphanumeric formats.

```
         Name:   JOHN SMITH
         Street: 612 PINE ST.
```

- Right-justify lists of numeric data.

```
         Basic:      965
         Surcharge:   82
         Total:    1,047
```

- Identical data should be consistent despite its origin.

```
   Company: 71         Company: ATLAS STEEL
   Company: ATLAS STEEL  Company: ATLAS STEEL
   Company: AS         Company: ATLAS STEEL
```

- Consider not displaying captions or data for fields whose values are "none," "zero," or blank.

- Consider creating "data statements" where the caption and data are combined.

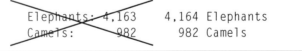

```
   Elephants: 4,163    4,164 Elephants
   Camels:      982      982 Camels
```

Visually emphasize data fields. Data fields should be visually emphasized to attract attention. This will enable the screen user immediately to find and begin scanning the display for the relevant information. High intensity is recommended to accomplish this.

Display directly usable information. Whereas data on an entry screen is often keyed in the form of a code, data on the display/inquiry screen should be displayed fully spelled out. An entry code, for example, might be keyed "AS," but the inquiry screen should display "Atlas Steel." Again, this will reduce learning requirements for the screen viewer.

Figure 6.20. Control Caption/Data Field Arrangement.

Shown below is a series of screens in a variety of formats containing either entry fields or display/inquiry fields. The author's comments are found with each screen. What are your thoughts?

6-20A. Entry screen with captions above single data fields. Captions distinctive from data but poor alignment and organization of fields. Left-to-right orientation and no groupings. Fair readability.

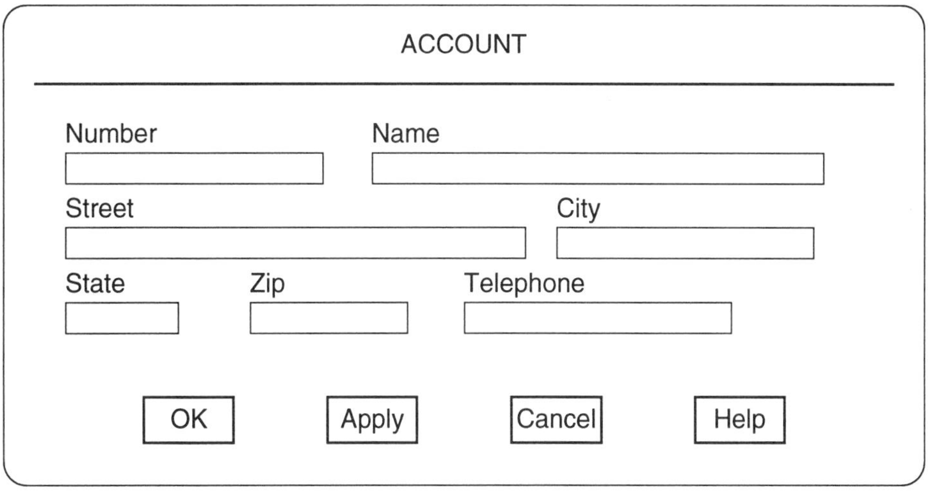

```
                          ACCOUNT
       ─────────────────────────────────────────────

       Number                Name
       [              ]      [                        ]
       Street                          City
       [                          ]    [              ]
       State        Zip            Telephone
       [      ]     [      ]       [                ]

             [ OK ]    [ Apply ]   [ Cancel ]   [ Help ]
```

6-20B. Display/Inquiry screen maintaining same structure as 6-20A. Extremely poor differentiation of captions and data. Crowded look and extremely poor readability.

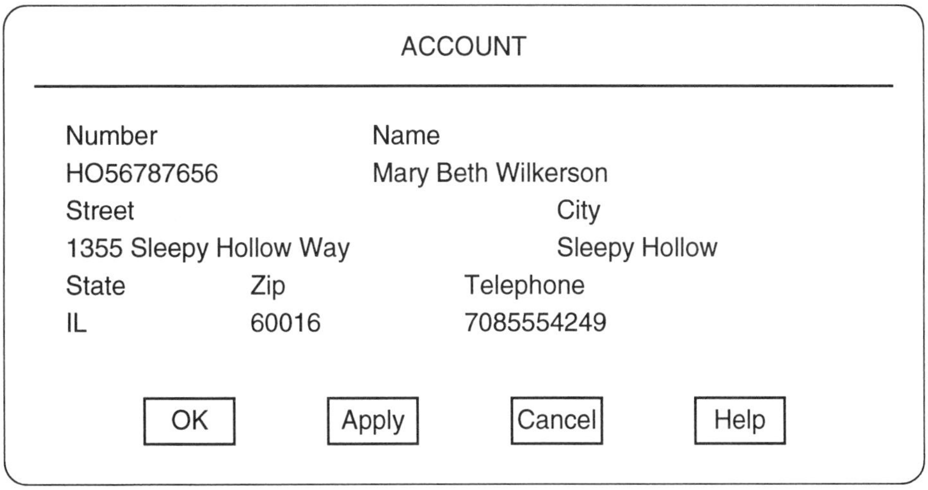

```
                          ACCOUNT
       ─────────────────────────────────────────────

       Number                Name
       HO56787656            Mary Beth Wilkerson
       Street                          City
       1355 Sleepy Hollow Way             Sleepy Hollow
       State        Zip            Telephone
       IL           60016         7085554249

             [ OK ]    [ Apply ]   [ Cancel ]   [ Help ]
```

6-20C. Entry screen in 6-20A with colons attached to captions. Captions somewhat more distinctive but still poor alignment and organization of fields, left-to-right orientation and no groupings. Fair readability.

ACCOUNT

Number: Name:

Street: City:

State: Zip: Telephone:

[OK]   [Apply]   [Cancel]   [Help]

6-20D. Display/Inquiry screen maintaining same structure as 6-20C. Somewhat better differentiation of captions and data than 6-20B but still a crowded look and poor readability.

ACCOUNT

Number: Name:
HO56787656   Mary Beth Wilkerson
Street: City:
1355 Sleepy Hollow Way   Sleepy Hollow
State: Zip: Telephone:
IL   60016   7085554249

[OK]   [Apply]   [Cancel]   [Help]

6-20E.   Entry screen with captions to left of single data fields. Captions distinctive from data but poor alignment and organization of fields. Left-to-right orientation and no groupings. Fair readability.

```
╭──────────────────────────────────────────────────────────────╮
│                          ACCOUNT                              │
│  ──────────────────────────────────────────────────────────  │
│                                                               │
│   Number [            ]      Name  [                      ]   │
│                                                               │
│   Street [                         ]    City [            ]   │
│                                                               │
│   State [  ]    Zip [         ]    Telephone [          ]     │
│                                                               │
│                                                               │
│          [  OK  ]    [ Apply ]   [Cancel]    [ Help ]         │
│                                                               │
╰──────────────────────────────────────────────────────────────╯
```

6-20F.   Display/Inquiry screen maintaining same structure as 6-20E. Extremely poor differentiation of captions and data. Less crowded look than previous display/inquiry screens but still poor readability.

```
╭──────────────────────────────────────────────────────────────╮
│                          ACCOUNT                              │
│  ──────────────────────────────────────────────────────────  │
│                                                               │
│   Number HO56787656        Name Mary Beth Wilkerson           │
│                                                               │
│   Street 1355 Sleepy Hollow Way        City Sleepy Hollow     │
│                                                               │
│   State IL        Zip 60016      Telephone 7085554249         │
│                                                               │
│                                                               │
│          [  OK  ]    [ Apply ]   [Cancel]    [ Help ]         │
│                                                               │
╰──────────────────────────────────────────────────────────────╯
```

6-20G. Entry screen in 6-20E with colons attached to captions. Captions somewhat more distinctive but still poor alignment and organization of fields, left-to-right orientation and no groupings. Fair readability.

ACCOUNT

Number: [　　　　　　]　　Name: [　　　　　　　　　　　]

Street: [　　　　　　　　　　]　　City: [　　　　　　　]

State: [　]　Zip: [　　　　]　Telephone: [　　　　　]

[OK]　[Apply]　[Cancel]　[Help]

6-20H. Display/Inquiry screen maintaining same structure as 6-20G. Somewhat better differentiation of captions and data than 6-20F but still poor readability.

ACCOUNT

Number: HO56787656　　Name: Mary Beth Wilkerson

Street: 1355 Sleepy Hollow Way　　City: Sleepy Hollow

State: IL　　Zip: 60016　　Telephone: 7085554249

[OK]　[Apply]　[Cancel]　[Help]

6-20I. Entry screen with much better alignment and readability than previous screens. Captions crowd data fields, however. Also, no groupings and does not maintain Post Office suggested format for City, State, and Zip.

```
┌──────────────────────────────────────────────────────────────┐
│                          ACCOUNT                             │
│  ──────────────────────────────────────────────────────────  │
│         Number:                                              │
│         [          ]                                         │
│         Name:                              ┌──────┐          │
│         [                            ]     │  OK  │          │
│         Street:                            └──────┘          │
│         [                            ]     ┌───────┐         │
│         City:                              │ Apply │         │
│         [                     ]            └───────┘         │
│         State:                             ┌────────┐        │
│         [    ]                             │ Cancel │        │
│         Zip:                               └────────┘        │
│         [          ]                       ┌──────┐          │
│         Telephone:                         │ Help │          │
│         [          ]                       └──────┘          │
└──────────────────────────────────────────────────────────────┘
```

6-20J. Display/Inquiry screen maintaining same aligned structure as 6-20I. Captions not very distinctive and poor readability. Again, it looks very dense and crowded.

```
┌──────────────────────────────────────────────────────────────┐
│                          ACCOUNT                             │
│  ──────────────────────────────────────────────────────────  │
│         Number:                                              │
│         HO56787656                                          │
│         Name:                              ┌──────┐          │
│         Mary Beth Wilkerson                │  OK  │          │
│         Street:                            └──────┘          │
│         1355 Sleepy Hollow Way             ┌───────┐         │
│         City:                              │ Apply │         │
│         Sleepy Hollow                      └───────┘         │
│         State:                             ┌────────┐        │
│         IL                                 │ Cancel │        │
│         Zip:                               └────────┘        │
│         60016                              ┌──────┐          │
│         Telephone:                         │ Help │          │
│         7085554249                         └──────┘          │
└──────────────────────────────────────────────────────────────┘
```

6-20K. Entry screen with the better alignment and readability of 6-20I. Caption positioned to left, however, resulting in more distinctive data fields. Still no groupings, though, and does not maintain Post Office suggested format for City, State, and Zip.

ACCOUNT	
Number:	[ ]
Name:	[ ] OK
Street:	[ ]
City:	[ ] Apply
State:	[ ] Cancel
Zip:	[ ] Help
Telephone:	[ ]

6-20L. Display/Inquiry screen maintaining same alignment and positioning of captions of 6-20K. Captions and data much more distinctive. Still no groupings, though, and does not maintain Post Office suggested format for City, State, and Zip.

ACCOUNT	
Number:	HO56787656
Name:	Mary Beth Wilkerson OK
Street:	1355 Sleepy Hollow Way
City:	Sleepy Hollow Apply
State:	IL Cancel
Zip:	60016 Help
Telephone:	7085554249

6-20M. Entry screen providing alignment, groupings, and the suggested and familiar Post Office address format. Data fields also segmented to enhance readability (Number and Telephone).

```
┌─────────────────────────────────────────────────────────────┐
│                        ACCOUNT                                │
│   ─────────────────────────────────────────────────────      │
│                                                               │
│    Number:  □ – □   □                                         │
│                                                               │
│     Name:  [                              ]                   │
│                                                               │
│    Street:  [                             ]                   │
│                                                               │
│      City:  [                ]   State: □   Zip: [       ]     │
│                                                               │
│  Telephone: (□)  □ – □                                        │
│                                                               │
│        [ OK ]      [ Apply ]      [Cancel]    [ Help ]         │
│                                                               │
└─────────────────────────────────────────────────────────────┘
```

6-20N. Display/Inquiry screen maintaining same item alignment and positioning, and data field segmentation of 6-20M. Some data distinctiveness lost, and minor crowding occurs, however, because of the location of the captions for State and Zip between data fields.

```
┌─────────────────────────────────────────────────────────────┐
│                        ACCOUNT                                │
│   ─────────────────────────────────────────────────────      │
│                                                               │
│    Number:  HO –  5678  7656                                  │
│                                                               │
│     Name:  Mary Beth Wilkerson                                │
│                                                               │
│    Street:  1355 Sleepy Hollow Way                            │
│                                                               │
│      City:  Sleepy Hollow       State: IL      Zip: 60016     │
│                                                               │
│  Telephone:  (708)  555 – 4249                                │
│                                                               │
│        [ OK ]      [ Apply ]      [Cancel]    [ Help ]         │
│                                                               │
└─────────────────────────────────────────────────────────────┘
```

6-20O. Entry screen identical to 6-20M except that captions for State and Zip are stacked with City, enhancing distinctiveness and readability of the data fields. The screen also achieves a more compact and balanced look. The recommended style for this kind of entry screen.

```
┌──────────────────────────────────────────────────────────────┐
│                         ACCOUNT                                │
│  ────────────────────────────────────────────────────────     │
│                                                                │
│   Number:        ☐ – ☐  ☐                                      │
│                                                                │
│   Name:          ┌──────────────────────────┐                 │
│                  └──────────────────────────┘                 │
│   Street:        ┌──────────────────────────┐                 │
│                  └──────────────────────────┘                 │
│   City/State/Zip: ┌──────────────┐  ☐   ┌────────┐            │
│                                                                │
│   Telephone:    (☐) ☐ – ☐                                     │
│                                                                │
│        ┌──────┐   ┌───────┐  ┌───────┐   ┌──────┐             │
│        │  OK  │   │ Apply │  │Cancel │   │ Help │             │
│        └──────┘   └───────┘  └───────┘   └──────┘             │
│                                                                │
└──────────────────────────────────────────────────────────────┘
```

6-20P. Display/Inquiry screen maintaining same alignment, item positioning, and data segmentation as 6-20O. Good readability but the lengthy caption City/State/Zip does impinge upon the distinctiveness for the data.

```
┌──────────────────────────────────────────────────────────────┐
│                         ACCOUNT                                │
│  ────────────────────────────────────────────────────────     │
│                                                                │
│   Number:        HO – 5678  7656                               │
│                                                                │
│   Name:          Mary Beth Wilkerson                           │
│                                                                │
│   Street:        1355 Sleepy Hollow Way                        │
│                                                                │
│   City/State/Zip:  Sleepy Hollow        IL      60016          │
│                                                                │
│   Telephone:     (708) 555 – 4249                              │
│                                                                │
│        ┌──────┐   ┌───────┐  ┌───────┐   ┌──────┐             │
│        │  OK  │   │ Apply │  │Cancel │   │ Help │             │
│        └──────┘   └───────┘  └───────┘   └──────┘             │
│                                                                │
└──────────────────────────────────────────────────────────────┘
```

6-20Q.   Display/Inquiry screen identical to 6-20P except the captions Street, and City/State/Zip have been eliminated to improve data field distinctiveness. The content of the data should make the identity of these fields obvious. The recommended style for this kind of display/inquiry screen.

ACCOUNT

Number: HO – 5678 7656

Name: Mary Beth Wilkerson

                1355 Sleepy Hollow Way

                Sleepy Hollow   IL   60016

Telephone: (708) 555 – 4249

        [OK]   [Apply]   [Cancel]   [Help]

A data display should also reinforce the human tendency to break things into groups. People handle information more easily when it is in chunks.

Justification.   In general, columnized text and alphanumeric data should be left-justified, and numeric data should be right-justified. In aligning data fields, keep in mind how the fields will look in relation to one another when they contain information. The visual scan should flow relatively straight from top to bottom. This may require that some data fields be right-justified in the column that is created, not left-justified.

Consistency.   Identical data taken into the system in different formats should be displayed in the same formats on inquiry screens.

Consider not displaying fields containing no data.   Optional fields on data entry screens occasionally do not have data keyed into them. When displayed on an inquiry screen the data field may be blank or contain a value such as zero or none. In some situations it may not be important to the screen viewer to know that the field contains no data. In these cases consider not displaying both captions and data for these fields. Display on the screen only the fields containing data, thereby creating less cluttered screens.

If this alternative is chosen, space on the screen must be left for situations in which all fields contain data. In order to avoid large blank screen areas, a useful rule of thumb is to allow enough space to display clearly all data for about 90 percent of all possible screens. For screens containing an excessive amount of filled-in optional fields, paging to a second screen will be necessary.

This "nondisplay" alternative should only be considered if it is not important that the viewer know something is "not there." If it is important that the viewer know that the values in a field are zero or none, or that the field is blank, then the fields must be displayed on the inquiry screen.

Consider displaying "data statements." The traditional way to display data on an inquiry screen is the "caption: data" format, for example, "Autos: 61." Another alternative is to create data statements where the caption and data are combined: "61 Autos." This format improves screen readability and slightly reduces a screen's density. If this data statement format is followed, consider the statement as data and highlight it entirely.

Hardware Considerations in Screen Design

- Screen design must be compatible with the hardware capabilities of the system, including the following:
  — System power.
  — Screen size.
  — Screen resolution and graphics capability.
  — Displayable colors.

Screen design is affected by the physical characteristics of the display device itself. Important considerations include the following:

System power. A slow processing speed and small memory may inhibit effective use of windows. Feedback and animation capabilities may be limited, reducing the system's usability. A slow screen refresh rate will increase the user's chances of perceiving screen "flicker," which can be visually fatiguing. A system must be powerful enough to perform all necessary actions promptly, responsively, and meaningfully.

Screen size. Many of today's screens are not large enough in size to take full advantage of windowing capabilities. As a result, many windows are still of "post-it" dimensions. There is some evidence (Cooper, 1985; Johnson-Laird, 1985) that many users of personal computers expand their windows to cover a full screen. Either seeing all the contents of one window is preferable to seeing small parts of many windows or the operational complexity of multiple windows is not wanted.

Expanding screen size, though, may create other problems. A large display area will require longer control movements to reach all locations on the screen. The effect on user physical comfort, and the possibility of needing an expanded working area, must be considered. A larger screen also creates more opportunities for a more cluttered screen. Clearly, the screen size-usability tradeoff must be studied further.

Screen Resolution and Graphics Capability. Poor screen resolution and graphics capability may deter effective use of a graphical system by not permitting sharp and realistic drawings and shapes. Window structure and icon design may be severely affected. Adequate screen resolution and graphics capability is a necessity to achieve meaningful representations.

Colors. The color palette must be of a variety large enough to permit establishment of a family of discriminable colors. The colors used must be accurately and clearly presented in all situations. The contextual effect of colors must also be considered, as hues may change based on factors such as size and location in relation to other colors. Contextual effects are discussed in Chapter 13.

Software Considerations in Screen Design

- Utilize the toolkits and style guides provided by many graphical systems.
- Effectively use the various display features.

Style guides. A thrust for commonality in graphical system application design has emerged as providers have finally come to realize that design consistency is a virtue that has been ignored too long. To achieve this consistency in interface design, most providers have developed style guides, paper-based style guidelines for system developers. These guidelines specify the appearance and behavior of the user interface. They describe the windows, menus, and various controls available, including what they look like and how they work. They also provide some guidance on when to use the various components.

Examples of industry-produced guidelines include Apple's *Human Interface Guidelines: The Apple Desktop Interface* (1987), Digital Equipment Corporation's *XUI Style Guide* (1988), IBM's *System Application Architecture Common User Access (SAA-CUA)* (1987, 1989a, 1989b, 1991), and Sun Microsystems' *OPEN LOOK Graphical User Interface Application Style Guidelines* (1990), Open Software Foundation's *OSF/MOTIF Style Guide* (1990), and Microsoft's *The Windows Interface* (1992).

Toolkits. Also available for most graphical systems are "toolkits" to aid in GUI application development. Toolkits include a library of high-level routines that implement elements as specified in the applicable style guide. Toolkits allow developers to develop applications more quickly and consistently. Their use requires using both the toolkit software and its documentation.

Display features

Intensity

- Good attention-getting capability.
- Least disturbing features.
- Provide two levels only.
- Use brighter intensity for more important elements.

Mixed-Case Font

- Moderate attention-getting capability.
- Use for textual information.

Upper-Case Font

- Moderate attention-getting capability.
- Use for section headings and title.

Reverse Video

- Good attention-getting capability used in moderation.
- Can reduce legibility.
- Might increase eye fatigue.
- Use in moderation.
- Suggested uses:
  — Items selected.
  — Items in error.
  — Information being acted upon.
  — Information of current relevance.

Underlining

- Poor attention-getting capability.
- May reduce legibility.
- Use to emphasize (e.g., title or headings).

Blinking

- Excellent attention-getting capability.
- Reduces legibility.
- Distracting.
- Provide two levels only (on and off).
- Blink rate should be 2–5 Hz with minimum on interval of 50 percent.
- Suggested uses:
  — Urgent situations.
  — Situations where quick response required.
- Turn off when person has responded.

Multiple Fonts

- Moderate attention-getting capability.
- Provide no more than two styles or weights.
- Provide no more than three sizes.
- Use to differentiate screen components, with larger, bolder letters to designate higher-level pieces such as title and headings.

Thin/Thick/Double Rulings and Line Borders

- Provide no more than:
  — Three line thicknesses.
  — Two line styles.
- Suggested uses:
  — Break screen into groupings.
  — Guide eye through screen.

Monochromatic Phosphor Color

- At the standard viewing distance, white, orange, or green are acceptable colors.
- At a far viewing distance, white is the best choice.
- Over all viewing distances, from near to far, white is the best choice.

Colors

- Use no more than four to six colors at one time.

A wide range of display techniques are available to aid the screen design process. Before beginning design, the designer must be aware of what capabilities exist, how they may be most effectively used, and what their limitations are.

Often these features will be used to call attention to various items on the display. The attraction capability of a mechanism is directly related to how well it stands out from its surroundings. Its maximum value is achieved when it is used in moderation. Overuse is self-defeating, as contrast with the surroundings is reduced and distraction may even begin to occur. Use of too many features at one time may also lead to increased screen visual clutter. The design goal: Use only the features necessary to get the message effectively communicated to the user. As in many aspects of design, too little or too much is not desirable. Not all display features are ideal for all situations. Following are some recommended uses and limitations that currently exist.

Intensity. High intensity has a good attention-getting quality and no disturbing features. It is frequently used to indicate items in error on data entry screens and is an excellent vehicle for calling attention to data on inquiry screens. Do not use more than two levels on a screen. If it has a fault, it is that displays with improperly set manual screen contrast controls can diminish its effectiveness, even causing it to disappear. This can be a major problem for terminals placed in exceptionally bright viewing conditions.

Mixed-case font. Mixed case should be used for textual information since it is read faster than upper case. However, use it only if the character set contains true descenders (the line dropping from a *g* or *p* that makes it lower than an *a* or *o*) or ascenders (the upward line on a *b* or *d*). Words composed of characters without true ascenders and descenders (the bottom of the *p* is not longer than the bottom of the *o*) are harder to read than upper case since the structure of the word fits no pattern we have memorized. Without true ascenders and descenders, it is better to use upper case exclusively.

Upper-case font. Upper case is recommended for screen headings and titles.

Reverse video. Reverse video is a display feature that permits a screen to resemble the normal printed page (dark letters on a light background). Rooms with overhead lighting can cause disturbing screen reflections, a problem that is significantly reduced by reverse video because the reflection is masked by the light screen background. However, reverse video should be used with caution. The following are some potential problems:

- Excessively bright display caused by the large area of emitted light from the electron gun. The result is best described as "dazzle" to one's eyes that can be fatiguing. Paper viewing is accomplished by reflected light, which is not subject to this phenomenon (although a light source positioned close to a piece of paper can create reflected glare that also creates viewing problems).
- Light emitted by the display screen tends to bleed into the dark surrounding area, as perceived by the viewer's eyes. Therefore, a display with a light background results in the background bleeding into characters displayed. Light characters bleed into a dark background. Thus, a light character on a dark background will actually look larger to the viewer than do dark characters on a light background. If character size and resolution are not adequate, the reverse video characters may not be as legible as the light-on-dark characters.
- For a normal light character on dark background display, a display refresh rate of 60 cycles per second must be maintained so the viewer does not perceive a display flicker (which can be fatiguing to the eye). A full reverse video display is much more susceptible to the perception of flicker, and the refresh rate must be increased to 90 to 100 cycles per second to eliminate it. If reverse video is used on a display being refreshed at 60 cycles per second, flicker can become a problem.

Several studies comparing reverse video screens to the more prevalent light character on dark background screens have found no performance differences

(Cushman, 1986; Kühne et al., 1986; and Zwahlen and Kothari, 1986) and no differences in eye-scanning behavior and feelings of visual fatigue (Zwahlen and Kothari, 1986). One study did find reverse video more visually fatiguing (Cushman, 1986), while another (Wichansky, 1986) found green and orange phosphor reverse video screens easier to read but found no differences in white phosphor readability.

Given the above potential problems and conflicting study results, reverse video should be used with discretion. Before implementing it on a full-screen basis, it is necessary to verify whether or not these problems do actually exist. Some displays will be fully acceptable, while others will not. The number of different displays in existence makes it impossible to specify any all-encompassing conclusions. The safest general conclusion is to use reverse video in moderation. If reverse video is used to identify certain fields or highlight certain kinds of information, some additional cautions are warranted:

- If reverse video is used to identify one kind of field such as data entry, avoid what can best be described as the crossword puzzle effect—the haphazard arrangement of elements on the screen creating an image that somewhat resembles a typical crossword puzzle. An arrangement of elements might be created that tries to lead the eye in directions that the designer has not intended or causes elements to compete for the viewer's attention. The cause of this problem is using reverse video for too many purposes or by poor alignment and columnization of fields selected for this emphasis.

  Conservative use and alignment and columnization rules will minimize this effect.
- If reverse video is used to highlight information such as error messages or actions to be taken, allow an extra reversed character position on each side of the field. This will leave a margin around the information in the field, giving it a more pleasing look. This will also eliminate any degradation in information legibility caused by lines made up of wide characters being placed too close to the edge of the field.

Underlining. Underlining can reduce legibility, so it should be used with caution. One possibility is to emphasize titles or headings. Use underlining only if some space exists between the underlining and the word being underlined. On some displays the underline is part of the character itself, thereby reducing word legibility.

Blinking. Blinking has a very high attention-getting capability, but it reduces character legibility and is disturbing to most people. It often causes visual fatigue if used excessively. Therefore, it should be reserved for urgent situations and when quick response is necessary. A user should be able to turn off the blinking once his attention has been captured. The recommended blink rate is 2–5 Hz with a minimum "on" time of 50 percent. An alternative to consider is creating an "on" cycle considerably longer than the "off," a "wink" rather than a "blink."

Multiple fonts. Multiple fonts have moderate attention-getting capability. Their varying sizes and shapes can be used to differentiate screen components. Use larger, bolder letters to designate higher-level screen pieces, such as titles and headings. Use no more than two styles or weights, and three sizes, on a screen.

Thin / thick / double rulings and line borders. Use horizontal rulings as a substitute for spaces in breaking a screen into pieces. Use vertical rulings to convey to the screen viewer that a screen should be scanned from top to bottom. Line or graphical borders can also be drawn around elements to be grouped. Figure 6.21 illustrates identical screens with and without borders. While many groupings are obvious without borders, borders certainly reinforce their existence. Use no more than three line thicknesses or two line styles on a screen.

Monochromatic phosphor color. In a study by Hewlett-Packard (Wichansky, 1986), at the standard screen viewing distance (18–24 inches), no performance differences were found between white, orange, and green phosphor in either polarity (light characters on a dark background, or dark characters on a light background). Subjective ratings of ease of reading were highest for green and orange reverse video screens as compared to normal video (light character screens), while no differences in ease of reading were found for either polarity with white phosphor at this distance. At a far viewing distance (4–5 feet), orange and green phosphor reverse video screens could be seen more clearly than normal video screens, while white screens were equally legible in either polarity. More errors were found with green phosphor than the other two.

Green phosphor caused red or pink afterimages for 35 percent of the screen viewers; orange phosphor yielded blue afterimages for 20 percent; and white phosphor yielded afterimages for 5 percent. A 35 percent green phosphor afterimage for viewing was also found by Galitz (1968).

Some conclusions:

- At standard viewing distances, no significant performance differences exist for white, orange, or green. All are acceptable. Subjective preferences may vary, however, so providing the viewer a choice of any of these colors is desirable.
- At far viewing distances, white is the more legible color and therefore the best choice.
- Over all viewing distances, white phosphor is the best choice.
- White phosphor has the lowest probability for creating afterimages.

Colors. Use no more than 4 to 6 colors at one time on a screen. Color considerations will be extensively reviewed in Chapter 13.

Figure 6.21. The effect of line or graphical borders.

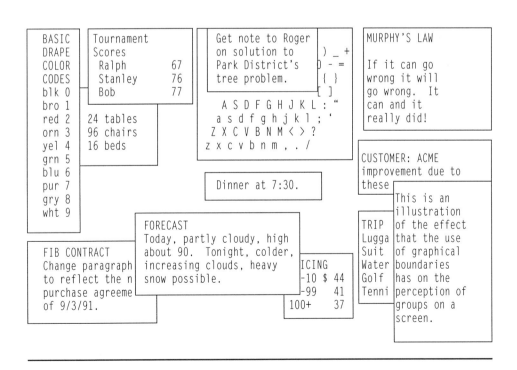

```
BASIC     Tournament              Get note to Roger       MURPHY'S LAW
DRAPE     Scores                  on solution to    ) _ +
COLOR       Ralph        67       Park District's   0 - =   If it can go
CODES       Stanley      76       tree problem.       { }   wrong it will
blk 0       Bob          77                           [ ]   go wrong.  It
bro 1                               A S D F G H J K L : "    can and it
red 2     24 tables                 a s d f g h j k l ; '    really did!
orn 3     96 chairs                 Z X C V B N M < > ?
yel 4     16 beds                   z x c v b n m , . /
grn 5                                                       CUSTOMER: ACME
blu 6                                                       improvement due to
pur 7                             Dinner at 7:30.           these
gry 8                                                              This is an
wht 9                                                              illustration
                          FORECAST                         TRIP  of the effect
                          Today, partly cloudy, high       Lugga that the use
FIB CONTRACT              about 90.  Tonight, colder,       Suit  of graphical
Change paragraph          increasing clouds, heavy   ICING Water boundaries
to reflect the n          snow possible.           -10 $ 44 Golf  has on the
purchase agreeme                                    -99   41 Tenni perception of
of 9/3/91.                                          100+   37       groups on a
                                                                    screen.
```

CHAPTER 6 EXAMPLE

Example 1.   Two pairs of display/inquiry screens from an insurance system. The first screen set is an example of good design in a text-based system. The second screen set illustrates how the same information might be presented in a graphical system.

Screen 1-1.   The first screen in this two screen text-based set summarizes the most important kinds of information a policyholder would want to know about an insurance policy. All information is aligned and columnized. The data is displayed brighter than the remaining screen elements. Groupings are strengthened by incorporating dashed lines between them. Navigation is accomplished through function keys. Messages are displayed in a message line at the bottom of the screen.

Field captions are omitted in the POLICY NUMBER/INSURED section at the top. Contextually, this information is self-explanatory. The information presented in the ENDORSEMENTS section reflects the principle of displaying something only if it is present or applicable. If one or more of these endorsements were not included with another similar policy, they would not be displayed at all. In that case, the applicable endorsements would fill this section beginning at its top. The descriptive information included with the top three endorsements reflects the conversion of the more customary "caption: data" format into simple data statements. The data statements are self-explanatory, captions are not required.

```
                      GAME RESERVE PROTECTION              Page 1 of 2
POLICY # / INSURED >>
                      24 681000
                      Swazi Game Reserve
                      East Track to Mozambique
                      Mbabane 1
                      Swaziland
_____
POLICY PERIOD >>                      | ENDORSEMENTS >>
       Effective Date:    07/21/92    |     Land Rover Extension
      Expiration Date:    07/21/93    |        7 Land Rovers
                                      |        $ 15,000 Limit
COVERAGES >>                          |
             Office: $    65,000      |     Game Ranger Business
              Cabin: $   125,000      |        Ace Rescue/Burial Services
          Liability: $ 5,000,000      |
         Deductible: $     1,000      |     Safari Survivor Benefits
                                      |        $  1,000 Minimum
                                      |        $ 99,000 Maximum
PREMIUMS >>                           |
              Basic: $     3,425      |
        Endorsement: $     9,250      |     Lion Bite Exclusion
              Total: $    12,700      |     Elephant Stampede Exclusion
                            (messages)

              F1=Help    F3=Exit   F7=Backward    F8=Forward
```

Screen 1-2. This second screen in the text-based pair includes the remaining, but less important, insurance policy information. The design philosophy, navigation, and message display philosophy is identical to the first screen. In content, policy number and insured name are carried forward to remind the viewer of the policy's identity.

```
                         GAME RESERVE PROTECTION                  Page 2 of 2
POLICY NUMBER/INSURED >>
                      24 681000
                      Swazi Game Reserve
_____

COMPANY / PRODUCER >>                  | RATING (Continued) >>
             Company: Hippopotamus     |    REST AREAS >
              Branch: Bulawayo         |                    Number:     5
            Producer: Shaka Zulu       |                   Fence Ht:   60 Ft
RATING >>                              |    TREES >
    SIZE/ROADS >                       |                    Number: 1,519
        Square Miles: 1,562            |           Ht of Tallest:    98 Ft
       Miles of Roads:    88           |       Tallest Climbable:   Yes
    NUMBER OF >                        |    SUBJECT TO >
               Lions:   413            |               Malaria:   No
           Elephants:   895            |                Floods:  Yes
              Hippos:    67            |                Famine:   No
               Caves:     3            |
_____

                              (messages)

              F1=Help   F3=Exit   F7=Backward   F8=Forward
```

Screen 1.3. The graphical equivalent to Screen 1-1. All important information is again displayed in one screen. Individual groupings are further strengthened by borders. Navigation is accomplished through the use of buttons. Messages will be displayed in a dialog box.

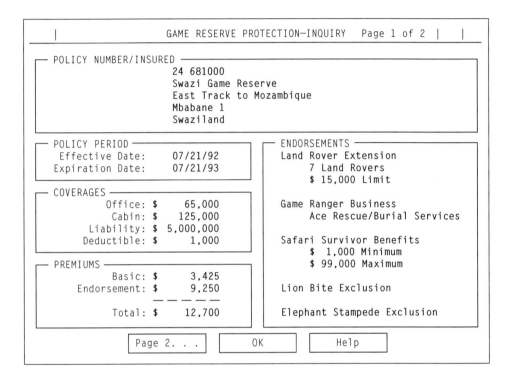

Screen 1-4. The graphical equivalent to screen 1-2, it presents the same information. The design and utilization philosophy are consistent with its sister screen, 1-3.

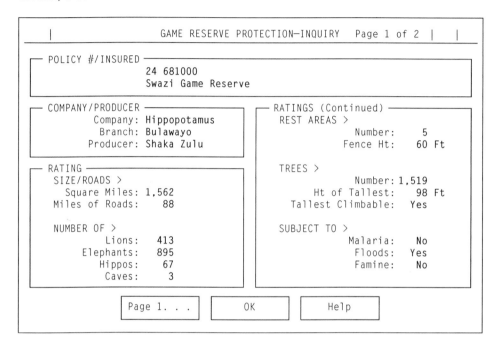

7

Application Considerations

An understanding of the user has now been obtained, as well as an understanding of the screen design considerations, including characteristics and limitations of the relevant hardware and software. Next, focus shifts to the application, including an analysis of the functions the system is to perform, a task analysis, and the development of a conceptual model for the system.

STEP 3

- *Perform a business definition and requirements analysis.*
- *Determine basic application functions.*
  - *— List major system functions.*
  - *— Describe the functions, including critical system inputs and outputs.*
  - *— Develop a flowchart of major functions.*
- Describe current user activities through task analysis.
- Develop a conceptual model of the system.
- Establish design standards or style guides.
- Establish system usability design goals.
- Define the kinds of training and documentation required.

The software development process, of which user interface design is a part, proceeds through a number of activities. An understanding of the application begins with the following:

BUSINESS DEFINITION AND REQUIREMENTS ANALYSIS

The objective of this phase is to establish the need for a system. A product description is developed and refined, based on input from users or marketing.

123

APPLICATION FUNCTIONAL SPECIFICATION

A detailed description of what the product will do is prepared. Major system functions are listed and described, including critical system inputs and outputs. A flowchart of major functions is developed. The user interface activities described in the previous chapter are usually performed concurrently with these steps.

Application Considerations

- Perform a business definition and requirements analysis.
- Determine basic application functions.
- *Describe current user activities through task analysis.*
  - *— Decompose functions down to the task level.*
  - *— Describe the tasks and related interactions.*
  - *— Develop flowcharts of the tasks and interactions.*
- Develop a conceptual model of the system.
- Establish design standards or style guides.
- Establish system usability design goals.
- Define the kinds of training and documentation required.

TASK ANALYSIS

The next step in interface design is to describe current user activities. This is accomplished through a task analysis. The task analysis may also be performed concurrently with the system functional specification.

Task analysis involves breaking down the user's activities to the individual task level. Work activities are studied and described by users. The goal is to obtain an understanding of "why" and "how" people currently do the things that will be automated. Knowing why establishes the major work goals; how provides details of actions performed to accomplish these goals. Task analysis also provides information concerning work flows, the interrelationships between people, objects, and actions, and the user's conceptual frameworks. The output of a task analysis is a complete description of all user tasks and interactions.

Task analyses may be accomplished through direct observation, interviews, questionnaires, or obtaining measurements of actual current system usage. Measurements, for example, may be obtained for the frequency in which tasks are performed or the number of errors that are made.

Application Considerations

- Perform a business definition and requirements analysis.
- Determine basic application functions.
- Describe current user activities through task analysis.

- *Develop a conceptual model of the system.*
  - *— Mental models.*
  - *— Guidelines for developing conceptual models.*
- Establish design standards or style guides.
- Establish system usability design goals.
- Define the kinds of training and documentation required.

CONCEPTUAL MODELS

The output of the task analysis is the creation of a conceptual model for the user interface.

A *conceptual model* is:

- The general conceptual framework through which the system's functions are presented.

A conceptual model describes how the interface will present objects, the relationships between objects, the properties of objects, and the actions that will be performed. A conceptual model is based on the user's mental model. A *mental model* is:

- An internal representation of a person's current conceptualization and understanding of something.

Mental models are gradually developed in order to understand, explain, and do something. Mental models enable a person to predict the necessary actions to do things if the action has been forgotten or has not yet been encountered.

The goal of the graphical system designer is to:

- Facilitate the development of a useful mental model of the system by presenting a meaningful interface conceptual model.

Mental models in using a system are derived from the system's behavior, including factors such as the system inputs, actions, outputs, including screens and messages, and its feedback and guidance characteristics. Documentation and training also play a formative role.

Guidelines for Designing Conceptual Models

- Reflect the user's mental model, not the designer's.
- Draw physical analogies or present metaphors.
- Comply with expectancies, habits, routines, and stereotypes.
- Provide action-response compatibility.
- Make invisible parts and process of a system visible.

- Provide proper and correct feedback.
- Avoid anything unnecessary or irrelevant.
- Provide design consistency.
- Provide documentation and a help system that will reinforce the conceptual model.
- Promote the development of both novice and expert mental models.

Since the term mental model refers to a person's current level of knowledge about something, people will *always* have them. They will be developed regardless of the particular design of a system, and they will be modified with experience. The goal of the designer is to design to *facilitate the process of developing an effective mental model.*

Unfortunately, little research is available to assist the software designer in creating conceptual models. Development of a user's mental model can be aided, however, by following these general guidelines for conceptual model development.

Reflect the user's mental model, not the designer's. A user will have different expectations and levels of knowledge than the designer. The mental models of the user and designer will be different.

Draw physical analogies or present metaphors. Replicate what is familiar and well known. Duplicate actions that are already well learned. The success of graphical systems can be attributed, in part, to its employing the "desktop" metaphor, a recreation of the desktop. A metaphor, to be effective, must be widely applicable within an interface. Metaphors that are only partially or only occasionally applicable should not be used. In the event a metaphor cannot be explicitly employed in a new interface, structure the new interface in terms of familiar aspects from the manual world.

Comply with expectancies, habits, routines, and stereotypes. Create a system that builds on knowledge, habits, routines, and expectancies that already exist. Use familiar associations, avoiding the new and unfamiliar. With color, for example, accepted meanings for red, yellow, and green are already well established. Use words and symbols in their customary ways. Replicate the language of the user, and create icons reflecting already known images.

Provide action-response compatibility. All system responses should be compatible with the actions that elicit them. Names of commands, for example, should reflect the actions that will occur. Organization of keys in documentation or help screens should reflect the ordering as they actually exist on the keyboard.

Make invisible parts of the system visible. Systems are comprised of parts and processes, many of which are invisible to the user. In creating a mental model, a person must make a hypothesis about what is invisible and how it relates to what is visible. New users of a system often make erroneous or incomplete assumptions about what is invisible and develop a faulty mental model. As more experience is gained, their mental models evolve to become more accurate and complete. Making invisible parts of a system visible will speed up the process of developing correct mental models.

An example of a process being made visible can be illustrated by moving a document between files. In a command language interface, the document must be moved through a series of typed commands. The file is moved invisibly and, the user assumes, correctly, unless an error message is received. In a graphical direct manipulation system, the entire process is visible, the user literally "picking up" the file in one folder and "dragging" it to another folder.

Provide proper and correct feedback. Be generous in providing feedback. Keep a person informed of what is happening, and what has happened, at all times.

- *Provide continuous indications of status.* Mental models are difficult to develop if things happen, or are completed, unknown to the user. During long processing sequences, for example, interim status messages such as "loading . . .," "opening . . .," or "searching . . ." enable the user to understand internal processes, more accurately predict how long something will take, are reassuring, and permit pinpointing of problems if they occur.
- *Provide visible results of actions.* For example, highlight selected objects, display new locations of moved objects, and show files that are closed.
- *Display actions in progress.* For example, show a window being changed in size actually changing, not simply the window in its changed form. This will strengthen cause-and-effect relationships in the mental model.
- *Present as much context information as possible.* To promote contextual understanding, present as much background or historical information as possible. For example, on a menu screen, maintain a listing of the menu choices selected to get to the current point. On a query screen, show the query criteria when displaying the query results.
- *Provide clear, constructive, and correct error messages.* Incomplete or misleading error messages may cause false assumptions that violate and weaken the user's mental model. Error messages should always be structured to reinforce the mental model. For example, error messages addressing an incomplete action should specify *exactly* what is missing, not simply advise a person that something is "incomplete."

Avoid the unnecessary or irrelevant. Do not display irrelevant information on the screen. People may try to interpret it and integrate it into their mental models, thereby creating a false one. Irrelevant information might be unneeded data fields, screen controls, system status codes, or error message numbers. If potentially misleading information cannot be avoided, point this out to the user.

Also, do not overuse display techniques, or use them in meaningless ways. Too much color, for example, may distract people and cause them to make erroneous assumptions as they try to interpret. The result will be a faulty and unclear mental model.

Provide design consistency. Design consistency reduces the number of concepts to be learned. Inconsistency requires the mastery of multiple models. If an occasional inconsistency cannot be avoided, explain it to the user. For example, if an error is caused by a user action that is inconsistent with other similar actions, explain in the error message that this condition exists. This will prevent the user from falsely assuming that the model he or she has been operating under is incorrect.

Provide documentation and a help system that will reinforce the conceptual model. Consistencies and metaphors should be explicitly described in the user documentation. This will assist a person in learning the system. Do not rely on the users to uncover consistencies and metaphors themselves. The help system should offer advice aimed at improving mental models.

Promote the development of both novice and expert mental models. Novices and experts are likely to bring to bear different mental models when using a system. It will be easier for novices to form an initial system mental model if they are protected from the full complexity of a system. Employ levels of functionality that can be revealed through "progressive disclosure."

Application Considerations

- Perform a business definition and requirements analysis.
- Determine basic application functions.
- Describe current user activities through task analysis.
- Develop a conceptual model of the system.
- *Establish design standards or style guides.*
- *Establish system usability design goals.*
  - *— Usability criteria.*
- *Define the kinds of training and documentation required.*

Specification of a system's functions also requires doing the following:

Establish design standards or style guides. This document defines the interface standards, rules, guidelines, and conventions that must be followed in detailed design. It will be based on the characteristics of the system's hardware and software, the principles of good screen design, the needs of system users, and any unique company or organization requirements that may exist.

The value of standards are:

- To users:
  - Faster performance.
  - Fewer errors.
  - Reduced training time.
  - Better system utilization.
  - Better satisfaction.
  - Better system acceptance.
- To designers:
  - Increased visibility to human-computer interface.
  - Simplified design.
  - More programming/design aids.
  - Reduced redundant effort.
  - Reduced training.

The published style guides vary in their ability to control compliance with the guidelines they present. Some present strict requirements leading to excellent consistency across applications (Apple); others provide little guideline compliance control. The style guides also are suffering growing pains because of their newness and the rapid pace of technology.

Terminology changes between versions can cause user confusion and learning problems (IBM SAA-CUA, 1989b, 1991). Terminology differences between guides lead to the same result. The screen background area in CUA is called the "desktop." In OPEN LOOK it is referred to as the "workspace." Window names in CUA are called "primary and secondary." In Microsoft Windows, "application and document."

In parallel with the development of guidelines has been some research looking at both how well guidelines are actually followed and methods to achieve most effective guideline utilization.

Research on guideline utilization has hardly been encouraging. Mosier and Smith (1986) found that only 58 percent of the users of a large interface guidelines document found the information they were looking for, and an additional 36 percent only sometimes found it. DeSouza and Bevan (1990) report that designers using a draft of the ISO menu interface standard violated 11 percent of the rules and had difficulties in interpreting 30 percent. Tetzlaff and Schwartz (1991) also report difficulties in interpreting guidelines from an interface style guide, although conformance with the guidelines was high. Thovtrup and Nielsen (1991) report designers were only able to achieve a 71 percent compliance with a two-page standard in a laboratory setting. In an evaluation of three real systems, they found that the mandatory rules of the company's screen design standard were violated 32 to 55 percent of the time.

Thovtrup and Nielsen, in analyzing why the rules in the screen design standard were broken, found a very positive designer attitude toward the standard, both in terms of its value and content. Rules were not adhered to, however, for the following reasons:

- An alternative design solution was better than that mandated by the standard.
- Available development tools did not allow compliance with the standard.
- Compliance with the standard was planned, but time was not yet available to implement it.
- The rule that was broken was not known or was overlooked.

Tetzlaff and Schwartz, in analyzing how their guidelines were used, found that designers depended heavily on the pictorial guideline examples, often ignoring the accompanying text.

The implications of these studies for a screen standard design are as follows:

- Include concrete examples of correctly designed screens.
- Provide development tools that support implementation of the screens that follow the standard.
- Provide a rationale for why the particular guidelines should be used.. This is especially important if the guideline is a deviation from a previous design practice.
- Provide a rationale describing the conditions under which various design alternatives are appropriate. The examples may illustrate alternatives and the tool kit may produce them, but when these various alternatives are appropriate may be difficult for designers to infer.
- Design the standards document following recognized principles for good document design. Provide good access mechanisms such as a thorough index, a table of contents, glossaries, and checklists.

Two questions often asked are, "Is it too late to develop and implement standards?" and "What will be the impact on systems and screens now being used?" To address these questions, Burns and Warren (1986) reformatted several alphanumeric inquiry screens to improve their comprehensibility and readability. When these reformatted screens were presented to expert system users, decision-making time remained the same but errors were reduced. For novice system users, the reformatted screens brought large improvements in speed and accuracy. Therefore, it appears, changes enhancing screens will benefit novice as well as expert users already familiar with the current screens. It is never too late to change.

Establish System Usability Design Goals. Human performance goals in system use, like any other design goal, should be stated in quantitative and measurable ways. Without performance goals you will never know if you achieved them. Clear goals also provide objectives for acceptance testing and assure that a faulty or unsatisfactory product will not be released.

The term "usability" to describe effectiveness of human performance was first used by Bennett (1979). In the following years a more formal definition was proposed by Shackel (1981, 1984) and modified by Bennett (1984). Finally, Shackel (1991) simply defined usability as "the capability to be used by humans easily and effectively, where,

easily = to a specified level of subjective assessment,
effectively = to a specified level of human performance."

He then presented the following criteria for measuring usability:

Usability Criteria

Effectiveness

- The required range of tasks must be accomplished at better than some required level of performance (e.g., in terms of speed and errors).
- By some required percentage of the specified target range of users.
- Within some required proportion of the range of usage environments.

Learnability

- Within some specified time from commissioning and start of user training.
- Based on some specified amount of training and user support.
- Within some specified relearning time each time for intermittent users.

Flexibility

- With flexibility allowing adaptation to some specified percentage variation in tasks and/or environments beyond those first specified.

Attitude

- Within acceptable levels of human cost in terms of tiredness, discomfort, frustration and personal effort.
- So that satisfaction causes continued and enhanced usage of the system.

Values for the various criteria should be specified in absolute terms. An absolute goal might be "Task A must be performed by a first-time user in 12 minutes with no errors with 30 minutes training and without referring to a manual." Goals may also be set in relative terms. For example, "Task B must be performed 50 percent faster than it was using the previous system."

The level of established goals will depend on the capabilities of the user, the capabilities of the system, and the objectives of the system. In addition to providing commitments to a certain level of quality, goals become the foundation for the system test plan.

Define the kinds of training and documentation required. System training and documentation needs will be based on user needs, system conceptual design, system learning goals, and system performance goals. It may include such tools as formal or video training, manuals, online tutorials, reference manuals, quick reference guides, and online help.

8

Windows

A window is an area of the screen, usually rectangular in shape, defined by a border that contains a particular view of some area of the computer or some portion of the user's dialogue with the computer. It can be moved, sized, and rendered independently on the screen. A window may be small, containing a short message or a single field, or it may be large, consuming most or all of the available display space. A display may contain one, two, or more windows within its boundaries.

STEP 4

- Organize window system functions.
- Determine the style, or styles, of windows to be presented.
- Divide the tasks into a series of windows.

CHARACTERISTICS

A window is seen to possess the following characteristics:

- A name or *title,* allowing it to be identified.
- A *size* in height and width (which can vary).
- A *state,* whether it is accessible or active or not accessible. (Only active windows can have their contents altered.)
- *Visibility*—the portion that can be seen. (A window may be partially or fully hidden behind another window, or the information within a window may extend beyond the window's display area.)
- A *location,* relative to the display boundary.

- *Presentation,* its arrangement in relation to other windows. It may be tiled, overlapping, or cascading.
- *Management capabilities,* methods for manipulation of the window on the screen.
- Its *highlight,* the part that is selected.
- Its *pointer,* a graphic representation of its location.
- The *application* or task it is dedicated to.

THE ATTRACTION OF WINDOWS

The value of windowing is best seen in the context of the typical office job. An office worker performs a variety of tasks, often in a fairly unstructured manner. The worker is asked to monitor and manipulate data from a variety of sources, synthesize information, summarize information, and reorganize information. Things are seldom completed in a continuous time frame. Outside events such as telephone calls, supervisor requests, and deadlines force shifts in emphasis and focus. Tasks start, stop, and start again. Materials used in dealing with the tasks are usually scattered about one's desk, being positioned in the workspace to make handling the task as efficient as possible. This spatial mapping of tools helps people organize their work and provides reminders of uncompleted tasks. As work progresses and priorities change, materials are reorganized to reflect the changes.

Single-screen technology supports this work structure very poorly. Since only one screen of information can be viewed at one time, comparing or integrating information from different sources and on different screens often requires extensive use of one's memory. To support memory, the worker is often forced to make handwritten notes or obtain printed copies of screens. Switching between tasks is difficult and interrupting and later returning to a task requires an extensive and costly restructuring of the work environment.

The appeal of windowing is that it allows the "display workspace" to mirror the "desk workspace" much more closely. This dramatically reduces one's short-term memory loads. A person's ability to do mental calculations is limited by how well one keeps track of one's place, one's interim conclusions and products, and, finally, the results. Windows act as external memories that are an extension of one's internal memory (Card et al., 1985). Windows also make it much easier to switch between tasks and to maintain one's context, since one does not have to reestablish one's place continually. Windows also provide access to more information than would normally be available on a single screen of the same size. This is done by overwriting or placing more important information on top of that of less importance at that moment.

While all the advantages and disadvantages of windows are still not well understood, they do seem to be useful in the following ways.

Presentation of different levels of information. Information can be examined in increasing levels of detail. A document table of contents can be presented in a window. A chapter, or topic, selected from this window can be simultaneously displayed in more detail in an adjoining window. Deeper levels are also possible on additional windows.

Presentation of multiple kinds of information. Variable information needed to complete a task can be displayed simultaneously in adjacent windows. An order-processing-system window could collect a customer account number in one window and return the customer's name and shipping address in another window. A third window could collect details of the order after which another window presents factory availability and shipping dates of the desired items. Significant windows remain displayed so that details may be modified as needed prior to order completion. Low stocks or delayed shipping dates might require changing the order.

Sequential presentation of levels or kinds of information. Steps to accomplish a task can be sequentially presented through windows. Successive windows are presented until all the required details are collected. Key windows may remain displayed, but others appear and disappear as necessary. This sequential preparation is especially useful if the information-collection process leads down different paths. An insurance application, for example, will include different coverages. A requested coverage might necessitate the collection of specific details about that coverage. This information can be entered into a window presented to collect the unique data. The windows disappear after data entry and additional windows appear when needed.

Access to different sources of information. Independent sources of information may have to be accessed at the same time. This information may reside in different host computers, operating systems, applications, files, or areas of the same file. For example, information may be presented on the screen alongside the problem, greatly facilitating its solution. Or, a writer may have to refer to several parts of text being written at the same time. Or, a travel agent may have to compare several travel destinations for a particularly demanding client.

Combining multiple sources of information. Text from several documents may have to be reviewed and combined into one. Pertinent information is selected from one window and copied into another.

Performing more than one task. More than one task can be performed at one time. While waiting for a long, complex procedure to finish, another can be performed. Tasks of higher priority can interrupt less important ones. The interrupted task can then be resumed with no "close down" and "restart" necessary.

Reminding. Windows can be used to remind the viewer of things likely to be of use in the near future. Examples might be menus of choices available, a history of the path followed or command choices to that point, or the time of an important meeting.

Monitoring. Changes, both internal and external, can be monitored. Data in one window can be modified and its effect on data in another window can be studied. External events, such as stock prices, out of normal range conditions, or system messages can be watched while another major activity is carried out.

Multiple representations of the same task. The same thing can be looked at in several ways—for example, alternative drafts of a speech, different versions of a screen, or different graphical representations of the same data.

CONSTRAINTS IN WINDOW SYSTEM DESIGN

Windowing systems, in spite of their appeal and obvious benefits, have failed to live up to their expectations, says Billingsley (1988) in her excellent review. Benest and Dukic (1989) describe the overall user interface as "chaotic" because of the great amount of time users must spend doing such things as pointing at tiny boxes in window borders, resizing windows, moving windows, closing windows, and so forth. Billingsley attributes the problems with windowing systems to three factors: historical considerations, hardware limitations, and human limitations.

Historical considerations. Historically, system developers have been much more interested in solving hardware problems than in user considerations. Since technical issues abound, they have received the strong focus of attention. There has been very little research addressing design issues and their impact on the usability of window systems. Therefore, there are few concrete window design guidelines to aid designers.

This lack of guidelines makes it difficult to develop acceptable and agreeable window standards. While some companies are developing style guides, they are very general and limited in scope to their products. Standardization is also made more difficult by the complexity and range of alternatives available to the designer. Without user performance data, it is difficult to compare realistically the different alternatives, and design choices become a matter of preference.

Standardization of the interface is also inhibited by other factors. Some software developers, who are proud of their originality, see standards as a threat to creativity and its perceived monetary rewards. Some companies are wary of standards because they fear other companies are promoting standards that reflect their own approach. Finally, some companies have threatened, or brought, legal action against anyone who adopts an approach similar to their own.

The result, Billingsley concludes, is that developers of new systems create another new variation each time they design a product, and users must cope with a new interface each time they encounter a new windowing system.

Hardware limitations. Many of today's screens are not large enough to take full advantage of windowing capabilities. As a result, many windows are still of "post-it" dimensions. There is some evidence (Cooper, 1985; Johnson-Laird, 1985) that many users of personal computers expand their windows to cover a full screen. Either seeing all the contents of one window is preferable to seeing small parts of many windows or the operational complexity of multiple windows is not wanted.

The slower processing speeds and smaller memory sizes of some computers may also inhibit use of windows. A drain on the computer's resources may limit feedback and animation capabilities, thereby reducing the system's usability. Poor screen resolution and graphics capability may also deter effective use of windows by not permitting sharp and realistic drawings and shapes.

Human limitations. A windowing system, because it is more complex, requires the learning and using of more operations. Much practice is needed to master them. These window management operations are placed on top of other system operations, and window management can become an end in itself. This can severely detract from the task at hand. In a study comparing full screens with screens containing overlapping windows (Davies et al., 1985), task completion times were longer with the window screens, but the nonwindow screens generated more user errors. After eliminating screen arrangement time, however, task solution times were shorter with windows. The results suggest that advantages for windows do exist, but they can be negated by excessive window manipulation requirements.

Benest and Dukic (1989) suggest that to be truly effective, window manipulation must occur implicitly as a result of user task actions, not as a result of explicit window management actions by the user.

Other limitations. Other possible window problems include the necessity for window borders to consume valuable screen space, and small windows providing access to large amounts of information can lead to excessive, bothersome scrolling.

WINDOWS AND WINDOW DESIGN STEPS

Windows

- *Components of a window:*
  - *— Border.*
  - *— Title bar.*
  - *— Work area.*
  - *— System menu button.*
  - *— Sizing buttons.*
  - *— Menu bar.*
  - *— Message area.*
  - *— Status area.*
  - *— Scroll bar.*
  - *— Split box and split bar.*
  - *— Control bar.*
  - *— Command area.*
- Window manipulation guidelines.

Window Design Steps

- Organize window system functions.
- Determine the style, or styles, of windows to be presented.
- Divide the tasks into a series of windows.

Components of a Window

A typical window may be comprised of up to a dozen or so elements. Some appear on all windows; others appear conditionally. For consistency purposes, these elements should always be located in the same position within a window. Most windowing systems provide consistent locations for elements in their own windows. Some inconsistencies do exist in element locations between different systems, however, as do some differences in what elements are named. What follows is a description of typical window components and their purposes. Illustrations are found beginning with Figure 8.1. Relevant design guidelines for these components will be found in later sections of this book.

Border

Description

- A frame, usually rectangular in shape, surrounding the window.
  - — When it fills the entire screen, however, the screen edge may become the border.
- Standard on all windows.

Purpose

- To define the area of the window and distinguish it from other windows.
- May be used to identify the type of window (by changing thickness or color).
- May be used to change the window's size (by grabbing with the cursor).

A window will have a border, usually rectangular in shape, to define its boundaries and distinguish it from other windows. The border is comprised of a line that may be variable in thickness and/or color. This variation can be used as an aid in identifying the type of window being displayed. Windows filling an entire screen may use the screen edge as the border. Another term commonly used for border is "frame."

Title Bar

Description

- The top line stretching the full width of the window.
- It will contain the window's title.
- It may also include:
  - — System menu button.
  - — Window-sizing buttons.
- Standard on all primary and secondary windows.

Figure 8.1. Examples of various screen components (from Microsoft Windows).

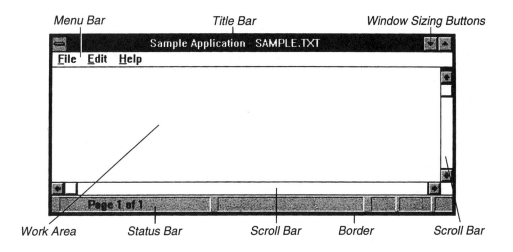

Purpose

- To identify a window and clarify its purpose.
- To display possible actions.
- To aid in moving a window (by grabbing with the cursor).

The title bar is the top line of the window. It contains a descriptive window title to identify the window's purpose and may possess, at the extreme left and right ends, control buttons for retrieving the system menu and performing window sizing. The area of the title bar used for displaying the title may be called the "title area" in some systems.

Work Area

Description

- The area of the window beneath the title bar and within the window's borders and other relevant window components.
- Standard on all windows.

Purpose

- To provide a working area for the application and the user.
- It may contain:
  — Application controls such as entry fields and lists.

— Customized forms such as spreadsheets.
— An open typing area for word processing applications.
— User-entered information.

The work area is the portion of the screen where the user performs tasks. It is the open area inside the window's border and other relevant peripheral screen components such as the menu bar and scroll bar. The work area may consist of an open area for typing, or it may contain application controls or customized forms. The work area may also be referred to as the "client area."

System Menu Button

Description

- A small button inscribed with a unique symbol located at the left side of the title bar.
  — The symbol is commonly a horizontal bar.

Purpose

- To present commands for manipulating the window (e.g., restore, move, minimize, close, etc.).

Located at the left corner of the title bar, the system menu button is used to retrieve a pull-down menu of commands for manipulating a window. The system menu is primarily an aid to keyboard users of a system, the mouse having direct access to all these actions. The system menu also serves as an aid to casual system users, reminding them of actions available. The symbol inscribed on the button is most commonly a horizontal bar, although versions using a form of inverted rectangle are also seen, as illustrated in Figure 8.2. The system menu may also be called the "window menu" or "control menu."

Figure 8.2.   Representative system menu icons.

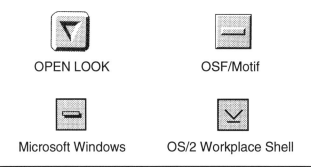

OPEN LOOK	OSF/Motif
Microsoft Windows	OS/2 Workplace Shell

Window Sizing Buttons

Description

- Three small buttons located at the right side of the title bar of primary windows.
  - The *minimize* button:
    - Is typically inscribed with a single downward-pointing arrow or small box.
    - Is located to the right end of the title bar, just to the left of the maximize button.
  - The *maximize* button:
    - Is typically inscribed with a single upward-pointing arrow or large box.
    - Is located to the far right end of the title bar, just to the right of the minimize button.
  - When a window has achieved its maximum size, the maximize button is replaced with a *restore* button.
    - The restore button is typically inscribed with a pair of arrows, one upward-pointing, the other downward-pointing, or another unique symbol.
    - When a window has been reduced from maximum size, the restore button is replaced with a maximize button.
- These buttons are graphical equivalents of the corresponding commands obtained through the system menu button.

Purpose

- The *maximize* button enlarges a window to its largest size.
- The *minimize* button reduces a window to its minimum size, usually an icon.
- The *restore* button returns a window to the size and location it had before it was minimized or maximized.

These buttons are used to manipulate the size of a window. The minimize button is used to reduce a window to its minimum size, usually an icon. It also hides all associated windows. The maximize button enlarges a window to its maximum size, usually the entire screen. When a screen is maximized, the restore button replaces the maximize button, since the window can no longer be increased in size. The restore button returns a window to the size it had before a minimize or maximize action was performed. These buttons are located in the upper-right corner of the title bar and take forms as illustrated by the examples in Figures 8.3 and 8.4. These buttons are graphical equivalents to the actions available through the system menu button.

Menu Bar

Description

- A "menu" or collection of menu titles provided by the application.
- Located at the top of the window in a horizontal row, just below the title bar.
- Each menu title will have a pull-down menu associated with it describing the exact actions that may be performed.
- Typically, each system provides a default set of menu bar actions (e.g., File, Edit, View, Window, Help).

Purpose

- To present titles of application features or choices to the screen user. They can be the following:
  — Commands.
  — Attributes or properties that apply to an object.

A menu bar is used to organize and provide access to application actions. It is located horizontally at the top of the window, just below the title bar. A menu bar contains a list of topics or titles of menus that, when selected, are displayed on a pull-down menu beneath the choice. A system will typically provide a default set of menu actions that can be augmented by an application. IBM SAA CUA previously called the menu bar an "action bar."

Figure 8.3.   Representative minimize icons.

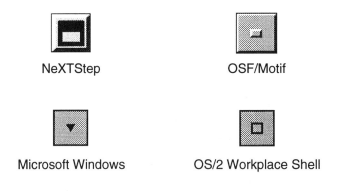

NeXTStep   OSF/Motif

Microsoft Windows   OS/2 Workplace Shell

Figure 8.4. Representative maximize icons.

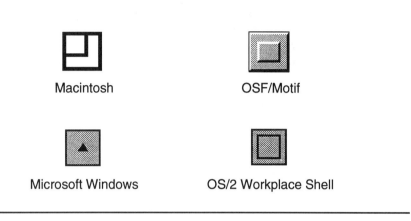

Macintosh   OSF/Motif

Microsoft Windows   OS/2 Workplace Shell

Message Area

Description

- An open area at the bottom of the window, located just below the horizontal scroll bar.
- Optional on all windows.

Purpose

- To display status information about a selection, command, or process.
- To explain menu items as they are highlighted.
- To request information from the user.
- To present help information.

Messages to the user can be displayed in a horizontal line at the bottom of the screen, below any included scroll bar. The kinds of messages displayed include statuses, explanations, or helps. Messages longer than the message bar should be displayed in a window. A message area, also referred to as the "message bar" or "information area," is illustrated in Figure 8.5.

Status Area

Description

- An open area of the window variously located:
  — Below the horizontal scroll bar at the screen bottom.
  — Below the title bar and, if included, the menu bar.
- Optional on all windows.

Figure 8.5. Example of a message area (from Microsoft Windows).

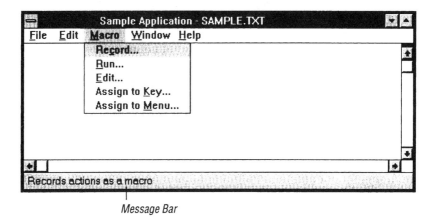

Message Bar

Purpose

- To display brief messages.
- To display information about the current state of the application.
  - Information about the current state of something displayed in the work area.
  - Cursor location.
  - Keyboard modes active.

A status area is useful when information about the current state of an application should be known. IBM SAA CUA (1991) recommends that the status bar be located just below the title bar, or just below the menu bar when it, too, is included in a window. Microsoft Windows (1992) positions the status bar at the bottom of the screen. The author recommends the IBM SAA CUA approach.

Scroll Bar

Description

- An elongated rectangular container consisting of:
  - A scroll area or shaft.
  - A slider box or elevator inside.
  - Arrows or anchors at each end.
- May be oriented:
  - Vertically at the far right side of the work area.
  - Horizontally, at the bottom of the work area (above the message area and/or command area).
- Optional on all windows.

Purpose

- To find and display information that takes more space than the allotted display space.

When all display information cannot be presented in a window, it must be found and made visible. This is accomplished by scrolling the display's contents through use of a scroll bar. A scroll bar is an elongated rectangular container consisting of a scroll area or shaft, a slider box or elevator, and arrows or anchors at each end. For vertical scrolling, the scroll bar is positioned at the far right side of the work area, extending its entire length. Horizontal scrolling is accomplished through a scroll bar located at the bottom of the work area.

Split Box and Split Bar

Description

- A *split box* is a solid button located:
  — Above the vertical scroll bar up arrow.
  — To the left of the left horizontal scroll bar arrow.
- A *split bar* is a double line separating pieces or panes of a split window.
- Optional on all windows.

Purpose

- A *split box* permits separating a window into two or more viewing areas to get multiple views of an object.
- A *split bar* identifies the separate viewing areas or panes.

A window can be split into two or more pieces or panes by manipulating a split box located above a vertical scroll bar or to the left of a horizontal scroll bar. The separate panes or viewing areas are delineated by a double-line separator, as illustrated in Figure 8.6.

Control Bar

Description

- A permanently displayed array of choices or commands, including the following:
  — Color/pattern palettes.
  — Toolboxes.
  — Rulers.
  — Ribbons.
- Occupy a fixed position in a primary window, usually to the side or bottom.
- Movable in supplemental windows and dialog boxes.
- Optional on all windows.

Purpose

- To provide quick and convenient access to frequently used choices and commands.

Control bars, illustrated in Figure 8.7, are permanently displayed arrays of choices or commands that must be accessed quickly. They usually occupy a fixed position in a primary window and are movable in other types of windows.

Command Area

Description

- An area for typing commands located below the scroll bar and above the information area/status bar.
- Optional on all windows.

Purpose

- To allow commands to be typed using the keyboard.

Figure 8.6. Example of split box and split bar (from IBM SAA CUA).

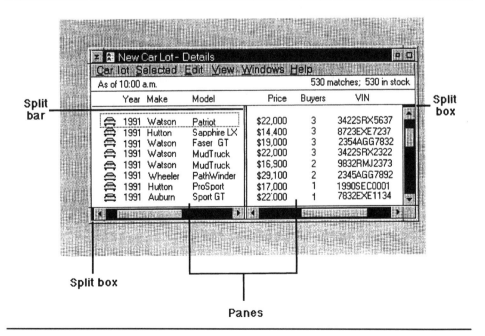

Figure 8.7. Examples of control bars (from Microsoft Windows).

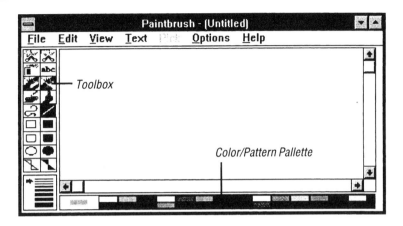

In situations where it is useful for a command to be typed into a screen, a command area can be provided. Locate the command area at the bottom of the window. If a horizontal scroll bar is included in the window, position the command area just below it. If a message area is included on the screen, locate the command area just above it, as illustrated in Figure 8.8.

Figure 8.8. Example of a command area (from OSF/Motif).

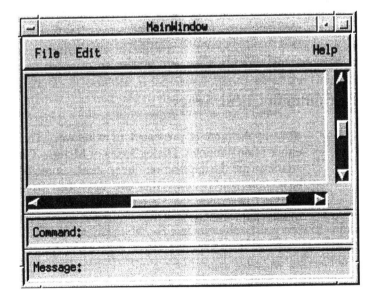

- They yield better user performance for tasks where the data requires little window manipulation to complete the task (Bly and Rosenberg, 1986).

Perceived disadvantages include the following:

- Only a limited number can be displayed in the screen area available.
- As windows are opened or closed, existing windows change in size. This can be annoying.
- As windows change in size or position, the movement can be disconcerting.
- As the number of displayed windows increases, each window can get very tiny.
- The changes in sizes and locations made by the system are difficult to predict.
- The configuration of windows provided by the system may not meet the user's needs.
- They are perceived as crowded and more visually complex because window borders are flush against one another. Crowding is accentuated if borders contain scroll bars and/or control icons. Viewer attention may be drawn to the border, not the data.
- They permit less user control because the system actively manages the windows.

Overlapping windows. Overlapping windows, illustrated in Figure 8.10, may be placed on top of one another like papers on a desk. They possess a three-dimensional quality, appearing to lie on different planes. Users can control the height, width, and location of these windows, as well as the plane in which they appear. Most new systems use this style of window. They have the following advantages:

- Visually, their look is three-dimensional, resembling the desktop that is familiar to the user.
- Greater control allows the user to organize the window to meet his or her needs.
- Windows can maintain larger sizes.
- Windows can maintain consistent sizes.
- Windows can maintain consistent positions.
- Screen space conservation is not a problem, as windows can be placed on top of one another.
- There is less pressure to close or delete windows no longer needed.
- The possibility exists for less visual crowding and complexity. Larger borders can be maintained around window information, and the window is more clearly set off against its background.
- They yield better user performance for tasks where the data requires much window manipulation to complete the task (Bly and Rosenberg, 1986).

Figure 8.10. Overlapping windows.

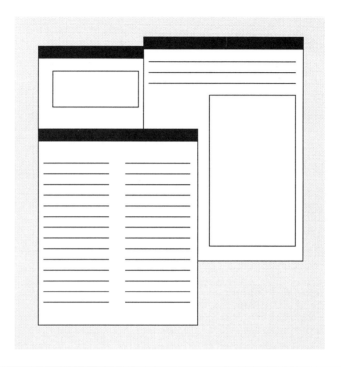

Disadvantages include the following:

- They are operationally more complex than tiled windows. More control functions require greater user attention and manipulation.
- Information in windows can be obscured behind other windows.
- Windows themselves can be lost behind other windows.
- Control freedom increases the possibility for greater visual complexity and crowding. Too many windows, or improper setoff, can be visually overwhelming.

Cascading windows. A special type of overlapping window has the windows automatically arranged in a regular progression. Each window is slightly offset from others, as illustrated in Figure 8.11. Advantages of this approach include the following:

- No window is ever completely hidden.
- Bringing any window to the front is easier.
- Simplicity in visual presentation and cleanness.

Figure 8.11. Cascading windows.

Presentation Styles of Windows

- Use tiled windows for:
  — Single task activities.
  — Tasks requiring little window manipulation.
  — Novice or inexperienced users.
- Use overlapping windows for:
  — Switching between tasks.
  — Tasks necessitating a greater amount of window manipulation.
  — Expert or experienced users.
  — Nonpredictable display contents.

Use of tiled windows. Tiled windows seem to be better for single task activities. Bly and Rosenberg (1986) found that tasks requiring little window manipulation can be carried out faster using tiled windows. They also found that novice users performed better with tiled windows, regardless of the task.

Use of overlapping windows. Overlapping windows seem to be better for situations that necessitate switching between tasks. Bly and Rosenberg concluded that tasks requiring much window manipulation could be performed faster with overlapping windows but only if user "window expertise" existed. For novice users, tasks requiring much window manipulation were found to be carried out faster with tiled windows. Therefore, the advantage to overlapping windows comes only after a certain level of expertise is achieved.

WINDOWS AND WINDOW DESIGN STEPS

Windows

- Components of a window.
- Window manipulation guidelines.

Window Design Steps

- Organize window system functions.
- Determine the style, or styles, of windows to be presented.
- *Divide the tasks into a series of windows.*
  - *— Primary or application window.*
    - *— To begin a user interaction.*
    - *— Should represent an independent function.*
  - *— Secondary, document, or supplemental window.*
    - *— To extend the interaction with users.*
    - *— To carry out most application features.*
  - *— Dialog boxes.*
    - *— To extend the interaction.*
    - *— Presenting brief information.*
    - *— Requesting specific actions.*

Determining the Types of Windows

User tasks must be structured into a series of windows. The type of window used will depend on the nature and flow of the task. Defining standard window types is difficult because of the varying terminology and definitions used by different windowing systems. In general, however, the different types exhibit the following characteristics. Summarized are a description of the window, its purpose, and its proper usage. Examples are shown in Figure 8.12. Any single system's windows may not behave exactly as presented, and some windows may exhibit characteristics common to more than one of those described window types.

Primary or Application Window

Description

- Appears first.
- Required for every application.
- Possesses a menu bar and some basic action controls.
- All subsidiary windows are associated with their primary window (directly or indirectly).
- Closing a primary window closes all windows in the application.

Figure 8.12. Examples of window types (from Microsoft Windows).

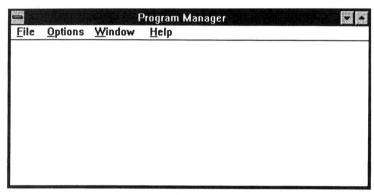

Primary

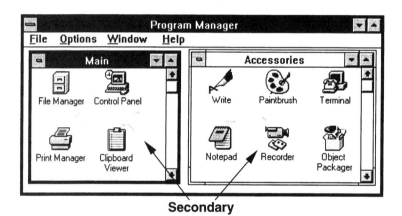

Secondary

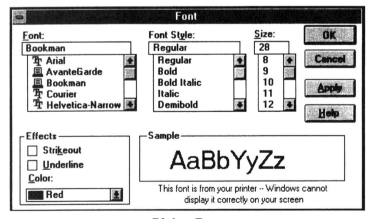

Dialog Box

Purpose

- To begin a user interaction.
- The framework for an application's commands and data.
- Contains data or provides top-level context for dependent windows.
- The main focal point of the user's activity.

Proper Usage

- Should represent an independent function (Application).
- Presenting constantly used window components and controls.
  — Menu bar items that are:
    — Used frequently.
    — Used by most, or all, primary or secondary windows.
  — Controls used by dependent windows.
- Presenting information that is continually updated.
  — For example, date and time.
- Providing context for dependent windows to be created.
- Do not:
  — Divide an independent function into two or more primary windows.
  — Present nonrelated functions in one primary window.

This type of window is the first that appears on a screen when an activity or action is started. It is required for every application, possessing a menu bar and some basic action controls. It should present the framework for an application's commands and data, and provide top-level context for dependent windows. It is variously referred to as the primary, application, or main window. It may also be referred to as the "parent" window if one or more "child" windows exist.

The primary window is the main focal point of the user's activities and should represent an independent function. Avoid dividing an independent function into two or more primary windows, and avoid presenting nonrelated functions in a single primary window. This tends to confuse people.

Independent functions should begin in a primary window. A primary window should contain constantly used window components such as frequently used menu bar items and controls used by dependent windows such as control bars. Also include in a primary window continually updated information like date and time.

Secondary, Document, or Supplemental Window

Description

- Always associated with a primary window.
- Can visually resemble a primary window.
- Appears on top of active window when requested.
- Sizable, movable, scrollable.
- Possesses some basic action controls but no menu bar.
  — Uses the menu bar of the primary window.

- May use other secondary windows to complete dialog.
- Removed when no longer needed.
  - Action completed.
  - Primary window closed or minimized.

Purpose

- To extend the interaction with the user.
- For continuing a work activity.
- For performing actions that are:
  - Subordinate.
  - Supplemental.
  - Ancillary (to the primary window).

Proper Usage

- Performing subordinate, supplemental, or ancillary actions extended or more complex in nature.
- Presenting frequently or occasionally used window components.

A window derived from the primary window, these "offspring" windows often contain the actual data being processed. They are typically associated with a single data object. They structurally resemble a primary window, but use the primary window's menu bar. Most systems permit the use of multiple secondary windows to complete a task.

Secondary windows are used to perform supplemental or subordinate tasks or tasks more extended in nature. Frequently or occasionally used window components should also be presented in them.

Dialog Boxes

Description

- Always displayed from another window:
  - Primary.
  - Secondary.
  - Another dialog box.
- Movable but not sizable or scrollable.
- May have a single size or alternate sizes.
- May possess some basic action controls.
- Does not have a menu bar.
- Two types: modal and modeless.

Purpose

- To extend the interaction with users.
- To complete an action within a limited context.
- To request information.

Proper Use

- Presenting brief information.
- Requesting specific, transient actions.
- Performing actions that:
    - — Take a short time to complete.
    - — Are not frequently changed.

Dialog boxes are also used to extend and complete an interaction within a limited context. They are used for presenting brief amounts of information such as messages to query users and to receive short user inputs. Dialog boxes are always displayed from another window, either primary or secondary, or another dialog box. They may possess some basic action controls but do not have a menu bar. Dialog boxes are of two kinds, modal and modeless.

Modal Dialog Boxes

Purpose

- To require completion of a supplemental action before interaction with another window is permitted.

Proper Usage

- When interaction with any other window must not be permitted.
- For:
    - — Presenting information.
        - — For example, messages (often called message box).
    - — Receiving user input.
        - — For example, data or information (often called prompt box).
    - — Asking questions.
        - — For example, data, information, or directions (often called question box).
- Automatically removed when interaction is completed.
- Should be used cautiously because it constrains what the user can do.

Most dialog boxes will be modal. A modal dialog box will not permit interaction with another window until the current dialog is completed. It remains displayed until the appropriate action is taken, after which it is removed from the screen. Modal dialog boxes typically request critical information or actions that must be reacted to before the dialog can continue. Since modal dialog boxes constrain what the user can do, they should be used cautiously.

Modeless Dialog Box

Purpose

- To permit performing other operations without dismissing the dialog box.

Proper Usage

- When interaction with other windows must be permitted.
  — For example, accessing help.
- When interaction with other windows must be repeated.
  — For example, a word search.
- Remains displayed on screen until removed by user.

A modeless dialog box permits the user to engage in parallel dialogs. Switching between the box and its associated window is permitted. Other tasks may be performed while a modeless dialog box is displayed, and it may be left on the screen after a response has been made to it. Actions leading to a modeless dialog box can be canceled, causing the box to be removed from the screen.

Active window. Most systems permit interaction with only one window at a time. The window that may be manipulated, and into which data may be keyed, is typically called the active window. The active window is usually identified in a visually distinctive way.

WINDOWS AND WINDOW DESIGN STEPS

Windows

- Components of a window.
- *Window manipulation guidelines.*
  - *General.*
  - *Interaction style.*
  - *Opening.*
  - *Positioning.*
  - *Sizing.*
  - *Active.*
  - *Moving.*
  - *Resizing.*
  - *Pointing, selecting, dragging and execution.*
  - *Shuffling.*
  - *Keyboard control/mouseless operation.*
  - *Closing.*
  - *Number to display.*

Window Design Steps

- Organize window system functions.
- Determine the style, or styles, of windows to be presented.
- Divide the tasks into a series of windows.

WINDOW MANIPULATION GUIDELINES

Guidelines for manipulating windows are slowly evolving. Because of the paucity of research data, many of the guidelines are more anecdotal and intuitive than scientific. Guidelines will continue to develop and probably change as our understanding of, and experiences with, the windows interface increases. Today, the following seem appropriate.

General Manipulation Considerations

- Design easy to use and learn windowing operations.
- Minimize the number of window operations necessary to achieve a desired effect.
- Make navigating between windows particularly easy and efficient to do.
- Make setting up windows particularly easy to remember.
- In overlapping systems, provide powerful commands for arranging windows on the screen in user-tailorable configurations.

Mayhew (1992), in a review of window system research (Bly and Rosenberg, 1986; Davies et al., 1985; Gaylin, 1986), presents the following guidelines.

Design easy to use and learn window operations. The complexity of a windowing system should not cancel out its potential advantages. Operations must be carefully designed to achieve simplicity. As Benest and Dukic (1989) have suggested, the ideal is that window manipulations should occur *implicitly* as a result of the user's task actions, not as a result of explicit window management actions.

Minimize the number of window operations to achieve a desired effect. Establish the kinds of window operations that people are likely to want and minimize the number of operations that must be performed to attain these configurations from any other.

Make navigating between windows easy and efficient. Gaylin (1986) found that navigation between windows was the most frequent manipulation activity performed. High-frequency operations should always be easy to do.

Make setting up windows easy to remember. Gaylin (1986) also found that window arrangement (opening, resizing, moving, etc.) was a less frequent activity. Low-frequency operations should always be easy to learn.

In overlapping systems, provide powerful commands for arranging windows in user-tailorable configurations. When an overlapping window system is used, provide easy operations to achieve desired windowing configurations. Specific configurations should be capable of being created, named, and recalled.

Interaction Style

- Direct manipulation seems to be a faster and more intuitive interaction style than indirect manipulation for many windowing operations.

This conclusion is presented by Billingsley (1988), but it is based on anecdotal evidence. She cautions that there is no empirical evidence to substantiate this observation and much research remains to be done.

Opening Windows

- Provide an iconic representation or textual list of available windows.
- When opening a window:
  - — Position in the most forward plane of the screen.
  - — Designate it as the active window.
  - — Set it off against a neutral background.
- If opening with an expansion of an icon, animate the icon expansion.
- If a primary window, also restore any secondary windows that were open when the primary window was closed.
- If more than one object is selected and opened, display each object in a separate window. Designate the last window selected as the active window.
- Display iconic representations of open windows in a visually highlighted manner on the screen.
- With tiled windows, provide an easy way to resize and move newly opened windows.

Typically, when windows are opened, they are designated as active and positioned in the most forward plane of the screen so that they can be used immediately. To focus attention on the newly opened window, display the screen background behind the window in a neutral or subdued manner. To indicate that a window is open, maintain the iconic representation on the screen and highlight in some manner. Keeping the open iconic representations visible helps the user keep track of the kind and number of windows actually open. This also reminds users of a window's existence if it is hidden behind another window. When opening windows from an iconic representation, gradually expand the window so that the movement is visible. This will aid association of the icon with the window in the mind of the viewer.

Opening tiled windows. The first opened tiled window will consume the entire screen. Subsequent windows are usually positioned by defaults in the system. The system positioning of these subsequent windows may not always be consistent with the user's needs. The system should allow the user to change the default positions, or provide a way for the user to move and resize the system-provided windows easily.

Positioning Windows

- Position a window so that it is completely visible.
- Position a window adjacent to information on the underlying screen or window it may relate to.

—If it is the initial window:
   — Preferred positions, in suggested order of placement, are below-right, below, right, top-right, below-left, top, left, top-left.
   — If it is a second window on top of another window:
      — Position it offset below-right so the underlying window title is fully visible.
   — If this second window is the result of a selection made on the previous window, leave the description of this choice fully (or partially) visible on the underlying window.
- Do not allow the window to cover:
   — Needed underlying screen information.
   — Underlying screen title.
   — Navigation controls that may be needed.
- If the window does not relate to items on an underlying screen, center the window on the screen.
- Permit the user to move the window, if necessary.

Position adjacent. Position a new window adjacent to the information on the underlying screen or window it may relate to. If the window is the initial window, preferred positions are essentially below and right. The suggested order of placement is below-right, below, right, top-right, below-left, top, left, top-left.

If it is a second window on top of another window, locate it offset below-right so the underlying window title is fully visible. If this second window is the result of a selection made on the previous window, leave the description of this choice fully (or partially) visible on the underlying window. This will provide a reminder about the origins of this window.

Do not cover needed information. Information needed on underlying screens or windows should always be visible. This includes underlying screen title and any needed navigation techniques.

Sizing Windows

- Provide large enough windows to:
   — Present all relevant information for the task.
   — Not obscure important information.
   — Not cause crowding or visual confusion.
   — Minimize the need for scrolling.
   — But less than the full size of the entire screen.
- Otherwise, make the window as small as possible.
   — Optimum window sizes:
      — For text, about 12 lines.
      — For alphanumeric information, about 7 lines.

Large enough windows should be provided to minimize the need for scrolling. Very small windows with a large number of scrollable items appear to increase decision-making time (Hendrickson, 1989).

Larger windows seem to have these advantages:

+ They permit display of more information.
+ They facilitate learning:
    — Data relationships are more obvious.
    — Groupings are more obvious.
+ Less window manipulation requirements exist.
+ Breadth is preferred to depth (based on menu research).
+ More efficient data validation and data correction can be performed.

Disadvantages:

— Longer pointer movements are required.
— Screens are more crowded.
— More visual scanning is required.
— Parts are more easily obscured by other windows.
— It is not as easy to hide inappropriate data.

Observations of people using windowing systems find that windows are often expanded to fill up the entire screen. This might indicate that window sizes, as they exist today, are not yet large enough for comfortable use.

Procedural text in window sizes of 6, 12, and 24 lines were evaluated by Desaulniers, et al. (1988). Fastest and most accurate completion occurred with the 12-line window. The retrieval of alphanumeric information was compared in 7-, 13-, and 19-line windows by Elkerton and Williges (1984). A 7-line window was found to be more than adequate.

Active Window

- Make moving to and designation of an active window as simple as possible.
- Visually differentiate the active window from other windows through:
    — A contrasting title bar.
    — A different border.
    — A different color background.
    — An "active" indicator.
- The visual cue should be moderate in intensity, not too powerful or too subtle.

Simple designation. Most systems permit communication with only one window at a time. This window, the "active" window, may be designated by the system or the user. Many systems make a window active when it is the object of another windowing operation. It is assumed that if the user wishes to change one aspect of a window's structure, they also wish to change its contents. The user should be permitted to move to and make any window active with as few steps as possible. This can be accomplished by simply allowing the user to move the selection cursor to the window's interior and then signaling by pressing a key or button. For hidden windows, a menu of open windows might be presented from which the user selects a new open window.

In some situations it may be desirable to allow multiple open windows. Hendrickson (1989) compared a single open window with multiple open windows in performing queries and found multiple open windows were related by people as more "natural." Performance was slower with multiple open windows, however. He concludes that if user acceptance is important, multiple open windows may be the better alternative. If speed of task handling is critical, a single active window is more desirable.

Visually differentiate the active window from other windows. It is important that the user be able to quickly identify the active window. Methods to do this include a contrasting window title bar, border, or background color. An "active" indicator in the window border, which is turned on or off, may also be used. A combination of two or more of these visual cues may also be used. The visual cue selected should be of moderate intensity, not too powerful or too subtle. Powerful cues will be distracting; subtle cues will be easily overlooked.

Moving Windows

- Permit the user to change the position of all windows.
- Change pointer shape to indicate the move selection is successful.
- Move the entire window as the pointer moves.
  - If it is impossible to move the entire window, move the window outline while leaving the window displayed in its original position.
- Permit moving a window without making it active.

Change cursor shape and move entire window. An indication that the move operation has been successfully selected, and that the move may begin, should be indicated to the user by changing the pointer's shape. This will provide the necessary feedback that it is safe to begin the move operation and avoid false starts. Ideally, the entire window should move along with the pointer. If the entire window cannot be moved, move the window outline while leaving the full window displayed on the screen. Displaying only the window's outline during the move operation, and not the window itself, may make it harder for the user to decide when the window has been repositioned correctly (Billingsley, 1988).

Permit moving without making a window active. It may sometimes be necessary for a window to be moved without being active. This should be possible.

Resizing Windows

- Permit the user to change the size of primary and secondary windows.
- Change the pointer shape to indicate the resizing selection is successful.
- The simplest operation is to anchor the upper-left corner and resize from the lower-right corner.
  — Permitting resizing from any point on the border is thought to be more complex for the user.
- Show the changing window as the pointer moves.
  — If it is impossible to show the entire window being resized, show the window outline while leaving the window displayed in its original position.
- When window size changes and content remains the same:
  — Change image size proportionally as window size changes.
- If resizing creates a window or image too small for easy use, do one of the following:
  — Clip (truncate) information arranged in some logical structure or layout when minimum size is attained, or
  — Format (restructure) information when no layout considerations exist as size is reduced, or
  — Remove less useful information (if it can be determined), or
  — When minimum size is attained, replace information with a message that indicates the minimum size has been reached and that the window must be enlarged to continue working.

Change pointer shape and anchor point. An indication that the resize operation has been successfully selected, and that the move may begin, should be indicated to the user by changing the pointer's shape. This will provide the necessary feedback that it is safe to begin the resizing and avoid false starts. The simplest operation for the user, conceptually, is always to resize from the lower-right corner and "anchor" the window in the upper-left corner. Resizing flexibility can be provided by permitting it to occur from any point on the border (the anchor is always opposite the pulling point), but conceptually this is more complex. Some people may have difficulty predicting which window sides or corners will be resized from specific pulling points (Billingsley, 1988).

Show the changing window. Ideally, the entire window should move along with the pointer. If the entire window cannot be moved, move the window outline while leaving the full window displayed on the screen. Displaying only the window's outline during the move operation, and not the window itself, may make it harder for the user to decide when the window has been repositioned correctly (Billingsley, 1988).

Effect on data. The effect of a resizing operation on the window's contents usually depends on the application. In enlarging, more data may be displayed, a larger image may be created, or blank space may be added around the image. In reducing, less data may be displayed, the image made smaller, blank space eliminated, or the data may be reformatted.

If resizing creates a window or image too small for easy use, clip or truncate information arranged in some logical structure, format, or layout. When no layout considerations exist, such as for text, format or restructure the displayed information.

Also consider removing less useful information, if it can be determined. When the minimum size is attained, for any additional attempts to reduce window size, replace the information with a message that indicates the minimum size has been reached and that the window must be enlarged to continue working.

Pointing, Selecting, Dragging, and Execution

Pointing

- Visually indicate the following in a unique and consistent manner:
  — What objects or choices on the screen are selectable.
  — When the object or choice is under the pointer and can be selected.
- If cursor pointing with a mouse or other similar pointing mechanism is the selection method used:
  — The selectable target area should be at least twice the size of the active area of the pointing device. In no case should it be less than six millimeters.
- If a touch screen with finger pointing is the selection method used:
  — The touch area must be a minimum of 20–30 millimeters square.
  — The touch area must encompass the entire choice or object plus one character surrounding it.
- Adequate separation must be provided between adjacent target areas.
- Pointer tracking with the mouse should be smooth and even.

Selecting

- Provide feedback concerning the operation to be performed.
  — If the action is a selection, highlight the object selected.
  — If the action is a movement, change the shape of the mouse pointer and highlight the object being moved.

Dragging

- Move the entire object as it is being moved.
  — Alternatively, move the object outline or some reasonable representation.
- The object being moved should not lag behind the pointer.

- Highlight or emphasize possible destination locations as the object being moved is dragged over them.
- Change the pointer shape to reflect the operation that will result if the dragged object is dropped in the current location (e.g., move, copy).
- Indicate invalid destination locations by providing a unique and meaningful pointer shape as the object being moved is dragged over them.

Execution

- Provide separate steps for selecting and executing actions.
- Permit canceling the choice before execution.
- Selection and the performance of actions should be accomplished in a consistent manner.

In a graphics environment, elements on a screen can be selected by pointing at them through movement of one of the pointing/input devices. The touch screen and light pen are called direct pointers because they are positioned directly on the screen. The others, graphic tablet, mouse, trackball, and joystick, are called indirect pointers because they exist in another plane, usually the desktop. A movement of these indirect pointers causes a pointer displayed on the screen also to move in the same direction. With most devices, an indication of an action to be performed requires pressing of one or more keyboard keys. Some devices, such as the mouse, signal actions by pressing one or more buttons located on the mouse itself.

Pointing

Visual indication. Visually indicate in a unique and consistent manner what objects or choices on the screen are selectable. This can be accomplished through highlighting selectable options or lowlighting nonselectable options. Also indicate in another visually distinctive way when an object or choice is under the pointer and can be selected. This can be accomplished by highlighting (if not used for selectable options), reversing the item's polarity, or changing the shape of the cursor itself. Indicating when an item is under the pointer provides direct visual feedback that the proper choice has been selected, reducing the probability for errors in choice selection.

Cursor selection. If cursor pointing with a mouse or other indirect pointing mechanism is the selection method used, the selectable target area should be at least twice the size of the active area of the pointing device. It should never be less than six millimeters. Indirect device movements tend to be faster and more ballistic in nature than cursor movement through the keyboard. Larger target areas are needed to reduce the potential for errors.

Touch screens. If a touch screen with finger pointing is the selection method used, the touch area must be larger, a minimum of 20–30 millimeters square.

The touch area must encompass the entire choice or object plus one character surrounding it. Again, this is needed to reduce the potential for errors.

Adequate separation. Because of the faster, less precise movements associated with these devices, adequate separation must be provided between adjacent target areas to minimize unintended activation of the wrong item.

Smooth tracking. The movement of the screen pointer with the mouse should be smooth and even.

Selecting.

To indicate that an item on the screen has been selected, highlight it in another distinctive way. If the selection action also involves a movement, the shape of the mouse pointer may also be changed in a distinctive manner.

Dragging

In a dragging operation, show the entire object being moved on the screen. If movement of the entire object cannot be shown, minimally show the outline of the object being moved. The object being moved should not lag behind the pointer as it is dragged across the screen.

When moving an object, also highlight or emphasize possible destination locations as the object is dragged over them. Change the pointer shape to reflect the operation that will result if the dragged object is dropped in the current location (e.g., move, copy). Indicate invalid destination locations by changing the pointer to a unique and meaningful shape as the object is dragged over them.

Execution

Separate actions. Provide separate steps for selecting and executing actions. Using a mouse, for example, requires moving the cursor to the option to select and then pressing a button to execute.

Election canceling. Always permit erroneous selections to be canceled or "undone" before execution. This will prevent unwanted actions.

Consistency. All actions must be accomplished in a consistent manner with consistent results. Control actions that are inconsistent in procedure and result are very confusing.

Window Shuffling

- Window shuffling should be easy to accomplish.

Window shuffling should be easy to perform in as few steps as possible. OPEN LOOK, for example, permits toggling of the two most recent windows displayed. Microsoft Windows and Presentation Manager permit rapid window shuffling and swapping of the front window and the second or back window.

Keyboard Control/Mouseless Operation

- Window actions should be capable of being performed through the keyboard as well as with a mouse.
- Keyboard alternatives should be designated through use of mnemonic codes, as much as possible.
- Keyboard designations should be capable of being modified by the user.

All window actions should be capable of being performed using the keyboard as well as the mouse. This will provide a more efficient alternative for applications that contain tasks that are primarily keyboard oriented, for users skilled in touch typing, and for any other situations in which frequent movement between keyboard and mouse may be required. The use of mnemonic codes to reflect window mouse actions will greatly aid user learning of the keyboard alternatives. To provide the user flexibility, all keyboard designations should be capable of being user modified.

Closing Windows

- Close a window when:
  — The user requests it to be closed.
  — The user performs the action required in the window.
  — The window has no further relevance.
- If a primary window, also remove its secondary windows.
- When a user closes a window, save its current state, including size and position, for use when the window is again opened.
  — When closing to an iconic representation of the window, animate the icon contraction.
  — Display iconic representations of closed windows in a visually subdued manner on the screen.

The close operation provides a way of temporarily setting aside a window without having to remove it from the screen. When no longer needed and closed, the window should be placed in a storage area of the screen and "shrunk" into a meaningful icon. These icons conserve screen space and serve as reminders of the window's existence. Closed-window icons should have some visual display different from that of open-window icons. This can be done by displaying them subdued or grayed.

Close a window when the user requests it to be closed, the action required in the window is performed, or the window has no further relevance. If the closed window is a primary window, also close its associated secondary windows. When a user closes a window, it is important that its current state, including size and position, be saved for use when the window is again opened.

Number of Windows to Display

- Display no more than two or three windows at one time.

Guidelines concerning the maximum number of windows to display that appeared in early stages of window evolution were quite generous, a limit of seven or eight being suggested. As experience with windows has increased, these numbers have gradually fallen. One study (Gaylin, 1986) found the mean number of windows maintained for experienced users was 3.7. Today, based on expressions of window users, a recommendation of no more than two or three at one time seems most realistic. The exact number of windows a person can effectively deal with at one time will ultimately depend on both the capabilities of the user and the characteristics of the task. Some users and situations may permit handling of more than three windows; for other users and situations, three windows may be too many.

Menus

A system contains large amounts of data and performs a variety of functions. Regardless of its purpose, the system must provide some means to tell people about the information it possesses or the things it can do. This is accomplished by displaying listings of the choices or alternatives the user has at appropriate points while using the system, or creating a string of listings that lead a user from a series of general descriptors through increasingly specific categories on following listings until the lowest level listing is reached. This lowest level listing provides the desired choices. The common name for these kinds of listings are menus.

Menus are effective because they utilize the more powerful human capability of recognition rather than the weaker recall. Working with menus reminds users of available options and information that they may not be aware of or have forgotten.

Menus are not without problems, however. New system users might find learning larger systems difficult because information often must be integrated across a series of displays (Engel and Granda, 1975; Dray et al., 1981; Billingsley, 1982; and Miller, 1981). If each menu is viewed in isolation, relationships between menus are difficult to grasp. Words and phrases with multiple meanings may be interpreted incorrectly because of the inability to see relationships (Bower et al., 1969). Ambiguities may be resolved on the basis of assumptions about menu structure that are incorrect (Cuff, 1980; Durding et al., 1977). The frequent result is that users make mistakes and get lost in the hierarchical structure.

Experienced system users, while finding menus helpful at first, may find them tedious as they learn the system. Continually having to step through a series of menus to achieve the desired objective can be time consuming and frustrating.

Therefore, the design of menu systems must consider the conflicting needs of both inexperienced and experienced users.

MENU SELECTION AND DESIGN

STEP 5

- Understand the principles of menu design.
- Establish kinds of menus needed to perform the tasks.
- Determine what system-provided default menu items are available and use them, if applicable.
- Determine what critical functions are not represented by the default items and add new menu items.
- Design menus using established design guidelines.

GRAPHICAL SYSTEM MENUS

Graphical systems are heavily menu oriented. They are used to designate commands, properties that apply to an object, documents, and windows. When selected, a graphical menu item may lead to another menu, cause a window to be displayed, or directly cause an action to be performed. To accomplish these goals, a graphical system presents a variety of menu styles to choose from. Included are entities commonly called menu bars, pull-downs, pop-ups, cascades, tearoffs, and iconic. In this chapter graphical system menus will be addressed. The various styles will be described, their purpose presented, recommendations for their proper usage given, and relevant specific design guidelines summarized.

MENU SELECTION AND DESIGN STEPS

Understand the principles of menu design.
- Establish kinds of menus needed to perform the tasks.
  - Menu bar.
  - Pull-down menus.
  - Cascading menus.
  - Pop-up menus.
  - Iconic menus.
- Determine what system-provided default menu items are available and use them, if applicable.
- Determine what critical functions are not represented by the default items.
  - Add any new required menu items.
  - Design new commands as necessary.
- Design menus using established design guidelines.

Before addressing specific graphical menus, a series of general menu design guidelines will be presented. The human-computer interface has a rich history of menu experimental studies, the results of which can and have been applied to graphical menu design and presentation.

MENU DESIGN GUIDELINES

The following summary is derived from Galitz (1992). The reader seeking additional detail should refer to it.

Display

- If continual or frequent reference to menu options are necessary, permanently display the menu in an area of the screen that will not obscure other screen data.
- If only occasional references to menu options are necessary, the menu may be presented on demand.
  — Critical options should be continuously displayed, however.

Whether to display a menu continually, or on demand, is determined by the menu's frequency of use. Always permanently display menus that are frequently referenced, while occasionally needed menus may be presented on request via pop-ups or pull-downs. Critical options should always be continuously displayed.

Organization

- Provide a general or main menu.
- Display:
  — All relevant alternatives.
  — Only relevant alternatives.
    — Delete or gray-out inactive choices.
- Match the menu structure to the structure of the task.
  — Organization should reflect the most efficient sequence of steps to accomplish a person's most frequent or likely goals.
- Minimize number of levels within limits of clarity.
  — Without logical groupings of elements, limit choices to four–eight.
  — With logical groupings, nine or more choices may be displayed.
- Provide users an easy way to restructure a menu according to how work is accomplished.

Provide a general menu. The top-level menu in a hierarchical menu scheme should be a general or main menu consisting of basic system options. This will provide a consistent starting point for all system activities and a "home-base" to which the user may always return.

Relevant alternatives. A menu screen, or screens, should provide all relevant alternatives, and only relevant alternatives, at the point at which it is displayed. Including nonrelevant choices on a menu screen increases learning requirements and has been found to interfere with performance (Baker and Goldstein, 1966). There are two exceptions to this rule, however. Alternatives that are conditionally nonactive may be displayed along with the conditionally active choices, if the active choices can be visually highlighted in some manner (such as through high intensity or reverse video). A recent study (Francik and Kane, 1987), however, found that completely eliminating nonactive alternatives on a menu resulted in faster choice access time, when compared to leaving nonactive alternatives on a menu but displayed in a subdued manner. This study concludes that eliminating conditionally nonactive choices from a menu appears to be the best approach.

Options to be implemented in the future may also be displayed if they can be visually marked in some way (through a display technique or some other annotation). Mayhew (1992), however, suggests that while deletion does provide an advantage to expert users of keyboard-driven menus, graying out seems to be advantageous to novices and systems using pointer-driven selection devices. She concludes that since menus are geared toward novices, graying appears to be the best overall choice.

Match menu structure to the tasks. Menus should be organized according to how people structure their tasks. They should reflect the most efficient sequence of steps to accomplish a person's most frequent or likely goals.

Minimize number of levels within limits of clarity. The issue that must be addressed in creating a multilevel menu structure is determining how many items will be placed on one menu (its breadth) and how many levels it will consume (its depth). In general, the more choices contained on a menu (greater breadth), the less will be its depth; the fewer choices on a menu (less breadth), the greater will be its depth.

The advantages of a menu system with greater breadth and less depth are:

- Fewer steps and shorter time to reach one's objective (Seppala and Salvendy, 1985).
- Fewer opportunities to wander down wrong paths.
- Easier learning by allowing the user to see relationships of menu items.

A broad menu's disadvantages are:

- A more crowded menu that may reduce the clarity of the choice wording.
- Increased likelihood of confusing similar choices because they are seen together.

The advantages of greater depth are:

- Less crowding on the menu.
- Fewer choices to be scanned.
- Easier hiding of inappropriate choices.
- Less likelihood of confusing similar choices since there is less likelihood that they will be seen together.

Greater depth disadvantages are:

- More steps and longer time to reach one's objective (Seppala and Salvendy, 1985).
- More difficulties in learning since relationships between elements cannot always be seen.
- More difficulties in predicting what lies below, resulting in increased likelihood of going down wrong paths or getting lost.
- Higher error rates (Tullis, 1985; Snowberry et al., 1983; Kiger, 1984; Seppala and Salvendy, 1985).

A good number of studies have looked at the breadth-depth issue in recent years. Some have concluded that breadth is preferable to depth in terms of either greater speed or fewer errors (Landauer and Nachbar, 1985; Tullis, 1985; Wallace, 1987), that a low number of levels (2 to 3) and an intermediate number of choices (4 to 8) results in faster, more accurate performance as opposed to fewer or greater numbers of levels and choices (Miller, 1981; Kiger, 1984), and that four to eight choices per menu screen is best (Lee and MacGregor, 1985). Another study found that one level was easiest to learn (Dray et al., 1981), and a couple of studies have concluded that a menu could contain up to 64 items if it were organized into logical groups (Snowberry et al., 1983; Paap and Roske-Hofstrand, 1986). The least desirable alternative in almost all cases was deep-level menu screens that simply presented the user with a binary choice (select one of two alternatives) on each screen.

The conclusion that one might derive from these studies is this: Fewer levels of menus aid the decision-making process, but trying to put too many choices on a single menu also has a negative impact. The final solution is a compromise: Minimize the number of levels within limits of clarity. What is clarity? The studies seem to indicate that if the choices to be displayed cannot be segmented into logical categories, then confine the number of alternatives displayed to four to eight per menu. If logical categorization is possible, and meaningful, logical category names can be established, then a larger number of choices can be presented. The maximum number of alternatives will, however, be dependent upon the size of the words needed to describe the alternatives to the user. "Wordy" captions will greatly restrict the number of alternatives capable of being displayed.

Provide an easy way to restructure menus. Menus should be capable of being restructured according to how people work. Not everyone works the same way.

Groupings

- Create hierarchical groupings of items that are logical, distinctive, meaningful, and mutually exclusive.
- Categorize in such a way as to:
  — Maximize the similarity of items within a category.
  — Minimize the similarity of items across categories.
- If meaningful categories cannot be developed and more than eight options must be displayed on a screen, create arbitrary visual groupings that:

- — Consist of about four or five but never more than seven options.
- — Are of equal size.
- Separate groupings created through either:
  - — Wider spacing.
  - — A thin ruled line.
- Provide immediate access to critical or frequently chosen items.

Items displayed on menus should be logically grouped to aid learning and speed up the visual search process (Card, 1982). Liebelt et al. (1982) have demonstrated that logically categorized menus are easier to learn and result in faster and more accurate performance. McDonald et al. (1983) have found similar results comparing versions of a 64-item menu either structured into logical categories, arranged alphabetically, or randomly arranged. They speculate that a categorical organization may facilitate the transition from novice to expert user because information is visually represented in the way people think about it.

Shneiderman (1987) states that in addition to containing logically similar items, groupings should cover all the possibilities and contain items that are nonoverlapping. While some collections of information will be easily partitioned into logical groups, others may be very difficult to partition. Some users may not understand the designer's organizational framework, and there may be differences among users based on experience. Thus, no perfect solution may exist for all, and extensive testing and refinement may be necessary to create the most natural and comprehensible solution.

Visual groupings. Noncategorized menus should be broken in arbitrary visual groupings through the use of space or lines. Groups should be of as equal size as possible and consist of about four or five options. Groupings should never exceed more than seven options.

Finally, choices that are critical or frequently chosen should be accessible as quickly and through as few steps as possible.

Ordering

- Order lists of choices by their natural order, or
- For lists with a small number of options (seven or less), order by
  - — Sequence of occurrence.
  - — Frequency of occurrence.
  - — Importance.
- Use alphabetic order for:
  - — Long lists (eight or more options).
  - — Short lists with no obvious pattern or frequency.
- Separate potentially destructive actions from frequently chosen items.
- If option usage changes, do not reorder menus.
- Maintain a consistent ordering of options on all related menus.
  - — For variable-length menus, maintain consistent relative positions.
  - — For fixed-length menus, maintain consistent absolute positions.

Within categories included on a menu, or in menus in which categories are not possible, options must be ordered in meaningful ways. When a menu contains categories of information, category ordering will follow these same principles.

Natural ordering. If items have a natural sequence, such as chapters in a book, months in the year, or physical properties such as increasing or decreasing sizes or weights, the ordering scheme should follow this natural sequence. These ordering schemes will have already been well learned by the screen viewer.

Small number of options. For groupings with a small number of options (about seven or less), sequence of use, frequency of use, or importance of the item is the best ordering scheme.

Alphabetic order. For a large number of options, alphabetic ordering of alternatives is desirable. Alphabetic ordering is also recommended for small lists where no frequency or sequence pattern is obvious.

It has been found that alphabetically ordered menus can be searched much faster than randomly ordered menus (Card, 1982; McDonald et al., 1983; Perlman, 1985). Card, for example, found that an 18-item alphabetic menu was visually searched four times faster than a randomly organized menu. Search time was a function of saccadic eye movements through the display. Search patterns were random, but fewer eye movements were required with the alphabetic arrangement. After twenty trials, however, only one eye movement was required for all conditions and search time was the same. Learning does take place, but it will be greatly aided by the ordering scheme.

Do not reorder menus. Adaptivity is thought to be a desirable quality of a computer system. This may not be so for menu option ordering. Mitchell and Shneiderman (1989) compared static or fixed menus with dynamic menus whose options were continually reordered based upon the frequency in which they were chosen. Dynamic menus were slower to use and less preferred than static menus. The continual reordering interfered with menu order learning, which occurred quickly.

Consistency between menus. Options found on more than one menu should be consistently positioned on all menus. If menus are of variable length, maintain relative positioning of all item options (for example, place EXIT at the bottom or end of the list). If menus are of fixed length, place options in the same physical position within the list.

Initial Cursor Positioning

- If one option has a significantly higher probability of selection, position the cursor at that option.
- If repeating the previously selected option has the highest probability of occurrence, position the cursor at this option.

- If no option has a significantly higher probability of selection, position the cursor at the first option.

When a menu is first displayed, position the cursor at the most likely option to be chosen, or the first option in the list.

Control

- Permit only one selection per menu.
- When levels of menu are used, provide one simple action to:
  — Return to the next higher level menu.
  — Return to the main menu.
- Where access of a lower-level menu is possible through multiple pathways, provide these pathways.

One selection per menu. Requiring more than one choice per displayed menu can be confusing to the novice user.

Simple key actions. Navigation through menu levels should be accomplished through simple key actions. It shold always be very easy to return to the next higher level menu and the main or general menu.

Provide multiple pathways. If it is logical to access levels within a menu structure by meaningful and relevant multiple pathways, provide for access through such pathways.

Menu Navigation Aids

- To aid menu navigation and learning, provide:
  — A "look-ahead" at the next level of choices, alternatives that will be presented when a currently viewed choice is selected.
  — Menu maps or overviews of the menu hierarchy.

Provide "look-aheads." Menu navigation and learning will be assisted if a person is able to browse the next level of choices before the currently displayed choice is selected. As the cursor moves across a menu bar, for example, the pull-down menu may be automatically dropped, permitting review of the choices available if that menu bar item is selected. Look-aheads are useful if ambiguity exists at high-level choice points. They have been found to decrease errors and improve satisfaction. Menu search time may be longer, however.

Provide menu maps. It is often difficult to maintain a sense of position or orientation as one wanders deeper into a multilevel menu system. The result is that "getting lost" in the menu maze is quite easy to do. The value of a menu map in reducing disorientation has been demonstrated in three studies (Billingsley, 1982; Parton et al., 1985; Kaster and Widdell, 1986). In all cases, providing a graphic representation of the menu in map form, either in hard copy or online, resulted in fewer errors or wrong choices, faster navigation, and/or greater user satisfaction when compared to no guides or simply providing indexes or narrative descriptions of the menu structure. Kaster and Widdell also found that being able to view on the screen just the "path" one was following improved performance and learning.

Paap and Roske-Hofstrand (1988) suggest that the display of a list of choices selected is especially valuable if the system has many levels and the user frequently has to navigate down new pathways. Maps of the menu structure, they say, are very useful when there is high ambiguity at high-level choice points.

So, menu maps or graphic representations of the menu structure are desirable. These maps should be included in the system documentation and also should be available through a HELP function.

Menu Title

- Create a short, simple, clear, and distinctive title representing the purpose of the entire series of choices.
- Locate it at the top of the listing of choices.
- Spell out fully using an upper-case font.

The menu title should immediately orient the viewer to the menu's content and purpose. It should be at the top and displayed in upper-case letters for emphasis.

Menu Item Descriptions

- Can be names of actions, properties, documents, or windows.
- Provide familiar, fully spelled-out descriptions of choices available.
- Item descriptions may be single words, compound words, or multiple words.
  — Exception: Menu bar items should be a single word (if possible).
- The first letter of each item description word should be capitalized.
- A menu item must never have the same wording as the menu title.
- Item descriptions should be unique within a menu.
- Identical items on different menus should be named identically.
- Items should not be numbered.
  — Exception: If the listing is numeric in nature, graphic, or a list of varying items, it may be numbered.
- If menu options will be used in conjunction with a command language, the capitalization and syntax of the captions should be consistent with the command language.

Menu item descriptions should comprise familiar, fully spelled-out words. While abbreviations may occasionally be necessary, they should be kept to a minimum. Descriptions should also be concise, containing as few words as possible, and distinctive, constructed of words that make its intent as clear as possible.

Use high-imagery key words, words that elicit a mental image of the object or action. Avoid low-imagery key words, words more general in connotation. For example, when obtaining a printout of a screen, the term "print" is much more descriptive than "list."

Arrange multi-item descriptions so that the descriptive and unique words appear at its beginning. This optimizes scanning and recognition while the user is learning the menu. Description phrasing and wording should also be consistent across all menus to aid learning further.

Capitalize the first letter of each item description word. A menu item must never have the same wording as the menu title. Item descriptions should be unique within a menu, but identical items on different menus should be named identically. Also, items should not be numbered unless the listing is numeric in nature, graphic, or a list of varying items. If menu options will be used in conjunction with a command language, the capitalization and syntax of the captions should be consistent with the command language.

In creating menu item descriptions, never assume the description chosen by the designer will have the same meaning to the user. Furnas et al. (1982) found that the probability of two people choosing the same name or description for something ranged from 8 to 18 percent. Names chosen by experts were no better than nonexperts. Therefore, iteratively test and refine the choices to achieve as much agreement as possible.

Item Arrangement

- Align alternatives or choices into columns whenever possible.
  - — Orient for top-to-bottom reading.
  - — Left-justify descriptions.
- If a horizontal orientation of descriptions must be maintained:
  - — Organize for left-to-right reading.

For scanning ease, options should be left-justified and aligned into columns. Parkinson et al. (1985) and Backs et al. (1987) have found columnar menus searched significantly faster than horizontally oriented menus.

When menus are included on other screens, space constraints often exist, and the menu must be arrayed horizontally. In this case, always present the menu in the same location and use distinctive display techniques to contrast the menu with the remainder of the screen. Display techniques must, of course, be compatible with those used for other purposes on the remainder of the screen. A good way to set a menu off from the remainder of the screen is to enclose it in a box or, if it is at the screen's top or bottom, separate it with a horizontal line. Techniques chosen should be consistent throughout the system.

If a single-row (horizontal) orientation is necessary, organize for left-to-right reading based on one of the ordering principles described earlier. If two or more rows are available for displaying choices, organize for top-to-bottom, left-to-right reading to facilitate visual scanning.

Intent Indicators

Cascade Indicator

- To indicate that selection of an item will lead to a sub-menu, place a triangle or right-pointing solid arrow immediately following the choice.
- Every cascaded menu must be indicated by a cascade indicator.

To a Window Indicator

- For choices that result in displaying a window, place an ellipsis (. . .) immediately following the choice.
- Every menu item that is followed by a window must have an ellipsis following it.

Direct Action Items

- For choices that directly perform an action, no special indicator should be placed on the menu.

Predictability and exploration of a graphical system can be enhanced by providing an indication of what will happen when the menu item is selected. If an item leads to another lower-level menu, include a cascade indicator, a right-pointed arrow following the item description. If an item leads to a window, include an ellipsis following the item description. Items causing a direct action will have no indicator. These intent indicators are illustrated in Figure 9.1. IBM SAA CUA calls choices leading to sub-menus or windows "routing" choices, and items causing direct actions as "action" choices.

Line Separators

- Separate vertically arrayed groupings with subtle solid lines.
- Separate vertically arrayed sub-groupings with subtle dotted or dashed lines.
- Left-justify the lines under the first letter of the columnized item descriptions.
- Right-justify the lines under the last character of the longest item description.

Indicate groupings and sub-groupings of vertically arrayed related choices by inscribing subtle solid or dashed lines between each group. The line or lines

Figure 9.1.   Intent Indicators

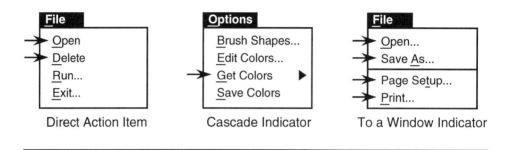

Direct Action Item   Cascade Indicator   To a Window Indicator

Figure 9.2.   Recommended line separators.

Figure 9.3.   Extended line separators.

should only extend from the first character of the descriptions to the end of the longest description, as shown in Figure 9.2. Many systems extend the line from border to border, as illustrated in Figure 9.3. This extended line results in too strong a visual separation between menu parts. Visual separation should exist, but it should not be too overpowering.

Unavailable Choices

- Unavailable choices should be dimmed or "grayed out."
- Do not add or remove items from a menu unless the user takes explicit action to add or remove them through the application.

Choices available to the user should be made visually distinctive by dimming or graying them. They must not compete with relevant items for the user's attention. Items should not be added or removed from a menu unless the user takes explicit action to do so. Allowing the system to change menu items takes control away from the user and can also lead to confusion.

Keyboard Equivalents

- Each menu item should be assigned a keyboard equivalent mnemonic to facilitate keyboard selection.
- The mnemonic should be the first character of the menu item's description.
  — If duplication exists in first characters, for duplicate items use another character in the item description.
  — Preferably choose the first succeeding consonant.
- Designate the mnemonic character by underlining it.

The ability to select a menu alternative through the keyboard should always be provided. This is accomplished by providing a keyed equivalent for each menu alternative. Keyboard equivalents that have meaningful associations with their corresponding choices will be more easily learned and remembered. Studies (Ehrenreich, 1985; Grudin and Barnard, 1985) have found that simple truncation is a good method for creating mnemonics. Therefore, the first letter of the item description is the recommended mnemonic. Unfortunately, following this method duplications easily occur so an alternative principle must also be provided. A simple scheme is to use the second consonant for duplicate items. This duplication-breaking scheme need not always be faithfully followed, however. Occasionally another letter in the menu item may be more meaningful to the user. In these cases, it should be selected.

Mnemonic codes can be visually indicated in a number of ways. The recommended method is an underline beneath the proper character within the

Figure 9.4. Keyboard equivalents.

choice. Other methods, a different character color, a different character intensity, or a contrasting color bar through the relevant character are visually more complex. See Figure 9.4.

Keyboard Accelerators

- For frequently used items, provide a keyboard accelerator to facilitate keyboard selection.
- The accelerator may be one function key or a combination of keys.
- Pressing no more than two keys simultaneously is preferred.
  — Do not exceed three simultaneous keystrokes.
- Accelerators should have some associative value to the item.
- Identify the keys by their actual keytop engraving.
- Use a plus (+) sign to indicate that two or more keys must be pressed at the same time.
- Separate the accelerator from the item description by three spaces.
- Right-align the key descriptions.
- Do not use accelerators for menu items that have cascaded menus.

Accelerators are keys, or key combinations of keys, that invoke an action regardless of cursor or pointer position. They are most commonly used to activate a menu item without opening the menu. They are most useful for frequent activities performed by experienced users.

For frequently used items, assign a key, or combination of keys, to accomplish an action. Pressing no more than two keys simultaneously is preferred, three keystrokes is the maximum. Accelerators should have some associative value to the item and be identified by their actual keytop engraving. Use a plus (+) sign to indicate that two or more keys must be pressed at the same time.

Display the accelerator right-aligned and enclosed in parentheses to the right of the choice. Incorporating these key names within parentheses indicates that they are prompts (which they actually are) and that they may easily be ignored when not being used. Most graphic systems do not place them within parentheses, giving them too strong a visual emphasis. See Figure 9.5.

Figure 9.5. Keyboard accelerators.

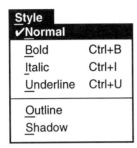 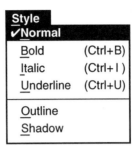

Item Selection

Pointers

- Select the choice by pointing at it with a pointing mechanism such as the cursor, light pen, or finger.
- Indicate:
  — Which options are selectable.
  — When the option is under the pointer and can be selected.
- Visually distinguish single- and multiple-choice menus.
- If cursor pointing is the selection method used,
  — The selectable target area should be at least twice the size of the active area of the pointing device, or displayed pointer. In no case should it be less than six millimeters square.
  — Adequate separation must be provided between adjacent target areas.
- If the finger pointing is the selection method used,
  — The touch area must be a minimum of 20 to 30 millimeters square.
  — The touch area must encompass the entire caption plus one character around it.

Keyboard

- The up and down arrow keys should move the cursor up or down vertically oriented menu options.
- The left and right cursor keys should move the cursor left or right between horizontally oriented menu options.
- Either upper- or lower-case typed entries should be acceptable.

Selection/Execution

- Provide separate actions for selecting and executing menu options.
- Indicate the selected choice through either:
  — Highlighting it with a distinctive display technique.
  — Modifying the shape of the cursor.

- Permit unselecting choice before execution.
  - If a multiple-choice menu, permit all options to be selected before execution.

Combining Techniques

- Permit alternative selection techniques to provide flexibility.

Pointers. The pointer is moved to the designated item through use of a "mouse", or the user's finger is used to make the selection (if the screen is touch sensitive). Depressing a key such as TRANSMIT or ENTER or a mouse button signals the choice to the computer. Indicate which options are selectable and when the option is under the pointer and can be selected. Visually distinguish single- and multiple-choice menus.

If cursor pointing is the selection method used, an adequate target area should be provided. This area should be at least twice the size of the active area of the pointing device or the displayed pointer. In no case should it be less than six millimeters square. To avoid unintended activation of the wrong option, provide adequate separation between selectable areas. Highlighting of the selected choice will also provide indication of an incorrect choice.

If finger pointing is the selection method used, an even larger touch area must be provided, a minimum of 20–30 millimeters. Single-character positions on a screen make poor targets for most fingers. Also, keep in mind that using a finger to signify a choice can be taxing on arm muscles, so this approach should only be used in casual or infrequent use situations.

Keyboard. The up and down arrow keys should move the cursor up and down a vertical column of menu options. The left and right arrow keys should move the cursor left and right across a horizontal array of options. In typing, the mnemonics should be acceptable in any case (upper and lower mixed).

Selection/Execution. Provide separate actions for selecting and executing menu options. For example, require typing the mnemonic to select and then pressing the enter or return key to execute. Or, with a mouse, require moving the pointer to the option to select and then "clicking" to execute. Always permit erroneous selections to be unselected and, in a multiple-choice menu, all options to be selected before execution.

The item selected should be highlighted in some way through a distinctive display technique such as reverse polarity. An alternative is to change the shape of the pointer itself. These methods provide direct visual feedback that the proper choice has been selected, reducing the probability of errors in choice selection.

Combining techniques. Permit alternative selection techniques to provide flexibility. If a pointing method is used, also provide a keyboard alternative to accomplish the same task. Pointing will probably be easier for the novice, but many experts prefer the keyboard alternative.

MENU SELECTION AND DESIGN STEPS

- Understand the principles of menu design.
- *Establish kinds of menus needed to perform the tasks.*
  - *— Menu bar.*
  - *— Pull-down menus.*
  - *— Cascading menus.*
  - *— Pop-up menus.*
  - *— Iconic menus.*
- Determine what system-provided default menu items are available and use them, if applicable.
- Determine what critical functions are not represented by the default items.
  - — Add any new required menu items.
  - — Design new commands as necessary.
- Design menus using established design guidelines.

DETERMINING STYLES OF MENUS

Providing the proper kinds of menus to perform system tasks is critical to system success. The best kind of menu to use in each situation depends on several factors. The following must be considered:

- The number of items to be presented in the menu.
- How often the menu is used.
- How often the menu contents may change.

Graphical menus will be described in terms of purpose, advantages and disadvantages, and suggested proper usage. Design guidelines for each kind are also presented.

MENU BAR

Description

- A "menu" or collection of menu titles provided by the application.
- Located at the top of the display in a horizontal row.
- Each menu title will have a pull-down menu associated with it describing exact actions that may be performed.
- Typically, each system provides a default set of menu bar commands (e.g., File, Edit, View, Window, Help).

Purpose

- To present application alternatives or choices to the screen user. They can be:
  — Commands.
  — Properties that apply to an object.

Advantages/Disadvantages

+ Always visible, reminding user of existence.
+ Easy to browse through.
+ Easy to locate consistently on the screen.
+ Usually does not obscure the screen working area.
+ Usually not obscured by windows and dialog boxes.
+ Allows for use of keyboard equivalents.

− Consumes a full row of screen space.
− Requires looking away from main working area to find.
− Requires moving pointer from main working area to select.
− Menu options are smaller than full-size buttons, slowing selection time.
− Horizontal orientation less efficient for scanning.
− Horizontal orientation limits number of choices that can be displayed.

Proper Usage

- To identify and provide access to common and frequently used application actions that take place in a wide variety of different windows.

Description.   The highest-level graphical system menu is commonly called the menu bar. A menu bar consists of a collection of action descriptions arrayed in a horizontal row at the top of a window. Each menu bar item will have a pull-down menu associated with it detailing specific actions that may be performed. Menu bars often consist of a series of textual words as represented in Figure 9.6. Examples of this textual approach are illustrated by Macintosh, Presentation Manager, and Windows 3.0.

Some products have placed the choices within buttons as represented in Figure 9.7. An example of this approach is Sun Microsystems' OPEN LOOK, which calls them "menu buttons."

There are also combinations of both. OSF/Motif presents a list of textual choices, but when one is selected, it resembles a button. Motif refers to these as "cascade buttons."

Purpose.   Menu bars are used to present application alternatives or choices to the screen user. Menu bar item descriptions are sometimes referred to as the "titles" of the associated pull-down items. Typically, each system provides a default set of menu bar commands (e.g., File, Edit, View, Window, Help).

Figure 9.6. Menu bar comprised of text.

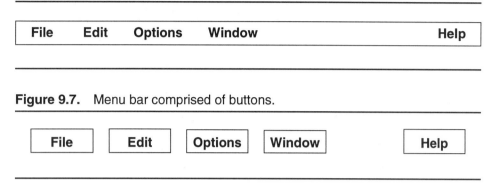

Figure 9.7. Menu bar comprised of buttons.

Advantages/Disadvantages. Menu bars are also visible, reminding the user of actions available. They permit browsing and do not obscure the screen working area. On the other hand, they do consume screen space and require looking away from the screen working area to read, and moving the pointer some distance to activate.

Proper usage. Menu bars are most effectively used for presenting common or frequent actions to be used on many windows in a variety of circumstances.

Menu Bar Guidelines

Display

- All primary windows must have a window bar.
- Do not allow the user to turn off the display of the menu bar.
- If all the items in its associated pull-down menu are disabled, then disable the menu bar item.
  - — Display the disabled item in a visually subdued manner.
  - — However, the disabled pull-down menu must always be capable of being pulled down so that the choices may be seen.

All primary windows must have a menu bar. Secondary windows and dialog boxes may use their primary window bar. Never permit the menu bar to be turned off, as reminders of system actions will be eliminated and possibly forgotten by inexperienced users.

If all the items in its associated pull-down menu are disabled, then disable the menu bar item but continue to display it in a visually subdued manner. The disabled pull-down menu must always be capable of being pulled down so that the choices may be seen. This will facilitate system exploration and learning.

Location

- Position choices horizontally over the entire row at the top of the screen, just below the screen title.
  — A large number of choices may necessitate display over two rows.

Choices should be positioned horizontally across the top of the screen below the screen title. A typical bar is comprised of about seven or eight choices, although more or less are sometimes seen. Due to screen space constraints, and human information processing capabilities, a maximum of seven or eight is reasonable. In the event more are needed, a second line of choices may be added.

Title

- The window title will be the menu bar title.

The window title will serve as the menu bar title.

Item Descriptions

- The menu item descriptions must clearly reflect the kinds of choices available in the associated pull-down menus.
  — Menu item descriptions will be the "titles" for pull-down menus associated with them.
- Use mixed-case letters to describe choices.
- Use single-word choices whenever possible.
- Do not display choices that are never available to the user.

The menu item descriptions must clearly reflect alternatives available in the associated pull-down menus. Choices should be composed of mixed-case single words. Typically, only the first letter of the choice is capitalized. Acronyms, abbreviations, or proper nouns that are normally capitalized may be capitalized. Choices should never be numbered.

If a multiple-word item must be used for clarity, consider including a hyphen (-) between the multiple words to associate the words and differentiate them from other items. Never display choices that are not available to the user.

Organization

- Order choices left-to-right with:
  — Most frequent choices to the left.
  — Related information grouped together.
- Choices found on more than one menu bar should be consistently positioned.

- Left-justify choices within the line.
- When choices can be logically grouped, provide visual logical groupings, if possible.

- Help, when included, should be located to the right side of the bar.

File	**Edit**	**Options**	**Window**	**Help**

Order all choices left-to-right, with most frequently elected choices to the left and related information grouped together. Choices found on more than one menu bar should be consistently positioned.

Left-justify all choices within the line (as opposed to centering when there are not enough choices to completely fill the line). However, always locate Help when included, to the far right side. Right-side positioning will always keep Help in a consistent location within the bar. Also, provide visual groupings of all related choices, if space permits on the bar.

Layout

- Indent the first choice one space from the left margin.
- Leave at least three spaces between each of the succeeding choices (except Help and/or Exit, which will be right-justified).
- Leave one space between the final choice and the right margin.

xTabsxxx**Justification**	**Spacing**	**Left**	**Right**	**Carriage**	**Help**x

The spacing recommendations above are intended to provide clear delineation of choices, leave ample room for the selection cursor, provide a legible selected choice, and provide efficiency in bar design.

Separation

- Separate the bar from the remainder of the screen by:
  — A different background, or
  — Solid lines above and below.

In addition to being identified by its location at the top, the bar should be identifiable by a contrasting display technique. The most effective way to do this is through use of a different background, either reversed polarity (black on white for the bar contrasted with white on black for the screen body), or a color different from the adjacent title and screen body. When a color is used, it must be chosen in conjunction with good color principles in Chapter 13. Affecting the background color choice will be the foreground or choice description color, the selection indicator to be described next, and the screen body background color. The contrast of the bar to the remainder of the screen should be moderate, neither too vivid nor too subtle.

Other Components

- Keyboard equivalent mnemonics should be included on menu bars.
- Keyboard accelerators, to a window, and cascade indicators need not be included.

While keyboard mnemonics should be included on menu bars, keyboard accelerators and other intent indicators should not because a menu bar selection will always lead to a pull-down menu.

Selection Indication

Keyboard Cursor

- Use a reverse video, or reverse color, selection cursor to surround the choice.
- Cover the entire choice, including one blank space before and after the choice word.

File	**Edit**	**Options**	**Window**	**Help**

Pointer

- Use reverse video, or reverse color, to highlight the selected choice.

When using the keyboard, the selection cursor should be indicated by a contrasting reverse video or reverse color bar surrounding the choice. The cursor should extend at least one space to each side of the choice word. When using a pointer, use a reverse video or reverse color to highlight the choice when it is selected.

The recommended reverse color combination is simply to reverse the foreground and background colors of the nonselected choices. Colors chosen must be those that are completely legible in either polarity. Some good combinations would include: black-white, blue-white, and black-cyan.

Other contrasting-color combinations may, of course, also be used. Since limitations exist in the number of colors that may be used on a screen, however, the colors chosen for menu bars must be performed in conjunction with the colors of other screen components. Since a menu bar can be identified by its location, the use of a completely different color to identify it can be redundant and unnecessary. It is more practical to reserve the use of color for other less identifiable screen components.

PULL-DOWN MENU

Description

- A vertically arrayed listing of menu items that appear beneath the menu bar when a menu bar choice is selected.

Purpose

- To present alternatives or choices to the screen user. They can be:
  — Commands.
  — Properties that apply to an object.

Advantages/Disadvantages

+ Reminder of existence cued by menu bar.
+ May be located relatively consistently on the screen.
+ No window space consumed when not used.
+ Easy to browse through.
+ Vertical orientation most efficient for scanning.
+ Vertical orientation most efficient for grouping.
+ Vertical orientation permits more choices to be displayed.
+ Allows for display of both keyboard equivalents and accelerators.

− Requires searching and selecting from another menu before seeing options.
− Requires looking away from main working area to read.
− Requires moving pointer out of working area to select (unless using keyboard equivalents).
− Items are smaller than full-size buttons, slowing selection time.
− May obscure screen working area.

Proper Usage

- For frequently used application actions that take place on a wide variety of different windows.
- For a small number of items.
- For items best represented textually.
- For items that rarely change.

Description. Selection of an alternative from the menu bar results in the display of the exact actions available to the user. These choices are displayed in a vertically arrayed listing that appears to pull down from the bar. Hence, these listings, as illustrated in Figure 9.8, are typically referred to as "pull-downs."

Figure 9.8. Action/Menu bar pull-down.

Tabs	Justification	Spacing	Left	Right	Carriage	Help
	None					
	Left					
	Center					
	Right					

Other identification terms may be used: OSF/Motif, for example, calling them "drop-downs."

Purpose. Pull-down menus are used to provide access to common and frequently used application actions that take place on a wide variety of different windows.

Advantages/Disadvantages. That a pull-down series of choices is available is indicated by the permanently displayed menu bar. They do not consume any space when not used and are easy to browse. Their vertical orientation permits easy visual scanning and grouping of related elements. Disadvantages include having to make another selection before they appear, having to look away from the main working area to read, and moving the pointer away from the working area to select.

Proper usage. They are most useful for a small number of rarely changing items, usually about five to 10. Larger numbers of choices become awkward to use, being best handled by incorporating cascade menus (see discussion that follows). Pull-downs are best suited for items represented textually, but graphical presentations, such as colors, patterns, and shades, may also be used.

PULL-DOWN MENU GUIDELINES

Display

- Display all possible alternatives.
- Items that cannot be chosen due to the current state of an application must be indicated by graying out or dimming.

Display all possible alternatives on a pull-down. Items that cannot be chosen due to the current state of an application must be indicated by graying out or dimming. If all items are, at any one point, conditionally not applicable, they must still be capable of being retrieved for perusal through the menu bar.

Location

- Position the pull-down directly below the selected action/menu bar choice.

The pull-down will be located directly below the action/menu bar choice by which it is selected.

Size

- Restrict to no more than five to ten choices, preferably eight or less.

A typical pull-down is comprised of about five to ten choices, although more or less are sometimes seen. Because of their vertical orientation, there is space for more choices containing longer descriptions than on a menu bar, and they can easily be positioned on one screen.

Title

- Not necessary on a pull-down menu. The title will be the name of the menu bar item chosen.

The name of the item chosen on the menu bar serves as the title of a pull-down menu.

Item Descriptions

- Use mixed-case letters to describe choices.
  - If the choices can be displayed graphically, such as fill-in patterns, shades, or colors, textual descriptions are not necessary.
- Do not:
  - Identify a menu item by the same wording as its menu title.
  - Change the meaning of menu items through use of the shift key.
  - Use scrolling in pull-downs.
  - Place instructions in pull-downs.

Choices should be composed of mixed-case letters. Typically, only the first letter of the choice is capitalized. For multiword-choice descriptions, capitalize the first letter of each significant word. Acronyms, abbreviations, or proper nouns that are normally capitalized may be capitalized. If the choices can be displayed graphically, such as fill-in patterns, shades, or colors, textual descriptions are not necessary.

Never identify a pull-down menu item by the same wording as its menu bar title. The menu bar title must reflect *all* the items within the pull-down. Never change the meaning of items through use of the shift key. Shift key activations are extremely error prone, and their use should be reserved for key accelerators. Also, do not use scrolling in, or place instructions within, a pull-down.

Organization

- Align choices into columns, with:
  — Most frequent choices toward the top.
  — Related choices grouped together.
  — Choices found on more than one pull-down consistently positioned.
- Left-align choice descriptions.
- Multi-column menus are not desirable. If necessary, organize top-to-bottom, then left-to-right.

Align all pull-down choices into columns with their descriptions left-aligned. Locate most frequently chosen alternatives toward the top and group-related choices together. Choices found on more than one pull-down should be consistently positioned.

Layout

- Leave the menu bar choice leading to the pull-down highlighted in the selected manner (reverse video or reverse color).
- Physically, the pull-down menu must be wide enough to accommodate the longest menu item description and its cascade or accelerator indicator.
- Align the first character of the pull-down descriptions under the second character of the applicable action bar choice.
- Horizontally, separate the pull-down choice descriptions from the pull-down borders by two (2) spaces on the left side and at least two spaces on the right side.
  — The left-side border will align with the left side of the action bar highlighted choice.
  — The right-side border should extend, minimally, to the right side of its highlighted action bar choice.

Tabs	Justification	Spacing	Left	Right	Carriage	Help
	None					
	Left					
	Center					
	Right					

  — Pull-downs for choices on the far-right side of the action bar, or long pull-down descriptions, may require alignment to the left of their menu bar choice to maintain visibility and clarity.

Page	Source	Destination	Init-String	Margins	Name	Other	Help

Space-Compression
Attributes
Format
Top-Labels
Left-Labels
No-Labels

The menu bar choice leading to the pull-down should remain highlighted in the selected manner. Pull-down columnized descriptions should be aligned beginning under the second character position of the applicable bar choice. Pull-down borders should be positioned for balance and for maximum legibility and clarity of the choice descriptions. Leave two spaces to the left of the descriptions to align the left pull-down border with the left border of the selected action/menu bar choice. Leave a minimum of two spaces after the longest description and the right pull-down border. Minimally, the right pull-down border should extend to the right border of the highlighted action bar choice. Menu bar choices located at the far right, or long pull-down choice descriptions, may require alignment to the left of the applicable action bar choice, however.

Groupings

- Provide groupings of related pull-down choices:
  — Incorporate a solid line between major groupings.
  — Incorporate a dotted or dashed line between sub-groups.
  — Left-justify the lines under the first letter of the columnized choice descriptions.
  — Right-justify the lines under the last character of the longest choice description.
  — Display the solid line in the same color as the choice descriptions.

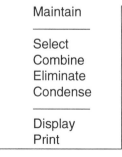

Indicate groupings of related choices by inscribing a line between each group. The line, or lines, should only extend from the first character of the descriptions to the end of the longest description, as shown above.

SAA CUA recommends that the line extend from pull-down border to border. Many other system pull-downs also follow this border-to-border approach. This extended line, however, results in too strong a visual separation between pull-down parts. The parts should be separated but not too strongly.

Settings

- If a menu item establishes or changes the attributes of data or properties of the interface, mark the pull-down choice or choices whose state is current or active ("on").
  - For nonexclusive items, display a check mark (✔) to the left of the item description.
    - If the two states of a setting are not obvious opposites, a pair of alternating menu item descriptions should be used to indicate the two states.
  - For exclusive choices, precede the choice with a contrasting symbol such as a diamond (♦) or circle (●).

If a menu item is made permanently active or "on" when selected, this can be made clear to the user by providing a mark by the item. For nonexclusive items, display a check mark (✔) to the left of the item description. For exclusive choices, precede the choice with a different and contrasting symbol such as a diamond (♦) or circle (●).

If a setting containing two states is not clear and obvious opposites, a pair of alternating menu item descriptions should be used to indicate the two states.

Pull-Downs Leading to Another Pull-Down

- If a pull-down choice leads to another pull-down, provide a cascade indicator:
  - Place an arrow or right-pointing triangle (▶) after the choice description.
  - Separate the triangle from the description by one space.
  - Display the triangle in the same color as the choice descriptions.

```
Font ▶
Spacing ▶
Size ▶
Intensity ▶
```

Occasionally a secondary or second level pull-down (or cascading pull-down as it is frequently called) may be desirable if the first pull-down leads to another short series of choices. Or, it may be desirable if the first pull-down has a large number of choices that are capable of being logically grouped. The existence of this second level, and hidden, pull-down should be indicated to the user on the first pull-down in a consistent manner. A simple way to do this is to include a right-pointing triangle to the right of the applicable choice description. These triangles can be seen displayed directly adjacent to their choice description, or they can be positioned aligned to the right side of the pull-down. The recommended method is adjacent for position consistency with the location of the pop-up window indicator to be described next.

Pull-Downs Leading to a Pop-Up Window

- For pull-down choices leading to a pop-up window:
  - Place an ellipsis (three dots) after the choice description.
  - Do not separate the dots from the description by a space.
  - Display the ellipsis in the same color as the choice descriptions.

```
Change . . .
Delete . . .
Copy . . .
Move . . .
```

When a pop-up window results from the selection of a pull-down choice, a visual indication of this fact is desirable. An ellipsis inscribed after the choice description is a good indicator that a window will appear.

Keyboard Equivalents and Accelerators

- Provide unique mnemonic codes by which choices may be selected through the typewriter keyboard.
  - Indicate the mnemonic code by underlining the proper character.
- Provide key accelerators for choice selection.
  - Identify the keys by their actual key top engravings.
  - Use a plus (+) sign to indicate two or more keys must be pressed at the same time.
  - Enclose the key names within parentheses ().
  - Right-align the key names, beginning three positions to the right of the longest choice description.
  - Display the key alternatives in the same color as the choice descriptions.

Maintain	(Alt+Backspace)
Select	(Shift+Ins)
Combine	
Eliminate	
Condense	
Display	
Print	

Enabling the user to select pull-down choices through the keyboard provides flexibility and efficiency in the dialogue. One method of doing this is to provide single-character mnemonic codes which, when typed, will also cause the choice to be invoked. Mnemonic codes can be visually indicated in a number of ways. The recommended method is an underline beneath the proper character within the choice.

Another method is to assign accelerators, one key, or a combination of keys, to accomplish the action. Identify these keys exactly as they are engraved on the keyboard, indicate simultaneous depression through use of a plus sign, and right-align and position to the right of the choice descriptions.

Separation

- Separate the pull-down from the remainder of the screen, but visually relate it to the menu bar by:
  — Using a background color the same as the menu bar.
  — Displaying choice descriptions in the same color as the menu bar.
  — Incorporating a solid-line border completely around the pull-down in the same color as the choice descriptions.
- A drop shadow (a heavier shaded line along two borders that meet) may also be included.

In addition to being identified by its position below the menu bar, the pull-down should visually relate to the menu bar and also visually contrast with the screen body. The most effective way to do this is to use the same foreground and background colors that are used on the menu bar but ensure that these colors adequately contrast with the screen body background. Because good contrasting background colors are often limited, a solid-line border of the same color as the choice descriptions will clearly delineate the pull-down border. A drop shadow, when included, will give the pull-down a three-dimensional effect.

Selection Cursor

- Use a reverse video, or reverse color, selection cursor the same color as the action/menu bar to surround the choice.
- Create a consistently sized cursor as long as the longest choice plus one blank space before and after.

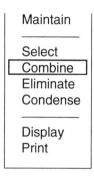

- — If ellipses, right-pointing arrows, or keyboard accelerators are displayed, the cursor should extend one space beyond the longest one.

The selection cursor should be a contrasting reverse video or reverse color bar of a consistent size surrounding the selected choice, including ellipses, arrows, or keyboard accelerators. The reverse color combination should be the same as appears within the menu bar.

CASCADING MENUS

Description

- A sub-menu derived from a higher-level menu.
- This higher-level menu may be a pull-down, pop-up, or another cascading menu.
- Cascading menus are located to the right of the menu item on the previous menu that they are related to.
- Menu items that lead to cascading menus are indicated by a right-point triangle.

Purpose

- To reduce the number of choices that are presented together for selection (reduce menu breadth).
- When a menu specifies many alternatives and the alternatives can be grouped in meaningful related sets on a lower-level menu.
- When a choice leads to a short, fixed list of single-choice properties.

- When there are several fixed sets of related options.
- To simplify a menu.

Advantages/Disadvantages

+ The top-level menus are simplified because some choices are hidden.
+ More first-letter mnemonics are available because menus possess fewer alternatives.
+ High-level command browsing is easier because sub-topics are hidden.

− Access to sub-menu items requires more steps.
− Access to sub-menu items requires a change in pointer movement direction.
− Exhaustive browsing is more difficult; some alternatives remain hidden as pull-downs become visible.

Proper Usage

- For mutually exclusive choices.
- To simplify a higher-level menu.
- To provide easier browsing of a higher-level menu.
- Do not place commands on cascading menus.

Description. A cascading menu is a sub-menu derived from a higher-level menu, most typically a pull-down. Cascades may also be attached to other cascades or pop-up menus, however. Cascading menus are located to the right of the menu item on the previous menu that they are related to. Menu items that lead to cascading menus are typically indicated by a right-pointing triangle.

Purpose. Cascading menus are developed to simplify menus by reducing the number of choices that appear together on one menu. Cascades can be used when many alternatives exist that can be grouped meaningfully. The top-level menu may contain the grouping category headings and the cascaded menu the items in each group. Any menu choices with a fixed set of related options may utilize cascades.

Advantages/Disadvantages. In addition to simplifying menus, cascades reduce visual clutter and make high-level command browsing easier because lower-level topics are hidden. More first-character mnemonics are also possible.

Cascades reduce breadth but at the cost of greater menu depth. This additional depth requires more choices to be made and more physical movements to the desired choice. Exhaustive browsing is also more difficult, necessitating more actions to accomplish. Cascades, while useful, must be used carefully and conservatively, consisting of only a few levels.

Proper usage. Cascaded menus should be used to reduce the number of choices presented and to permit easier browsing of high-level mutually exclusive alternatives.

CASCADING MENU GUIDELINES

Cascade Indicator

- Place an arrow or right-pointing triangle (>>, > >) to the right of each menu choice description leading to a cascade menu.
- Separate the indicator from the choice description by one space.
- Display the indicator in the same color as the choice descriptions.

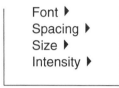

To indicate that another lower-level menu will appear when a menu item is selected, place an arrow or right-pointing triangle immediately to its right. Display the cascade indicator in the same color as the choice descriptions.

Location

- Position the first choice in the cascading menu immediately to the right of the selected choice.
- Leave the choice leading to the cascading menu highlighted.

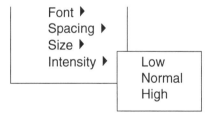

Cascading menus should be positioned so that the first choice in the cascading menu is immediately to the right of the selected choice. The choice leading to the cascade should remain highlighted in some way so that the cascade path is obvious.

Levels

- Do not exceed three levels whenever possible.
  — Only one cascading menu is preferred.

Each additional cascade level presented reduces ease of access and increases visual clutter. The number of cascade levels presented should represent a balance between menu simplification, ease in menu comprehension, and ease in item selection. Whenever possible, do not exceed three levels of menus (original and two cascades), as suggested by DECwindows. Try to maintain only one cascade, as recommended by Apple. If too many cascade levels are derived, use more pull-down menus or a dialog box for alternatives.

Title

- Not necessary on the cascading menu.
  - The title will be the name of the higher-level menu item chosen.

The title of the cascading menu will be the choice selected on the menu from which it cascades.

Other Guidelines

- Follow the organization, content, layout, separation, and selection cursor guidelines for the kind of menu from which the menu cascades.

Design of a cascade menu should follow all relevant guidelines for the family of menus to which it belongs. Included are organization, content, layout, and selection cursor.

POP-UP MENUS

Description

- A floating vertically arranged listing of choices that appears when specifically requested.
- The items displayed depend on where the pointer was positioned when the menu was requested.
  - Within a "hot" section of the working area.
  - On an icon.

Purpose

- To present alternatives or choices within the context of the task.

Advantages/Disadvantages

- + Appears in working area.
- + Does not use window space when not displayed.

+ No pointer movement needed if selected by button.
+ Vertical orientation for most efficient scanning.
+ Vertical orientation most efficient for grouping.
+ Vertical orientation allows more choices to be displayed.
+ May be able to remain showing ("pinned").
+ Allows for display of both keyboard equivalents and accelerators.

− Existence must be learned and remembered.
− Means for selecting must be learned and remembered.
− Requires a special action to see the menu (mouse click).
− Items are smaller than full-size buttons, slowing selection time.
− May obscure screen working area.
− Display locations may not be consistent.

Proper Usage

- For frequent users.
- For frequently used contextual commands.
- For a small number of items.
- For items that infrequently change.
- For items that require a small amount of screen space.

Description. Choices may also be presented to the user on the screen through "pop-up" menus, vertically arrayed listings that only appear when specifically requested. Pop-up menus may be requested when the mouse pointer is positioned over a designated or "hot" area of the menu (a window border, for example) or over a designated icon. In looks, they resemble pull-down menus, as shown in Figure 9.9.

Figure 9.9. Pop-up menu.

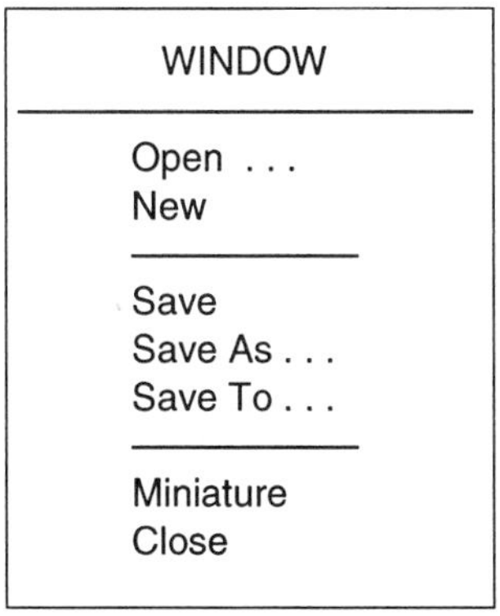

Purpose. The kinds of choices displayed in pop-up menus are context sensitive, depending on where the pointer is positioned when the request is made. They are most useful for presenting alternatives within the context of the user's immediate task. If positioned over text, for example, a pop-up might include text-specific commands.

Advantages/Disadvantages. A pop-up menu's biggest advantage is that it does not appear until needed, reducing visual clutter in the work area. It is also efficient, appearing at the point on the screen where the user's attention is focused, and it is vertically arrayed for easy grouping of elements, scanning, and display of keyboard equivalents and accelerators. A disadvantage of a pop-up menu is that, because it is usually hidden, its existence must be learned and remembered. One must also remember how to retrieve and display it. The actions available through pop-ups, therefore, are shortcuts and must also be capable of being accomplished in other clearly obvious ways. Pop-up menus must never be relied on for new or casual users.

Proper usage. Present, for experienced users, an alternative to retrieve frequently used contextual choices in pop-up menus. Choices should be limited in number and stable or infrequently changing in content.

POP-UP MENU GUIDELINES
Display

- Provide a pop-up menu for common, contextual actions.
  - If the pointer is positioned over an object possessing more than one quality (for example, both text and graphics), at minimum present actions common to all object qualities.
- Items that cannot be chosen due to the current state of an application should not be displayed.
- Continue to display a pop-up until:
  - A choice is selected.
  - An action outside the pop-up is initiated.
  - The pop-up is removed by the user.

Provide a pop-up menu for common, contextual actions. If, when requested, the pointer is positioned over an object possessing more than one quality (for example, both text and graphics), at minimum present actions common to all object qualities. Items that cannot be chosen due to the current state of an application should not be displayed.

Continue to display a pop-up until the user selects a choice, initiates an action outside the pop-up, or physically asks that the pop-up be removed.

Location

- Position the pop-up as follows:
  - Centered and to the right of the object from which it was requested.
  - Close enough to the pointer so that the pointer can be easily moved onto the menu.
  - But not so close that the pointer is positioned on an item, possibly leading to accidental selection.
  - If the pointer is positioned in such a manner that the pop-up would appear off-screen or clipped, position the menu:
    - As close as possible to the object, but not covering the object.
    - So that it appears fully on the screen.

Position a pop-up menu in a consistent location relative to the object from which it is requested. The preferable location is centered to the right. Locate the pop-up close enough to the pointer so that the pointer can be easily moved onto the menu. Positioning of the pointer on the menu itself could lead to accidental selection of an action.

If the pointer is positioned in such a manner that a right-centered position would force the pop-up partially or fully off the screen, locate the pop-up fully on the screen as close as possible to the object. Do not move the pointer to make a menu fit in the most desirable location.

Size

- Restrict to no more than five to 10 choices, preferably eight or less.

Limit pop-up menus to about 8 choices. If a large number of choices are needed, consider creating cascading menus. Minimize the number of levels of cascades, however, to provide ease of access and prevent visual clutter.

Title

- Not always necessary on a pop-up menu.
- If included, clearly describe the menu's purpose.
- Locate in a centered position at the top.
- Display in capital letters.
- Separate from the menu items by a line extending from the left menu border to the right border.

Titles on pop-up menus should clearly reflect the menu's purpose. This will avoid any possible confusion that may occur if the wrong menu is accidentally selected and displayed. The title should be set off from the item descriptions by capitalization and a separator line.

Other Guidelines

- Arrange logically organized and grouped choices into columns.
- If items are also contained in pull-down menus, organize pop-up menus in the same manner.
- Left-align choice descriptions.
- Use mixed-case letters to describe choices.
- Separate groups with a solid line the length of the longest choice description.
- If the choice leads to a pop-up window, place an ellipsis after the choice description.
- If keyboard accelerators are shown:
  — Indicate the mnemonic code by underlining the proper character.
  — Set apart key alternatives by placing them within parentheses.
- To separate the pop-up from the screen background:
  — Use a contrasting, but complementing, background.
  — Incorporate a solid line border around the pull-down.
- Use a reverse video, or reverse color, selection cursor slightly longer than the longest choice.

Follow the relevant pull-down menu guidelines for organization, content, layout, separation, and selection cursor.

TEAR-OFF MENUS

Description

- A pull-down menu that has been "torn-off" and positioned on the screen for constant referral.

Purpose

- To present alternatives or choices to the screen user that are needed infrequently at some times and heavily at other times.

Advantages/Disadvantages

- + No space consumed on screen when not used.
- + When needed, can remain continuously displayed on screen.

- − Requires extra steps to retrieve.
- − May obscure screen working area.

Proper Usage

- For items sometimes frequently selected and other times infrequently selected.
- For a small number of items.
- For items best represented textually.
- For items that rarely change.

Description. A tear-off menu is a pull-down menu that has been "torn-off" and positioned on the screen for constant referral. As such it possesses all the characteristics of a pull-down.

Purpose. To present alternatives or choices to the screen user that are needed infrequently at some times and heavily at other times.

Advantages/Disadvantages. No space is consumed on the screen when the menu is not needed. When needed, it can remain continuously displayed. It does require extra steps to retrieve and it may obscure the screen working area.

Proper usage. Use in situations where the items are sometimes frequently selected and other times infrequently selected. Items should be small in number and rarely change in content. A typical use would be to display a tool set when needed.

TEAR-OFF MENU GUIDELINES

- Follow all relevant guidelines for pull-down menus.

Since a tear-off menu is a pull-down, all pull-down guidelines will be followed.

ICONIC MENUS

Description

- A graphic or pictorial representation of menu items or objects.

Purpose

- To remind users of the commands, attributes, or application choices available.

Advantages/Disadvantages

- + Pictures help facilitate memory of applications.
- + Larger size increases speed of selection.

- Can consume considerable screen space.
- Difficult to organize for scanning efficiency.
- Drawing meaningful icons requires:
  - Artistic skills.
  - Additional time.
  - Special software.

Proper Usage

- To designate applications available.
- To designate special functions within an application.

Description. An iconic menu is the portrayal of menu items or objects in a graphic or pictorial form, as illustrated in Figure 9.10.

Purpose. To remind users of the commands, attributes, or application choices available.

Advantages/Disadvantages. Pictures help facilitate memory of applications and their larger size increases speed of selection. Pictures do, however, consume considerably more screen space than text, and they are difficult to organize for scanning efficiency. To create meaningful icons requires special skills and an extended amount of time.

Proper usage. To designate applications or special functions within an application. When a window is minimized it can take the form of an icon.

Figure 9.10. Iconic menu (from Microsoft Windows).

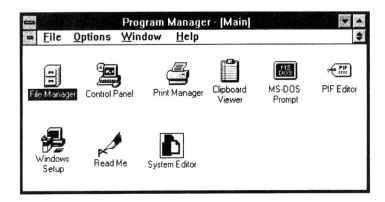

ICONIC MENU GUIDELINES

- Create icons that:
  — Help enhance recognition and hasten option selection.
  — Are concrete and meaningful.
  — Clearly represent choices.

Icons must be meaningful and clear. See Chapter 14 for a complete review of icon design guidelines.

Table 9.1. Menu proper usage summary.

MENU BAR

- To identify and provide access to:
  — Common and frequently used application actions.
  — Actions that take place in a wide variety of different windows.

PULL-DOWN MENU

- For frequently used application actions that take place in a wide variety of different windows:
  — A small number of items (5–10).
  — Items rarely changing in content.

CASCADING MENU

- To simplify a higher-level menu.
- To provide easier browsing of a higher-level menu.
- For mutually exclusive choices.
- Restrict to 1–2 cascades.

POP-UP MENU

- For:
  — Frequent users.
  — Frequently used contextual commands.
  — A small number of items (5–10).
  — Items rarely changing in content.
  — Items that require a small amount of screen space.

TEAR-OFF MENU

- For items:
  — Sometimes frequently selected.
  — Sometimes infrequently selected.
  — Small in number (5–10).
  — Rarely changing in content.

ICONIC MENU

- To designate applications available.
- To designate special functions within an application.

MENU SELECTION AND DESIGN STEPS

- Understand the principles of menu design.
- Establish kinds of menus needed to perform the tasks.
  — Menu Bar.
  — Pull-Down Menus.
  — Cascading Menus.
  — Pop-up Menus.
  — Iconic Menus.
- *Determine what system-provided default menu items are available and use them, if applicable.*
- Determine what critical functions are not represented by the default items.
  — Add any new required menu items.
  — Design new commands as necessary.

DETERMINING DEFAULT MENU ITEMS AVAILABLE

Every system will provide a set of standard menu items. Using the default items will reduce design time and encourage interface consistency. System learning time will also be reduced. Microsoft Windows (1992), for example, provides the following standard and optional menu bar items and pull-down actions:

File. A standard element, the file menu provides all the commands needed to open, create, and save files. The standard file functions are:

- New.
- Open.
- Save.
- Save As.
- Print.
- Print Setup.
- Exit.

Edit. A standard element, the edit menu provides commands that affect the state of selected objects. The standard edit functions are:

- Undo.
- Cut.
- Copy.
- Paste.
- Paste Links.
- Links.

View. An optional element, the view menu provides commands that affect the perspective, details, and appearance of the application. They affect the view, not the data itself. The view functions are application specific and include the following:

- Magnify.
- Zoom In.
- Zoom Out.
- Grid Points.

Window. The window menu, an optional element, provides commands to manipulate entire windows. Included are items such as:

- New Window.
- Arrange All.
- Hide.
- Show.

Help. The Help menu, a standard element, provides Help commands including:

- Contents.
- Search for Help On.
- How to Use Help.
- About (Application).

These standard menu items also have a prescribed order on the menu bar: File, Edit, View, Window, and Help. Items on their related pull-down menus also follow standard orders.

Standard menus and items should always be used when creating an application. Refer to a system's design documentation for exact details concerning what menu items are available and how they are used.

MENU SELECTION AND DESIGN STEPS

- Understand the principles of menu design.
- Establish kinds of menus needed to perform the tasks.
  - — Menu Bar.
  - — Pull-Down Menus.
  - — Cascading Menus.
  - — Pop-up Menus.
  - — Iconic Menus.
- Determine what system-provided default menu items are available and use them, if applicable.
- *Determine what critical functions are not represented by the default items.*
  - *— Design new commands as necessary.*
  - *— Add any new required menu items.*
- *Design menus using established design guidelines.*

Determine necessary new functions. Having established the usability of the standard menu functions, additional system functions must be identified.

Commands to accomplish these functions must be created and added to the pertinent menus.

Design menus. Finally, menus must be designed following principles of good menu design.

CHAPTER 9 EXAMPLES

Example 1.   A sequence of menu bars and pull-down menus are illustrated. An evolution of design, from poor to good, is shown.

Menu 1-1.   What are the problems in the way this menu bar and pull-down menu are presented? (1) Keyboard mnemonics are designated by capital letters. Note the uncommon shape of "foRmat," "cuT," and "clEar" when the mnemonic is not the first letter of the word. (2) Item groupings do not exist in the pull-down. The differences in basic functions are not obvious and the more destructive operations (Undo, Clear, and Delete) are positioned close to standard actions, increasing the potential for accidental selection. (3) The keyboard accelerators are adjacent to the choice descriptions and not set off in any way. Therefore, these alternative, and supplemental, actions visually compete with choice descriptions for the viewer's attention.

I			**OFFICE SYSTEM**			I I
File	**Edit**	**foRmat**	**View**	**Options**		**Help**

```
      Undo      Alt+Backspace
      cuT       Shift+Delete
      Copy      Ctrl+Ins
      Paste     Shift+Ins
      clEar
      Delete
```

Menu 1-2.   Keyboard mnemonics are designated by underlines, not capital letters. Choice descriptions now assume more common and recognizable shapes.

I			**OFFICE SYSTEM**			I I
File	**Edit**	**Format**	**View**	**Options**		**Help**

```
      Undo      Alt+Backspace
      Cut       Shift+Delete
      Copy      Ctrl+Ins
      Paste     Shift+Ins
      Clear
      Delete
```

Menu 1-3. Groupings through use of white space are established for choices in the pull-down. The different functions are much more obvious and separation is provided for the destructive actions.

I	OFFICE SYSTEM		I	I

File	Edit	Format	View	Options	Help

Undo Alt+Backspace

Cut Shift+Delete
Copy Ctrl+Ins
Paste Shift+Ins

Clear
Delete

Menu 1-4. The different groupings are visually reinforced through use of separating lines. The lines are not extended to the pull-down border so as not to completely disassociate the choices.

I	OFFICE SYSTEM		I	I

File	Edit	Format	View	Options	Help

Undo Alt+Backspace
―――――――――――――
Cut Shift+Delete
Copy Ctrl+Ins
Paste Shift+Ins
―――――――――――――
Clear
Delete

Menu 1-5. Keyboard alternatives are right-aligned to move them further from the choice descriptions. They are also enclosed in parentheses to deemphasize them, thereby reducing their visual competition with the choices. Choice descriptions are now more obvious.

I	OFFICE SYSTEM		I	I

File	Edit	Format	View	Options	Help

Undo (Alt+Backspace)
―――――――――――――
Cut (Shift+Delete)
Copy (Ctrl+Ins)
Paste (Shift+Ins)
―――――――――――――
Clear
Delete

Example 2. Alternative poor and good versions of an "Office System" menu bar are illustrated.

Menu 2-1. A very poor menu bar. All alternatives are presented creating a very crowded series of choices in a difficult-to-scan horizontal array. No groupings are provided and an alphabetic order causes intermixing of what appear to be different functions. While menu breadth is preferred to excessive menu depth, too many choices are presented here.

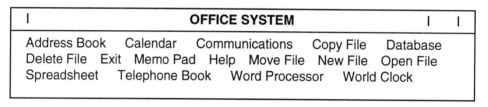

Menus 2-2 and 2-3. Another poor menu bar. While "File," "Function," and "Help" are now presented separately, the cascading "Function" menu requires an excessive number of steps to complete selection. Note the number of levels needed to access the address or telephone book. Excessive levels of depth are difficult to scan and lead to one's getting lost. Some have referred to this problem as "cascade confusion."

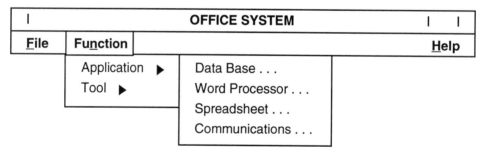

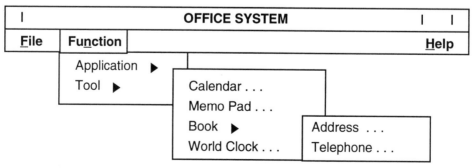

Menus 2-4, 2-5, and 2-6.   A more reasonable solution. "Application" and "Tool" menu bar items are created and all alternatives now exist on one pull-down menu. The number of steps necessary to reach any alternative is minimized and easier scanning of all items is permitted.

I	OFFICE SYSTEM	I I
<u>F</u>ile	<u>A</u>pplication <u>T</u>ool	<u>H</u>elp

<u>N</u>ew . . .
<u>O</u>pen . . .
<u>M</u>ove . . .
<u>C</u>opy . . .
<u>D</u>elete

———————

E<u>x</u>it

I	OFFICE SYSTEM	I I
<u>F</u>ile	<u>A</u>pplication <u>T</u>ool	<u>H</u>elp

<u>D</u>ata Base . . .
<u>W</u>ord Processor . . .
<u>S</u>preadsheet . . .
<u>C</u>ommunications . . .

I	OFFICE SYSTEM	I I
<u>F</u>ile	<u>A</u>pplication <u>T</u>ool	<u>H</u>elp

<u>M</u>emo Pad . . .
<u>C</u>alendar . . .
<u>T</u>elephone Book . . .
<u>A</u>ddress Book . . .
<u>W</u>orld Clock . . .

Device-Based Controls

Device-based controls are the mechanisms through which people communicate their desires to the system. The evolution of graphical systems has seen a whole new family of devices provided to assist and enhance this communication. These new mechanisms are most commonly referred to as pointing devices.

STEP 6

- Identify the characteristics and capabilities of various device-based controls.
  - Trackball.
  - Joystick.
  - Graphic tablet.
  - Touch screen.
  - Light pen.
  - Mouse.
  - Keyboard.
- Select the proper controls for the user and tasks.

For years the device of choice in display-based systems was the standard keyboard. As graphical systems evolved, emphasis shifted to another device, the mouse. A number of other kinds of devices have also been around and have seen extended service through the years, including the joystick, trackball, light pen, and graphic tablet. Another entity, animate in nature—one's finger—has also been used in conjunction with touch-sensitive screens. The various alternatives have both strengths and weaknesses. Selecting the proper device-based control to do the required job is critical to system success. A good fit between user and control will lead to fast, accurate performance. A poor fit will result in lower productivity, more errors. and possibly user fatigue.

We'll begin by reviewing the kinds of tasks being performed using graphical systems. We will discuss each device and identify its advantages and disadvantages. Then, we'll focus on the most popular control, the mouse, describing it in more detail and presenting a series of design guidelines for its use. The keyboard, because of its versatility and usefulness for text entry tasks, will also be examined in more detail. Finally, pertinent research will be reviewed and guidelines presented to aid in selecting the proper device.

GRAPHICAL DEVICES

Several specific tasks are performed using graphical systems. The first is to point at an object on the screen. Next is to select the object or identify it as the focus of attention. It is also possible to drag an object across the screen or draw something free-form on the screen. Moving objects may be tracked or followed. Objects may also be oriented or positioned. Data or information may be entered or manipulated.

The alternative devices vary in how well they can perform these actions. A summary of their capabilities follows.

Trackball

Description

- A spherical object (ball) that rotates freely in all directions in its socket.
- Direction and speed tracked and translated into cursor movement.

Advantages/Disadvantages

- + Direct relationship between hand and cursor movement in terms of direction and speed.
- + Does not obscure vision of screen.
- + Does not require additional desk space (if mounted on keyboard).

- − Movement indirect, in plane different from screen.
- − No direct relationship between hand and cursor movement in terms of distance.
- − Requires a degree of eye-hand coordination.
- − Requires hand to be removed from keyboard keys.
- − Requires different hand movements.
- − Requires hand be removed from keyboard (if not mounted on keyboard).
- − Requires additional desk space (if not mounted on keyboard).
- − May be difficult to control.
- − May be fatiguing to use over extended time.

Description. Commonly used with portable PCs, the trackball is a ball that rotates freely in all directions in its socket. The ball is rotated with the finger tips, and its direction and speed are tracked and translated into equivalent screen cursor movement.

Advantages and Disadvantages. In terms of direction and speed, a trackball possesses a direct relationship between how it is rolled and how the cursor moves on the screen. The cursor moves in the same direction and speed ratio as the ball is rotated. Many trackballs are mounted on the keyboard itself, permitting the user's hands to remain close to the keyboard itself. Trackballs on the keyboard do not require additional desk space, although the keyboard must be expanded to allow for their inclusion.

Trackballs share a common problem with several other controls: control movement is in a different plane from the screen. The cursor, or pointer, is separated from the control itself—the pointer being on the screen, the control on the keyboard. These controls, where the control and pointer are separated, are referred to as indirect pointing devices. To effectively use a trackball requires learning the proper psychomotor skills, fine finger movements for accurate pointing, and gross hand movements for moving longer distances. The fine finger movements necessary to use them can be difficult to do. Over longer periods of use, they can be fatiguing. When paired with keyboard tasks, they require a shift in motor activity from keystrokes to finger/hand movement.

Joystick

Description

- A stick or bat-shaped device anchored at the bottom.
- Variable in size, smaller ones being operated by fingers, larger ones requiring the whole hand.
- Variable in cursor direction movement method, force joysticks respond to pressure, movable respond to movement.
- Variable in degree of movement allowed, from horizontal-vertical only to continuous.

Advantages/Disadvantages

+ Direct relationship between hand and cursor movement in terms of direction.
+ Does not obscure vision of screen.
+ Does not require additional desk space (if mounted on keyboard).

− Movement indirect, in plane different from screen.
− Indirect relationship between hand and cursor in terms of speed and distance.
− Requires a degree of eye-hand coordination.

– Requires hand to be removed from keyboard keys.
– Requires different hand movements to use.
– Requires hand to be removed from keyboard (if not mounted on keyboard).
– Requires additional desk space (if not mounted on keyboard).
– May be fatiguing to use over extended time.
– May be slow and inaccurate.

Description. A joystick, like its aircraft namesake, is a stick or bat-shaped device usually anchored at the bottom. They come in variable sizes, smaller ones being operated by fingers, larger ones requiring the whole hand. The smaller joysticks require fine motor coordination, the larger ones more gross coordination. Some, called force joysticks, are immovable, responding to pressure exerted against them. The direction and amount of pressure is translated into pointer movement direction and speed. Others, called movable joysticks, can be moved within a dish-shaped area. The direction and distance of the movements creates a similar pointer movement on the screen. Some kinds of joysticks permit continuous movements, others only horizontal and vertical movements. Joysticks may also be mounted on the keyboard.

Advantages/Disadvantages. Joysticks typically possess a direct relationship between hand and cursor movement in terms of direction. When mounted on the keyboard, they do not require additional desk space.

Joysticks are also indirect devices, the control and its result being located in different planes. They require developing a skill to use and can be slow and inaccurate. Use over extended time may also be fatiguing. When paired with keyboard tasks, they require a shift in motor activity from keystrokes to finger/ hand movement.

Graphic Tablet

Description

- Pressure-, heat-, light-, or light-blockage-sensitive horizontal surfaces that lie on the desktop.
- May be operated with fingers, light pen, or objects like a stylus or pencil.
- Cursor imitates movements on tablet.

Advantages/Disadvantages

+ Direct relationship between touch movements and cursor movements in terms of direction, distance, and speed.
+ More comfortable horizontal operating plane.
+ Does not obscure vision of screen.

– Movement indirect, in plane different from screen.

- Requires hand be removed from keyboard.
- Requires hand to be removed from keyboard keys.
- Requires different hand movements to use.
- Requires additional desk space.
- Finger may be too large for accuracy with small objects.

Description. A graphic tablet, also called a touch tablet, is a device with a horizontal surface sensitive to pressure, heat, light, or the blockage of light. It lies on the desk and may be operated with fingers, light pen, or objects like a pencil or stylus. The screen pointer imitates movement on the tablet.

Advantages/Disadvantages. With graphic tablets, a direct relationship exists between touch movements and pointer movements in terms of direction, distance, and speed. The screen mimics the tablet. When used with objects like styluses, light pens, or pencils, the operational angle, horizontal, is more comfortable than those vertically oriented.

Tablets are also indirect controls, creating coordination problems. To use them requires moving one's hand from the keyboard and, if using another device, picking it up. If the finger is the tablet-activation object, accuracy with small objects is difficult. Tablets also require desk space.

Touch Screen

Description

- A special surface on the screen sensitive to finger or stylus touch.

Advantages/Disadvantages

- + Direct relationship between hand and cursor movement in terms of direction, distance, and speed.
- + Movement direct, in same plane as screen.
- + Requires no additional desk space.
- + Stands up well in high use environments.

- − Finger may obscure part of screen.
- − Finger may be too large for accuracy with small objects.
- − Requires moving the hand far from the keyboard to use.
- − Very fatiguing to use for extended period of time.
- − May soil or damage the screen.

Design Guidelines

- Screen objects should be at least 3/4″ × 3/4″ in size.
- Object separation should be at least 1/8″.
- Provide visual feedback in response to activation. Auditory feedback may also be appropriate.

- When the consequences are destructive, require confirmation after selection to eliminate inadvertent selection.

Description. A touch screen is a screen comprised of a special surface sensitive to finger or stylus touch. Objects on the screen are pointed to and touched to select.

Advantages/Disadvantages. Touch screens possess a direct relationship between hand and pointer movement in terms of direction, distance, and speed. This relationship is direct, however, not indirect, because the control (finger or stylus) is on the same plane as the pointer. Another significant advantage of a touch screen is that it does not require any additional desk space.

A disadvantage of touch screens is that they are fatiguing to use over an extended period of time. If a finger is the touch mechanism, it may obscure part of the screen and be too large to be accurate with small objects. A stylus is usually more accurate than the finger. Fingers may also soil the screen, and a stylus may damage it. Both finger and stylus require moving of a hand from the keyboard to operate, and a stylus must also be picked up.

Design Guidelines. When using touch screens, larger screen objects should always be provided to foster accuracy in use. Minimally, objects should be 3/4" square and separated by at least 1/8". Visual, and perhaps auditory, feedback should be provided in response to activation. When the consequences of selection are destructive, require a confirmation to avoid inadvertent selection (Brown, 1988).

Light Pen

Description

- A special surface on the screen sensitive to touch of a special stylus or pen.

Advantages/Disadvantages

+ Direct relationship between hand and cursor movement in terms of direction, distance, and speed.
+ Movement direct, in same plane as screen.
+ Requires minimal additional desk space.
+ Stands up well in high-use environments.
+ More accurate than finger touching.

− Hand may obscure part of screen.
− Requires picking up to use.
− Requires moving the hand far from the keyboard to use.
− Very fatiguing to use for extend period of time.

Description. A light pen also utilizes a touch screen but is sensitive in a specific way to one kind of pen or stylus.

Advantages/Disadvantages. Advantages and disadvantages are similar to those of the touch screen. Touch screens possess a direct relationship between hand and pointer movement in terms of direction, distance, and speed, and are also classified as direct pointing devices because the control (pen or stylus) is on the same plane as the pointer. Another advantage of a touch screen is that it does not require any additional desk space, except for the pen to rest.

A disadvantage is that they are also fatiguing to use over an extended period to time. A light pen is usually more accurate than the finger. Light pens require moving a hand from the keyboard to pick up and use.

Mouse

Description

- A rectangular or dome-shaped, movable, desktop control containing from one to three buttons used to manipulate objects and information on the screen.
- Movement of cursor mimics mouse movement.

Advantages/Disadvantages

- + Direct relationship between hand and cursor movement in terms of direction, distance, and speed.
- + Selection mechanisms included on mouse.
- + Does not obscure vision of screen.

- − Movement indirect, in plane different from screen.
- − Requires hand be removed from keyboard.
- − Requires additional desk space.
- − May require long movement distances.
- − Requires a degree of eye-hand coordination.

Description. A mouse is a rectangular or dome-shaped, movable, desktop control containing from one to three buttons used to manipulate objects and information on the screen. The movement of the screen pointer mimics the mouse movement.

Advantages/Disadvantages. There is a direct relationship between hand and cursor movement in terms of direction, distance, and speed. The mouse itself contains some basic controls (buttons) useful for manipulating screen objects.

Disadvantages are that they are also indirect devices, the control and its result being located in different planes. They require developing a skill to use and, when paired with keyboard tasks, they require movement away from the keyboard and a shift in motor activity from keystrokes to finger/hand movement. The mouse also requires extensive additional desk space and long positioning movements.

Mouse Configurations, Functions, and Operations

Configurations

- One, two, or three buttons.

Functions

- Select—To manipulate controls and select alternatives or objects.
- Menu—To request and display a pop-up menu.
- Adjust—To extend or reduce number of items selected.

Operations

- To *point* is the movement and positioning of the mouse pointer over the desired screen object.
  — Prepares for selection or control operation.
- To *press* is to press and hold the button down without releasing it.
  — Identifies the object to be selected.
- To *click* is to press and immediately release a button without moving the mouse.
  — Selects item or insertion point.
  — Operates control.
  — Activates inactive window or control.
- To *double-click* is to perform two clicks within a predefined time limit without moving the mouse.
  — Shortcut for common operations (e.g., activates icon, open file, etc.).
- To *drag* is to press and hold the button down, and then move the pointer in the appropriate direction.
  — Identifies range of objects.
  — Moves or resizes items.
- To double-drag is to perform two clicks and hold the button down, and then move the pointer in the appropriate direction.
  — Identifies selection by larger unit (e.g., words).

The mouse comes in a variety of configurations, performs some basic functions, and is operated in several ways.

Configurations. A mouse may possess one, two, or three buttons. Most, but not all, windowing systems permit operation using all configurations. Buttons are used to perform the three functions to be described. When three mouse buttons are not available, the pointer location or keyboard qualifiers must be used to determine the function to be performed. A multibutton mouse permits a more efficient operation, but a person must remember which button to use to perform each function. A multibutton mouse may usually be configured for left- or right-hand use.

Functions. The functions performed by a mouse are select, menu, and adjust. The SELECT function is used to manipulate controls, select alternatives and data, and select objects that will be affected by actions that follow. Select is a mouse's most important function and is the function assigned to a one-button mouse. For a multibutton mouse, it is usually assigned to the leftmost button (assuming a right-handed operation).

The MENU function is typically used to request and display a pop-up menu on a screen. A menu appears when the button is depressed within a particular defined area of the screen. This area may be, for example, the entire screen, within a window, or on a window border. This button eliminates the need for a control icon, which must be pointed at and selected. The user, however, must remember that a menu is available.

The ADJUST function extends or reduces the number of items selected. It is the least used of the three functions and is usually assigned last and given the least prominent location on a mouse.

Operations. Several operations can be performed with a mouse button. The first, point, is the movement and positioning of the mouse pointer over the desired screen object. It prepares for a selection or control operation. To press is to press and hold the button down without releasing it. It identifies the object to be selected.

To click is to press and immediately release a button without moving the mouse. This operation typically selects an item or insertion point, operates a control, or activates an inactive window or control. To double-click is to perform two clicks within a predefined time limit without moving the mouse. It is used as a shortcut for common operations such as activating an icon or opening a file.

To drag is to press and hold the button down, and then move the pointer in the appropriate direction. It identifies a range of objects or moves, or resizes items. To double-drag is to perform two clicks and hold the button down, and then move the pointer in the appropriate direction. It identifies a selection by a larger unit, such as a group of words.

Mouse Usage Guidelines

- Provide a "hot zone" around small or thin objects that might require extremely fine mouse positioning.
- Never use double-clicks or double-drags as the only means of carrying out essential operations.
- Do not require a person to point at a moving target.

If an object is very small and might require fine mouse positioning, provide a "hot zone" around it. This will increase target size and speed selection. Do not require double-clicks or double-drags as the only way to carry out essential operations. Rapid double-pressing is difficult for some people. Do not require a person to point at a moving target, except, of course, for a game.

Keyboard

Description

- Standard typewriter keyboard and cursor movement keys.

Advantages/Disadvantages

- + Familiar.
- + Accurate.
- + Does not take up additional desk space.
- + Very useful for:
    - ++ Entering text and alphanumerics.
    - ++ Inserting in text and alphanumerics.
    - ++ Keyed shortcuts—accelerators.
    - ++ Keyboard mnemonics—equivalents.
- + Advantageous for:
    - ++ Performing actions where less than three mouse buttons exist.
    - ++ Using with very large screens.
    - ++ Touch typists.

- − Slow for non-touch typists.
- − Slower than other devices in pointing.
- − Requires discrete actions to operate.
- − No direct relationship between finger or hand movement on the keys and cursor movement on screen in terms of speed and distance.

Description. The standard typewriter keyboard and associated cursor movement and function keys.

Advantages/Disadvantages. The standard keyboard is familiar, accurate, and does not consume additional desk space. It is useful and efficient for entering or inserting text or alphanumeric data. For tasks requiring heavy text or data entry, shifting hands between a keyboard and an alternative control such as a mouse can be time consuming and inefficient, especially for a touch typist. The keyboard is flexible enough to accept keyed shortcuts, either keyboard accelerators or mnemonic equivalents. Some systems also permit navigation through a screen through use of keyboard keys like the space bar, arrows, tab, and enter.

Inefficiencies in using other graphical device-based controls can occur in other ways. A mouse with a limited number of buttons will require use of the keyboard to accomplish some functions, possibly causing frequent shifting between devices. Operations that are being performed on very large screens may also find keyboard window management preferable to the long mouse movements frequently required. Therefore, to compensate for these possible inefficiencies, many windowing systems provide alternative keyboard operations for mouse tasks.

Disadvantages of a keyboard include their requiring discrete finger actions to operate instead of the more fine positioning movements. As a result, no direct relationship exists in terms of speed and distance between finger or hand movement on the keys and cursor movement on the screen. Depending on the layout of the keyboard cursor control keys, direct relationship direction problems may also exist as fingers may not move in the same direction as the cursor. Keyboards will also be slower for non-touch typists and slower than other controls in pointing tasks.

Keyboard Guidelines

- Provide keyboard accelerators.
  - Assign single keys for frequently performed, small-scale tasks.
  - Assign SHIFT + key combinations for actions that extend or are complementary to the actions of the key or key combination used without the SHIFT key.
  - Assign CTRL + key combinations for:
    - Infrequent actions.
    - Tasks that represent larger-scale versions of the task assigned to the unmodified key.
- Provide keyboard mnemonics.
  - Use the first letter of the item description.
    - If first letter conflicts exist, use:
      - Another distinctive consonant in the item description.
      - A vowel in the item description.
- Provide window navigation through use of keyboard keys.

Keyboard Accelerators. Accelerators provide a way to access menu elements without displaying a menu. They are useful for frequent tasks performed by experienced users. Keys assigned for accelerators should foster efficient performance and be meaningful and conceptually consistent to aid learning.

Microsoft Windows (1992) suggests frequently performed, small-scale tasks should be assigned single keys as the keyboard alternative. Actions that extend or are complementary to the actions of a key (or key combination) should be assigned a SHIFT key in conjunction with the original action. Microsoft, for example, uses a single key, F6, as the key to move clockwise to the next pane of an active window. To move counterclockwise to the next pane, SHIFT + F6.

Infrequent actions, or tasks that represent larger-scale versions of the task assigned to the unmodified key, should be assigned CTRL + key combinations. The left arrow key in Microsoft Windows, for example, moves the cursor one character; CTRL + left arrow moves it one word.

Keyboard Mnemonics. Keyboard mnemonics enable selecting a menu choice through the keyboard instead of by pointing. This enables a person's hands to remain on the keyboard during extensive keying tasks. Keyboard mnemonics should be chosen in a meaningful way to aid rememberability and foster predictability of those things that may be forgotten. Mnemonics need only be unique within a menu. A simple rule is always to use the first letter of a menu item description. If the first letter of one item conflicts with that of another, choose another distinctive consonant in the item description, preferably, but not always necessarily, the second in the item word (occasionally another consonant may be more meaningful). The last choice would be a vowel in the item description.

Window Navigation. Also provide ways of navigating through windows by use of keyboard keys.

CONTROL RESEARCH

Which devices work better for which tasks and under what conditions has been addressed by a number of investigators. A survey of the research literature comparing and evaluating different devices was done by Greenstein and Arnaut (1988). They provide the following summarization concerning tasks involving pointing and dragging:

- The fastest tools for pointing at stationary targets on screens are the devices that permit direct pointing, the touch screen and light pen. This is most likely due to their high level of eye-hand coordination and because they use an action familiar to people.
- In positioning speed and accuracy for stationary targets, the indirect pointing device, the mouse, trackball, and graphic tablet, do not differ greatly from one another. The joystick is the slowest, although it is as accurate as the others. Of most importance in selecting one of these devices will be its fit to the user's task and working environment.
- A separate confirmation action that must follow pointer positioning increases pointing accuracy but reduces speed. The mouse offers a very effective design configuration for tasks requiring this confirmation.
- For tracking small, slowly moving targets, the mouse, trackball, and graphic tablet are preferred to the touch screen and light pen because the latter may obscure the user's view of the target.

Another common manipulation task is dragging an object across the screen. Using a mouse, graphic tablet, and trackball for this task, as well as pointing, was studied by MacKenzie, et al. (1991). They report the following:

- The graphic tablet yielded best performance during pointing.
- The mouse yielded best performance during dragging.
- The trackball was a poor performer for both pointing and dragging, and it had a very high error rate in dragging.

GUIDELINES FOR SELECTING THE PROPER DEVICE-BASED CONTROL

- Consider the characteristics of the task.
  - Provide keyboards for tasks involving:
    - Heavy text entry and manipulation.
    - Movement through structured arrays consisting of a few discrete objects.
  - Provide an alternative pointing device for graphical or drawing tasks. The following are some suggested best uses:
    - Mouse—pointing, selecting, drawing, and dragging.
    - Joystick—pointing, selecting, tracking, and dragging.
    - Trackball—pointing, selecting, and tracking.
    - Touch screen—pointing and selecting.
    - Graphic tablet—pointing and selecting.
  - Provide touch screens under the following conditions:
    - The opportunity for training is minimal.
    - Targets are large, discrete, and spread out.
    - Frequency of use is low.
    - Desk space is at a premium.
    - Little or no text input requirement exists.
- Consider user characteristics and preferences.
  - Provide keyboards for touch typists.
- Consider the characteristics of the environment.
- Consider the characteristics of the hardware.
- Consider the characteristics of the device in relation to the application.
- Provide flexibility.
- Minimize eye and hand movements between devices.

Selection of the proper device for an application, then, depends on a host of factors.

Task Characteristics. Is the device suited to the task? For tasks requiring text entry and manipulation, standard typewriter keyboards are always necessary. Keyboards (cursor control keys) are usually faster when moving through structured arrays consisting of a few discrete objects.

For graphical and drawing tasks, alternative pointing devices are easier and faster. Use a mouse, joystick, trackball, or graphic tablet for pointing, selecting, drawing, dragging, or tracking. The devices best suited for each kind of task are summarized above (Mayhew, 1992).

Provide touch screens where the opportunity for training is minimal; targets are large, discrete, and spread out; frequency of use is low; desk space is at a premium; and little or no text input requirement exists (Mayhew, 1992).

User Characteristics and Preferences. Will the user be able to easily and comfortably operate the control? Are the fine motor movements required by some devices capable of being performed? Is the user familiar with the standard keyboard? What are the user's preferences? While preferences do not always correspond to performance, it is important that the user be comfortable with the selected device.

Environmental Characteristics. Will the device fit easily into the work environment? If desk space is necessary, does it exist and is it large enough?

Hardware Characteristics. Is the device itself of a quality that permits easy performance of all the necessary tasks? Joysticks, for example, are quite variable in their movement capabilities.

The Device in Relation to the Application. Is the device satisfactory for the application? Table 10.1 based on a table presented by Greenstein and Arnaut (1988), summarizes a variety of characteristics and capabilities of the alternative devices.

Flexibility. Often, task and user needs will vary within an application. Providing more than one kind of device will give the user choices in how to most efficiently accomplish whatever tasks must be performed. A keyboard paired with another kind of pointing device is almost always necessary.

Minimize Eye and Hand Movements. When multiple devices are used, eye and hand movements between them must be minimized. Structure the task, if possible, to permit the user to stay in one working area. If shifts must be made, they should be as infrequent as possible.

POINTER GUIDELINES

- The pointer:
  - Should be visible at all times.
  - Should contrast well with its background.
  - Should maintain its size across all screen locations and during movement.
  - The hotspot should be easy to locate and see.
  - Location should not warp (change position).
    - The user should always position the pointer.
- The shape of a pointer:
  - Should clearly indicate its purpose and meaning.
  - Should be constructed of already-defined shapes.

Table 10.1 Advantages and disadvantages of the standard pointing/input devices (from Greenstein and Arnaut, 1988).

Legend: + Advantage
         o Neutral
         – Disadvantage

	Touch Screen	Light Pen	Graphic Tablet	Mouse	Trackball	Joystick
Eye-hand Coordination	+	+	o	o	o	o
Unobstructed View of Screen	–	–	+	+	+	+
Ability to Attend to Display	+	o	+	o	+	+
Freedom from Parallax Problems	–	–	+	+	+	+
Input Resolution Capability	–	–	+	+	+	+
Flexibility of Placement in Workplace	–	–	o	o	+	+
Minimal Space Requirements	+	+	–	–	+	+
Minimal Training Requirements	+	o	o	o	o	o
Comfort in Extended Use	–	–	o	o	+	+
Absolute Mode Capability	+	+	+	–	–	o
Relative Mode Capability	–	–	+	+	+	o
Capability to Emulate Other Devices	–	–	+	–	–	–
Suitability for:						
• Pointing	+	+	+	+	+	–
• Rapid Pointing	+	+	o	o	o	–
• Pointing with Confirmation	–	o	o	+	o	–
• Drawing	–	–	+	o	–	–
• Tracing	–	–	+	–	–	–
• Continuous Tracking of:						
— Slow Targets	o	o	+	+	+	–
— Fast Targets	–	–	o	o	o	+
• Alphanumeric Data Entry	–	–	–	–	–	–
Dragging (From MacKenzie, et al., 1991)	o	o	+	+	–	o

— Should not be used for any other purpose other than its already-defined meaning.
— Do not create new shapes for already-defined standard functions.
• Use only as many shapes as necessary to inform the user about current location and status. Too many shapes can confuse a person.

The focus of the user's attention in most device operations is most often the pointer. As such, the pointer image should be used to provide feedback concerning the function being performed, the mode of operation, and the state of the system. For example, the pointer shape image can be changed when it is positioned over a selectable object, signaling to the user that a button action may be performed. When an action is being performed, the pointer can assume the shape of a progress indicator such as a sand timer, providing an indication of processing status.

A pointer should contrast well with its background and be visible at all times. The user should always be in control of its location on the screen. The shape of a pointer should clearly indicate its purpose and meaning. Always use predefined shapes provided by graphical systems. Microsoft Windows (1992), for example, provides about two dozen, some of which are illustrated in Table 10.2. To aid learning and avoid user confusion, never create new shapes for already-defined standard functions or use a shape for any purpose other than its previously defined meaning. Also, use only as many shapes as absolutely necessary to keep the user informed about current position and status. Too many shapes can confuse a person.

Table 10.2. Suggested movement pointers from Microsoft Windows.

Shape	Screen Location	Movement
↖	On item	Unconstrained
↕	On item	Vertical
↔	On item	Horizontal
⬌⬍	On item	Vertical or horizontal

Screen-Based Controls

Screen-based controls are the elements of screens that permit the user to interact with data. They typically contain some form of identification, usually a caption or label, and the data or information itself, its content. Some controls also have special buttons that permit their data to be manipulated in certain ways. Controls are almost always located in the work area of the screen.

STEP 7

- Identify the characteristics and capabilities of various screen-based controls.
  — Buttons.
  — Entry fields.
  — Selection fields.
  — Combination entry/selection fields.
  — Settings.
- Select the proper controls for the user and tasks.

The screen designer is presented an array of screen-based controls to choose from. Selecting the right one for the user and the task is often difficult. But, as with device-based controls, making the right choice is critical to system success. A proper fit between user and control will lead to fast, accurate performance. A poor fit will result in lower productivity, more errors, and probably dissatisfaction.

CONTROLS

We'll start by describing the types of controls and identifying their advantages, disadvantages, and proper usage. Control design guidelines will also be presented. We'll finish by providing some guidance in choosing the proper kind of control to enable the tasks to be performed quickly and efficiently by the user.

Buttons

Description

- A rectangular shape with text inside that shows the action to be taken when selected.
- A square or rectangular shape with a symbol inside. The symbol, when learned, identifies the action to be performed when selected.

Purpose

- To execute commands directly.
- To display a menu or manipulate a window.

Advantages/Disadvantages

Textual or Alphanumeric Labels

- + Always visible, reminding user of existence.
- + Convenient and logically located in work area.
- + Provide meaningful descriptions of the actions that will be performed.
- + Larger size generally provides faster selection target.
- + 3-D appearance:
  - ++ Adds an aesthetically pleasing style to the screen.
  - ++ Provides visual feedback through button movement when activated.
- + Easily permit use of keyboard equivalents and accelerators.
- + Faster than using a two-step menu bar/pull-down sequence.

- − Consume screen space.
- − Larger size limits the number that may be displayed.
- − Require looking away from main working area to activate.
- − Require moving the pointer to select.

Symbol Labels

- + Always visible, reminding user of existence.
- + Consume little screen space.
- + Allow for use of keyboard accelerators.

- − Usually located away from main work area at window edges.
- − Usually smaller than other menu styles, causing slower selection.
- − Do not allow for keyboard equivalents.
- − Label is a symbol whose meaning must be learned and remembered.

Proper Usage

- Use buttons for frequently used actions that are specific to a window.
  — To cause something to immediately happen.
  — To display a menu of options.
  — To display another window.

Description and Purpose. A button comes in two styles. The first resembles the control commonly found on electrical or mechanical devices and are sometimes called pushbuttons. They are rectangular shaped with text inside that shows the action to be taken when they are selected. These buttons are usually placed within a window, and activating them causes the action or command described on them to be immediately performed. This kind of button may take a variety of forms, some of which are illustrated in Figure 11.1.

The second style is square or rectangular in shape with a symbol inscribed inside. The symbol, when learned, identifies the button and the action to be performed when the button is selected. These buttons are located in the borders of windows and are used to do such things as obtaining a system menu or resizing a window. They have already been described in more detail in Chapter 8.

Advantages/Disadvantages. The advantages of textual-labelled buttons are that they are always visible, providing a reminder of their existence. They can be conveniently and logically located in the work area and inscribed with meaningful descriptions of what they do. Their larger size speeds selection and their 3-D appearance is aesthetically pleasing and also can be used to provide meaningful feedback through movement of the button when activated. Their activation is faster than using a two-step menu bar/pull-down sequence.

Among the disadvantages of textual-labelled buttons is their large size, which consumes considerable screen space and limits the number that can be displayed.

Advantages of symbol-labelled buttons include their continuous visibility and the small amount of space they use. Disadvantages include their location away from the main work area, their small size that slows down selection, and the necessity of learning and remembering what they are used for.

Figure 11.1. Examples of buttons.

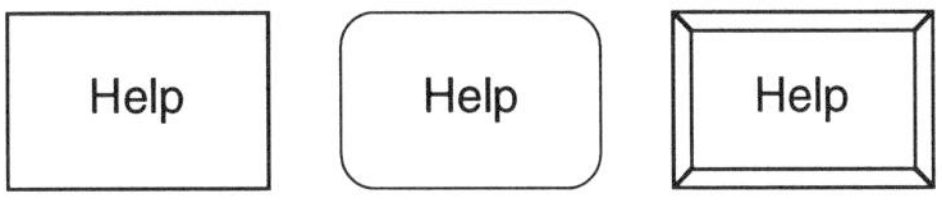

Proper Usage. Buttons are best for frequently used actions in a window. They can be used to cause actions to occur immediately, such as saving a document, quitting a system, or deleting text. They can be used to display a menu of options, such as colors or fonts. Buttons can also be used to display other secondary windows or dialog boxes.

BUTTON GUIDELINES

Structure

- Make the button a rectangular-shaped box with the caption inscribed inside. Design alternatives include:
  — a square-cornered rectangle.

  — a rounded-corner rectangle.

  — beveled edges.

  — drop shadows.

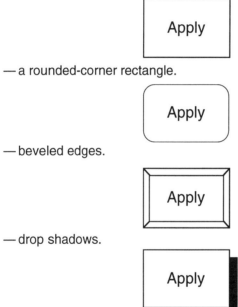

- Maintain consistency in style through an application.

The shape of a button can vary. Generally, rectangular-shaped buttons are preferred because they provide the best fit for horizontally arrayed textual captions. Square-cornered rectangles are found in OSF/Motif, and rounded-corner rectangles are found in OPEN LOOK, Presentation Manager, and suggested in IBM's SAA CUA. Drop Shadows will be found in OPEN LOOK and in NeXTStep. OSF/Motif uses beveled edges. The button style chosen is mostly a matter of preference. The button style chosen should be consistently maintained throughout an application, however.

Labels

General

- Use standard button labels when available.

Textual or Alphanumeric

- For application buttons, provide meaningful descriptions of the actions that will be performed.
- Use single-word labels whenever possible.
- Use mixed-case letters with the first letter of each label word capitalized.
- Display labels
  - In the regular system font.
  - In the same size font.
- Labels should not be numbered.
- When a button leads to display of:
  - A window, include an ellipsis (. . .) after the label.

Open . . .

  - A menu, include a right-pointed arrow (>>) after the label.

Colors > >

- Center the label within the button borders leaving at least two pixels between the text and the button border.
- Provide consistency in button labeling across all screens.

Symbol

- Use standard symbols whose meaning is widely known.
- Use pictures that clearly represent the object or action.

Textual button labels should be clearly spelled out, with meaningful descriptions of the actions they will cause to be performed. Choices should be composed of mixed-case single words. Multiple words are preferred, however, to single words lacking clarity in their intent. If multiple-word labels are used, capitalize the first letter of each word. When a button action leads to another window, include the ellipsis indicator; to a menu, include menu arrow indicators. Center each label within the button borders, leaving at least two pixels between the text and the border.

Symbol buttons should contain clear, readily learnable, easily memorized symbolic labels.

Common button functions should have standard names and uses. IBM's SAA CUA, for example, provides these standard names and definitions:

OK	— Any changed information in the window is accepted and the window is closed.
APPLY	— Any changed information in the window is accepted and again displayed in the window.
RESET	— Cancels any changed information that has not been submitted.
CANCEL	— Closes window without performing nonsubmitted changes.
HELP	— Displays, if available, contextual help for the item on which the cursor is positioned.
	— If no contextual help is available, help for the entire window is displayed.

Size

- Buttons must be wide enough to accommodate the longest label.
- Maintain consistency in button size whenever possible.

Buttons must be wide enough to accommodate the longest label. Leave at least two pixels between labels and button borders. Create equal-sized buttons on each window whenever possible, but never reduce the font size of some labels to create equal-sized buttons. In this case, buttons of different widths are preferable.

Number

- Keep number of buttons to six or fewer.

The maximum number of buttons on a window must reflect a balance between application effectiveness, real estate efficiency, and operational simplicity. No more than six buttons on a window seems to appropriately balance these issues.

Location

- Locate buttons in one of two ways:
  - Position buttons horizontally aligned in the lower part of the window.

— Position the buttons vertically stacked along the right side of the window.

- Place buttons in only one row or column.
- Maintain consistency in button location between windows.
- If there is a contingent relationship between a button and other controls, place the button adjacent to the related controls.
  — Exact positioning is dependent upon sequence of use, the preferred location being to the left or above the related controls.

The preferred button location is horizontally across the lower part of the window. This is consistent with one's top-to-bottom movement through the window. If the lower portion of the window is not available, locate the buttons vertically along the window's right side.

Position buttons in only one row or column and try consistently to locate buttons on all windows. If there is a contingent relationship between a button and other controls, place the button adjacent to the related controls. The preferred position is to the left or above the related controls.

Organization

- Order the buttons based on common and customary grouping schemes.
  — For buttons ordered left to right, place most frequent actions to the left.
  — For buttons ordered top to bottom, place most frequent actions at the top.
- Keep related buttons grouped together.
- Separate potentially destructive buttons from frequently chosen selections.
- Buttons found on more than one window should be consistently positioned.
- The orders should never change.

Buttons should be ordered logically, such as by frequency of use, sequence of use, or importance. For buttons arrayed left to right, start ordering from left to right. For buttons arrayed top to bottom, start ordering from top to bottom. Ordering, as recommended by IBM's SAA CUA, is:

Application specific pushbuttons:

OK
APPLY
RESET
CANCEL
HELP

Keep related buttons together and separate potentially destructive buttons from frequently chosen selections. The same buttons included on different windows should always be consistently positioned.

Layout

- Horizontally aligned buttons should be:
  — Centered at the bottom of the window.
  — Of the same height and width.
    — Exception: Buttons containing excessively long labels may be wider.

- Vertically stacked buttons should be:
  — Positioned beginning at the top right side of the window.
  — Of the same height and width.

- Provide equal and adequate spacing between adjacent buttons.
- Place related buttons in common, discernible groupings.
  — Use extra white space between button groups.

- Do not place a border around a grouping of buttons.
- Provide adequate spacing between buttons and the screen body controls.
- It is not necessary to align buttons with other screen body controls because they should form their own visual group.

To create visual appeal, do the following. Make horizontally arrayed buttons the same height and vertically arrayed buttons the same width. Also, provide equal and adequate spacing (two or more spaces) between adjacent buttons and create logical visual groups whenever possible. Finally, center horizontal buttons at the bottom of the screen and locate vertical buttons beginning at the right side of the window.

To avoid visual clutter, do not place a border around a grouping of buttons. To set off the buttons from the screen body, leave sufficient space between the buttons and the body controls. It is not necessary to align buttons with other screen body controls. Buttons will form their own visual group.

Dynamic and Unavailable Choices

- If the nature of the action represented by a button changes depending on circumstances, a button label can be modified to reflect that change.
- Unavailable choices should be dimmed or "grayed out."

Buttons should be dynamically changed to reflect the current conditions. If the nature of the action represented by a button changes depending on circumstances, a button label can be modified to reflect that change. For example, the label of the CANCEL button can be changed to CLOSE after an action that cannot be cancelled is carried out. Choices currently not available should be dimmed or "grayed out."

Keyboard Equivalents

- Each button should be assigned a keyboard equivalent mnemonic to facilitate keyboard selection.
- The mnemonic should be the first character of the button's label.
  — If duplication exists in first characters, for duplicate items, use another character in the label.
  — Preferably, choose the first succeeding consonant.
- Designate the mnemonic character by underlining it.

> **Apply**

- Maintain the same mnemonic on all identical buttons on other screens.

Enabling the user to select button actions through the typewriter keyboard provides flexibility and efficiency in the dialogue. To do this, provide single-character mnemonic codes which, when typed, will cause the action to be performed. The suggested method to indicate the accelerator is by underlining the proper character in the button label.

Scrolling

- If a window can be scrolled, do not scroll the buttons.

Never scroll buttons—they should be available at all times.

Button Activation

Pointing

- Highlight the button in some visually distinctive manner when the pointer is resting on it and the button is available for selection.

Activation

- Call attention to the button in another visually distinctive manner when it has been activated or pressed.
- If a button can be pressed continuously, permit the user to hold the mouse button down and repeat the action.

Default

- When a window with buttons is first displayed, provide a default action.
- Indicate the default action by displaying the button with a bold or double border.
- The default action should be a positive response such as "OK."
- If a destructive action is performed (such as "DELETE"), the default should be "CANCEL."
- If none of the buttons are destructive in nature, the default button should be the one most frequently selected.
- Locate the initial default button:
  — At the left side of horizontally aligned buttons.
  — At the top of vertically stacked buttons.

Pointing. Highlight the button in some visually distinctive manner when the pointer is resting on it and the button is available for selection. This will provide the user feedback that the selection process may be performed. Some systems, such as Sun's OPEN LOOK, display a brighter button.

Activation. Highlight the button in another visually distinctive manner when it has been activated or pressed to indicate that the action is successful. OPEN LOOK subdues or grays the button. OSF/Motif has raised beveled buttons that appear to sink into the screen when selected. Another alternative is to move the button slightly as if it had been depressed. If a button can be pressed continuously, permit the mouse button to be held down and the action repeated.

Default. When a window with buttons is first displayed, provide a default action and identify the button through a bolder border. For example, DECwindows uses a double border to indicate the default button; IBM's SAA CUA recommends using a bold border. The default action should be a positive response such as "OK." If the default is a destructive action (such as "DELETE"), the default should be "CANCEL," requiring the user to change the selection in order to perform the destructive action.

If none of the buttons are destructive in nature, the default button should be the one most frequently selected. Locate the initial default button at the left side of horizontally aligned buttons and at the top of vertically stacked buttons.

ENTRY FIELDS

General

Description

- A control consisting of a rectangular box into which users type information and, almost always, a caption describing the kind of information to be keyed.
- Two types exist:
  — Single line.
  — Multiple line.
- When first displayed, the field may be blank or contain an initial value.

Purpose

- To permit typing of information into a screen.

Advantages/Disadvantages

- + Very flexible.
- + Familiar.
- + Consumes little screen space.

- − Requires use of typewriter keyboard.
- − Requires user to remember what must be keyed.

Proper Usage

- Most useful for data that is:
  — Unlimited in scope.
  — Difficult to categorize.
  — Of a variety of different lengths.
- When using a selection list is not possible.

Single Line

Description

- A two-part control consisting of a caption and a one-line entry field for typing.

Purpose

- To make alphanumeric entries when the information can be contained on one line of the screen.

Typical Uses

- Typing the name of a file to save.
- Typing the path of a file to copy.
- Typing variable data on a form.
- Typing a command.

Multiple Line

Description

- A two-part control consisting of a caption and a multi-line rectangular box for typing.

Purpose

- To type, edit, and read passages of text.

Typical Uses

- Creating or reading an electronic mail message.
- Displaying and editing text files.

An entry field is a control consisting of a rectangular box into which information is typed and, almost always, a caption describing the kind of information to be keyed. Entry fields are familiar, flexible, and consume little screen space. They do require a typewriter keyboard, which to some is an advantage and to others a disadvantage. One disadvantage to all is that what is keyed into an entry field must be remembered.

Two types of entry fields exist: single line and multiple line. They are most useful for data that is difficult to categorize or unlimited in scope, or when use of a selection field is not possible. An entry field's display and organizational principles are similar to those for text-based screens.

ENTRY FIELD GUIDELINES

Captions

Structure and Size

- Provide a descriptive field caption to identify the kind of information to be typed into the field.
- Use a mixed-case font.
- Display in normal intensity or in a color of moderate brightness.

Formatting

- Single fields:
  - Position the field caption to the left of the entry field.
    - Place a colon (:) immediately following the caption.
    - Separate the colon from the entry field by one space.

    Organization: ☐

  - Alternatively, the caption may be placed above the entry field.
    - Place a colon (:) immediately following the caption.
    - Locate above the upper-left corner of the entry field, flush with the left edge.

    Organization:
    ☐

- Multiple occurrence fields:
  - For data entry fields:
    - Locate the caption left-justified one line above the column of entry fields.

    Office:
    ☐

  - For display or inquiry fields:
    - If the data field is fixed-length, or the displayed data is about the same length, center the caption above the displayed data.

    Date:

    01/26/89
    07/21/90
    11/18/91

    - If the data displayed is alphanumeric and quite variable in length, left-justify the caption above the displayed data.

    City:

    Alice Springs
    Darwin
    Traralgon
    Wagga Wagga
    Whyalla

— If the data field is numeric and variable in length, right-justify the caption above the displayed data.

Balance:

1.26
53.98
45,345.00
2,509.04

Structure and size.   Screen captions must be understandable to the screen user. Fully spell out all captions in a language meaningful to the user. In general, abbreviations and contractions should not be used. To achieve the alignment recommendations (to be discussed shortly), however, an occasional abbreviation or contraction may be necessary. If so, choose those that are common in the everyday language of the application or those that are meaningful or easily learned. Use mixed-case text in the caption, capitalizing only the first letter of each word (except for articles, conjunctions, and prepositions—a, the, and, for, etc.). Acronyms, abbreviations, or proper nouns that are normally capitalized, however, may be capitalized. If the caption is of a sentence-style nature, sentence-style capitalization should be followed. In this case, capitalize only the first letter of the first word of the caption.

In relation to the entry field, the caption should be of normal intensity or consist of a moderately bright color. Visual emphasis should be given to the entry field.

Formatting.   For single fields, it is recommended that the caption should precede the entry field. Place a colon (:) directly following the caption to visually separate the caption from the data.

For multiple-occurrence fields, the captions should be positioned above the columnized entry fields. The exact location of the caption will depend on the kind of screen and the kind of data displayed. For data entry screens, the caption should be left-justified above the columnized entry fields. This will signal the starting point of the entry field and assure the caption is positioned directly above the keyed data.

For display or inquiry screens where information already exists in the entry field, positioning of the caption depends on the kind of information displayed within the field. The goal is to center the caption over the data. If the field is fixed-length, or the information to be displayed within it usually fills, or almost fills, the field, center the caption above the data. If the information is alphanumeric and can be quite variable in length, left-justify the caption. This will keep the caption directly above the data when it appears in the field. Similarly, for numeric fields, right-justify the caption to keep it above the data that will be right-justified when it appears.

Entry Fields

Structure

- Identify entry fields by underscores or underlining

  Account: _____

  or a rectangular box.

  Account: [_____]

- Break up long fields through incorporation of slashes (/), dashes (–), spaces, or other common delimiters.

  Date: __/__/__
  Telephone Number: (___) ___ ____

  Date: [___/___/___]
  Telephone Number: [(   )   –   ]

Size

- Entry fields for fixed-length data must be large enough to contain the entire entry.
- Entry fields for variable-length data must be large enough to contain the majority of the entries.
  - Where entries may be larger than the entry field, scrolling must be provided to permit keying into, or viewing, the entire field.
  - Employ word wrapping for continuous text in multiple-line entry fields.

Highlighting

- Call attention to the entry fields through a highlighting technique.
  - If the entry field is indicated by an underscore or underline, display the data in a higher intensity or brighter color than the caption.
    - If color is used, choose one that contrasts well with the screen background.
  - If the entry field is indicated through a box, choose a box color that both complements the screen background and provides good contrast with the color chosen for the entry field data.

Structure.   Entry fields should attract attention, not detract from the entry legibility, provide some indication of the kind of desired response, and indicate the appropriate number of characters required for the entry. Savage et al. (1982) found that a broken underscore is a good technique for entry fields. Graphic terminals also permit the use of rectangular boxes. Both resemble the coding areas most frequently found on paper forms. To make the entry fields more readable, it is desirable to break them up into logical pieces. Slashes, dashes, and spaces should be inserted into the entry fields as illustrated above.

Size.   Entry fields for fixed-length data must be long enough to contain the entry. Variable-length entry fields should be large enough to contain the majority of the entries. The size of variable-length entry fields will be dependent on field alignment, space utilization, and aesthetics. If an entry field is not large enough to key, or view, the entire entry, it must be scrollable. Scrolling, however, should be avoided whenever possible.

Highlighting.   Entry fields and data (as opposed to captions) are the most important part of a screen. Call attention to them through highlighting techniques. If an underline or underscore is the field delimiter, display them in high intensity with monochrome screens. With color screens, use the brightest colors. As will be described in Chapter 13, the brightest colors are white and yellow. If a box is the delimiter, choose a background color that complements the screen body background and provides good contrast with the color chosen for the entry field data. Again, see Chapter 13 for more detail.

Entry Field Alignment

- Vertically left-align entry fields into columns.

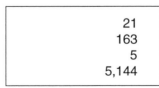

- If the entry field is numeric and is being used for display or inquiry purposes, right-align the field by its decimal point (or implied decimal point).

```
                        21
                       163
                         5
                     5,144
```

Fields should always be columnized. Left-align all entry fields. If a field is numeric and is used for inquiry or display purposes, right-align on the decimal point or implied decimal point. This will make the entry process more efficient by reducing eye movements and permitting reading of more than one piece of data at a time with one eye fixation. When reading screen data, this also makes it easier and faster to find and compare the data of interest. When space permits the creation of two or more columns on a screen, the entry process should flow in a columnar orientation, from top to bottom, then left to right. Top-to-bottom visual scanning is always more efficient than left-to-right scanning.

Caption Justification

1. First Approach:
- Left-align captions.
- Leave one space between the longest caption and the entry field column.

```
Name:          [                                    ]
Organization:x [                                    ]
Location:      [                    ]
Building:      [        ]
```

2. Second Approach:
- Right-align captions.
- Leave one space between each caption and entry field.

```
        Name:x [                                    ]
Organization: [                                    ]
    Location: [                    ]
    Building: [        ]
```

Field justification can be accomplished in either of two ways. Approach 1 results in both captions and entry fields being left-aligned into columns. Approach 2 right-aligns the captions up against the left-justified column of entry fields. Each approach has advantages and disadvantages, as previously discussed in Chapter 6. Whichever approach is chosen should be consistently followed in a family of screens.

Horizontal Spacing

- Provide horizontal separation of columns of data by:
  — Leaving a minimum of five spaces between the longest entry field in one column and the leftmost caption in an adjacent column.

Make:	xxxxx Warranty:
Model:	Period:
Year:	Labor:
Color:	Parts:

  — Separating adjacent columns with a vertical solid line.

Make:	Warranty:
Model:	Period:
Year:	Labor:
Color:	Parts:

Columns of data on a screen must be separated to maintain their own visual identity. This is done by separating adjacent columns by at least five spaces. To reinforce the vertical nature of entry and visual scanning, solid lines can also be drawn between adjacent columns. With lines, spacing between columns need not be as great.

Vertical Spacing

- Leave at least one space line between columnized "groups" of related information.

Driver Name:
License Number:
Restrictions:
Expires:

Make:
Model:
Year:
Color:

- For long columns of related elements, leave a space line after every fifth row. (If space permits, leave a space line after every third row.) Never exceed seven rows without a space line.

Policy Number:

Account Number:

Effective Date:

Expiration Date:

Policy Status:

Policy Form:

Property:

Liability:

Deductible:

Endorsement:

Status:

Occasional space lines on screens will improve the screen's readability and reduce the screen's density.

Dependent Fields

- Position a conditional field or fields to the right of the field to which it relates, or below the field to which it relates.
- Either:
  — Do not display these conditional fields until the selection to which it relates is chosen.
  — Display these conditional fields but in a subdued or grayed manner. When it is relevant, return it to a normal intensity.
- Inscribe a filled-in arrow between the selected choice and its dependent fields to relate them visually to each other.
  — Leave two spaces between the choice description and the arrow for horizontally arrayed dependent fields.
  — Leave two spaces between the arrow and the caption of the dependent field.

Number of Children: [ ] ▶ Names: [   ]

Number of Children: [ ]
        ▶ Names: [   ]

In some circumstances, a field may be conditionally active. Only when a particular response is made is this additional information needed. For example, a question such as "Do you have any children?" might necessitate knowing their names. If this question is answered affirmatively, a field requesting their names can be displayed at that point on the screen. A "No" response will cause the cursor to move to the next field, and the children names field will not appear.

Locate dependent or conditional fields to the right of or below the field or choice that necessitates it. The displayed arrow serves to tie the dependent field to the triggering field. The field may either be shown in a grayed or subdued manner, or not displayed at all until it is needed.

Displaying an area as grayed or subdued allows the user to be aware of its existence but reduces the visual competition between it and other needed information on the screen. Not displaying dependent fields until they are triggered reduces screen clutter. Hiding their existence, however, does not give the screen user a full picture of all the possible needed data and the relationships that may exist. By hiding them, then, there may be a slight learning price to pay, depending upon the complexity of the needed data.

SELECTION FIELDS

A selection field is a field that displays on the screen all the possible alternatives, conditions, or choices that may exist for a data element or action. From those displayed, the relevant choice, or choices, are selected. Several styles exist.

Radio Buttons

Description

- A two-part control consisting of the following:
  — Small circles, diamonds, or rectangles.
  — Choice text.
- When a choice is selected:
  — The option is highlighted.
  — Any existing choice is automatically un-highlighted and de-selected.

Purpose

- To set one of a small set of mutually exclusive options.

Advantages/Disadvantages

+ Easy to access choices.
+ Easy to compare choices.

– Consume screen space.
– Limited number of choices.

Proper Usage

- For setting attributes, properties, or values.
- For mutually exclusive choices (i.e., only one can be selected).
- Where adequate screen space is available.
- Most useful for data and choices that are:
  — Discrete.
  — Small and fixed in number.
  — Not easily remembered.
  — In need of a textual description to describe meaningfully.
  — Most easily understood when the alternatives may be seen together and compared to one another.
  — Infrequently selected.
  — Never changed in content.
- Do not use:
  — For commands.
  — Singly to indicate the presence or absence of a state.

Description. Controls of this type take several different physical forms. They are most often called radio buttons because of their resemblance to similar controls on radios. Microsoft Windows, however, refers to them as option buttons. One common display method consists of a circle associated with each choice description. When an alternative is selected, the center of the circle is partially filled in to provide a visual indication that it is the active choice. Macintosh, OS/2 Presentation Manager, Microsoft Windows, DECwindows, and IBM's SAA CUA follow this approach. Other styles of radio buttons may also be seen. NeXTStep uses small circular buttons that look recessed when not selected and are raised when selected. OSF/Motif uses small diamond-shaped buttons that look raised when not selected and depressed when selected. These various radio button styles are illustrated in Figure 11.2.

A different method for presenting exclusive choices is the butted box or button where the alternatives are inscribed in adjoining rectangles horizontally arrayed, and the selected alternative is highlighted in some way. Xerox's Star, OPEN LOOK (which calls them "two state exclusive settings"), and Silicon Graphics's SGI use this approach. Butted boxes or buttons are illustrated in Figure 11.3.

Deciding on which style to use seems to be more a matter of preference than performance. No published comparison studies are available for guidance.

Purpose. Radio buttons are used to designate one of a small set of mutually exclusive options.

Advantages/Disadvantages. With radio buttons, all alternatives are always visible. Therefore, it is easy to access and compare choices. They do, however,

Figure 11.2.   Representative radio button styles.

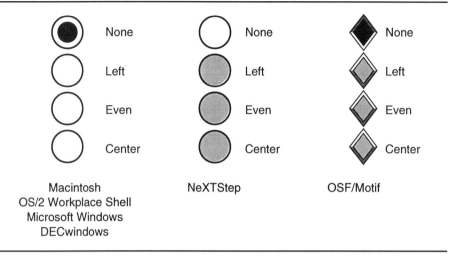

Figure 11.3   Examples of butted box or buttons.

None	Left	Even	Center

consume a certain amount of screen real estate, limiting the number of alternatives that can be displayed.

Proper Usage. Radio buttons are useful for setting attributes, properties, or values where adequate screen space is available. The alternatives should be discrete, small in number, and in need of a textual description to identify meaningfully. Radio buttons are helpful in situations where the alternatives cannot always be easily remembered or, if displaying the alternatives together, aid understanding and selection of the proper choice. The alternatives presented should be those that do not require frequent selection and change by the user. The choices displayed should be stable, never changing in content.

Do not use radio buttons for implementing commands. Do not use one radio button by itself to indicate the presence or absence of a state. A check box is recommended for this purpose.

RADIO BUTTON GUIDELINES

Selection Descriptions

- Provide meaningful, fully spelled-out choice descriptions.
- Display using mixed-case letters.
- Locate descriptions associated with a radio button, or similar small button-

type indicator, to the right of the button. Separation by one space is usually sufficient.

- Locate descriptions for rectangular-shaped boxes within the box.

Choice descriptions must be clear, meaningful, fully spelled out, and displayed in a mixed-case text. For multiword descriptions, capitalize the first letter of each significant word. Small button-type indicators should be located to the left of the choice description; rectangular-shaped boxes will find the description within the box. Small buttons associated with text are advantageous when the choice description must be lengthy. Descriptions in boxes impose restrictions on the number of words that can be inscribed within them.

Size

- Show a minimum of two choices, a maximum of seven or eight.

Selection fields of this style should not present more than eight choices. Displaying more than eight is usually not efficient, being wasteful of screen space. If the number of field choices exceeds this maximum, consider using a list box or a drop-down list box.

Structure

- A columnar orientation is the preferred manner.
  - If radio buttons are used, left-align the buttons and choice descriptions.

        ○ None
        ○ Left
        ○ Even
        ○ Center

  - If rectangular boxes are used:
    - Create boxes of equal height.
    - Position the boxes adjacent to, or butted up against, one another.

None
Left
Even
Center

- If vertical space on the screen is limited, orient the choices horizontally.
  - If small buttons are used, provide adequate separation between choices

so that the buttons are associated with the proper description. A distance equal to three spaces is usually sufficient.

    ◯ NonexxxO Left   ◯ Even   ◯ Center

— If rectangular boxes are used:
  — Create boxes of equal width.
  — Position the boxes adjacent to, or butted up against, one another.

None	Left	Even	Center

The preferred orientation of selection fields is columnar. This aids visual scanning and choice comparison. Fields with small button indicators usually fit best in this manner because choice descriptions are not restricted in size. Rectangular boxes should be of equal height and/or width and be butted up against one another. This will distinguish them from nonexclusive choice fields that will be separated from one another.

Organization

- Arrange selections in expected orders or follow other patterns such as frequency of occurrence, sequence of use, or importance.
  - For selections arrayed top to bottom, begin ordering at the top.
  - For selections arrayed left to right, begin ordering at the left.
- If, under certain conditions, a choice is not available, display it subdued or less brightly than the available choices.

Selection choices should be organized logically. If the alternatives have an expected order, follow it. Other ordering schemes such as frequency of use, sequence of use, or importance may also be considered. Always begin ordering at the top or left. If, under certain conditions, a choice is not available, display the nonselectable choice subdued or less brightly than the available choices.

Captions

- Provide a caption for each selection field.
  - In screens containing only one selection field, the screen title may serve as the caption.
- Display the caption fully spelled out using mixed-case letters. A slightly larger type size may also be used.

Columnar Orientation

- Position the field caption left-justified above the selection descriptions.

— If small buttons are used to designate the choices, separate the caption from the choice descriptions by a space line.

Justification: Justification:

○ None | None |
○ Left | Left |
○ Even | Even |
○ Center | Center |

- Alternatively, the caption may be located to the left of the topmost choice description.

Justification: ○ None   Justification: | None |
                   ○ Left | Left |
                   ○ Even | Even |
                   ○ Center | Center |

Horizontal Orientation

- The preferred location of the field caption is to the left of the selection descriptions.

Justification: ○ None   ○ Left   ○ Even   ○ Center

| Justification: | None | Left | Even | Center |

- Alternatively, the caption may be located above the topmost choice description.
  — If small buttons are used to designate the choices, separate the caption from the choice descriptions by a space line.

Justification:

○ None   ○ Left   ○ Even   ○ Center

Justification:

| None | Left | Even | Center |

- Be consistent in caption style and orientation within an application.

Figure 11.4. Ways to, and not to, present radio buttons.

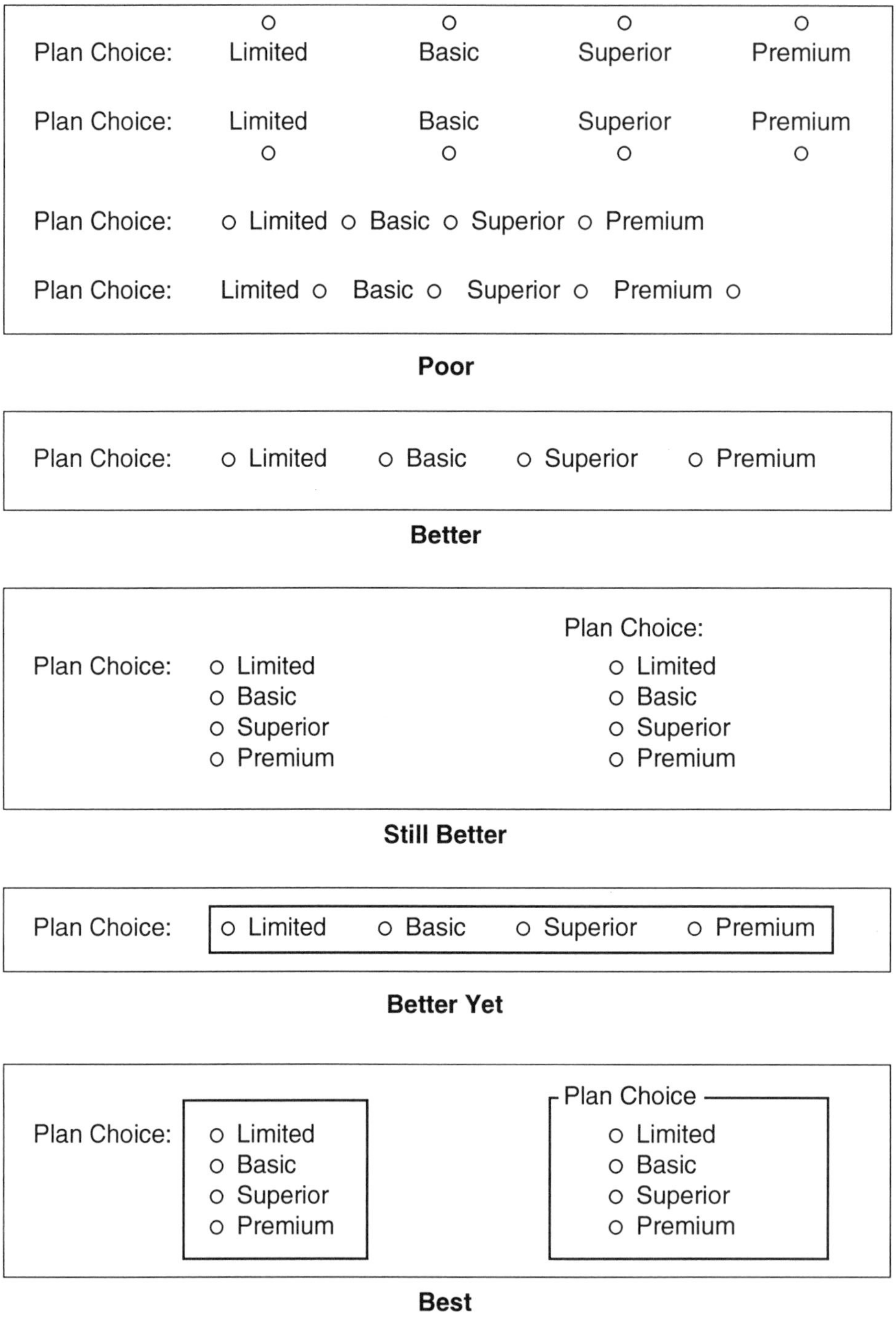

Plan Choice: ○ Limited   ○ Basic   ○ Superior   ○ Premium

Plan Choice: Limited   Basic   Superior   Premium   ○   ○   ○   ○

Plan Choice: ○ Limited ○ Basic ○ Superior ○ Premium

Plan Choice: Limited ○   Basic ○   Superior ○   Premium ○

Poor

Plan Choice: ○ Limited   ○ Basic   ○ Superior   ○ Premium

Better

                              Plan Choice:

Plan Choice: ○ Limited   ○ Limited
                   ○ Basic   ○ Basic
                   ○ Superior   ○ Superior
                   ○ Premium   ○ Premium

Still Better

Plan Choice: | ○ Limited   ○ Basic   ○ Superior   ○ Premium |

Better Yet

                             ⌐ Plan Choice ⎯⎯⎯⎯⎯

Plan Choice: | ○ Limited | | ○ Limited
            | ○ Basic | | ○ Basic
            | ○ Superior | | ○ Superior
            | ○ Premium | | ○ Premium

Best

Display the caption fully spelled out using mixed-case letters. Some occasional common abbreviations may be used, however, to achieve the alignment goals to be specified. A slightly larger type size may also be used for captions, if available. The preferred location of a field caption is above columns and to the left of horizontal selection descriptions. This will help achieve screen efficiency, minimize viewer eye movements, and provide caption and choice distinctiveness. If the screen contains only one field, the screen title may serve as the field caption. Be consistent in caption style and orientation within an application.

Keyboard Equivalents

- Assign a keyboard mnemonic to each choice.
  - Designate the mnemonic by underlining the letter.

  Justification: ○ <u>N</u>one
                   ○ <u>L</u>eft
                   ○ <u>E</u>ven
                   ○ <u>C</u>enter

Assign unique keyboard mnemonics for each alternative in the standard way, choosing the first letter (or another) and designating it by character underlining.

Selection Method and Indication

Pointing

- The selection target area should be as large as possible.
  - If a small button is the selection indication method used, the target area should include the button and the choice description text.
- Highlight the selection choice in some visually distinctive way when the pointer is resting on it and the choice is available for selection.
  - If a small button is the selection indication method used, a reverse video, reverse color, or dotted or dashed box selection cursor or bar may be used to surround the selected choice description.
  - This cursor should be as long as the longest description plus one space at each end. Do not place the cursor over the small button.

  ○ Left

  ⊙ | Even |

  ○ Center

- Alternatively, change the shape of the pointer to signal that a selection can be performed.

Activation

- When a choice is selected, distinguish it visually from the nonselected choices.
  — A radio button should be filled in with a solid dark dot.
  — A small button should be made to look depressed, or higher, through use of drop shadows.
  — A rectangular box can be highlighted in a manner different from when it is pointed at, or a bolder border can be drawn around it.
- When a choice is selected, any other selected choice must be deselected.

Defaults

- If a selection field is displayed with a choice previously selected or a default choice, display the currently active choice in the manner used when it is selected.

Pointing. The selection target area should be as large as possible in order to make it easy to move to. If a small button is the selection indication method used, the target area should include the button and the choice description text. If the rectangular box selection method is used, the entire box should be the target.

Highlight the selection choice in some visually distinctive way when the pointer is resting on it and the choice is available for selection. If a small button is the selection indication method used, a distinctive reverse video, reverse color, or dotted or dashed box selection cursor or bar may be used to surround the selected choice description. This cursor should be as long as the longest description plus one space at each end. The cursor should not cover the small button. An alternative method to indicate that the selection can be performed is to change the shape of the pointer when it is positioned correctly over a selection.

Activation. When a choice is selected, distinguish it visually from the non-selected choices. A radio button should be filled in with a solid dark dot. Other methods include making the button look depressed or higher than the others through the use of drop shadows. A rectangular box can be highlighted in a manner different from when it is pointed at, or a bolder border can be drawn around it. When a choice is selected, any other selected choice must be deselected or made inactive.

Defaults. If a selection field is displayed with a choice previously selected or a default choice, display the currently active choice in the same manner shown when it is selected.

Check Boxes

Description

- A two-part control consisting of:
  - — A square box.
  - — Choice text.
- Each option acts as a switch and can be either "on" or "off."
  - — When an option is selected (on), an "X" appears within the square box or it is highlighted in some other manner.
  - — Otherwise the square box is unselected or empty (off).
- Each box can be:
  - — Switched on or off independently.
  - — Used alone or grouped in sets.

Purpose

- To set one or more options as either on or off.

Advantages/Disadvantages

+ Easy to access choices.
+ Easy to compare choices.

- Consume screen space.
- Limited number of choices.

Proper Usage

- For setting attributes, properties, or values.
- For nonexclusive choices (i.e., more than one can be selected).
- Where adequate screen space is available.
- Most useful for data and choices that are:
  - — Discrete.
  - — Small and fixed in number.
  - — Not easily remembered.
  - — In need of a textual description to describe meaningfully.
  - — Most easily understood when the alternatives may be seen together and compared to one another.
  - — Infrequently selected.
  - — Never changed in content.

Description. Controls of this type differ from radio buttons in that they permit selection of more than one alternative. Each option acts as a switch and can be either "on" or "off." When an option is selected (on), an "X" or "check" appears within the square box or it is highlighted in some other manner. When not selected, the square box is unselected or empty (off). Each box can be switched on or off independently. Check boxes may be used alone or grouped in sets.

Check boxes, too, may take different physical forms and be called by different names. The most common name is "check boxes," used, for example, by Macintosh, OS/2 Presentation Manager, Microsoft Windows, and IBM's SAA CUA. Others include "toggle buttons" (OSF/Motif and DECwindows), "switches" (NeXTStep), and "two state nonexclusive settings" (OPEN LOOK). As their names differ, differences also exist in the way these fields are presented on screens. One very common display method is the check box, which, resembling its namesake, consists of a square placed adjacent to each alternative. When the choice is selected, some systems place an "X" in the square to provide a visual indication that it is active. Macintosh, OS/2 Presentation Manager, and Microsoft Windows follow this approach. Others place a check mark (✓) in the square (IBM SAA CUA, NeXTStep), fill in the selected square (DECwindows), or make it look depressed when selected (OSF/Motif). Examples of these styles are illustrated in Figure 11.5.

Another style for this type of field is a button or box with the choice description inscribed inside. When selected, the alternative is highlighted in some way.

Figure 11.5.   Representative check box style nonexclusive choice fields.

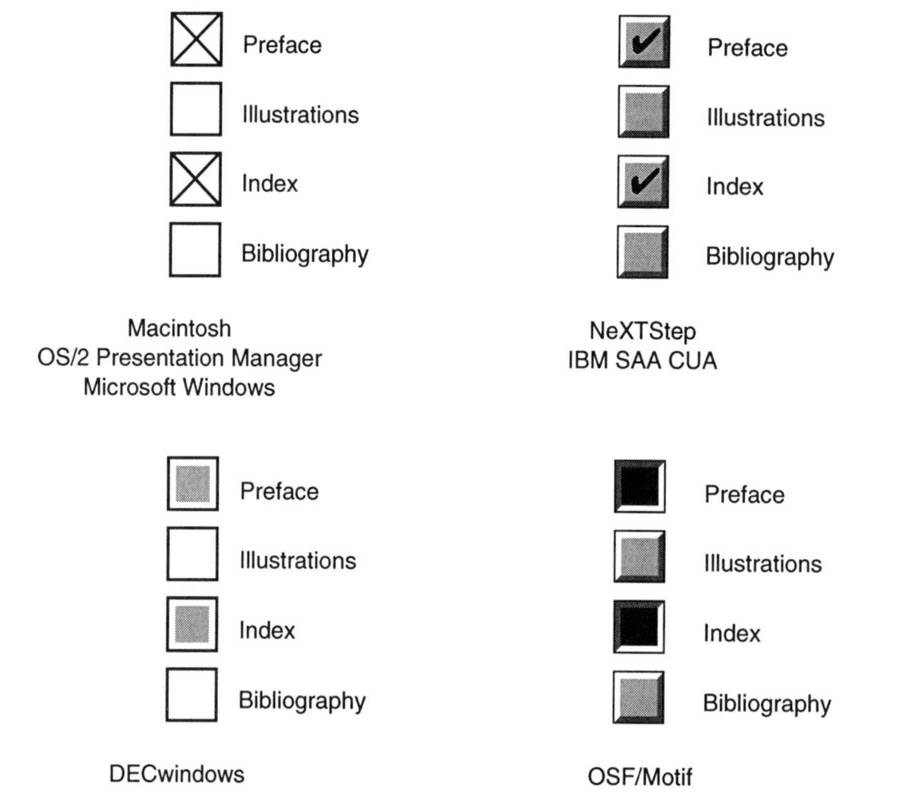

Figure 11.6. Examples of box or button nonexclusive selection fields.

| Preface | Illustrations | Index | Bibliography |

To distinguish these fields visually from similarly constructed fields presenting mutually exclusive choices, the buttons are not adjacent to, or butted up against, one another. OPEN LOOK also uses this approach. Examples of rectangular boxes or buttons are illustrated in Figure 11.6.

Again, deciding on which style to use seems to be more a matter of preference than performance. No published comparison studies are available for guidance.

Purpose. Check boxes are used to designate one or more of a small set of options as either "on" or "off."

Advantages/Disadvantages. With check boxes, all alternatives are always visible. Therefore, it is easy to access and compare choices. They do, however, consume a certain amount of screen real estate, limiting the number of alternatives that can be displayed.

Proper Usage. Check boxes are useful for setting attributes, properties, or values where adequate screen space is available. The alternatives should be discrete, small in number, and in need of a textual description to identify meaningfully. Check boxes are helpful in situations where the alternatives cannot always be easily remembered, if displaying the alternatives together aids understanding and selection of the proper choice. The alternatives presented should be those that do not require frequent selection and change by the user. The choices displayed should be stable, never changing in content.

A check box may be used by itself to indicate the presence or absence of a state.

CHECK BOX GUIDELINES

Selection Descriptions

- Provide meaningful, fully spelled-out choice descriptions.
- Display using mixed-case letters.
- Locate descriptions associated with a check box, or similar small box-type indicator, to the right of the box. Separation by one space is usually sufficient.
- Locate descriptions for rectangular-shaped boxes within the box.

Choice descriptions must be clear, meaningful, fully spelled out, and displayed in a mixed-case text. For multiword descriptions, capitalize the first letter of each significant word. Small box-type indicators should be located to the left of the choice description, rectangular-shaped boxes will find the description within the box. Small boxes associated with text are advantageous when the choice description must be lengthy. Descriptions in boxes impose restrictions on the number of words that can be inscribed within them.

Size

- Show a minimum of one choice, a maximum of seven or eight.

Selection fields of this style should not offer more than eight choices. Displaying more than eight is usually not efficient as it wastes screen space.

Structure

- A columnar orientation is the preferred style.
  - If check boxes are used, left-align the check boxes and choice descriptions.

<pre>
                    ☐ Preface
                    ☐ Illustrations
                    ☐ Index
                    ☐ Bibliography
</pre>

  - If rectangular boxes are used:
    - Create boxes of equal width.
    - Separate the boxes from one another by small equidistant spaces.

<pre>
        ┌─────────────────┐
        │ Preface   │
        └─────────────────┘

        ┌─────────────────┐
        │ Illustrations   │
        └─────────────────┘

        ┌─────────────────┐
        │ Index   │
        └─────────────────┘

        ┌─────────────────┐
        │ Bibliography   │
        └─────────────────┘
</pre>

- If vertical space on the screen is limited, orient the choices horizontally.
  - If check boxes are used, provide adequate separation between choices so that the boxes are associated with the proper description. A distance equal to three spaces is usually sufficient.

☐ Prefacexxx☐ Illustrations ☐ Index ☐ Bibliography

— If rectangular boxes are used:
  — Create boxes of equal height.
  — Separate the boxes from one another by small equidistant spaces.

Preface	Illustrations	Index	Bibliography

The preferred orientation of selection fields is columnar. This aids scanning and choice comparison. Fields with check box indicators usually fit best in this manner because choice descriptions are not restricted in size. Rectangular boxes should be of equal width and separated from one another by small and equidistant spaces. This will distinguish them from mutually exclusive choices that will be butted up against one another.

Organization

- Arrange selections in logical order or follow other patterns such as frequency of occurrence, sequence of use, or importance.
  - For selections arrayed top to bottom, begin ordering at the top.
  - For selections arrayed left to right, begin ordering at the left.
- If, under certain conditions, a choice is not available, display it subdued or less brightly than the available choices.

Selection choices should be organized logically. If the alternatives have an expected order, follow it. Other ordering schemes such as frequency of use, sequence of use, or importance may also be considered. Always begin ordering at the top or left. If, under certain conditions, a choice is not available, display the unavailable choice subdued or less brightly than the available choices.

Captions

- Provide a caption for each selection field.
  - In screens containing only one selection field, the screen title may serve as the caption.
- Display the caption fully spelled out using mixed-case letters. A slightly larger type size may also be used.

Columnar Orientation

- Position the field caption left-justified above the selection descriptions.
  - If check boxes are used to designate the choices, separate the caption from the choice descriptions by a space line.

Contents: Contents:

☐ Preface   ┌─────────────────┐
☐ Illustrations   │ Preface   │
☐ Index   └─────────────────┘
☐ Bibliography
                        ┌─────────────────┐
                        │ Illustrations │
                        └─────────────────┘

                        ┌─────────────────┐
                        │ Index   │
                        └─────────────────┘

                        ┌─────────────────┐
                        │ Bibliography   │
                        └─────────────────┘

- Alternatively, the caption may be located to the left of the topmost choice description.

Contents: ☐ Preface
            ☐ Illustrations
            ☐ Index
            ☐ Bibliography

Contents: ┌─────────────────────┐
            │ Preface   │
            └─────────────────────┘

            ┌─────────────────────┐
            │ Illustrations   │
            └─────────────────────┘

            ┌─────────────────────┐
            │ Index   │
            └─────────────────────┘

            ┌─────────────────────┐
            │ Bibliography   │
            └─────────────────────┘

Horizontal Orientation

- The preferred location of the field caption is to the left of the selection descriptions.

Contents: ☐ Preface   ☐ Illustrations   ☐ Index   ☐ Bibliography

Contents: ┌──────────┐ ┌──────────────┐ ┌────────┐ ┌──────────────┐
           │ Preface │ │ Illustrations│ │ Index │ │ Bibliography │
           └──────────┘ └──────────────┘ └────────┘ └──────────────┘

- Alternatively, the caption may be located above the topmost choice description.
  - If small buttons are used to designate the choices, separate the caption from the choice descriptions by a space line.

Contents:

☐ Preface   ☐ Illustrations   ☐ Index   ☐ Bibliography

Contents:

| Preface | Illustrations | Index | Bibliography |

- Be consistent in caption style and orientation within an application.

Display the caption fully spelled out using mixed-case letters. Some common abbreviations may be used, however, to achieve the alignment goals to be specified. A slightly larger type size may also be used for captions, if available. The preferred location of a field caption is above columns and to the left of horizontal selection descriptions. This will help achieve screen efficiency, minimize viewer eye movements, and provide caption and choice distinctiveness. If the screen contains only one field, the screen title may serve as the field caption. Be consistent in caption style and orientation within an application.

Keyboard Equivalents

- Assign a keyboard mnemonic to each choice.
  — Designate the mnemonic by underlining the letter.

  Contents: ☐ Preface
  ☐ Illustrations
  ☐ Index
  ☐ Bibliography

Assign unique keyboard mnemonics for each alternative in the standard way, choosing the first letter (or another) and designating it by character underlining.

Selection Method and Indication

Pointing

- The selection target area should be as large as possible.
  — If a check box is the selection indication method used, the target area should include the button and the choice description text.
- Highlight the selection choice in some visually distinctive way when the pointer is resting on it and the choice is available for selection.
  — If a check box is the selection indication method used, a reverse video, reverse color, or dotted or dashed box selection cursor or bar may be used to surround the selected choice description.
  — This cursor should be as long as the longest description plus one space at each end. Do not place the cursor over the check box.

☐   Preface

☐ | Illustrations |

☐   Index

- Alternatively, change the shape of the pointer to signal that a selection can be performed.

Activation

- When a choice is selected, distinguish it visually from the nonselected choices.
  — A check box should be marked with an "X", or check mark (✓), or filled in.
  — A small button should be made to look depressed, or higher, through use of drop shadows.
  — A rectangular box can be highlighted in a manner different from when it is pointed at, or a bolder border can be drawn around it.
  — The style chosen should be consistently applied throughout an application or system.

Defaults

- If a selection field is displayed with a choice previously selected or a default choice, display the currently active choice in the manner used when it is selected.

Pointing. The selection target area should be as large as possible in order to make it easy to move to. If a check box is the selection indication method used, the target area should include the box and the choice description text. If the rectangular box selection method is used, the entire box should be the target. Highlight the selection choice in some visually distinctive way when the pointer is resting on it and the choice is available for selection. If a check box is the selection indication method used, a distinctive reverse video, reverse color, or dotted or dashed box selection cursor or bar may be used to surround the selected choice description. This cursor should be as long as the longest description plus one space at each end. The cursor should not cover the check box. An alternative method to indicate that the selection can be performed is to change the shape of the pointer when it is positioned correctly over a selection.

Activation. When a choice is selected, distinguish it visually from the nonselected choices. A check box may be marked with an "X" or check or filled in. Other methods include making the button look depressed or raised through appropriate use of drop shadows. A rectangular box can be highlighted in a manner different from when it is pointed at, or a bolder border can be drawn around it. The style chosen must be consistently applied throughout an application or system.

Figure 11.7.   Ways to, and not to, present check boxes.

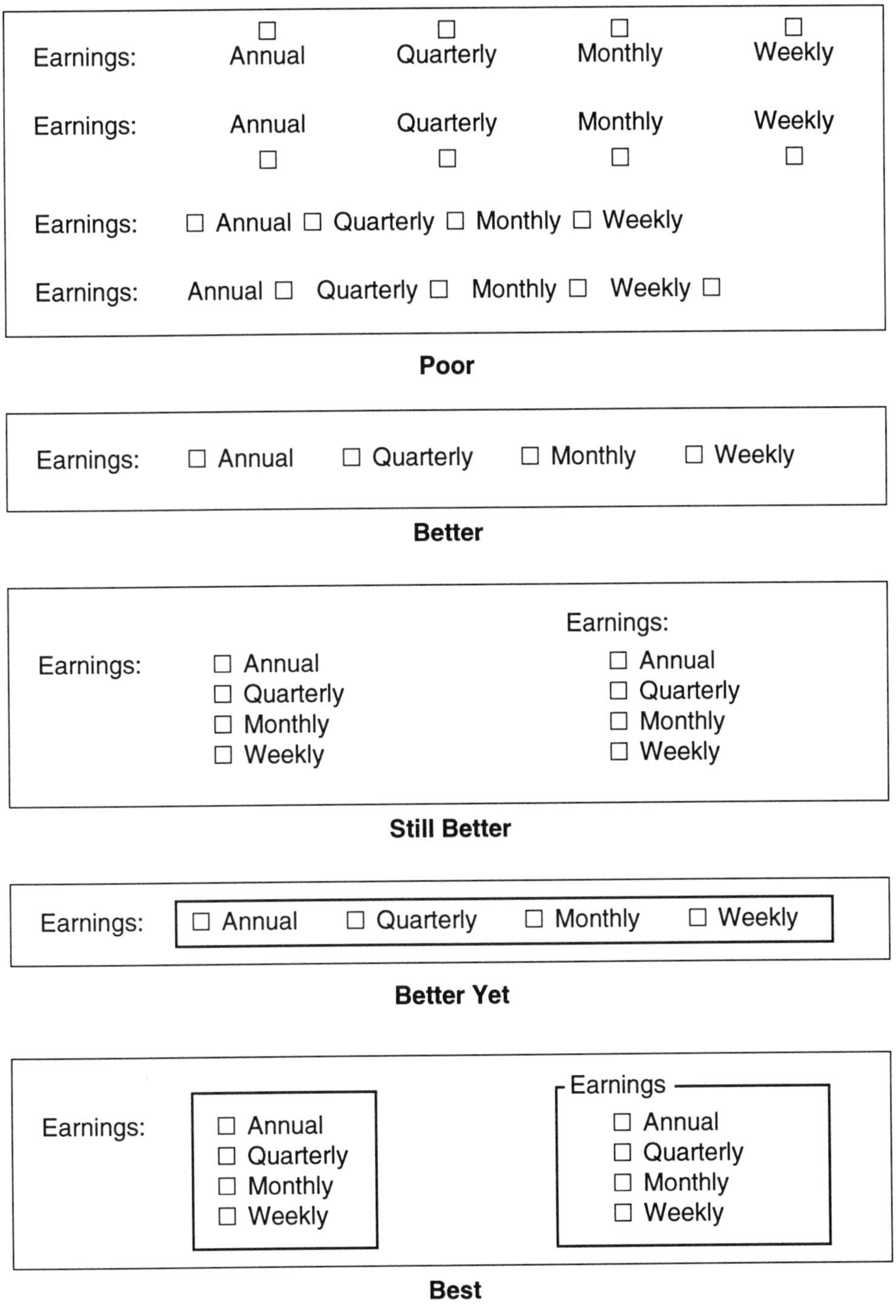

Earnings: □ Annual   □ Quarterly   □ Monthly   □ Weekly

Earnings: Annual   Quarterly   Monthly   Weekly
               □   □   □   □

Earnings: □ Annual □ Quarterly □ Monthly □ Weekly

Earnings: Annual □   Quarterly □   Monthly □   Weekly □

Poor

Earnings: □ Annual   □ Quarterly   □ Monthly   □ Weekly

Better

                                              Earnings:
Earnings: □ Annual   □ Annual
               □ Quarterly   □ Quarterly
               □ Monthly   □ Monthly
               □ Weekly   □ Weekly

Still Better

Earnings: □ Annual   □ Quarterly   □ Monthly   □ Weekly

Better Yet

                                        ┌ Earnings ─────────┐
Earnings: ┌─────────────┐   □ Annual
               │ □ Annual   │   □ Quarterly
               │ □ Quarterly │   □ Monthly
               │ □ Monthly   │   □ Weekly
               │ □ Weekly   │
               └─────────────┘

Best

Defaults. If a selection field is displayed with a choice previously selected or a default choice, display the currently active choice in the same manner shown when it is selected.

PALETTES

Description

- A control consisting of a series of graphical alternatives. The choices themselves are descriptive, being comprised of the following:
  — Icons, such as scissors for cutting.
  — Graphical reproductions, such as colors or shades.
- In addition to being a standard screen control, a palette may also be presented on a pull-down or pop-up menu.

Purpose

- To set one of a series of mutually exclusive options that are presented graphically or pictorially.

Advantages/Disadvantages

- \+ Pictures aid comprehension.
- \+ Easy to compare choices.
- \+ Usually consume less screen space than textual equivalents.

- – Limited number of choices can be displayed.
- – Difficult to organize for scanning efficiency.
- – Requires skills and time to design meaningful and attractive graphical representations.

Proper Usage

- For setting attributes, properties, or values.
- For mutually exclusive choices (i.e., only one can be selected).
- Where adequate screen space is available.
- Most useful for data and choices that are:
  — Discrete.
  — Frequently selected.
  — Limited in number.
  — Variable in number.
  — Not easily remembered.
  — Most easily understood when the alternatives may be seen together and compared to one another.
  — Most meaningfully represented pictorially or by example.
  — Can be clearly represented pictorially.
  — Rarely changed in content.
- Display the palette in the proper manner:
  — If the attributes on the palette need to be available at all times, use a standard control or fixed palette.

> — If the attributes on the palette are sometimes used frequently and other times used infrequently, use a floating palette from a pop-up or tear-off menu.
> — Do not place frequently used palettes on pull-down menus.
- Do not use:
  - — Where the alternatives cannot be meaningfully and clearly represented pictorially.
  - — Where words are clearer than icons.
  - — Where the choices are going to change.

Description. Like radio buttons, palettes can also be used to present two or more mutually exclusive alternatives. The choices presented, however, are visually descriptive within themselves. No choice descriptions are needed to identify them. Examples of palettes might be fill-in colors, patterns, or different shades of colors. A palette may also be referred to as a value set. A value set is illustrated in Figure 11.6. In addition to being a standard screen control, a palette may also be presented on a pull-down or pop-up menu.

Purpose. A palette is used to set one of a series of mutually exclusive options that can be represented graphically or pictorially.

Advantages/Disadvantages. Palettes are preferable to radio buttons in that they take up less space and allow the viewer to focus on the visual characteristics of the choice itself, instead of having to read the choice text and cross-referencing it to a radio button. Some qualities, such as colors, patterns, and shades, are much more easily comprehended when they are actually seen.

While a larger number of choices can be presented than with radio buttons, there is still a limit to how many can be practically displayed. Because of their larger size, they are also most difficult to organize for scanning efficiency. Palettes also require skill and time to design meaningful and attractive graphical representations.

Proper Usage. Palettes are used for setting attributes, properties, or values of mutually exclusive choices where adequate screen space is available. Consider using a palette when the choices have qualities that can be best described

Figure 11.6. A palette.

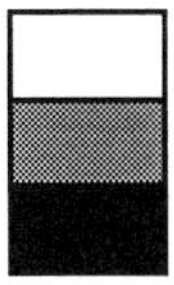

---

by actual illustration. They are useful for data and choices that are discrete and limited in number. They are most useful when the choices, being seen together and compared to one another, aid identification and selection of the proper alternative. They are also most useful when the alternatives can be meaningfully and clearly represented pictorially or by example. Palettes are usually frequently used but should rarely change in content.

Palettes should be displayed in the proper manner. If the attributes on a palette must be available at all times, place them on a standard control or fixed palette. If the attributes on the palette are sometimes used frequently and other times used infrequently, place them on a pop-up or tear-off menu. Do not place frequently used palettes on pull-down menus.

Also, from a presentation perspective, do not use a palette if the alternatives cannot be meaningfully and clearly represented pictorially. In addition, do not use one where words are clearer than icons, or in situations where the choices are going to change.

PALETTE GUIDELINES

Graphical Representations

- Provide meaningful, accurate, and clear illustrations or representations of choices.
- Create images large enough to:
  — Clearly illustrate the available alternatives.
  — Permit ease in pointing and selecting.
- Create images of equal size.
- Always test illustrations before implementing.

Provide meaningful, accurate, and clear illustrations or representations of alternative choices. Create equal size images large enough to illustrate clearly the available alternatives and permit ease in pointing and selecting. Always test illustrations with users before implementing to assure they will work satisfactorily.

While most palettes will not possess textual choice descriptions, under certain circumstances textual descriptions may be needed. For example, a choice might require selection of a style of font. The palette may contain the names of the available styles (like Roman) with the text displayed as the font style would actually appear.

Size

- Present all available alternatives within limits imposed by:
  — The size of the graphical representations.
  — The screen display capabilities.

Since palettes will consume less screen space, more are capable of being displayed in the same area of a screen than can be displayed using textual choice descriptions. Present all available alternatives within limits imposed by how big the graphical representations must be and the capabilities of the display hardware in creating clear illustrations. Human limitations in ability to differentiate accurately the kinds of graphical representations being presented must also be considered.

Layout

- Create boxes large enough to:
  — Effectively illustrate the available alternatives.
  — Permit ease in pointing and selecting.
- Create boxes of equal size.
- Position the boxes adjacent to, or butted up against, one another.
- A columnar orientation is the preferred manner.

- If vertical space on the screen is limited, orient the choices horizontally.

Palette boxes must be large enough to illustrate effectively the available alternatives and to maximize ease in selecting. Created boxes should be of equal size and positioned adjacent to, or butted up against, one another, since they are mutually exclusive choices. Columns are preferred, but horizontal rows can be used if space constraints exist on the screen.

Organization

- Arrange palettes in expected or normal orders.
  — For palettes arrayed top to bottom, begin ordering at the top.
  — For palettes arrayed left to right, begin ordering at the left.
- If an expected or normal order does not exist, arrange choices by frequency of occurrence, sequence of use, importance, or alphabetically (if textual).
- If, under certain conditions, a choice is not available, display it subdued or less brightly than the other choices.

Palettes should be organized logically. If the alternatives have an expected order, follow it. Colors, for example, should be ordered from the right or top by their spectral position: red, orange, yellow, green, blue, indigo, and violet. If an expected or normal order does not exist, arrange choices by frequency of occurrence, sequence of use, or importance. Palettes with text may be arranged alphabetically. If, under certain conditions, a choice is not available, display the unavailable choice subdued or less brightly than the available choices.

Captions

- Provide a caption for each palette.
  - — In screens containing only one value set, the screen title may serve as the caption.
- Display the caption fully spelled out using mixed-case letters.

Columnar Orientation

- The field caption may be located above the palette.

- Alternatively, the caption may be located to the left of the topmost alternative.

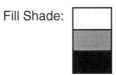

Horizontal Orientation

- The field caption may be located above the palette.

Fill Shade:

- Alternatively, the caption may be located to the left of the alternatives.

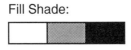

Provide a caption for each palette. In screens containing only one value set, the screen title may serve as the caption. Display the caption fully spelled out using mixed-case letters, although some abbreviations may be used to achieve the alignment goals to be specified. Field captions may be located above, or to the left of, the value set.

Selection Method and Indication

Pointing

- Highlight the choice in some visually distinctive way when the pointer or cursor is resting on it and the choice is available for selection.
- Also, change the shape of the pointer to indicate that a selection can be performed.

Activation

- When a choice is selected, distinguish it visually from the nonselected choices by highlighting it in a manner different from when it is pointed at, or by placing a bold border around it.

Defaults

- If a palette is displayed with a choice previously selected or a default choice, display the currently active choice in the manner used when selected.

Pointing. The selection target should be as large as possible in order to make it easy to move to. Highlight the selection choice in some visually distinctive way when the pointer or cursor is resting on it and the choice is available for selection. Also, change the shape of the pointer to indicate that a selection can be performed.

Activation. When a choice is selected, distinguish it visually from the non-selected choices by highlighting it in a manner different from when it is pointed at, or by placing a bolder border around it.

Defaults. If a palette is displayed with a choice previously selected or a default choice, display the currently active choice in the manner used when selected.

FIXED LIST BOX

Description

- A rectangular box containing a list of attributes or objects from which:
  - A single selection is made (mutually exclusive), or
  - Multiple selections are made (non-mutually exclusive).

- The choice may be text, pictorial representations, or graphics.
- Selections are made by using a mouse to point and click.
- Capable of being scrolled to view large lists of choices.
- No entry field exists in which to type text.
- A single-selection list box may be associated with a display field where the selected choice is displayed.

Purpose

- To select from a large set of choices that may be:
  — Mutually exclusive options.
  — Non-mutually exclusive options.

Advantages/Disadvantages

- + Unlimited number of choices.
- + Reminds users of available options.
- + Box always visible.

- − Consumes some screen space.
- − All choices not always visible, may require scrolling.
- − The list content may change, making it hard to find items.
- − The list may be ordered in an unpredictable way, making it hard to find items.
- − Generally, requires more work on the part of the user than many other controls.

Proper Usage

- For selecting objects or setting attributes.
- For choices that are:
  — Mutually exclusive (e.g., only one can be selected).
  — Non-mutually exclusive (i.e., one or more may be selected).
- Where screen space is available.
- For data and choices that are:
  — Best represented textually.
  — Infrequently selected.
  — Not well known, easily learned, or remembered.
  — Ordered in a non-predictable fashion.
  — Frequently changed.
  — Large in number.
  — Fixed or variable in list length.
- When screen space or layout considerations make radio buttons or check boxes impractical.

Description. A fixed list box is a rectangular-shaped box containing a list of attributes or objects from which single or multiple selections are made. The choice is usually text, but it may be pictorial representations or graphics as well. A fixed list box may be scrollable to view large lists, and selections are made by using a mouse to point and click. No entry field exists in which to type text, but a single-selection list box may be associated with a display field where the selected choice is displayed. While single- and multiple-selection fixed list boxes often look alike, they should be visually differentiated in some way.

The term "fixed list box" is used in this text to indicate that they are always permanently displayed or "fixed" on a screen, and to differentiate them clearly from other kinds of list boxes, notably drop-down/pop-up list boxes. IBM's SAA CUA uses the term "list box" for these kinds of fields. OSF/Motif refers to them as simply "lists." Examples of list boxes are illustrated in Figure 11.7.

Purpose: To select from a large set of choices that may be mutually exclusive or non-mutually exclusive options.

Advantages/Disadvantages. Fixed list boxes are always visible, reminding users of the choices available. They permit an unlimited number of options to be displayed.

Among their disadvantages are the excessive screen space they consume and the possible necessity for scrolling to see all items. Since the list content can change, and items can be ordered in an unpredictable way, it can be hard to find items. Generally, fixed list boxes require more work on the part of the user than many other screen-based controls.

Proper Usage. Fixed list boxes are used for selecting objects or setting attributes, either mutually exclusive or non-mutually exclusive, where sufficient screen space is available to display them.

Their best use is for data and choices that are textual, large in number, fixed or variable in list length, not well known, easily learned or remembered, and ordered in a non-predictable fashion. Fixed list box items should not have to be selected frequently, but when they are, they may be changed often.

Figure 11.7. List boxes. "Location" is not scrollable; "destination" is scrollable vertically.

Location:

| Amphitheater |
| Chicago Stadium |
| Comiskey Park |
| Dyche Stadium |
| Melbourne Cricket Ground |
| Soldier Field |
| Stagg Field |
| Wrigley Field |

Destination:

FIXED LIST BOX GUIDELINES

Selection Descriptions

- Selection descriptions will reflect the choices available. They should be meaningful and spelled out as fully as possible.
  — Graphical representations must clearly represent the options.
- If a particular choice is not available in the current context, it should be omitted from the list.
  — Exception: If it is important that the existence and non-availability of a list item be communicated, display the choice dimmed or grayed instead of deleting it.
- Organize the descriptions left-aligned in columns.
- Order the descriptions in a meaningful way or in alphabetical order.
- Display the descriptions using mixed-case letters.
- If associated with a display field, display the descriptions in the same color as the display field text.

Selection descriptions will reflect the selection alternatives available. They should be meaningful, fully spelled out, and organized in columns. Meaningful ordering schemes include logical order, frequency of use, sequence of use, or importance. If no such pattern exists, arrange the list alphabetically. Display the list of choices using mixed-case letters.

If a particular choice is not available in the current context, it should be omitted from the list. If it is important that the existence and nonavailability of a list item be communicated, however, display the choice dimmed or grayed instead of deleting it. If the list is associated with a display field and the screen uses color, the color scheme of the display field and the list box should be consistent.

List Size

- Not limited in size.
- Present all available alternatives.

A list being displayed in a fixed list box has no size limit. All available alternatives should be capable of being displayed.

Fixed List Box Size

- A fixed list box should be long enough to display six to eight choices without requiring scrolling.
  — If screen space constraints exist, the box may be reduced in size to display at least three items.

- — If more items are available than are visible in the box, provide vertical scrolling to display all items.
- The list box should be wide enough to display the longest possible choice.
  - — Avoid horizontal scrolling whenever possible.
  - — If horizontal scrolling is ever necessary, provide a scroll bar at the bottom of the box.

The exact size of a fixed list box will depend on the application and screen space constraints. Generally, boxes should be restricted to no more than eight choices at one time. Slightly larger boxes that eliminate the need for scrolling, however, are preferable to list boxes that require a little scrolling. If screen space constraints exist, the box may be reduced in size to display at least three items. If scrolling is necessary, include a scroll bar on the right side of the box. The list box should be wide enough to display fully all selection choices. If horizontal scrolling is necessary, provide a scroll bar at the bottom of the list box.

Layout and Separation

- Enclose the choices in a box with a solid border.
  - — The border should be the same color as the choice descriptions.
- Leave one blank character position between the choice descriptions and the left border.
- Leave one blank character position between the longest choice description in the list and the right border, if possible.
- If associated with a display field, use the same background color for the box as is used in the display field.

```
┌─────────────────┐
│ Australia       │
│ Canada          │
│ England         │
│ France          │
│ Germany         │
│ Hong Kong       │
│ New Zealand     │
│ Netherlands     │
│                 │
└─────────────────┘
```

Enclose the box in a solid border in the color of the choice descriptions. To provide adequate legibility, leave one space between the choice descriptions and the left border, and one space between the longest choice description and the right border. If the box is associated with a display field, visually relate the box to the entry field by using the same background color for the box as is used in the display field box. Also incorporate a solid line border around the fixed list box in the same color as the choice descriptions.

Captions

- Display using mixed-case letters.
- The preferred location of the field caption is above the upper-left corner of the fixed list box.

Location:

```
Amphitheater
Chicago Stadium
Comiskey Park
Dyche Stadium
Melbourne Cricket Ground
Soldier Field
Stagg Field
Wrigley Field
```

- Alternatively, the caption may be located to the left of the topmost choice description.

Location:
```
Amphitheater
Chicago Stadium
Comiskey Park
Dyche Stadium
Melbourne Cricket Ground
Soldier Field
Stagg Field
Wrigley Field
```

- If used with a display field, the list box field caption should be worded similarly to the display field caption.

Location: [   ]

Location:
```
Amphitheater
Chicago Stadium
Comiskey Park
Dyche Stadium
Melbourne Cricket Ground
Soldier Field
Stagg Field
Wrigley Field
```

- Be consistent in caption style and orientation within an application.

To identify the fixed list box, a field caption in mixed-case letters with each significant word capitalized is necessary. Place this caption either above the upper-left corner of the box or to the left of the first choice description. If the list box is associated with a display field, this caption must be worded similarly to the display field caption. The caption style chosen, above or left, should be consistent within an application.

Selection Method and Indication

Pointing

- Highlight the selection choice in some visually distinctive way when the pointer or cursor is resting on it and the choice is available for selection.

Activation

- Use a reverse video or reverse color bar to surround the choice description when it is selected.
- The cursor should be as wide as the box itself.

Destination:

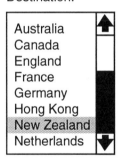

Selection Indication

- For multiple selection (nonexclusive) choice list boxes:
  - — For active choices, include a check mark or checked box to the left of the choice description.
  - — Provide a field indicating how many choices selected.
    - — Locate field to right of box caption.

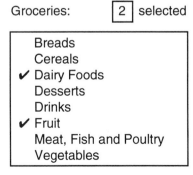

- For single selection (exclusive) choice list boxes:
  - For active choice, indicate by highlighting or marking with circle or diamond to left of choice description.

Dictionaries in Use

Defaults

- When the list box is first displayed:
  - If a choice has been previously selected, display the currently active choice in the same manner used when it was selected.
  - If a choice has not been previously selected, provide a default choice and display it in the same manner that is used in selecting it.

Pointing. Highlight the selection choice in some visually distinctive way when the pointer or cursor is resting on it and the choice is available for selection. One method for this is a bold border around the choice.

Activation. Indicate the selected choice through use of a reverse video or reverse color bar, as wide as the box itself.

Selection Indication. Visually differentiate multiple (non-exclusive) from single (mutually exclusive) choice fixed list boxes: For multiple choice, include a check mark or checked box to the left of the active choice descriptions and provide a field indicating how many choices have been selected to the right of the box caption. The field will indicate how many active choices may not be visible. For single-selection fixed list boxes, indicate an active choice by highlighting it or marking it with a circle or diamond to left of choice description.

Defaults. When the list box is first displayed, the active selection will depend on previous activities. If a choice has been previously selected, display the currently active choice in the same manner used when it was selected. If a choice has not been previously selected, provide a default choice and display it in the same manner that is used in selecting it. If properly organized, the default choice will be the first alternative in the list.

Location

- If a standalone field, position the list box in its logical sequence within the elements on the screen.

- If associated with a display field, locate the list box below, and as close as possible to, the display field to which it applies.
  — If multiple list boxes are included on the screen, they should be in the same order (top to bottom or left to right) as the display fields appear.

Destination: | Australia |

Location: | Melbourne Cricket Ground |

Destination:

| Australia ▲ |
| Canada |
| England |
| France |
| Germany |
| Hong Kong |
| New Zealand |
| Netherlands ▼ |

Location:

| Amphitheater |
| Chicago Stadium |
| Comiskey Park |
| Dyche Stadium |
| Melbourne Cricket Ground |
| Soldier Field |
| Stagg Field |
| Wrigley Field |

Position the list box or boxes in the logical sequence of elements found within the screen. If the box is associated with an entry field, locate the list box below and as close as possible to the entry field to which it relates. For screens containing multiple boxes, arrange the boxes in the same order as the entry fields appear on the screen. If the entry fields are in a top-to-bottom orientation, leave them that way. If this cannot be accomplished, orient them left to right.

DROP-DOWN/POP-UP LIST BOX

Description

- A single rectangular field with a small button to the side and an associated hidden list of options.
  — The button provides a visual cue that an associated selection box is available but hidden.
- When requested, a larger associated rectangular box appears containing a scrollable list of choices from which one is selected.
- Selections are made by using the mouse to point and click.
- No entry field exists in which to type text.

Purpose

- To select one item from a large list of mutually exclusive options when screen space is limited.

Advantages/Disadvantages

+ Unlimited number of choices.
+ Reminds users of available options.
+ Conserves screen space.

– Requires extra step to display list of choices.
– When displayed, all choices not always visible. May require scrolling.
– The list content may change, making it hard to find items.
– The list may be ordered in an unpredictable way, making it hard to find items.
– Generally, requires more work on the part of the user than many other controls.

Proper Usage

• For selecting objects or setting attributes.
• For choices that are mutually exclusive (i.e., only one can be selected).
• Where screen space is limited.
• For data and choices that are:
  — Best represented textually.
  — Infrequently selected.
  — Not well known, easily learned, or remembered.
  — Ordered in a non-predictable fashion.
  — Frequently changed.
  — Large in number.
  — Variable or fixed in list length.
• When screen space or layout considerations make radio buttons or fixed list boxes impractical.

Description. A drop-down/pop-up list box is a single rectangular field with a small button to the side and an associated hidden list of options. The button provides a visual cue to the user that an associated selection box of choices is available but hidden. When requested, a larger associated rectangular box appears containing a scrollable list of choices from which one is selected. Selections are made by using the mouse to point and click. No entry field exists in which to type text.

Fields of this nature go by many different names. IBM's SAA CUA refers to them as "drop-down lists" because they appear to drop-down from the single selection field. Xerox's Viewpoint calls them "pull-down lists." Other list boxes of this type seem to pop-up on the screen, either next to or over the selection field. OSF/Motif calls list boxes of this style "option menus," and DECwindows uses the term "list boxes." NeXTStep refers to them as "pop-up lists."

A selection field with a drop-down list, similar to those described in SAA CUA, is illustrated in Figure 11.8. Figure 11.9 shows a pop-up list.

Purpose. To permit selection from a large set of mutually exclusive choices when screen space is scarce.

Figure 11.8.   Drop-down list box. A drop-down iconic indicator is associated with the "Sport" field in the left grouping of fields. The right grouping shows the drop-down list box.

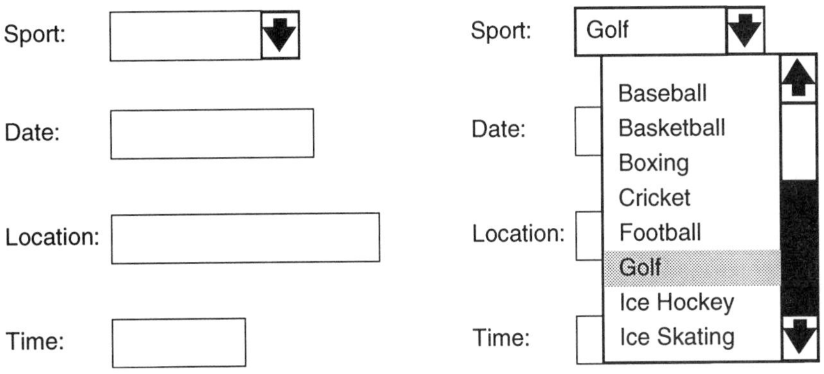

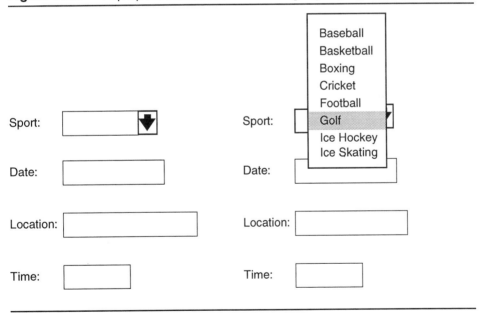

Figure 11.9.   Pop-up list box illustrated in the right grouping.

Advantages/Disadvantages. Drop-down/pop-up list boxes are useful in that they conserve screen space. They may be retrieved on demand, reminding users of the choices available. They permit an unlimited number of options to be displayed.

A significant disadvantage is that they necessitate an extra step to display the available options. Scrolling may also be necessary to see all items. Since the list content can change, and items can be ordered in an unpredictable way, it can be hard to find items. Generally, drop-down/pop-up list boxes require more work on the part of the user than many other screen-based controls.

Proper Usage. Drop-down/pop-up list boxes are used much like fixed list boxes, except the choices are not visible at all times. They are used for selecting objects or setting attributes when sufficient screen space is not available to display the choices permanently.

Their best use is for data and choices that are textual, large in number, fixed or variable in list length, not well known, easily learned or remembered, and ordered in a non-predictable fashion. Items should not have to be selected frequently, but when they are, they may be changed often.

DROP-DOWN/POP-UP LIST BOX GUIDELINES

Prompt Button

- Provide a visual cue that a list box is hidden by including a downward pointing arrow, or other meaningful icon, to the right of the selection field.
  — Position the button directly against the selection field.

  — When the arrow or icon is selected by the user and the list appears, reverse its polarity, using either reverse video or reverse color.

Many systems indicate the presence of a drop-down or pop-up list by associating a meaningful icon with the applicable field. This icon can be seen positioned to the left of the selection field (OPEN LOOK), within the selection field (NeXTStep), or to the right of the selection field (IBM's SAA CUA). Others do not provide any visual indication that a hidden list is available (OSF/Motif and DECwindows).

An indication to the user that a drop-down or pop-up list is available should be indicated on the screen. This is especially critical if not all fields have associated hidden lists. The best location is to the right of the selection field where it is out of the way until needed. To differentiate it from a drop-down/pop-up combination box, position the button abutting the selection field. (A drop-down/pop-up combination box button will be separated by a space.) The indicator should be large enough to provide a good pointing target. When the list is selected, reverse the polarity of the indicator using either reverse video or reverse color.

Selection Descriptions

- Selection descriptions will reflect the choices available. They should be meaningful and spelled out as fully as possible.

- — Graphical representations must clearly represent the options.
- If a particular choice is not available in the current context, it should be omitted from the list.
  - — Exception: If it is important that the existence and non-availability of a list item be communicated, display the choice dimmed or grayed instead of deleting it.
- Organize the descriptions left-aligned in columns.
- Order the descriptions in a meaningful way or in alphabetical order.
- Display the descriptions using mixed-case letters.
- If associated with a display field, display the descriptions in the same color as the display field text.

Selection descriptions will reflect what may be placed in the selection field. They should be meaningful, fully spelled out, and organized in columns. Meaningful ordering schemes include logical order, frequency of use, sequence of use, or importance. If no such pattern exists, arrange the list alphabetically. Display the list of choices using mixed-case letters. Descriptions should be displayed in the same color as the selection field text.

If a particular choice is not available in the current context, it should be omitted from the list. If it is important that the existence and nonavailability of a list item be communicated, however, display the choice dimmed or grayed instead of deleting it.

List Size

- Not limited in size.
- Present all available alternatives.

A list being displayed in a drop-down/pop-up list box has no size limit. All available alternatives should be capable of being displayed.

Box Size

- Restrict the number of choices visible at one time to eight or less.
  - — If more than eight choices are available, provide scrolling to display all choices.
  - — If scrolling is necessary, provide a scroll bar on the right side of the box.

Pop-up or drop-down list boxes should be restricted to eight or less choices. If more must be displayed, permit scrolling and include a scroll bar on the right side of the box.

Location

- Locate:
  — A drop-down list box beneath the selection field to which it applies.

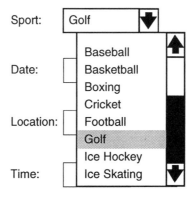

  — A pop-up list box:
  — Adjacent to the selection field to which it applies, or
  — Over the selection field to which it applies.

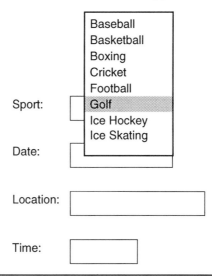

Locate a drop-down list box directly beneath the selection field to which it applies. Pop-up lists should be positioned adjacent to, or over, the selection field. If the list is located over the selection fields, position the selected or default choice in the list directly over the selection field, as illustrated above. This means the box will slightly change position as selection field entries change. Never reorder the list.

Layout and Separation

- Enclose the choices in a box composed of a solid line border.
  - — The border should be the same color as the choice descriptions.
- Left-align the choices in the list.
- Leave one blank character position to the left of the column of choices.
- Leave one blank character position to the right of the longest choice description in the list.
- Extend the listing box to the right edge of the prompt button.
- Use the same background color for the box as is displayed in the selection field.

To provide adequate legibility, leave one space between the choice descriptions and the left border, and one space between the longest choice description and the right border. Extending the listing box to the right edge of the prompt button allows the user to move easily from the button to the list. To set off the box from the screen body background, use the same color background for the box as is used in the entry field. Also incorporate a solid line border around the box in the same color as the choice descriptions.

Captions

- Display using mixed-case letters.
- Position the caption to the left of the display field.
- Inscribe a colon (:) following the caption.

The control caption should appear in the standard way, in mixed-case letters to the left of the display field.

Selection Method and Indication

Pointing

- Highlight the selection choice in some visually distinctive way when the pointer or cursor is resting on it and the choice is available for selection.

Activation

- Highlight a selected choice by using a reverse video or reverse color bar to surround the selected item.
- The bar should be as wide as the box itself.

Defaults

- When the list box is first displayed:
  - —If a choice has been previously selected, display the currently active choice in the same manner used when it was selected.
  - — If a choice has not been previously selected, provide a default choice and display it in the same manner that is used in selecting it.

Pointing. Highlight the selection choice in some visually distinctive way when the pointer or cursor is resting on it and the choice is available for selection.

Activation. Highlight a selected choice by using a reverse video or reverse color bar to surround the selected item. The bar should be as wide as the box itself.

Defaults. When the list box is first displayed, the active selection will depend on previous activities. If a choice has been previously selected, display the currently active choice in the same manner used when it was selected. If a choice has not been previously selected, provide a default choice and display it in the same manner that is used in selecting it.

COMBINATION ENTRY/SELECTION FIELDS

It is possible for a control to possess the characteristics of an entry field and a selection field. In this type of control, information may either be typed into the field or selected and placed within it. The following varieties of combination entry/selection fields exist.

Spin Box

Description

- A single-line field followed by two small, vertically-arranged buttons.
  - — The top button has an arrow pointing up.
  - — The bottom button has an arrow pointing down.
- Selection/entry is made by:
  - — Using the mouse to point at one of the directional buttons and clicking. Items will change by one unit or step with each click.
  - — Keying a value directly into the field itself.

Purpose

- To make a selection by either scrolling through a small set of meaningful predefined choices or typing by keying text.

Advantages/Disadvantages

+ Consume little screen space.
+ Flexible, permitting selection or typed entry.

– Difficult to compare choices.
– Useful only for certain kinds of data.

Proper Usage

• For setting attributes, properties, or values.
• For mutually exclusive choices (i.e., only one can be selected).
• When the task requires the option of either key entry or selection from a list.
• When the user prefers the option of either key entry or selection from a list.
• Where screen space is limited.
• Most useful for data and choices that are:
— Discrete.
— Infrequently selected.
— Well known, easily learned or remembered, and meaningful.
— Ordered in a predictable, customary, or consecutive fashion.
— Infrequently changed.
— Small in number.
— Fixed or variable in list length.

Description. A spin box, also called a spin button, is a single-line field followed by two small, vertically arranged buttons inscribed with up and down arrows. Selection of an item is accomplished using the mouse to point at one of the buttons and clicking. Items in a listing in the display field will change by one unit or step in the direction selected with each click. The list is searched as the ring or circle of alternatives "spins" by. A spin box may also be completed by keying a value directly into the field itself. A spin box is illustrated in Figure 11.10.

Purpose. A spin box is used to make a selection by scrolling through a meaningful small set of predefined choices or by keying through typing text.

Advantages/Disadvantages. Spin boxes are flexible, permitting either selection or typed entry. They also consume little screen space. On the other hand, spin boxes are useful only for certain kinds of data, predictable or consecutive. Because only one item is displayed at a time, it is difficult to compare choices.

Figure 11.10. Spin box.

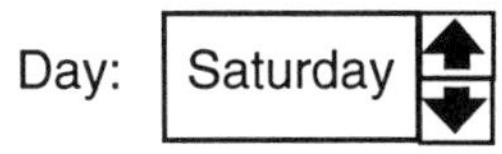

Day: | Saturday ▲▼

Proper Usage. Spin boxes are used for setting attributes, properties, or values that are mutually exclusive. They are useful when the task requires, or user prefers, the option of key entry or selection from a list.

Spin boxes are useful for data and choices that are discrete and small in number. The choices themselves should be well known, easily learned or remembered, and meaningful. Choices should be ordered in a predictable, customary, or consecutive fashion so people can anticipate the next not-yet-visible choice. Items in spin boxes should be selected infrequently, and the array of items listed should change infrequently.

SPIN BOX GUIDELINES

List Size

- Keep the list of items relatively short.
- To reduce the size of potentially long lists, break the listing into subcomponents, if possible.

Since the list must be manipulated to display its contents, it should be as short as feasible. To reduce the size of potentially long lists, break the listing into subcomponents whenever possible. A date, for example, may be broken into its pieces, month, day, and year.

List Organization

- Order the list in the customary, consecutive, or expected order of the information contained within it.
  - Assure that the user can always anticipate the next (not-yet-visible) choice.
- When first displayed, the field should contain a default choice.

Spin boxes are most effective when the values they contain have a customary or consecutive order that is predictable. Information can be letters or numbers with a customary or expected order. Examples would be days of the week, months of the year, shoe sizes, and so on. The user must always be able to anticipate the next choice before it is displayed. The field should always contain a default value when first displayed.

Field Size

- The spin box should be wide enough to display the longest entry or choice.

Fully display all alternatives within the spin box.

Spin Indicator

- Provide an indication that a spin button is available by placing up and down arrows immediately to the right of the entry field.

Day: | Saturday ⬆⬇ |

The clue to the user that the field is a spin button is the up and down arrows adjacent to the field. Locate the arrows to the right of the field.

Entry and Selection Methods

- Permit field completion by:
  — Typing directly into the field.
  — Scrolling and selecting with a mouse.
  — Scrolling and selecting with the up/down arrow keys.
- For alphabetical values:
  — Move down the order using the down arrow.
  — Move up the order using the up arrow.
- For numeric values or magnitudes:
  — Show a larger value using the up arrow.
  — Show a smaller value using the down arrow.

Field completion should be possible by typing directly into the field or by scrolling and selecting with a mouse or keyboard keys. When spinning alphabetical values, move down the order using the down arrow and up the order using the up arrow. For numeric values or magnitudes, display a larger value using the up arrow and a smaller value using the down arrow.

ATTACHED COMBINATION BOX

Description

- A single rectangular entry field, beneath which is a larger rectangular box (resembling a drop-down list box) displaying a list of options.
- The entry field permits a choice to be keyed within it.
- The larger box contains a list of mutually exclusive choices from which one may be selected for placement in the entry field.
  — Selections are made by using a mouse to point and click.
- Combines the capabilities of both an entry field and a fixed list box.
- Any information keyed does not have to match the list items.

Purpose

- To allow either typed entry or selection from a list of options in a permanently displayed box attached to the field.

Advantages/Disadvantages

+ Unlimited number of entries and choices.
+ Reminds users of available options.
+ Flexible, permitting selection or typed entry.
+ Entries not restricted to items selectable from box.
+ Box always visible.

- Consume some screen space.
- All box choices not always visible, may require scrolling.
- Users may have difficulty recalling sufficient information to type entry, making entry field unusable.
- The list may be ordered in an unpredictable way, making it hard to find items.
- Might require more work on the part of the user than some other controls.

Proper Usage

- For entering or selecting objects or values or setting attributes.
- For information that is mutually exclusive (i.e., only one can be entered or selected).
- When users may find it practical to, or prefer to, type information rather than selecting from a list.
  — Predominantly keyboard-oriented tasks.
- When users can often recall and type information faster than selecting from a list.
- When it is useful to provide the users a reminder of the choices available.
- Where data must be entered that is not contained in the selection list.
- Where screen space is available.
- For data and choices that are:
  — Best represented textually.
  — Somewhat familiar or known.
  — Ordered in a non-predictable fashion.
  — Frequently changed.
  — Large in number.
  — Variable or fixed in list length.

Description. An attached combination box is a single rectangular entry field, beneath which is a larger rectangular box (resembling a drop-down list box) displaying a list of options. The entry field permits a choice to be keyed within it while the larger box contains a list of mutually exclusive choices from which one may be selected for placement in the entry field. An attached combination box combines the capabilities of both an entry field and a fixed list box. It visually resembles a drop-down list box or drop-down combination box (to be described). When keying into the field, the information keyed does not have to match the list items.

Attached combination boxes are sometimes simply referred to as combination boxes. One is illustrated in Figure 11.11.

Purpose. To allow either typed entry or selection from a list of options in a permanently displayed box attached to the field.

Advantages/Disadvantages. Attached combination boxes are flexible, permitting selection or typed entry. Alternatives are always visible, or retrievable, reminding people of the available options. An unlimited variety of entries and choices are possible. Entries are not restricted to items selectable from a box.

Attached combination boxes do consume quite a bit of screen space. Because all box choices may not be visible, some scrolling may be required. It is always possible that people may have difficulty recalling sufficient information to type, making the entry field unusable. The list may also be ordered in an unpredictable way, making it hard to find items. Additional work is required of the user if selection scrolling must be performed.

Proper Usage. Attached combination boxes are useful for entering or selecting objects or values or setting attributes that are mutually exclusive. They are of most value when users may find it practical to, or prefer to, type information rather than selecting from a list but where reminders of alternatives available must occasionally be provided. They are also useful when the listings are dynamic and changeable, permitting the user to key items not contained on the list in the box. They do require that screen space be available to display them but eliminate the extra steps involved in retrieving drop-down lists.

Figure 11.11. Attached combination box.

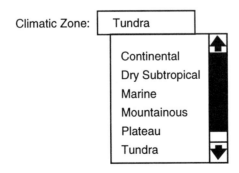

Attached combination boxes are useful for textual data and choices that are frequently changed and somewhat familiar or known, fostering keyed entry. The lists may be long, variable, and ordered in a non-predictable fashion.

ATTACHED COMBINATION BOX GUIDELINES

For the entry field, see *Single Line Entry Field* guidelines. For the box, see *Drop-Down/Pop-Up List Box* guidelines.

DROP-DOWN/POP-UP COMBINATION BOX

Description

- A single rectangular entry field with a small button to the side and an associated hidden list of options.
  - The button provides a visual cue that an associated selection box is available but hidden.
- When requested, a larger associated rectangular box containing a scrollable list of choices from which one is selected.
  - Selections are made by using the mouse to point and click.
- Information may be keyed into the field.
- The information keyed does not have to match list items.
- Combines the capabilities of both an entry field and a selection field.

Purpose

- To allow users either to type an entry or select from a list of options in a list box that may be retrieved as needed.

Advantages/Disadvantages

- \+ Unlimited number of entries and choices.
- \+ Reminds users of available options.
- \+ Flexible, permitting selection or typed entry.
- \+ Entries not restricted to items selectable from box.

- − Conserves screen space.
- − Requires extra step to display list of choices.
- − When displayed, all box choices not always visible. May require scrolling.
- − User may have difficulty in recalling what to type.
- − The list content may change, making it hard to find items.
- − The list may be ordered in an unpredictable way, making it hard to find items.
- − Generally, requires more work on the part of the user than many other controls.

Proper Usage

- For entering or selecting objects or values or setting attributes.
- For information that is mutually exclusive (i.e., only one can be entered or selected).
- When users may find it practical to, or prefer to, type information rather than selecting from a list.
  — Predominantly keyboard-oriented tasks.
- When users can recall and type information faster than selecting from a list.
- When it is useful to provide the users an occasional reminder of the choices available.
- Where data must be entered that is not contained in the selection list.
- Where screen space is limited.
- For data and choices that are:
  — Best represented textually.
  — Somewhat familiar or known.
  — Ordered in a non-predictable fashion.
  — Frequently changed.
  — Large in number.
  — Variable or fixed in list length.

Description. A drop-down/pop-up combination box is a single rectangular field with a small button to the side and an associated hidden list of options. The button provides a visual cue to the user that an associated selection box of choices is available but hidden. When requested, a larger associated rectangular box appears containing a scrollable list of choices from which one is selected. Selections are made by using the mouse to point and click. It closely resembles a drop-down/pop-up list box.

Information, however, may also be keyed into the field itself. The information keyed does not have to match items in the list. A drop-down/pop-up combination box, therefore, combines the capabilities of both an entry field and a selection field. A drop-down combination box is illustrated in Figure 11.12.

Purpose. A drop-down/pop-up combination box allows users to either type an entry or select from a list of options in a list box that may be retrieved as needed.

Advantages/Disadvantages. Drop-down/pop-up combination boxes are flexible, permitting selection or typed entry. They conserve screen space, but alternatives are always retrievable, reminding people of the available options. An unlimited variety of entries and choices are possible. Entries are not restricted to items selectable from a box.

In terms of disadvantages, they necessitate an extra step to display the available options. Scrolling may also be necessary to see all items. Since the list content can change, and items can be ordered in an unpredictable way, it can be hard to find items. It is always possible also that people may have

Figure 11.12.   Drop-down combination box.

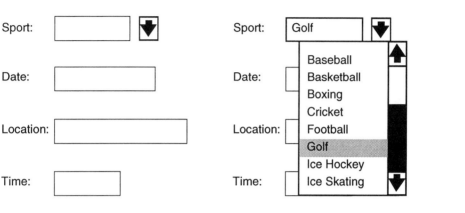

difficulty recalling sufficient information to type, making the entry field unusable. Generally drop-down/pop-up combination boxes require more work on the part of the user than many other screen-based controls.

Proper Usage. Drop-down/pop-up combination boxes are useful for entering or selecting objects or values or setting attributes that are mutually exclusive. They are of most value when users may find it practical to, or prefer to, type information rather than selecting from a list but where reminders of alternatives available must occasionally be provided. The box may only be retrieved as needed, thereby conserving screen space. They are also useful when the listings are dynamic and changeable, permitting the user to key items not contained on the list in the box.

Drop-down/pop-up combination boxes are useful for textual data and choices that are frequently changed and somewhat familiar or known, fostering keyed entry. The list may be long, variable, and ordered in a non-predictable fashion.

DROP-DOWN/POP-UP COMBINATION BOX GUIDELINES

Prompt Button

- Provide a visual cue that a list box is hidden by including a downward-pointing arrow to the right of the entry field.
  — Position the button separated by a space from the entry field.

- When the list is selected and the list appears, reverse the polarity of the arrow using either reverse video or reverse color.

Provide a visual cue that a list box is hidden by including a downward-pointing arrow to the right of the entry field. Position the button separated by a space from the entry field, differentiating it from the similar drop-down/pop-up list box whose button will be directly adjacent to its selection field. When the list is selected and the list appears, reverse the polarity of the arrow using either reverse video or reverse color.

OTHER GUIDELINES

For the entry field, see the *Single Line Entry Field* guidelines. For the box and selection components, see *Drop-Down/Pop-Up List Box* guidelines.

OTHER CONTROLS

Other screen-based controls include sliders, mark toggles, and scroll bars.

SLIDER

Description

- A scale exhibiting more or less of a quality on a continuum.
- Includes the following:
  - A shaft or bar.
  - A range of values with appropriate labels.
  - An arm indicating relative setting through its location on the shaft.
  - Optionally, a pair of buttons to permit incremental movement of the slider arm.
  - Optionally, an entry/display field for typing and displaying an exact value.
  - Optionally, a detent position for special values.
- Selected by using the mouse to:
  - Drag a slider across the scale until the desired value is reached.
  - Point at the buttons at one end of the scale and clicking to change the value.
  - Keying a value in the associated entry/display field.

Purpose

- To make a setting when a continuous qualitative adjustment is acceptable and it is useful to see the current value relative to the range of possible values.

Advantages/Disadvantages

- + Spatial representation of relative setting.
- + Visually distinctive.

- Not as precise as an alphanumeric indication.
- Consumes screen space.
- Can be more complex than other controls.

Proper Usage

- To set an attribute.
- For mutually exclusive choices.
- When an object has a limited range of possible settings.
- When the range of values is continuous.
- When graduations are relatively fine.
- When the choices can increase or decrease in some well-known, predictable, and easily understood way.
- When a spatial representation enhances comprehension and interpretation.
- When using a slider provides sufficient accuracy.

Description. A slider is a scale exhibiting more or less of a quantity or quality on a continuum. A slider incorporates the range of possible values and includes a shaft or bar representing the range, the values themselves with appropriate labels, and a visual indication of the relative setting through the location of a sliding arm. Optionally, sliders also may include a pair of buttons to permit incremental movement of the slider arm, an entry/display field for typing and displaying an exact value, and a detent position for special values.

Slider values can be set by using the mouse to drag a slider across the scale until the desired value is reached. A visual indication of the relative setting is seen as the setting movement is made. In addition, some sliders may also be set by pointing at slider buttons located at one end of the scale and incrementally moving the arm through button clicks. Finally, some sliders may also be set by keying a value in an associated field.

Examples of how sliders may be used are for adjusting the volume of a beep or the speed of the mouse cursor, or setting the saturation level of a particular color. Some sliders are illustrated in Figure 11.13.

Purpose. A slider is used to make a setting when a continuous qualitative adjustment is acceptable, and it is advantageous to see the current value relative to all possible values.

Advantages/Disadvantages. A slider displays a spatial representation of a relative setting, providing an excellent indication of where a value exists within a range of values. They are also visually distinctive and very recognizable.

Figure 11.13.   Sliders.

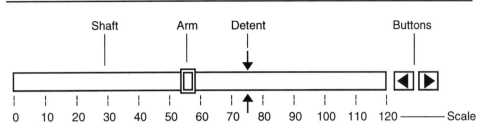

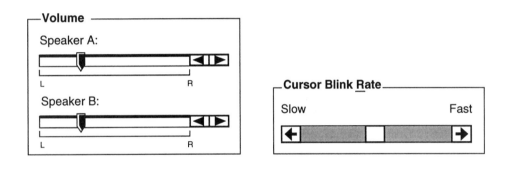

Sliders, however, are not as precise as an alphanumeric indication, unless an entry field is provided. They also consume more screen space than other kinds of fields, and they can be more complex to operate.

Proper Usage. Sliders are used to set an attribute when a limited range of continuous, relatively fine, possible settings exist. The choices must increase or decrease in some well-known, predictable, and easily understood way. Spatial representation of the attribute should enhance comprehension and interpretation and be sufficiently accurate.

SLIDER GUIDELINES

General

- Use standard sliders whenever available.

Use of standard system sliders will speed system learning.

Labels

- Provide meaningful, clear, and consistent labels.

Labels should clearly reflect the quality being displayed.

Scale

- Show a complete range of choices.
- Mark the low, intermediate, and high ends of the scale.
- Provide scale interval markings, where possible.
- Provide consistent increments.
- Permit the user to change the units of measure.
- If the precise value of a quantity represented is important, display the value set in an adjacent entry/display field.

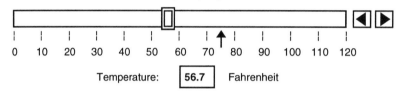

Provide a complete range of choices on the scale. Mark the low, intermediate, and high ends of the scale. For example, volumes may be indicated by low, normal, and high. Provide scale interval markings at consistent increments. Allow the user to change the units of measure, for example, a temperature from Fahrenheit to centigrade. If the precise value of a quantity represented is critical, display the set value in an adjacent entry/display field. This will also permit typed entry of the desired value.

Slider Arm

- If the user cannot change the value shown in a slider, do not display a slider arm.

If the user cannot change the value shown in a slider, do not display a slider arm. Fill in the shaft in a distinctive way to indicate relative setting, as illustrated in the guideline for Proportions.

Slider Buttons

- Provide slider buttons to permit movement by the smallest increment.
- If the user cannot change the value shown in a slider, do not display slider buttons.

Provide slider buttons to permit movement by the smallest increment. Movement is achieved by pointing and clicking. If the user cannot change the value shown in a slider, do not display slider buttons.

Detents

- Provide detents to set values that have special meaning.
- Permit the user to change the detent value.

For values that have special meaning, provide detents that can be changed by the user.

Proportions

- To indicate the proportion of a value being displayed, fill the slider shaft in some visually distinctive way.
  — For horizontal sliders, fill from left to right.
  — For vertical sliders, fill from bottom to top.

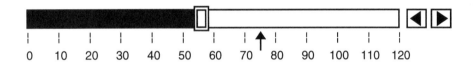

When the proportion of a value is also important, provide proportional indicators by filling in the slider shaft in a distinctive way. Fill from left to right and bottom to top.

MARK TOGGLES

Description

- A menu item that toggles between being active and not active.
- When the item is active:
  — For non-exclusive choices, a check mark (✔) is displayed next to the item description.
  — For mutually exclusive choices, another distinctive symbol such as a diamond (◊) or circle (o) is displayed next to the item description.
- When the item is not active, no mark or symbol appears.

Purpose

- To activate or deactivate an attribute by setting one menu item.

Advantages/Disadvantages

+ Provides visual indication of state of item.
+ Provides quick access.

− Not always visible.

Proper Usage

- To designate that an item or feature be active or inactive over a relatively long period of time.
- To provide a reminder that an item or feature is active or inactive.

Description. Mark toggles, illustrated in Figure 11.14, are menu items that toggle between active and not active. When it is active, an indicator is displayed adjacent to the item description. For non-exclusive choices, a check mark (✔) is displayed; for mutually exclusive choices, another distinctive symbol such as a diamond (◊) or circle (○) is displayed. When the item is not active, no mark or symbol will appear.

Examples of items using mark toggles might be: having a specific application automatically loaded after the system is loaded, having windows automatically reduced to icons when they are made inactive, or to make a setting without requiring a dialog box.

Purpose. To activate or deactivate an attribute by setting one menu item.

Advantages/Disadvantages. Mark toggles provide a visual indication of state of item. They are accessed quickly but may not always be visible.

Proper Usage. Mark toggles are best suited to items or features that remain active or inactive over relatively long periods of time. They provide good reminders of the state that exists.

Figure 11.14. Mark toggles.

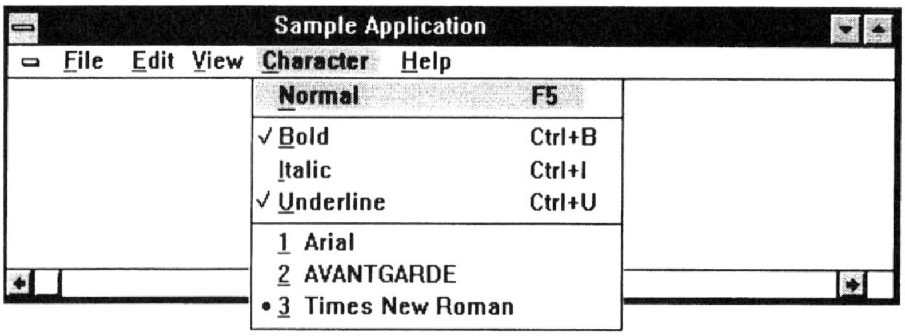

MARK TOGGLE GUIDELINES

- Position the indicator directly to the left of the option.
- For situations where several non-exclusive choices may be selected, consider including one alternative that deselects all the items and reverts the state to the "normal" condition.

Position the mark toggle indicator directly to the left of the menu option. In situations where several non-exclusive choices may be selected on one menu, consider including one alternative that deselects all the items and reverts the state to the "normal" condition, as illustrated in Figure 11.14.

TOGGLED MENU ITEMS

Description

- One menu item command that toggles between the current state and its alternative state.
- When the menu item is first displayed, it reflects the alternative state to the condition that currently exists.
- When the displayed menu item is selected, the menu item changes to reflect the opposite action.

Purpose

- To use a single menu item to activate one alternative of a two-state command setting.

Advantages/Disadvantages

- + Shortens menus.
- + Decreases visual clutter.
- + Faster comprehension of action.
- + Provides quick access.

- − Not always visible.
- − Limited in use to commands.

Proper Usage

- To designate two opposite commands that are accessed frequently.
- When the menu item displayed will clearly indicate that the opposite condition currently exists.

Figure 11.15.   Toggled menu items.

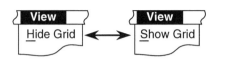

Description. Toggled menu items are one menu item command that toggles back and forth between the current state and its alternative state. When the menu item is first displayed, it reflects the alternative state to the condition that currently exists. For example, in Figure 11.15, if a background grid is currently being displayed, the menu item reads "Hide Grid." When Hide Grid is selected, the grid is removed and the menu item dynamically changes to reflect the opposite action. It will now read "Show Grid." When a grid is again requested, it will change back to Hide Grid.

Purpose. To use a single menu item to designate and activate the one, opposite, alternative of a two-state command setting.

Advantages/Disadvantages. Toggled menu items shorten menus, decrease visual clutter, provide quicker access, and foster faster comprehension of the command action. Because they are on a menu, however, the actions themselves are not always visible. The opposite action reflecting the current state of the attribute, since it too is not visible, can cause uncertainty for novice users concerning what the state actually is. Toggled menu items are also limited in use to commands only.

Proper Usage. Use toggled menu items to designate two opposite commands that are accessed frequently. The menu item displayed must be one that clearly indicates that the opposite condition currently exists.

TOGGLED MENU ITEM GUIDELINES

- Provide a meaningful, fully spelled out description of the action.
- Begin with a verb that unambiguously represents the outcome of the command.
- Use mixed-case letters with the first letter of each word capitalized.

The menu captions should clearly state what will happen when the menu item action is requested. It is most meaningful to begin the command with a verb.

SCROLL BAR

Description

- An elongated rectangular container consisting of:
  — A scroll area.
  — A slider box or elevator inside.
  — Arrows or anchors at either end.
- Available, if needed, in primary and secondary windows, and some controls.
- May be oriented vertically or horizontally at the window's edge.

Purpose

- To find and view information that takes more space than the allotted display space.

Advantages/Disadvantages

- + Permit viewing data of unlimited size.

- – Consumes screen space.
- – Can be cumbersome to operate.

Proper Use

- When more information is available than the window space for displaying it.

Description. A scroll bar is an elongated rectangular container consisting of a scroll area, a slider box, or elevator inside the scroll bar, and arrows or anchors at either end. They may be placed, if needed, in primary and secondary windows and some controls. They may be oriented vertically or horizontally at the right or bottom of a window. Scroll bars come in a variety of styles, as illustrated in Figure 11.16.

Purpose. Scroll bars are used to find and view information that occupies more space than the allotted display space.

Advantages/Disadvantages. While they permit viewing data of unlimited size, they do consume screen space and can be cumbersome to operate.

Proper Use. Use a scroll bar, or bars, when more information is available than the window space for displaying it.

SCROLL BAR GUIDELINES

General

- Provide a scroll bar when nonvisible information must be seen.

Scroll Area or Container

- To indicate that scrolling is available, a scroll area or container should be provided.
    - It should be constructed of a filled-in bar displayed in a technique that visually contrasts with the window and screen body background.

Scroll Slider Box or Handle

- To indicate the location and amount of information being viewed, a slider box or handle should be provided.
    - It should be constructed of a movable and sizable open area of the scroll area displayed in a technique that contrasts with the scroll area.
    - It should indicate by its position, spatially, the relative location in the file of the information being viewed.
    - It should indicate by its size, proportionately, the percentage of the available information in the file being viewed.

Scroll Directional Arrows

- To indicate the direction that scrolling may be performed, directional arrows should be provided.
    - They should be constructed of arrows in small boxes with backgrounds contrasting with the scroll area.

Selection

- When the slider box/handle has been selected, highlight it in some visually distinctive way.

Location

- A vertical (top-to-bottom) scroll bar should be positioned to the right of the window.
- A horizontal (left-to-right) scroll bar should be positioned at the bottom of the window.

Size

- A vertical scroll bar should be the height of the scrollable portion of the window body.
- A horizontal scroll bar should be at least one-half the width of the scrollable portion of the window body.

Current State Indication

- Whenever the window size or information position changes, the scroll bar components must also change, reflecting the current state.
- Include scroll bars in all sizable windows.

— If no information is currently available through scrolling in a particular direction, the relevant directional arrow should be subdued or grayed.

Directional Preference

- Where the choice exists, vertical (top-to-bottom) scrolling is preferred to horizontal (left-to-right) scrolling.

A scroll bar provides a method or control to permit display of information that may not always fit within a window displayed on a screen. One should only be included when scrolling may be necessary.

Components. In today's systems, scroll bars come in a variety of styles, as illustrated in Figure 11.16. Scroll bars consist of three elements: a scroll area or container, a slider box or handle that moves within a track made by the scroll area/container, and directional scroll arrows.

Scroll area or container. The scroll area or, as it is sometimes called, the scroll container, is an elongated rectangular-shaped bar. Its presence indicates scrolling is available. It usually is constructed of a filled-in area displayed in a technique that visually contrasts with the window and screen body background. The chosen display technique should be of moderate intensity, not too powerful or too subtle. A powerful technique will be distracting, a subtle technique may be overlooked.

Slider box or handle. To indicate the location and amount of information being viewed, a slider box or, as it is sometimes called, a scroll handle, is included within the scroll area/container. It is constructed of a movable and sizable portion of the scroll area displayed in a technique that contrasts with the scroll area. It should indicate by its position, spatially, the relative location in the file of the information being viewed. It should indicate by its size, proportionately, the percentage of the available information in the file being viewed. The usability of the slider box or handle can be further enhanced by displaying within it the page number of page-organized material being viewed.

Directional or scroll arrows. To indicate the direction that scrolling may be performed, directional or scroll arrows are also included. They are constructed of variously shaped arrows in small boxes with backgrounds contrasting with the scroll area/container. They are most often located at each end of the scroll bar, but some systems locate them adjacent to one another within the scroll area/container itself.

Placing directional arrows at opposite ends of the scroll bar, as is done by Macintosh, OSF/Motif, Microsoft Windows, and OS/2 Presentation Manager, is conceptually the clearest. The mouse pointer is moved in the same direction, away from the current position, when either the scroll arrow or scroll handle is manipulated. The distance the directional arrows are separated, however,

Figure 11.16. Representative scroll bars.

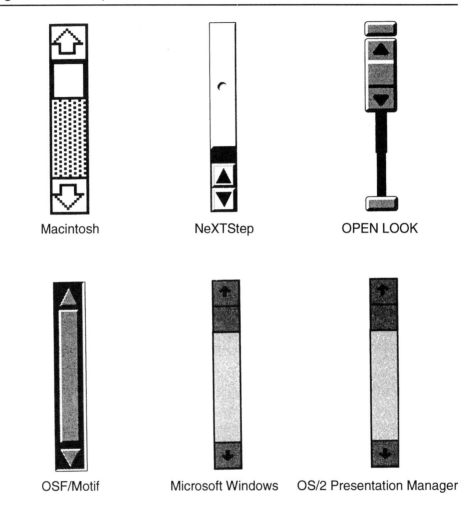

causes increased effort when a window's contents must be adjusted by scrolling in opposite directions.

NeXTStep solves the direction-switching problem by positioning the directional arrows adjacent to one another at one end of the scroll bar. While the forward-backward scrolling is made more efficient, the spatial correspondence between the beginning, middle, and end of the data is lost.

OPEN LOOK takes another approach, placing the directional arrows at opposite ends of the slider box/handle to maintain the desirable spatial correspondence while at the same time minimizing their separation. Since during a continuous scrolling operation the directional arrows move as the slider box/

handle moves, OPEN LOOK automatically moves the mouse pointer to keep it aligned with the scroll arrow. This eliminates the need for the user to move the pointer during the continuous scrolling operation, but it requires that the user relinquish control of the mouse operation and may be disorienting.

All of the advantages and disadvantages of these different approaches to scrolling are still not well understood and can only be experimentally resolved.

Scrolling operation.   The scrolling movement can be performed in several ways. The most common actions involve grabbing the slider box/handle and moving it in the desired direction, or selecting the proper directional arrow. Clicking a mouse button while selecting a directional arrow moves the contents of a window one line. Pressing the mouse button scrolls the window's contents continuously until the button is released. NeXTStep also provides another more efficient process. A region of the scroll area/container can also be selected, automatically moving the slider box/handle to that point and displaying the proper window contents.

Based upon scrolling research (see Bury et al., 1982), movement of the window data usually follows the window-up or telescope approach, whereby the window moves around over data that appears fixed in location. This causes the data in a window to move in the direction opposite the one indicated by the directional arrow or the direction of movement of the scroll container/handle. Scrolling using window systems, however, seems to be especially mistake prone, users often assuming the arrows will move the data in the same direction as the directional arrow or scroll container/handle. In other words, it is sensed that the data moves under the window, not the window over the data (Billingsley, 1988). Why this happens is open to conjecture. Billingsley speculates that because windows are seen to "move" physically on screens, when data scrolls or moves in a window, people may conclude the data must be moving because the window remains still during the scrolling operation. Or, because of the close physical proximity of the directional arrows in scroll bars to the data, people may feel the arrows are acting on the data, not the window. The implication is that the scrolling procedure should be rethought and restudied. Some recent applications have devised scrolling methods through actually pointing at the window data.

Selection.   When the slider box/handle has been selected, highlight it in some visually distinctive way. Most systems do provide some visual feedback of this kind. NeXTStep, however, does not.

Location.   While again no universal agreement exists, the majority of systems locate the vertical (top-to-bottom) scroll bar to the right of the window and the horizontal (left-to-right) scroll bar at the bottom of the window.

Size.   A vertical scroll bar should be the height of the scrollable portion of the window body. A horizontal scroll bar should be at least one-half the width of the scrollable portion of the window body.

Current state indication.   Whenever the window size or information position changes, the scroll bar components must also change, reflecting the current state of the scrolling process. Providing accurate information about the scrolling location facilitates user navigation and makes it easier to reposition the slider box/container. Include scroll bars in all sizable windows.

If scrolling cannot be performed in a particular direction, the relevant arrow box should be reduced in contrast or grayed.

If all the information in a window is displayed and no information is available for scrolling, both directional arrows should be reduced in contrast or grayed. OPEN LOOK is one of the few systems that takes this action.

Directional preferences.   Where the choice exists, people prefer and deal better with vertical (top-to-bottom) scrolling rather than horizontal (left-to-toright) scrolling.

COMMANDS

Purpose

- Actions that manipulate objects in ways described by the command label.
- They are immediately executed when selected.
- Once executed they cease to be relevant.

Presentation Methods

- Commands may be presented as:
  — Buttons.
  — Items in a menu.

Commands are actions that manipulate objects in ways described by the command label, for example "print" to print a document, "open" to open a file. They are immediately executed when selected, at which point they cease to be relevant. Commands may be presented in two different controls, buttons or menu items.

COMMAND GUIDELINES

Labels

General

- Provide a label for each command.
- Use labels that indicate:
  — The purpose of the command, or
  — The result of what happens when the command is selected.
- Use familiar, short, clear, concise words.
- Use distinctive wording.

- Use mixed-case, with the first letter capitalized.
- Begin commands with verbs or adjectives, not nouns.
- Preferably, use only one word.
  — If multiple words are required for clarity, capitalize the first letter of each significant word.
  — Do not use sentences as labels.
- Provide an ellipsis (. . .) to indicate that another window will result from selection of a command.
  — Do not use the ellipsis when the following window is a confirmation or warning.

Dynamic Labels

- As contexts change, dynamically change the label wording to make its meaning clearer in the new context.
  — For example, after a cut operation, "Undo" may be changed to "Undo Cut."

Provide a clear label for each command indicating the purpose of the command, or the result of what happens when the command is selected. Preferably, use single-word commands. If multiple words are required for clarity, capitalize the first letter of each significant word. Provide an ellipsis to indicate that another window will result from selection of a command, but do not use the ellipsis when the resulting window is a confirmation or warning. As contexts change, dynamically change the label wording to make its meaning clearer in the new context (toggled item). For example, after a cut operation, "Undo" may be changed to "Undo Cut."

Disabled Commands

- When a command is not available, indicate its disabled status by displaying it grayed or subdued.
- If selection of a disabled command is attempted, provide a message in the information area that the "Help" function will explain why it is disabled.

When a command is not available, indicate its disabled status by displaying it grayed or subdued. If selection of a disabled command is attempted, provide a message in the information area that the "Help" function will explain why it is disabled. Help, of course, must provide the proper explanation.

Navigation and Selection

General

- Permit multiple methods for selecting commands.

Keyboard Equivalents

- Assign a mnemonic for each command.
- A mnemonic should be as meaningful as possible. Use:
  - The first letter of the command, or if duplications exist,
  - The first letter of another word in the command, or
  - Another significant non-vowel letter in the command.
- For standard commands, use mnemonics provided by the tool set.

Keyboard Accelerators

- Assign keyboard accelerators for frequently used commands.
- For standard commands, use keyboard accelerators provided by the tool set.

Permit commands to be implemented through the keyboard as well. Provide keyboard equivalents or accelerators.

SELECTING THE PROPER CONTROLS

Providing the proper control or controls is critical to system success. The proper control will enable a person to make needed selections, entries and changes fast, efficiently, and with few mistakes. Improper selection most often leads to the opposite result.

This section will begin with a survey of some research addressing selection of the proper control. Then, the criteria that must be considered in control selection will be summarized. Finally, some selection guidelines will be presented.

ENTRY FIELDS VERSUS SELECTION FIELDS—A COMPARISON

Experimental determinations of the advantages and disadvantages of using either entry fields or selection fields for data collection on a screen have rarely been attempted. Two studies (Gould et al., 1988; Greene et al., 1988) have performed such a comparison.

Choosing a Type of Field

- For familiar, meaningful data, choose the technique that, in theory, requires the fewest number of keystrokes to complete.
- If the data is unfamiliar, or prone to typing errors, choose a selection technique.

Both studies found that if the data to be entered was familiar, the technique that required the minimum theoretical number of keystrokes to complete the task was the fastest. Theoretical keystrokes are the minimum number possible, excluding miskeys and erroneous cursor or selection movements. However, as the data became less familiar or became subject to spelling or typing errors, the minimum keystroke principle broke down. Selection techniques, and the reminders and structure they provide, become advantageous. The point at which the changeover occurs is not known, and it would be influenced by the nature of the task and the nature of the user.

These studies point out the advantages of the techniques that permit both typed entry and selection to enter the data (spin box, drop-down combination box, and attached combination box).

Aided Versus Unaided Entry

Greene at al. (1988) also compared unaided typed entry (the entire field had to be keyed) with aided entry (the system automatically and immediately completed the field when enough characters were keyed to make the desired data known). They found that autocompletion was preferred over unaided entry methods, and it was also the fastest. Autocompletion was also preferable to, and faster than, some selection methods.

The result is that, where possible, autocompletion of entry fields should be provided. Autocompletion will minimize the user's effort by reducing input time and keystrokes. It should also enhance the user's opinion of the system.

CONTROL SELECTION CRITERIA

Selection of the proper control depends on several factors. First is the structure and characteristics of the property or data itself. Other considerations include the nature of the task, the nature of the user, and the limitations of the display screen itself.

Property or data considerations reflect the characteristics of the data itself. Some kinds of controls are very restrictive in that they permit only specific kinds of information with specific qualities to be presented within them. Some kinds of controls may not be as restrictive concerning a data's qualities, but they are not well suited to the kind of data being used. Data considerations include the following:

- Is the property or data *mutually exclusive* or *nonexclusive*? Does entry/selection require single or multiple items?
- Is the property or data *discrete* or *continuous*? Discrete data can be meaningfully specified and categorized, while continuous cannot.
- Is the property or data *limited* or *unlimited* in scope? If limited, how many items will the data normally not exceed?
- Is the property or data *fixed* or *variable* in list length? Is there always a fixed number of items, or will it vary?
- Is the property or data ordered in a *predictable* or *non-predictable* fashion? If predictable, will the user be able to anticipate the next, non-visible, item?

- Can the property or data be *represented pictorially*? Will a picture or graphic be as meaningful as a textual description?

Task considerations reflect the nature of the job. Considerations include the following:

- *How often* is an item *entered* or *selected*?
- *How often* is an item *changed*?
- How *precise* must the item be entered or selected?

User considerations reflect the characteristics of the user. Important considerations:

- How much *training* in control operation will be provided?
- How *meaningful* or *known* is the property or data for the user?
- How *rememberable* or *learnable* is the property or data for the user?
- How *frequently used* will the system be?
- Is the user an *experienced typist*?

Display considerations reflect the characteristics of the screen and hardware.

- How much *screen space* is available to display the various controls?

Choosing a Control Form

In light of the above considerations, and the known characteristics of the various controls, some guidance in control selection can be presented.

Choosing an Entry Field or a Selection Field

Table 11.1 provides a decision chart contrasting standard entry field with selection fields. The term "selection field" is generic, referring to all members of the graphical system family of menus and controls recently described, except entry fields. Selection fields include menus like pull-downs and controls like radio buttons and fixed list boxes. The term selection field does not imply that a field cannot be completed using the keyboard, as some controls are combination fields, permitting selection or keyed entry. Some controls also provide keyboard accelerators.

Choosing a Type of Selection Control

Table 11.2 provides a series of recommendations for when to use the assorted graphical selection controls.

Table 11.1. Choosing a selection field or an entry field.

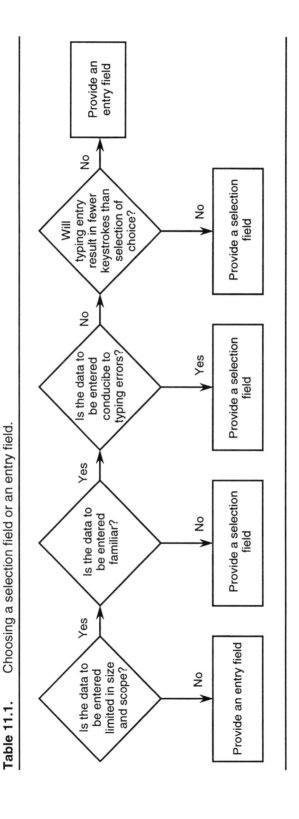

Table 11.2.   Suggested uses for graphical selection controls.

1.	*IF:*	*USE:*

- *Mutually exclusive* alternatives.
- Discrete data.
- Best represented verbally.
- Very limited in number (2–8).
- Typed entry is never necessary.

AND:
- Infrequently selected.
- Can never change.   } Radio buttons
- Adequate screen space is available.

OR:
- Infrequently selected.
- Rarely or never changes.   } Pop-up menu
- Adequate screen space not available.

OR:
- Frequently selected.   } Pull-down menu
- Rarely or never changes.

2.	*IF:*	*USE:*

- *Mutually exclusive* alternatives.
- Discrete data.
- Best represented verbally.
- Potentially large in number (9 or more).
- Can change frequently.
- Typed entry is never necessary.

AND:
- Adequate screen space is available   Fixed list box

OR:
- Adequate screen space not available   Drop-down/pop-up list box

3.	*IF:*	*USE:*

- *Mutually exclusive* alternatives.
- Discrete data.   } Palette
- Best represented graphically.
- Rarely change.

Table 11.2. *(Continued).*

4.	IF:	USE:

- *Mutually exclusive* alternatives.
- Infrequently selected.
- Infrequently changed.
- Well-known, easily remembered data.
- Predictable, consecutive data.
- Typed entry sometimes desirable.
- Adequate screen space not available.

Spin box

5.	IF:	USE:

- *Mutually exclusive* alternatives.
- Discrete data.
- Best represented verbally.
- Potentially large in number (9 or more).
- Can change frequently.
- Typed entry is sometimes desirable.

AND:
- Adequate screen space is available   Attached combination box

OR:
- Adequate screen space not available   Drop-down/pop-up combination box

6.	IF:	USE:

- *Mutually exclusive* alternatives.
- Continuous data with limited range of settings.
- Choices increase/decrease in a well-known, predictable way.
- Spatial representation enhances comprehension.

Slider

7.	IF:	USE:

- *Nonexclusive* alternatives.
- Discrete data.
- Best represented verbally.
- Very limited in number (2–8).
- Typed entry is never necessary.

Table 11.2. *(Continued).*

IF:	USE:
AND:	
• Infrequently selected.	
• Can never change.	Check boxes
• Adequate screen space is available.	
OR:	
• Infrequently selected.	
• Rarely or never changes.	Pop-up menu
• Adequate screen space not available.	
OR:	
• Frequently selected.	Pull-down menu
• Rarely or never changes.	

8. IF:	USE:
• *Nonexclusive* alternatives.	
• Discrete data.	
• Best represented verbally.	
• Potentially large in number (9 or more).	
• Can change frequently.	
• Typed entry is never necessary.	
AND:	
• Adequate screen space is available.	Fixed list box
OR:	
• Adequate screen space not available.	Drop-down/pop-up list box

Choosing Between Using Buttons or Menus for Commands

Determining the proper way to present a command also depends on several factors. The following considerations are involved in choosing the correct command form:

- Is the command part of a *standard tool set*?
- The total *number* of commands in the application.
- The *complexity* of the commands.
- The *frequency* with which commands are used.
- Whether or not the command is used in association *with another control*.

Guidelines for choosing the proper command form are presented in Table 11.3.

Table 11.3.   Choosing a command form.

If the commands:	Use:
• Are standard commands provided by a tool set.	Forms provided by the tool set
• Total seven or more, and can be arranged hierarchically into groups.	Menu bar and pull-downs
• Total six or fewer, and application is simple.	Buttons in a window
• Total six or fewer, are selected frequently, and affect an entire window.	Buttons in a window
• Are used with other controls, or are complicated and need to be simplified.	Buttons in a dialog box
• Are sometimes used frequently, and are sometimes used infrequently.	Buttons in a dialog box
• Are frequently accessed, and have only two conditions.	Toggled menu
• Are infrequently accessed, and have only two conditions.	Toggled command buttons

CHAPTER 11 EXAMPLES

Example 1. Improper and proper presentation of buttons in a dialog box.

Screen 1–1. Poor design and display of buttons. Problems include: (1) The buttons are split between the left and right side of the screen, causing a wide separation. Positioning to the left, from a screen usage and flow standpoint, is illogical. (2) Differences in sizes exist between buttons. "OK," a very frequently used button, is the smallest, slowing down selection speed if a pointer is used. (3) There appears to be redundancy in button use and purpose. How does "OK" differ from "Save?" What does "Edit" do? (4) From an organization standpoint, standard and application buttons appear to be intermixed. (5) The "Back" and "Next" actions are widely separated, making fast reversal of actions more difficult.

Screen 1–2.   A much better button design and presentation. Enhancements include: (1) The buttons are located at the bottom of the screen, in a position following the screen usage flow. (2) Button size is standardized, presenting generally larger targets. (3) The seemingly redundant buttons are eliminated. (4) Application buttons are grouped separately from standard buttons. Button groupings are created through a slightly larger spacing between "Next" and "OK." (5) "Back" and "Next" are positioned together for fast paging reversal.

Example 2.   Improper and proper use of a control.

Control 1.   The names of states must be selected using radio buttons. Problems include: (1) The large number of choices presented makes scanning very difficult. (2) Are all the state abbreviations familiar to you, and all users? (3) The organization of states must have been established by a lottery. The name of the state I want is Mississippi. How do I find it in the array?

```
┌─ State: ─────────────────────────────────────────┐
│                                                   │
│   o ME      o NH      o LA      o WA      o MA     │
│                                                   │
│   o AK      o MI      o ID      o IN      o AL     │
│                                                   │
│   o HI      o IL      o NC      o TX      o MO     │
│                                                   │
│   o NY      o VT      o CA      o WI      o ND     │
│                                                   │
│   o IA      o MD      o CT      o AR      o OH     │
│                                                   │
│   o FL      o KY      o SC      o NV      o NM     │
│                                                   │
│   o AZ      o MT      o WV      o NE      o VA     │
│                                                   │
│   o CO      o KS      o NJ      o PA      o OR     │
│                                                   │
│   o SD      o GA      o TN      o DE      o OK     │
│                                                   │
│   o RI      o UT      o WY      o MS      o MN     │
│                                                   │
└───────────────────────────────────────────────────┘
```

Control 2.   A much better alternative, a drop-down/pop-up combination box. If the state name is known, it can be typed in the field. Ideally, typing the state code, if known, will also be acceptable. If the name of a particular state is unknown, or its spelling unclear, the drop-down/pop-up can be retrieved and the state name selected from the list presented. Ideally, also, a misspelled keyed state name will still be correctly identified by the system and displayed properly.

State: | Mississippi | ▼

Example 3. Improper and proper use of a control.

Screen 3–1. A listing of names is being collected. Courtesy title selected through list box, last name, first name, and middle initial are typed. The problem: The task is heavily keyboard intensive. To select a title requires shifting to an alternative device control such as a mouse. This slows down the keying process and is awkward.

Name

Title:
- Chief
- Doctor
- Miss
- Mrs
- Mister
- Ms
- Professor

Last: [_____]

First: [_____]

Middle Initial: [____]

[OK]   [Apply]   [Cancel]

Screen 3–2. The solution: Collect courtesy title using a pop-up/drop/down combination box. Familiar titles may be keyed, along with the remainder of the name data. Rare or unusual titles may be identified by selecting, displaying and searching the listing of all alternatives. The title may then be entered in the field by selecting from the list or keying it into the field.

Name

Title: [_____▼]

Last: [_____]

First: [_____]

Middle Initial: [____]

[OK]   [Apply]   [Cancel]

Example 4.   Improper and proper use of controls.

Screen 4–1. A collection of seashells is being cataloged by class and order. Entry fields are provided for the task. The catalog process includes typing words like "Cephalopoda" and "Eulamellibranchia." The process is slow and conducive to spelling errors.

```
┌─────────────────────────────────────────────────────────────┐
│                         Seashells                            │
│  ──────────────────────────────────────────────────────     │
│                                                              │
│        Item Number:    [            ]                        │
│                                                              │
│        Class:          [                                ]    │
│                                                              │
│        Order:          [                                ]    │
│                                                              │
│                                                              │
│              [  OK  ]      [ Apply ]      [ Cancel ]         │
│                                                              │
└─────────────────────────────────────────────────────────────┘
```

Screen 4–2. The solution: Present "Class" and "Order" in fixed list boxes from which the proper varieties are selected. This will speed up the entry process and eliminate the possibility of spelling errors. To make the entire procedure a selection task, also make "Item Number" a selective and incrementable spin box.

```
┌─────────────────────────────────────────────────────────────┐
│                         Seashells                            │
│  ──────────────────────────────────────────────────────     │
│                                                              │
│          Item Number:    [          ] ▲▼                     │
│                                                              │
│                 Class:   ┌──────────────────┐                │
│                          │ Amphineura       │                │
│                          │ Cephalopoda      │                │
│                          │ Gastropoda       │                │
│                          │ [Pelecypoda]     │                │
│                          │ Scaphopoda       │                │
│                          └──────────────────┘                │
│                                                              │
│                 Order:   ┌──────────────────┐                │
│                          │ Eulamellibranchia │               │
│                          │ Filibranchia     │                │
│                          │ Palaeoconcha     │                │
│                          │ [Protobranchia]  │                │
│                          │ Septibranchia    │                │
│                          └──────────────────┘                │
│              [  OK  ]      [ Apply ]      [ Cancel ]         │
│                                                              │
└─────────────────────────────────────────────────────────────┘
```

Example 5.   Improper and proper use of a control.

Screen 5–1.   An international corporation is setting up a world-wide account data base. Names from dozens of different countries are added each day. Country is collected though using a spin box. Is this proper usage for a Spin Box?

Account

Name:

Street:

City/State/Post Cd:

Country:

OK   Apply   Cancel

Screen 5–2.   With a spin box, the following non-visible choice must be capable of being anticipated. If not, tedious clicking and searching to find the correct choice might have to be performed. (What country follows Greece in the worldwide alphabetical listing of countries today? Guatemala—at least at this writing). The data in spin boxes should be stable, not often changing. This quality does not accurately reflect the state of world countries today.

A better choice would be an attached combination box. Well-known country names can be typed and less well-known found in the listing. Due to the dynamic nature of country names, frequent reference to the list can be expected. Permanently displaying the list avoids the step of retrieving it when needed. The attached listing also permits scanning several names at one time, alleviating the predictability problem. Names can also be easily added or changed as needed.

12

Organizing and Laying Out Windows

Having determined what screen controls are needed and when they are needed, the controls must be presented clearly and meaningfully in the work area of the window. Proper presentation and organization will encourage quick and correct information comprehension and the fastest possible execution of application features.

A screen may, however, also contain a number of additional elements to aid in its use. Components like title, headings, borders, and prompting messages must be incorporated in the most effective manner possible.

STEP 8

- Identify other important window components.
  — Title.
  — Special fields.
  — Headings.
  — Window borders.
  — Prompting messages.
- Arrange controls to encourage quick and accurate information comprehension and control execution.
  — Provide organizational meaningfulness and efficiency.
  — Avoid visual clutter.
  — Create groupings.
  — Provide alignment and balance.

To begin, these other screens elements will be described and guidelines presented for their design and use. Then, screen organizational and layout principles will be detailed.

OTHER WINDOW COMPONENTS
Window Title

- All windows must have a title located in a centered position at the top.
  — Exception: Windows containing messages.
- Clearly and concisely describe the purpose of the window.
- Spell out fully using an upper-case font.
- If title truncation is necessary, truncate from right to left.
- If presented above a menu bar, display with a background that contrasts with the bar.

The window title should be positioned at the top center and fully spelled out using upper-case or capital letters. Using an upper-case font will give it the needed moderate emphasis, aiding setting it off from the screen body (IBM's SAA CUA displays the title, like all screen components, in mixed-case letters). Windows containing messages, however, need not have a title. The title should clearly and concisely describe the screen's purpose. If the window appears as a result of a previous selection, the title should clearly reflect the wording of the selection made to retrieve it. For small windows where title truncation is necessary, truncate from right to left.

If the title appears above menu bar, the title's background should contrast with that of the bar. A recommendation is to use the same background color and caption color as the screen body. A title can always be identified by its topmost location on the screen, so using a color different from other screen components may add to visual confusion.

Special Fields

- Display any special fields:
  — In the right corner of the title line if there is only one such field.
  — In the left and right corners of the title line if there are two fields.
- Use a mixed-case font.
- Maintain a consistent positioning of the same field on all screens.

Display special fields, such as file names, in a consistent location in all windows. Display in a mixed-case font, or the font style in which the information is normally found. If multiple special fields are needed, provide screen balance by displaying them in the left and right corners of the title line.

HEADINGS

Headings are used to give related controls a common identity. In addition to providing meaning, they foster the concept of grouping. Three kinds of headings may be incorporated on graphic screens: section, subsection or row, and field group.

Section Headings

- Locate section headings above their related screen controls, separated by one space line.
- Indent the captions a minimum of five spaces to the right of the start of the heading.
- Fully spell out in an upper-case font.
  — If a larger or bolder typeface is available, they may be displayed larger or bolder in mixed case.
- Display in normal intensity.
- Section headings may be left- or right-aligned.

        DOCUMENT
        xxxxxJustification: o None
                            o Left
                            o Even
                            o Center

                Contents: □ Preface
                            □ Illustrations
                            □ Index
                            □ Bibliography

Sections headings should be visually distinguishable through a combination of location and font style. They should not be overly emphasized, however. Displaying in upper case and positioning to the left will provide the moderate emphasis needed. Use of a slightly larger or slightly bolder typeface in mixed case is also acceptable, if available. IBM's SAA CUA gives visual emphasis to section headings through higher intensity in a mixed-case font. Higher intensity should be reserved for the more important screen data. Mixed case should only be used if it can be made slightly larger or bolder than the field captions.

If right-aligned or justified captions are used, an indention greater than five spaces may be necessary to set off the heading from the captions properly. Other techniques than positional cues may be used to set off section headings. Choices may include different style characters, underlining, etc. The method chosen should always permit easy, but subtle, discrimination of the section headings from other components of the screen. It should also be visually compatible with other screen components. Whatever methods are chosen, they should be consistently followed throughout a family of screens or a system.

Subsection or Row Headings

- Locate to the left of the:
  — Row of associated fields.
  — Topmost row of a group of associated fields.

- Fully spell out in an upper-case font.
- Separate from the adjacent caption through the use of a unique symbol, such as two "greater than" signs or a filled-in arrow.
- Separate the symbol from the heading by one space and from the caption by a minimum of three spaces.
- Display in normal intensity.
- Subsection or row headings may be left- or right-aligned.

AUTO ▶   Make: [   ]   Model: [   ]

                 Year: [   ]   Color: [   ]

REGISTRATIONx▶xxx Number: [   ] Expires: [   ]

A meaningful convention to designate subsection or row headings is a filled-in arrow or "greater than" sign. It directs the viewers attention to the right and indicates that everything that follows refers to this category. Subsections should be broken by space lines. They may also be right-aligned instead of left-aligned as follows:

AUTO ▶
REGISTRATION ▶

Field Group Headings

- Center field group headings above the captions to which they apply.
- Relate to those captions by a solid line.
- Spell out fully in an upper-case font.
- Display in normal intensity.

——————— AUTOMOBILE ———————
Driver   License Number

[   ]   [   ]

[   ]   [   ]

[   ]   [   ]

Occasionally a group heading above a series of multiple-occurring captions may be needed. It should be centered above the captions to which it applies and related to them through a solid line extending to each end of the grouping. This will provide closure to the grouping.

BORDERS

Line borders can be used in variety of ways on screens. Borders can enhance separation of elements, such as by setting a window off from a screen background. Borders can also strengthen groupings, by tying related elements together. Below are some general guidelines for using line borders, followed by some specific guidelines for windows and menu bars. Control borders will be described shortly.

General Considerations

- Incorporate rules or lines to create groupings of related information.
- Restrict line and border weights to a maximum of three variations.
- Create lines consistent in height and length.
- Use rules and borders sparingly.

Rules. Lines or rules assist in focusing attention on related information. They also aid in separating groupings of information from one another. Rules also serve to guide the viewer's eye in the desired direction. Use a standard hierarchy for rules, the thickest to differentiate major components, the thinnest for minor separation.

Minimize line thickness variations. Too many variations in line thicknesses on a screen create clutter and are distracting. Use no more than three line weights at one time.

Consistent line widths and heights. Similarly, variations in line widths and heights are distracting. Create horizontal lines of equal widths across the screen and vertical lines of equal height whenever possible.

Use lines and borders sparingly. Too many lines and borders on a screen also create clutter and can be distracting. Like any display technique, lines and borders must be used sparingly.

Window and Menu Bar Borders

- For menu bar pull-downs and windows:
  - — Incorporate surrounding borders.
  - — Leave a space frame, preferably two blank spaces but minimally one blank space, between the pull-down or window text and the border.

Surrounding borders aid in focusing attention on menu bar pull-downs and windows. They also isolate the contents of these elements. Include a line border around an element of a screen when it is presented and attention must be directed to it. Simple background differences in color or shade by themselves are not as effective in drawing attention. Line borders also make a screen appear less complicated.

Provide "breathing space" around text in pull-downs and windows. A common problem with windows is that the text within a window has no outer margins. The text from one window runs directly into the text from an underlying window, making reading more difficult and giving the screen a cluttered look. Preferably, leave a minimum of two spaces (but at least one space) between a window's text and its borders.

PROMPTING MESSAGES

- Incorporate prompting on a screen, as necessary:
  - In a position just preceding the part, or parts, of a screen to which they apply.
  - In a manner that visually distinguishes them, such as:
    - Displaying them in a unique type style.
    - Displaying them in a unique color.
  - In a position that visually distinguishes them by:
    - Left-justifying the prompt and indenting the related field captions (or headings) a minimum of three spaces to the right.
  - Leaving a space line between the prompt and the controls to which they refer, if possible.
  - Using a mixed-case font.

Type the following for changes only.

Kind: _____

Amount: _____

Effective Date: _____

Prompting messages are instructions to the screen user on what to do with, or how to work with, the screen being presented. They are analogous to instructions for filling out a paper form.

When it is necessary to place them on a screen, they must be identified as prompts. This will permit them to be easily ignored when they are not needed. Therefore, some visual aspect of the prompt must indicate that it *is* a prompt.

Displaying them in a unique color or in a unique font on all screens is one way to do this. If one of these methods is used, the cautions concerning the excessive use of color and different font styles must be heeded. Another method is to identify the prompt simply by its location. Begin the prompt to the left of the field captions (or headings) to which it applies. This left-justification will identify it as a prompt.

Try to leave a space line between the prompting message and the controls to which it relates, whenever possible. Screen space constraints may not always permit the space line, however. The prompt should be displayed in normal sentence-style capitalization.

ORGANIZATION AND LAYOUT PRINCIPLES

How a screen is organized, and how its information is actually presented, is crucial to achieving the design goals of fast and accurate comprehension and control execution. Following is a listing of several key screen design principles toward these ends. They have all been addressed in earlier chapters but are restated as a reminder of their importance. Several of the principles also contain additional design guidelines within the context of graphical screen layout.

A SUMMARY OF KEY PRINCIPLES

General

Amount of Information

- Present the proper amount of information on each screen.
  - Too little is inefficient.
  - Too much is confusing.

Organization

- Provide an ordering that:
  - Is logical and sequential.
  - Is rhythmic, guiding a person's eye through the display.
  - Encourages natural movement sequences.
  - Minimizes cursor and eye movement distances.

Distinctiveness

- Provide perceptually distinct individual controls and groups of controls

Aesthetics

- Provide an aesthetic appearance through:
  - Adequate use of white space.
  - Groupings.
  - Balance.
  - Alignment of elements.

Control Placement

- Position the most important and frequently used controls to the top left.
- Maintain a top-to-bottom, left-to-right flow.

- If one control enables or affects another, the enabling control should be above or to the left of the enabled control.
- Place the command buttons that affect the entire window horizontally, and centered, at the window bottom.

Navigation

- The flow of interaction:
  — Should require as little cursor travel as possible.
  — Should minimize the number of times a person's hand has to travel between the keyboard and the mouse.
- When a window is initially opened, position the cursor at the object most likely to be completed or changed.
- If a focus is returned to a window, position the cursor at the last object to have the cursor.
- Keyboard navigation should be consistent with the logical ordering of controls.
- The displayed cursor:
  — Should always be visible.
  — Should only be moved by the user.

Additional important principles include the following:

Logical Organization

- A window, or series of windows, must reflect the organization of the world in which the information is collected or used.

A person organizes information internally in meaningful and expected ways. When the screen reflects these patterns and expectancies, it will be handled faster and be less prone to errors. The screen organization should always reflect the experiences and expectancies of its user.

Window Size

- Present related data in a single window whenever possible.
- An initial window should be large enough:
  — To accommodate the amount of data a person would typically expect to see.
  — So that window scrolling is not required.
    — If the window cannot be made large enough:
      — Initially place less frequently used controls or data out of view.
      — Provide an indication of where the displayed controls or data are located in relation to all the window's controls.
      — Maintain column and row heading when scrolling/paging through tables.

- Do not make the default size of a window the full screen.
- Do not make dialog boxes that are larger than the default size of the primary window.
- If one dialog box calls another, make the new one movable whenever possible.

Present the proper amount of information on a screen. Too little is as bad as too much. In general, present all related information in a single window whenever it is possible to do so. An initial window should be large enough to accommodate the amount of data a person would typically expect to see. The needed information can only be determined through thorough task analysis.

The necessity for window scrolling should also be avoided whenever possible. If all the relevant controls or data cannot be placed within the confines of a single window, place that which is less frequently needed out of view, either on another window or obtainable through scrolling. Generally, location on another window is preferable to scrolling. Always provide an indication where the displayed data or controls are located in relation to all the required data or controls. With scrolling, this can be accomplished through position of the slider box or handle. With multiple windows, page numbers will be necessary.

Do not make the default size of a window the full screen. The option to maximize a window always exists. Do not make dialog boxes that are larger than the default size of the primary window so that the primary window can unknowingly be hidden. If one dialog box calls another, make the new one movable whenever possible so the underlying one can be seen in its entirety.

Window Separation

- Crisply, clearly, and pleasingly demarcate a window from the background of the screen on which it appears.
  - Provide a surrounding solid line border for the window.
  - Provide a window background that sets off well against the overall screen background.
  - Consider incorporating a drop shadow beneath the window.

Component separation is especially critical in a graphics environment because of the spatial layering that can occur. All windows must be clearly set off from the underlying screen or windows. The demarcation must be crisp and visually pleasing. A solid single-line border is recommended for this purpose. Also provide a window background that sets off well against the overall screen background. If color is used, exercise caution and choose compatible colors. (See Chapter 13.) Another alternative is to use for the window a lighter shade of the color used for the screen background. Changes in the density of shades are often more visually pleasing. To emphasize the three-dimensional aspects of graphic windows, incorporate a drop shadow beneath each window.

Avoiding Visual Clutter

- Maintain low screen density levels. Do not exceed 30 to 40 percent.
- Maintain distinctiveness of items.
  - Controls should not touch the window border.
  - Controls should not touch each other.
  - A button label should not touch the button border.
- Leave at least two blank character positions between the left and right borders and the widest element within the window.

Never cram information into a window. Keep the proportion of the window devoted to "information" or "ink" to no more than 30 to 40 percent of the window's entire area. Always leave a sufficient margin around all screen elements and between elements and the screen border. The window will look much more appealing to the viewer.

Creating Groupings

General

- Provide groupings of associated elements.
  - Elements of a radio button or check box control.
  - Two or more related fields or controls.
- Create groupings as close as possible to 5 degrees of visual angle.

White Space

- Provide adequate separation of groupings through liberal use of white space.
- Leave adequate space:
  - Around groups of related controls.
  - Between groupings and window borders.
- The space between groupings should be sufficiently greater than the space between fields within a grouping.

Headings

- Provide section headings and subsection headings for multiple control groupings.
- Provide headings that meaningfully and concisely describe the nature of the group of related fields.

Borders

- Enhance groupings through incorporation of borders around:
  - Elements of a single control.
  - Groups of related controls or fields.

- Individual control borders should be visually differentiable from borders delineating groupings of fields or controls.
  — Provide a border consisting of a thin line around *single* controls.
  — Provide a border consisting of a slightly thicker line around *groups* of fields or controls.
- Do not place individual field or control borders around:
  — Single entry fields.
  — Single list boxes.
  — Single combination boxes.
  — Single spin boxes.
  — Single sliders.
- Do not place group borders around command buttons.

General. Individual controls with multiple parts, such as radio buttons or check boxes, should be identifiable as a single entity. A series of related controls should also be presented as related. Create groupings to do this as often as possible. Groupings aid learning and provide visual appeal. The optimum group size is 5 degrees of visual angle. At the normal viewing distance of a screen this is a circle 1.67 inches in diameter. On a text-based screen this is equivalent to about 6 to 7 lines at a width of 12 to 14 characters. Examples of groupings are shown in Figure 12.1.

White Space. Groupings can be made visually obvious through liberal use of white space. Sufficient space should be left between all groupings of controls, and groupings and the window borders, as illustrated in Figure 12.2.

Figure 12.1. Groupings.

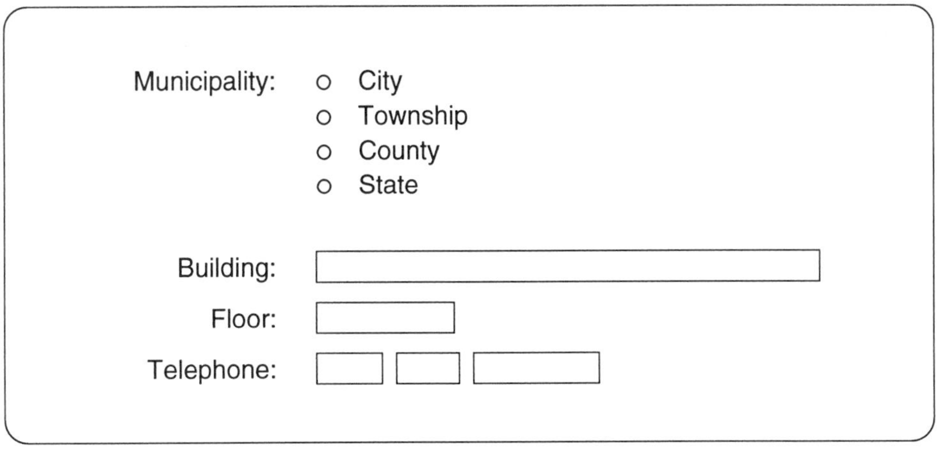

Figure 12.2. Groupings using white space.

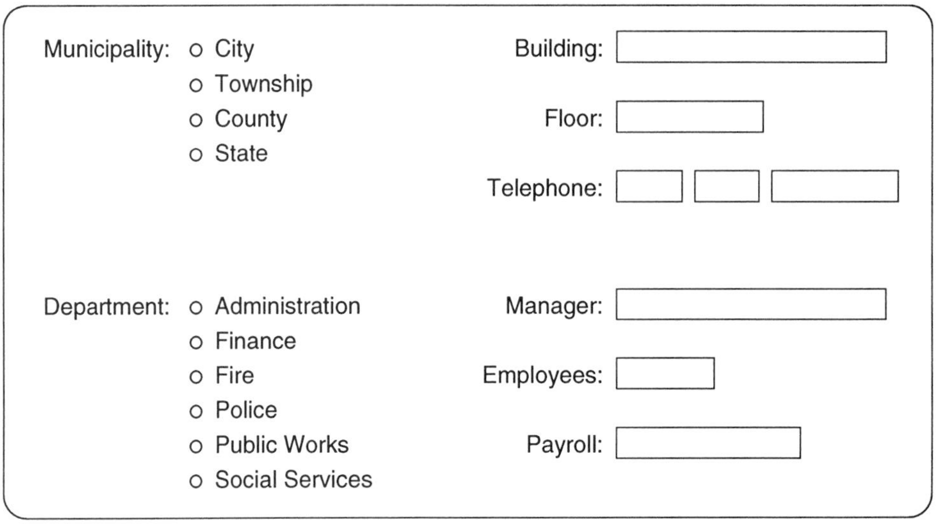

Headings. Headings should also be used to give groupings of controls or information an identity. This aids comprehension of what is presented. See Figure 12.3.

Figure 12.3. Groupings with section headings.

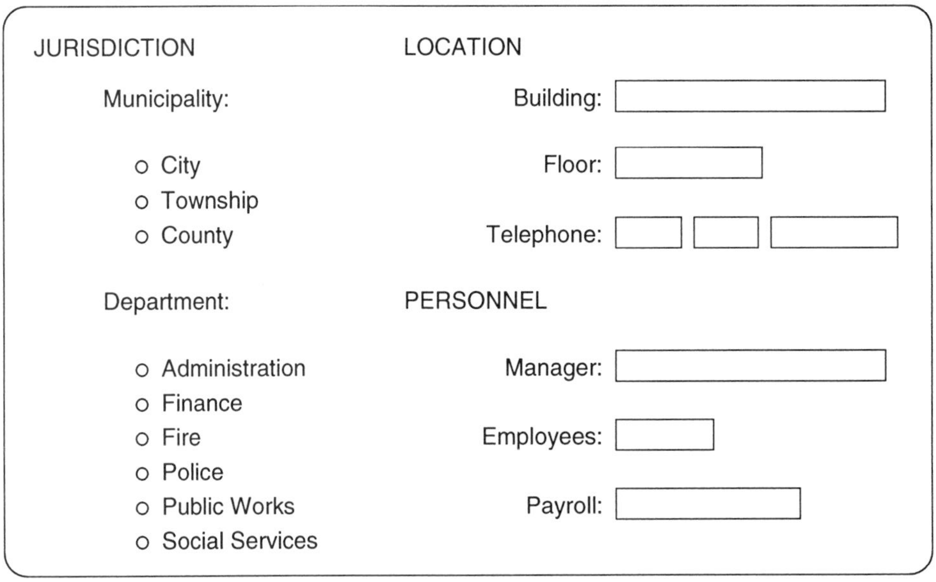

Borders. Groupings can be further enhanced through the use of borders. In-scribe line borders around elements of a single control such as a radio button or check box and/or groups of related controls or fields. Individual control borders should be visually differentiable from borders delineating groupings of fields or controls. Provide a border consisting of a thin line around single controls and a slightly thicker line around groups of fields or controls.

Control Borders

- Incorporate a thin single-line border around the elements of a selection control.
- For spacing:
  — Vertically, leave one space line above and below the control elements.
  — Horizontally:
    — Leave at least two character positions between the border and the left side of the control elements.
    — Leave at least two character positions between the border and the right side of the longest control element.
  — Locate the control caption in the top border, indented one character position from the left border.

```
┌─ Contents ──────┐
│                 │
│  □ Preface      │
│  □ Illustrations│
│  □ Index        │
│  □ Bibliography │
│                 │
└─────────────────┘
```

  — If the control caption exceeds the length of the choice descriptions, extend the border two character positions to the right of the caption.

```
┌─ Justification ─┐
│                 │
│  o None         │
│  o Left         │
│  o Center       │
│  o Right        │
│                 │
└─────────────────┘
```

Thin line borders may be used to surround some boxed-in controls, par-ticularly radio buttons and check boxes. Control captions should be located upper left within the border itself. The spacing guidelines are to avoid cramp-ing the text within the border. Some examples of control borders are illustrated in Figure 12.5.

Figure 12.5. Examples of controls without and with borders.

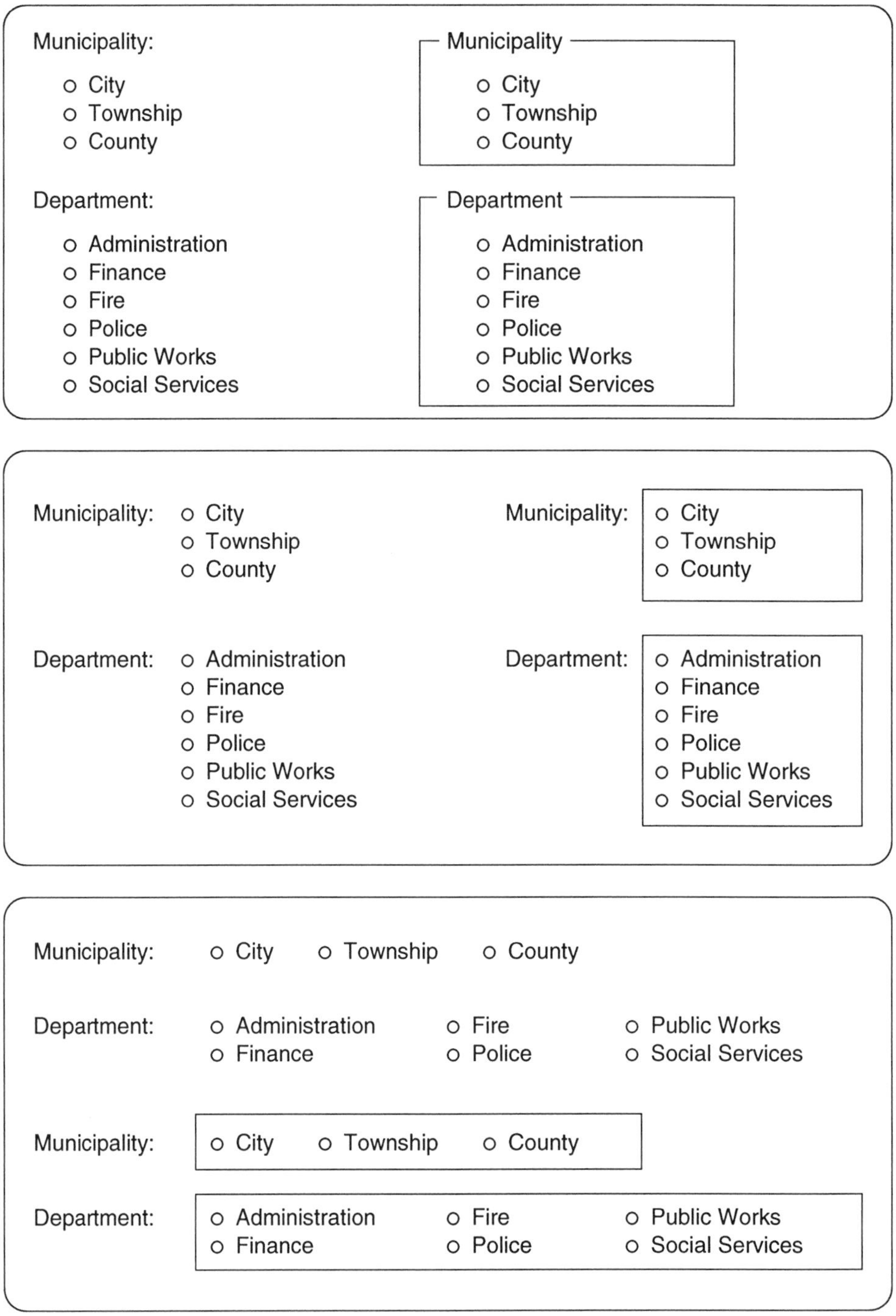

Section Borders

- Incorporate a thicker single-line border around groups of related entry or selection controls.
- For spacing:
  - — Vertically, leave one space line between the top and bottom row of the entry or selection control elements.
  - — Horizontally, leave at least four character positions to the left and right of the longest caption and/or entry field.
- Locate the section heading in the top border, indented two character positions from the left border.

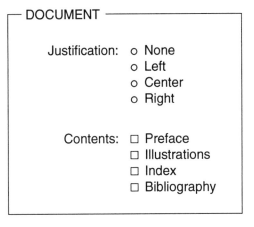

Line borders may be used to surround groupings of related controls. Section headings should be located upper left within the border itself. Display section headings in capital letters (or bolder type) to differentiate them easily from individual control captions. The spacing guidelines are to avoid cramping the text within the border. Examples of section borders are illustrated in Figure 12.6.

If both control borders and section borders are included on the same screen, make the section border slightly thicker, as illustrated in Figure 12.7.

Be conservative in the use of borders as too many can lead to screen clutter. Do not place individual field borders around the individual controls previously listed and illustrated in Figure 12.8. The nature of their design provides them with a border. Also, because of the potential for clutter, do not place a border around groups of pushbuttons.

Figure 12.6. Section Groupings using borders.

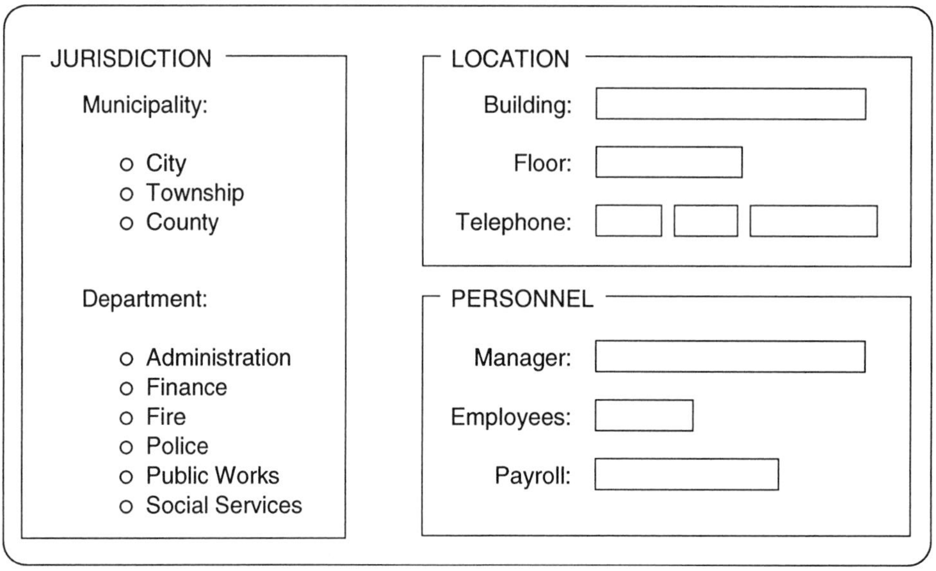

Figure 12.7. Differentiable control and section borders.

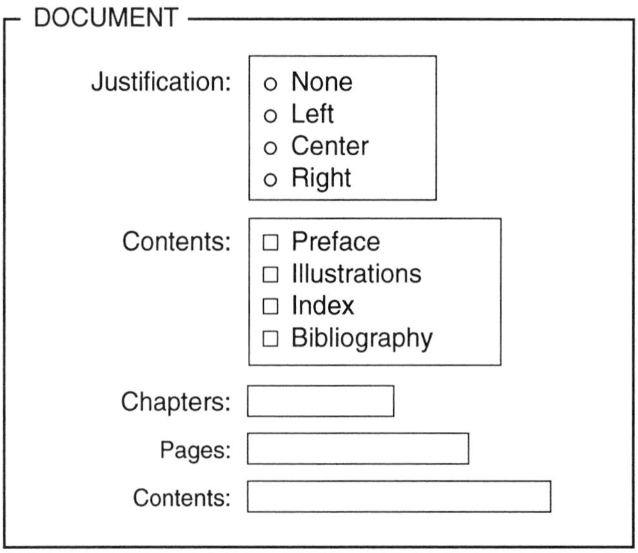

Figure 12.8. Kinds of borders to avoid.

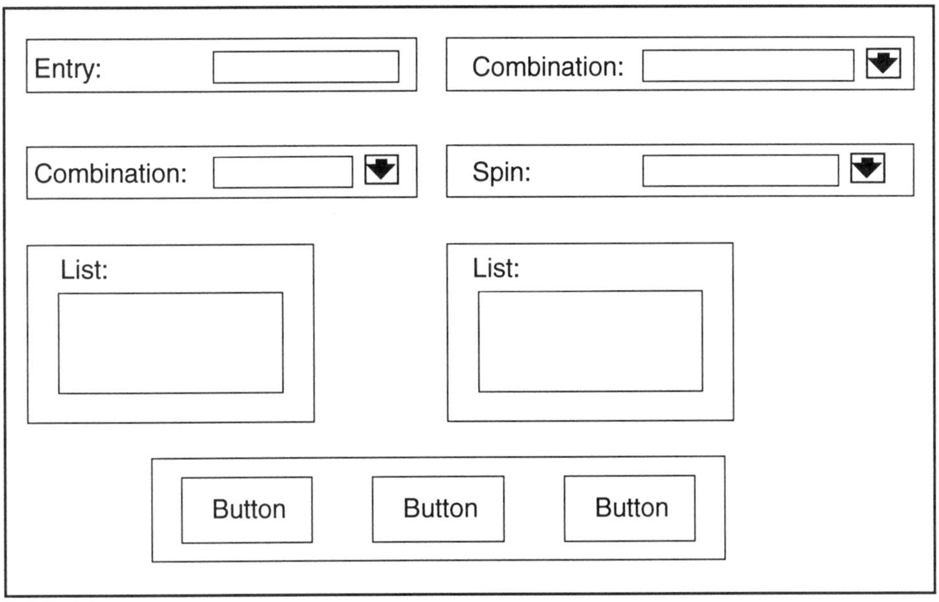

ALIGNING SCREEN ELEMENTS

General

- Minimize alignment points on a window.
  — Vertically.
  — Horizontally.

Fewer screen alignment points reduce a screen's complexity and make it more visually appealing. Aligning elements will also make eye and pointer movement through the screen much more obvious and reduce the distance both must travel. Screen organization will also be more consistent and predictable. Alignment is achieved by creating vertical columns of screen fields and controls and also horizontally aligning the tops of screen elements.

Fields or controls vertically columnized may be oriented in two directions, vertically or horizontally. Vertical orientation, a top-to-bottom flow through controls and control components, is the recommended structure.

Vertical Orientation and Vertical Alignment

Radio Buttons/Check Boxes

- Align both choice descriptions and selection indicators.
- Field captions may be left- or right-aligned.

Justification: o None
                 o Left
                 o Center
                 o Right

Contents: □ Preface
                 □ Illustrations
                 □ Index
                 □ Bibliography

With control borders:

- Also align the left borders of the boxes.

```
┌─ Sort by ──────────────┐
│   o Name               │
│   o Type               │
│   o Size               │
└────────────────────────┘
```

```
┌─ Style ────────────────┐
│   □ Bold               │
│   ☒ Italic             │
│   ☒ Underline          │
│   □ Strikeout          │
└────────────────────────┘
```

Entry Fields

- Left-align the entry fields.
  — If the screen will be used for inquiry or display purposes, numeric fields
    should be right-aligned.
- Field captions may be left- or right-aligned.

Number of Chapters: [   ]

Number of Pages: [   ]

Cost: [   ]

Fixed List Boxes

- Left-align fixed list boxes.

Dictionaries in Use:

```
┌─────────────────┬─┐
│ american.dic    │▲│
│ british.dic     │ │
│ user1.dic       │ │
│ user2.dic       │▼│
└─────────────────┴─┘
```

User Words:

```
┌─────────────────┬─┐
│ Edsel           │▲│
│ Honda           │ │
│ Nissan          │ │
│ Toyota          │▼│
└─────────────────┴─┘
```

Drop-down/Pop-up List Box, Spin Box, Combination Boxes

- Left-align selection/entry fields.
- Field captions may be left- or right-aligned.

Drop-down/Pop-up List Box:

Spin Box:

Attached Combination Box:

Drop-down/Pop-up Combo Box:

Mixed Entry and Selection Fields

- Left-align vertically arrayed:
  — Entry field fields.
  — Radio button buttons.
  — Check box boxes.
  — Drop-down/pop-up list box display fields.
  — Spin box selection entry fields.
  — Combination box entry fields.
  — Fixed list box left borders.
- Field captions may be left- or right-aligned.
- Leave one space between the longest columnized caption and the column of buttons, check boxes, and/or entry fields.

Entry Field:

Radio Buttons:
    o XXXXXXXXX
    o XXXXX
    o XXXXXXXXXX

Check Boxes:
    ☐ XXXXXX
    ☐ XXXXXXXXXX
    ☐ XXXX
    ☐ XXXXXXXXXXXXX

Fixed List Box:

Drop-down/Pop-up List Box:

Spin Box:

Attached Combination Box:

Drop-down/Pop-up Combo Box:

Elements and information should be organized vertically (top to bottom) as well. Two, and sometimes three, columns of controls and fields may occasionally be created. When multiple columns are presented and no section borders are used, column separation and downward flow may be emphasized through line borders, as illustrated in Figure 12.9.

In some cases, window space constraints may dictate a horizontal orientation of controls, most noticeably radio buttons and check boxes. Again the pattern created must be consistent, predictable, and distinct.

Figure 12.9.   Multicolumn controls/fields with separation borders.

```
┌──────────────────────────────────────────────────────────────┐
│  APPLICANT                    │  VEHICLE                        │
│     Name:    [            ]   │     Make:    [            ]      │
│     Occupation: [         ]   │     Model:   [            ]      │
│     Birth Date: [ ]–[ ]–[ ]   │     ID Number: [          ]      │
│                               │     Horsepower: [    ]           │
│  LICENSE                      │                                 │
│     Number:  [            ]   │     Annual Miles: [    ]         │
│     State:   [      ]         │     Use:      [          ]       │
│     Years:   [    ]           │     Miles to Work: [    ]        │
│     Restriction: [     ]      │     Symbol:  [     ]             │
└──────────────────────────────────────────────────────────────┘
```

Horizontal Orientation and Vertical Alignment

Radio Buttons/Check Boxes Selection Fields

- Align leftmost radio buttons and/or check boxes.
- Field captions may be left- or right-aligned.

Left-Aligned Captions

Justification:	o None	o Left	o Even	o Center

Contents:	☐ Preface	☐ Illustrations	☐ Index	☐ Bibliography

Right-Aligned Captions

Justification:	o None	o Left	o Even	o Center

Contents:	☐ Preface	☐ Illustrations	☐ Index	☐ Bibliography

Entry Fields

- Left-align entry fields into columns.
- Captions may be left- or right-aligned.

Left-Aligned Captions

Author: [   ]   Organization: [   ]

Location: [   ]   Building: [   ]

Right-Aligned Captions

Author: [   ]   Organization: [   ]

Location: [   ]   Building: [   ]

— Numeric data fields should be right-aligned.

Length: [   ]   Width: [   ]

Thickness: [   ]   Weight: [   ]

Mixed Entry and Selection Fields

- Align leftmost radio buttons and/or check boxes.
- Align leftmost entry field under leftmost choice description button or box.
- Captions may be left- or right-aligned.

Left-Aligned Captions

Justification: o None   o Left   o Even   o Center

Contents: □ Preface   □ Illustrations   □ Index   □ Bibliography

Author: [   ]   Organization: [   ]

Location: [   ]   Building: [   ]

Right-Aligned Captions

Justification: o None   o Left   o Even   o Center

Contents: □ Preface   □ Illustrations   □ Index   □ Bibliography

Author: [   ]   Organization: [   ]

Location: [   ]   Building: [   ]

For horizontally oriented controls, while the objective is to create as few vertical alignment points as possible, this is usually not practical. For check boxes and radio buttons, often the result will be indistinctiveness caused by the item descriptions being positioned too close to each other (Figure 12.10), too far from one another, and inconsistently spaced (Figure 12.11). Vertical alignment of items in several adjacent controls can also create a false "vertical orientation" perception, as illustrated in Figure 12.12. Final positioning will be a compromise between alignment and providing clear item distinctiveness as illustrated in Figure 12.13. With vertical orientation, these problems are avoided. Borders aid separation, as illustrated in Figure 12.14.

Figure 12.10.   Horizontally-arrayed control items with inadequate separation.

Municipality: o City o Township o County o State

Department: o Administration o Finance o Public Works o Social Services

Job Title: o Director o Manager o Professional o Clerical

Figure 12.11.   Horizontally-arrayed control items with too much separation.

Municipality: o City   o Township   o County   o State

Department: o Administration   o Finance   o Public Works   o Social Services

Figure 12.12.   Horizontally-arrayed control items with false "vertical orientation."

Municipality: o City   o Township   o County   o State

Department: o Administration   o Finance   o Public Works   o Social Services

Job Title: o Director   o Manager   o Professional   o Clerical

Figure 12.13.   Horizontally-arrayed control items comprising alignment and distinctiveness.

Municipality: o City   o Township   o County   o State

Department: o Administration   o Finance   o Public Works   o Social Services

Job Title: o Director   o Manager   o Professional   o Clerical

Figure 12.14. Horizontally-arrayed control items with borders to improve readability.

Municipality:	o City o Township o County o State

Department:	o Administration o Finance o Public Works o Social Services

Job Title:	o Director o Manager o Professional o Clerical

Figure 12.15. Vertical orientation of entry fields.

Justification: o None   o Left   o Even   o Center

Contents: □ Preface   □ Illustrations   □ Index   □ Bibliography

Author: [   ]

Location: [   ]

Organization: [   ]

Building: [   ]

Although the examples in the guidelines illustrate entry fields structured left to right, every attempt should be made to maintain a top-to-bottom orientation of entry fields. The entry fields in the example will be more effectively structured as illustrated in Figure 12.15.

Horizontal Alignment

Entry Fields

- Align by their tops horizontally adjacent entry fields.

Radio Buttons/Check Boxes

- Align by their tops horizontally adjacent radio button and/or check box controls.

Fixed List Boxes

- Align by their tops horizontally adjacent fixed list boxes.

Drop-down/Pop-up List Box, Spin Box, Combination Boxes

- Align by their tops horizontally adjacent entry/selection fields.

Entry Field: [   ] Entry Field: [   ]

Radio Buttons: o XXXXXXXXX Check Boxes: □ XXXXXX
                o XXXXX   □ XXXXXXXXXX
                o XXXXXXXXXX   □ XXXX
                                          □ XXXXXXXXXXXXXX

List Box: [   ] List Box: [   ]

Drop-down List: [▢] Entry Field: [   ]

Mixed Entry and Selection Fields

- Align by their tops:
  — Entry field fields.
  — Radio buttons.
     — If a control border exists, align by top border.
  — Check boxes.
     — If a control border exists, align by top border.
  — Drop-down/pop-up list box display fields.
  — Spin box selection/entry fields.
  — Combination box entry fields.
  — Fixed list box top borders.

Entry Field: [   ] Check Boxes: □ XXXXXX
Entry Field: [   ]   □ XXXXXXXXXX
                                         □ XXXX
                                         □ XXXXXXXXXXXXXX

Radio Buttons: o XXXXXXXXX Drop-down List 1: [▢]
                o XXXXX
                o XXXXXXXXXX Drop-down List 2: [▢]

Attach Combo: [   ] Spin Box: [▢]

Arrangement of controls horizontally always consists of aligning by their tops. Since controls may be of different heights, screen efficiency occasionally dictates that a control must be positioned in an area where it does not align horizontally with another control. When this occurs, attempt to align it horizontally with the bottom of an adjacent control, as illustrated by *drop-down list 2* in the above example. Do not cramp a control, however, to achieve bottom alignment.

Group Alignment

- Align by their left side vertically arrayed groupings containing group borders.
- Align by their top horizontally arrayed groupings containing group borders.

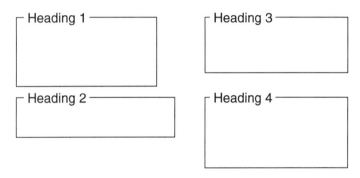

Groupings with borders should also be aligned vertically by their left border and horizontally by their top border. Controls within a grouping will, of course, be aligned following the alignment principles previously discussed.

BALANCING ELEMENTS

General

- Create balance by:
  - Equally distributing controls, spatially, within a window.
  - Aligning borders whenever possible.

Individual Control Borders

- If more than one control with borders is incorporated within a column on a screen:
  - Align the controls following the guidelines for multiple-control alignment.
  - Align the left and right borders of all groups.
  - Establish the left and right border positions by the spacing required for the widest element within the groups.

```
┌─ Contents ──────────────┐
│    □ Preface            │
│    □ Illustrations      │
│    □ Index              │
│    □ Bibliography       │
├─ Justification ─────────┤
│    o None               │
│    o Left               │
│    o Center             │
│    o Right              │
└─────────────────────────┘
```

With multigroupings and multicolumns, create a balanced screen by:
  — Maintaining equal column widths as much as practical.
  — Maintaining equal column heights as much as practical.

```
┌──────────────────┐    ┌──────────────────────┐
│                  │    │                      │
└──────────────────┘    │                      │
                        └──────────────────────┘
┌──────────────────┐    ┌──────────────────────┐
│                  │    │                      │
└──────────────────┘    │                      │
                        └──────────────────────┘
┌──────────────────┐
│                  │
└──────────────────┘
```

Grouping or Section Borders

  • If more than one section with borders is incorporated within a column on a
    screen:
      — Align the left and right borders of all groups.
      — Establish the left and right border positions by the spacing required by
        the widest element within the groups.

```
┌─ DOCUMENT ──────────────────────────────────┐
│                                              │
│   Justification:  o  None                    │
│              ˌ    o  Left                     │
│                   o  Center                   │
│                   o  Right                    │
│                                              │
│      Contents:   ☐ Preface                    │
│                  ☐ Illustrations              │
│                  ☐ Index                      │
│                  ☐ Bibliography               │
│                                              │
└──────────────────────────────────────────────┘


┌─ AUTHOR ────────────────────────────────────┐
│                                              │
│         Name:  [                    ]        │
│     Telephone:  [                    ]        │
│                                              │
└──────────────────────────────────────────────┘
```

— With multigroupings and multicolumns, create a balanced screen by:
  — Maintaining equal column widths as much as practical.
  — Maintaining equal column heights as much as practical.

Screen balance should be attained as much as possible. Do not sacrifice screen functionality to achieve balance, however. Never rearrange controls to simply make the screen "look nice." A meaningful order of elements is most important. The "look" will be the best that can be achieved within the limits imposed by functionality. Section border balance is illustrated in Figure 12.16.

Figure 12.16. Section border balance.

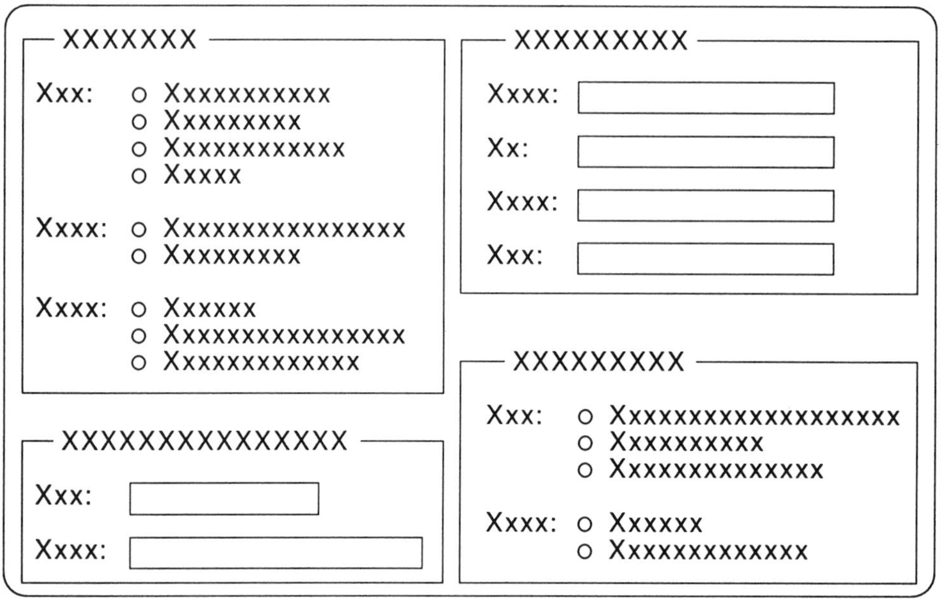

Example 1. A series of screens to illustrate the effect of including groupings, headings, and borders.

Screen 1-1. The screen controls are aligned and columnized. No groupings or headings exist.

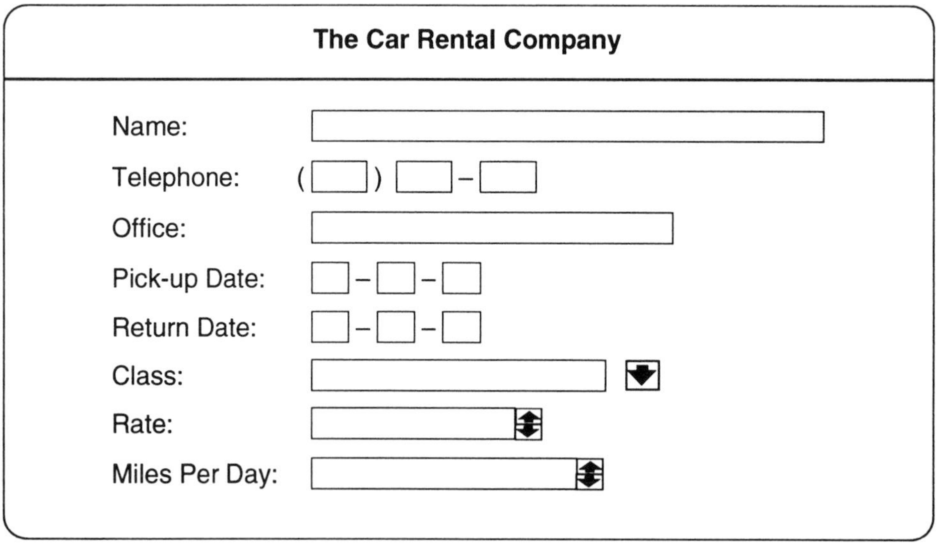

Screen 1-2. The utilization of space to create three groupings of controls.

The Car Rental Company

Name:

Telephone: ( ) –

Office:

Pick-up Date: – –

Return Date: – –

Class:

Rate:

Miles Per Day:

Screen 1-3. Section headings are added for each group. They are set off by indention and capitalization.

The Car Rental Company

RENTER
Name:

Telephone: ( ) –

LOCATION
Office:

Pick-up Date: – –

Return Date: – –

AUTOMOBILE
Class:

Rate:

Miles Per Day:

Screen 1-4. A different style of section heading, horizontally adjacent to the first control in each group. Headings are set off by capitalization and arrows.

Screen 1–5. The groupings are delineated by borders with the section heading located upper-left in each box.

Example 2. A poor combination display/inquiry and entry screen from a text-based system followed by examples of how the screen might be redesigned for use in a graphical system.

Screen 2–1. The initial text-based screen for establishing an inquiry. The kind of inquiry needed is selected from the listing of choices down the left side. Supplementary information needed to qualify the inquiry is found directly to the right of each inquiry choice. For example, to perform a "Basic Part Data" inquiry requires specifying the "Part Number."

Conceptually, the selection process for this screen is consistent. The inquiry choices are scanned down the left side and relevant qualifying data keyed in the fields to the right. Many problems exist however. A prominent feature at the screen's top is "Terminology Language Code." Close examination reveals that this is a prompt for the "Language Code" fields located at the screen's lower right side. This prompt is irrelevant, and screen *noise* for most screen usages, yet it forces attention to itself by its upper-left location. The inquiry choices themselves are not very distinctive due to the similarity in wording. The words part, data, and terminology are repeated many times. Distinctiveness is also lost because the inquiry choice descriptions are somewhat similar in length. Choices will have to be read closely to assure the correct alternative is selected. The entry field area of this screen has rather poor alignment. The word "supplier" sticks out awkwardly from the left-aligned field captions, unnecessarily calling attention to itself.

```
                O N   L I N E   I N Q U I R Y   S Y S T E M
     –TERMINOLOGY LANGUAGE CODE     (19-ENGLISH 28-FRENCH 29-GERMAN 39-ITALIAN
                                    (63-SPANISH 67-SWEDISH XX-ALL)


     BASIC PART DATA (MPL)          PART NUMBER:_____
     PART DATA RETRIEVAL (PDR)      CATEGORY:____ MAJOR:___ MINOR:___ METRIC:___
     PDR BY PART NUMBER             PART NUMBER:_____
     VENDOR PART LIST (VPL)          VENDOR PART NUMBER: _____
     SUPPLIER PART LIST (SPL)       SUPPLIER PART NUMBER: _____
     TERMINOLOGY BY TERM NAME        TERM:_____       LANG CODE:____
     TERMINOLOGY BY TERM CODE        CATEGORY & DESCR CODE: ____    LANG CODE:____
     TERMINOLOGY BY CAT CODE         CATEGORY CODE: _____           LANG CODE:____
     PART COST DATA INQUIRY          PRESS PF1 (OR ENTER/FOR BDX205 OR /FOR BDX206)
     SISE (STANDARDS INQUIRY)        PRESS PF2 (OR ENTER GOTO STDMENU)
```

Screens 2–2 and 2–3. Utilizing a graphical system, the inquiry choices can be greatly simplified by presenting them in a menu bar. Selection of a "Part Data Retrieval" inquiry is illustrated in Screen 7–2. Screen 7–3 illustrates the resulting window that presents exactly, and only, what is needed to perform the inquiry. The entry controls are columnized for easier entry and review.

```
┌─────────────────────────────────────────────────────────────────┐
│  │              ON-LINE INQUIRY SYSTEM              │   │        │
│ Part-Data │ Part-List  Terminology  Part-Cost  Standards   Help   │
│     Basic . . .                                                   │
│  [  Retrieval . . .           ]                                   │
│     Retrieval / Part # . . .                                      │
│     ─────────────────                                             │
│     Exit                                                          │
│                                                                   │
│                                                                   │
│                                                                   │
│                                                                   │
└─────────────────────────────────────────────────────────────────┘
```

```
┌─────────────────────────────────────────────────────────────────┐
│  │              ON-LINE INQUIRY SYSTEM              │   │        │
│ Part-Data   Part-List  Terminology  Part-Cost  Standards   Help   │
│       ┌───────────────────────────────────────────┐              │
│       │            PART DATA RETRIEVAL            │              │
│       │                                           │              │
│       │         Category:  [        ]             │              │
│       │            Major:  [     ]                │              │
│       │            Minor:  [     ]                │              │
│       │           Metric:  [      ]               │              │
│       │                                           │              │
│       │   [  OK  ]     [ Apply ]     [ Cancel ]   │              │
│       └───────────────────────────────────────────┘              │
└─────────────────────────────────────────────────────────────────┘
```

Screens 2–4 and 2–5. These screens illustrate a "Terminology by Category Code" inquiry request. The "Language Code" field on the original screen is presented simply as "Language" using an attached combination box. The language can either be typed or selected, as desired by the user. A code is no longer necessary.

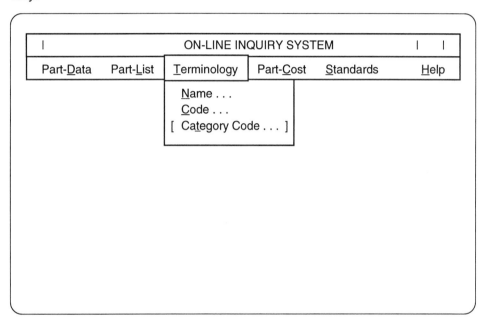

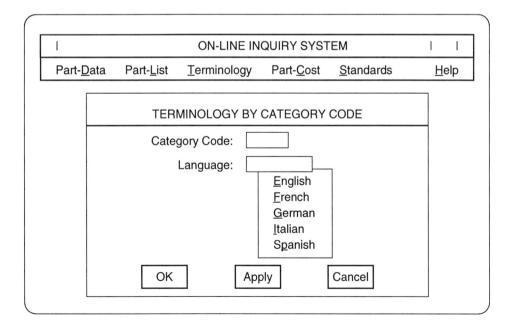

Example 3. A pair of screens containing a series of radio buttons and check boxes. A before and after design is presented.

Screen 3–1. A very poor screen. Captions are not discernible from choice descriptions and the initial choice descriptions are not left-aligned. The radio buttons and check boxes are not strongly associated with, and also *follow*, their respective descriptions, certainly causing selection confusions. The horizontal orientation of choices is not efficient for human scanning. No perception of groupings exists.

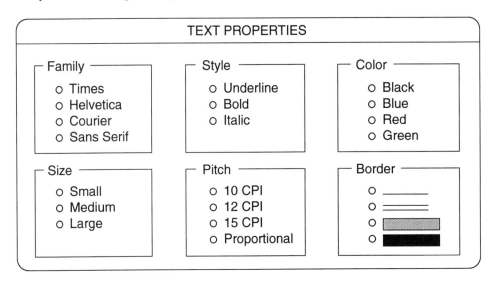

Screen 3–2. A much better screen. The title is capitalized to set it off from the remainder of the screen. The radio buttons and check boxes are arrayed vertically to facilitate scanning and comparison of alternatives. All controls are enclosed in borders to attract the viewer's attention. While the overall organization does not assist the viewer in establishing a scanning direction (horizontal or vertical), the kind of information presented does not make this critical. The screen can be effectively used left-to-right or top-to-bottom.

Example 4. A representation of an actual screen from Microsoft Windows. A before and after design is presented.

Screen 4–1. A screen with several faults. On a positive note, the captions on the left side are nicely aligned, as are the top four entry fields. The entry/selection field alignment, however, breaks down in the middle of the screen. Also, what appear to be captions (because they possess an ending colon) are really headings, communicating a false message to the viewer (Memory Requirements, EMS Memory and XMS Memory). The word "memory" repeated four times in succession seems redundant, indicating the potential for a heading. One radio button field (Video Memory) is arrayed horizontally, the others vertically (Display Usage and Execution). The control "Close Window on Exit" seems lost and is grasping for an identity (Am I a caption or data?)

		PIF Editor			

Program Filename:

Window Title:

Optional Parameters:

Start-up Directory:

Video Memory: o Text   o Low Graphics   o High Graphics

Memory Requirements: KB Required   [   ]   KB Desired   [   ]

EMS Memory: KB Required   [   ]   KB Limit   [   ]

XMS Memory: KB Required   [   ]   KB Limit   [   ]

Display Usage: o Full Screen   Execution: o Background
                 o Windowed   o Exclusive

☐ Close Window on Exit

Screen 4–2.   A much improved alternative. Groupings of elements are provided. Section borders, with titles, are included in the upper part of the screen to strengthen the perception of groupings. Control borders in the lower part of the screen serve the same purpose. Proper alignment of data fields is achieved in the top sections of the screen. The redundant word "memory" is incorporated as a section heading. Section headings are displayed capitalized to distinguish them from control captions. Sub-section headings are created in the Memory section where the heading-caption confusion previously existed. Sub-section headings are set off by capitalization and arrows.

The radio buttons/check boxes at the bottom of the screen are arrayed horizontally to provide screen balance. The "Close Window on Exit" field is given an (admittedly redundant) caption to allow a control border consistent with its neighbors and to create screen balance. The Video (Memory) control remains, as a trade-off, arrayed horizontally. It would have been desirable to organize its choices vertically, but the best overall fit within the screen is achieved by horizontal orientation.

```
┌─────────────────────────────────────────────────────────────────┐
│  |                        PIF EDITOR                  |      |    │
│  ┌─ APPLICATION ────────────────────────────────────────────┐    │
│  │   Program Filename:      ┌────────────────────────────┐   │    │
│  │                          └────────────────────────────┘   │    │
│  │   Window Title:          ┌────────────────────────┐       │    │
│  │                          └────────────────────────┘       │    │
│  │   Optional Parameters:   ┌────────────────────────────┐   │    │
│  │                          └────────────────────────────┘   │    │
│  │   Start-up Directory:    ┌────────────────────────────┐   │    │
│  │                          └────────────────────────────┘   │    │
│  └────────────────────────────────────────────────────────────┘   │
│  ┌─ MEMORY ─────────────────────────────────────────────────┐    │
│  │   REQUIREMENTS >  Required: ┌──────┐ Kb   Desired: ┌──────┐ Kb │
│  │   EMS >           Required: ┌──────┐ Kb   Limit:   ┌──────┐ Kb │
│  │   XMS >           Required: ┌──────┐ Kb   Limit:   ┌──────┐ Kb │
│  │   VIDEO >         Video:    o Text  o Low Graphics  o High Graphics │
│  └────────────────────────────────────────────────────────────┘   │
│  ┌─ Display Usage ─┐ ┌─ Execution ─┐ ┌─ Close Window ──────────┐  │
│  │  o Full Screen  │ │ o Background │ │ ☐ Close Window on Exit  │  │
│  │  o Windowed     │ │ o Exclusive  │ │                         │  │
│  └─────────────────┘ └─────────────┘ └─────────────────────────┘  │
└─────────────────────────────────────────────────────────────────┘
```

Example 5.   A representation of an actual screen from a banking system. A before and a pair of after designs are presented.

Screen 5–1.   A poor screen. The data fields are very poorly aligned, obscuring themselves as well as the screen captions. The "Name" field either has (1) no caption at all (nothing precedes it), or (2) its caption is located above. (Or is the text located above it a prompt?) The prompt for the "Date of Birth" field pushes the entry field unnecessarily far from its caption. The title seems awkward. We will not question what "Sex: Unknown" might be.

	Personal Details Customer			

1st Given Name   2nd Given Name (if any)   Surname

Courtesy Title: [   ] ⬇

Sex: o Male   o Female   o Unknown

Marital Status: o Married   o Single   o All Others

Date of Birth (dd/mm/yyyy): [   ]

Daytime Phone No: [   ]

Home Address: [   ]
[   ]

City/Town/Suburb: [   ]   Postcode: [   ]

Screen 5–2.   A much better screen. The "Name" field is given a caption and a single alignment point is established for both captions and data. Captions and data are now much more readable. Name format instructions (1st, 2nd, etc.) are established as prompts. This prompt designation is signalled by placing them in parentheses to subdue them visually. The prompt for "Birth Date" is placed to the right of the data field, out of the way but still easily viewable. This also permits the alignment point for the data fields to be moved closer to the captions. The date field is also segmented into its component pieces. "Sex" and "Marital Status" are arrayed vertically for easier scanning. Screen space constraints, however, require they be positioned horizontally adjacent to each other. The "Postcode" data field is right-aligned to the "Home Address" data field to achieve better balance.

```
┌──────────────────────────────────────────────────────────────────────┐
│  |                PERSONAL DETAILS CUSTOMER              |     |       │
│                                                                        │
│                  (1st)         (2nd-if any)      (Surname)             │
│     Name:        ┌──────────────────────────────────────────┐         │
│                  └──────────────────────────────────────────┘         │
│     Courtesy Title:  ┌────────────────────┐  ┌──┐                     │
│                      └────────────────────┘  │▼ │                     │
│                  ┌─ Sex ──────────┐  ┌─ Marital Status ──────┐        │
│                  │                │  │                        │        │
│                  │   o Male       │  │   o Married            │        │
│                  │   o Female     │  │   o Single             │        │
│                  │   o Unknown    │  │   o All Others         │        │
│                  └────────────────┘  └────────────────────────┘       │
│                                                                        │
│     Date of Birth:   ┌──┐┌──┐┌────────┐  (dd/mm/yyyy)                 │
│                      └──┘└──┘└────────┘                                │
│     Daytime Phone No: ┌──────────────────┐                            │
│                       └──────────────────┘                            │
│     Home Address:    ┌──────────────────────────────────────┐        │
│                      └──────────────────────────────────────┘        │
│                                                                        │
│     City/Town/Suburb: ┌─────────────────────┐  Postcode: ┌────────┐   │
│                       └─────────────────────┘            └────────┘   │
└──────────────────────────────────────────────────────────────────────┘
```

Screen 5.3.   Another good screen. Identical to Screen 5.2 except that the "Sex" and "Marital Status" choices are arrayed horizontally, permitting vertical alignment of all screen fields. Which screen arrangement do you prefer, 5.2 or 5.3?

	PERSONAL DETAILS CUSTOMER		

```
                          (1st)        (2nd-if any)      (Surname)

    Name:               [                                          ]

    Courtesy Title:     [                       ][▼]

    Sex:                [ o Male      o Female   o Unknown        ]

    Marital Status:     [ o Married     o Single   o All Others   ]

    Date of Birth:      [  ][  ][      ]  (dd/mm/yyyy)

    Daytime Phone No:   [                     ]

    Home Address:       [                                          ]
                        [                                          ]

    City/Town/Suburb:   [                      ]  Postcode: [      ]
```

Example 6. A series of screens containing the same entry fields, selection fields (check boxes and radio buttons), and buttons. An evolution in design, from poor to good, is illustrated.

Screen 6–1. A poor screen. Problems include poor alignment of entry and selection fields and poor visual differentiation of section headings from field captions. Equal spacing between selection field choice descriptions and check boxes/radio buttons makes association with correct description difficult. The variable widths of the buttons located to the right of the screen create a visually ragged edge, create inconsistent size selection targets, and, in one case, creates a very small selection target (OK button). The most desirable location of buttons is at the bottom of the screen.

```
                          Property
     Location
       Address: [_____]      ┌────────┐
                                                 │ OK     │
       Township: [_____]        │        │
                                                 ├────────┤
     Description                                  │ Reset  │
       Acres: [_____]                            │        │
                                                 ├────────┤
       Frontage: [_____]                         │ Cancel │
                                                 │        │
     Terrain: ☐ Open ☐ Wooded ☐ Level ☐ Rolling ☐ Water
                                                 ├────────┤
     Dwellings: ☐ House ☐ Garage ☐ Barn ☐ Store │ Help   │
                                                 └────────┘
     Zoning: ○ Agricultural ○ Commercial ○ Residential
```

Screen 6–2.   A better screen. The screen title and section headings are set off from the field captions through use of capital letters. The amount of indentation of the captions under the section headings is also increased. The entry fields and selection fields are aligned. The check boxes/radio buttons are properly associated with their choice descriptions through increased spacing between alternatives. The buttons are made equal in size, creating a more pleasing visual array and larger-size targets.

```
                            PROPERTY

   LOCATION
                                                        ┌─────────┐
       Address:  ┌──────────────────────────────┐      │   OK    │
                 └──────────────────────────────┘      └─────────┘
                                                        ┌─────────┐
       Township: ┌────────────────────────────┐        │  Reset  │
                 └────────────────────────────┘        └─────────┘
   DESCRIPTION                                          ┌─────────┐
                                                        │ Cancel  │
       Acres:    ┌───────────┐                          └─────────┘
                 └───────────┘                          ┌─────────┐
                                                        │  Help   │
       Frontage: ┌───────────┐                          └─────────┘
                 └───────────┘

       Terrain:   ☐ Open  ☐ Wooded  ☐ Level  ☐ Rolling  ☐ Water

       Dwellings: ☐ House  ☐ Garage  ☐ Barn  ☐ Store  ☐ Other

       Zoning:    ○ Agricultural  ○ Commercial  ○ Residential
```

Screen 6–3. A still better screen. Borders are included around groups of related information. Buttons are moved to the bottom of the screen.

```
┌─────────────────────────────────────────────────────────────────┐
│                          PROPERTY                                 │
│  ┌ LOCATION ────────────────────────────────────────────────┐    │
│  │    Address:  ┌──────────────────────────────────┐         │    │
│  │    Township: ┌──────────────────────────────┐              │    │
│  └──────────────────────────────────────────────────────────┘    │
│                                                                   │
│  ┌ DESCRIPTION ─────────────────────────────────────────────┐    │
│  │    Acres:    ┌──────┐                                     │    │
│  │    Frontage: ┌──────┐                                     │    │
│  │    Terrain:  ☐ Open  ☐ Wooded  ☐ Level  ☐ Rolling  ☐ Water│   │
│  │    Dwellings: ☐ House  ☐ Garage  ☐ Barn  ☐ Store  ☐ Other │    │
│  │    Zoning:   ○ Agricultural  ○ Commercial  ○ Residential   │    │
│  └──────────────────────────────────────────────────────────┘    │
│                                                                   │
│      ┌──────┐    ┌──────┐    ┌──────┐    ┌──────┐                 │
│      │  OK  │    │ Reset│    │Cancel│    │ Help │                 │
│      └──────┘    └──────┘    └──────┘    └──────┘                 │
└─────────────────────────────────────────────────────────────────┘
```

Screen 6–4. The best alternative. The entire screen, including the DESCRIP-TION section, is oriented for consistent top-to-bottom entry. The selection fields and alternatives are set off from another much better and more efficiently and easily scanned.

```
                                PROPERTY
   ┌─ LOCATION ─────────────────────────────────────────────────┐
   │      Address:   ┌──────────────────────────────────────┐    │
   │                 └──────────────────────────────────────┘    │
   │      Township:  ┌──────────────────────────────────┐        │
   │                 └──────────────────────────────────┘        │
   └─────────────────────────────────────────────────────────────┘

   ┌─ DESCRIPTION ──────────────────────────────────────────────┐
   │      Acres:     ┌──────────────┐  │ Dwellings:  ☐ House     │
   │                 └──────────────┘  │             ☐ Garage    │
   │      Frontage:  ┌────────────┐    │             ☐ Barn      │
   │                 └────────────┘    │             ☐ Store     │
   │      Terrain:   ☐ Open            │             ☐ Other     │
   │                 ☐ Wooded          │                         │
   │                 ☐ Level           │ Zoning:     ○ Agricultural│
   │                 ☐ Rolling         │             ○ Commercial │
   │                 ☐ Water           │             ○ Residential│
   └─────────────────────────────────────────────────────────────┘

        ┌─────────┐    ┌─────────┐    ┌─────────┐    ┌─────────┐
        │   OK    │    │  Reset  │    │ Cancel  │    │  Help   │
        └─────────┘    └─────────┘    └─────────┘    └─────────┘
```

Example 7.   A series of screens containing the same entry fields, selection fields, and buttons as shown in Example 6. The selection fields, however, are radio buttons and check boxes with field borders incorporated around them. An evolution in design, from poor to good, is again illustrated.

Screen 7–1.   A poor screen. Problems again include poor alignment of entry and selection fields. Required eye movement through the screen is inconsistent, flowing left to right through the first four fields, then switching down at Terrain, then back and to the right to Zoning, then across Zoning and then down and across Dwellings. Section headings are not included within the screen. The screen's overall appearance is irregular and disjointed. The buttons located at the bottom of the screen are not centered and inconsistent in size, in one case, creating a very small selection target (OK button).

Screen 7–2. A better screen. Section headings have been added and they, and the title, are set off from the field captions through use of capital letters. The entry fields and selection fields are aligned, space constraints dictating that the DESCRIPTION section maintain a left-to-right ordering. The buttons are made equal in size and centered, creating a more pleasing visual array and larger size targets.

Screen 7–3. The best alternative. Thick line borders are incorporated around the two sections. The selection fields (Terrain, Dwellings, and Zoning) are made equal size for balance and symmetry.

```
┌──────────────────────────────────────────────────────────────┐
│                          PROPERTY                              │
│  ┌ LOCATION ─────────────────────────────────────────────────┐ │
│  │                                                           │ │
│  │   Address: [                                     ]        │ │
│  │                                                           │ │
│  │   Township: [                            ]                │ │
│  │                                                           │ │
│  └───────────────────────────────────────────────────────────┘ │
│  ┌ DESCRIPTION ──────────────────────────────────────────────┐ │
│  │                                                           │ │
│  │   Acres: [      ]   Frontage: [      ]                    │ │
│  │                                                           │ │
│  │   ┌ Terrain ──────┐ ┌ Dwellings ───┐ ┌ Zoning ─────────┐  │ │
│  │   │ ☐ Open        │ │ ☐ House      │ │ ○ Agricultural  │  │ │
│  │   │ ☐ Wooded      │ │ ☐ Garage     │ │ ○ Commercial    │  │ │
│  │   │ ☐ Level       │ │ ☐ Barn       │ │ ○ Residential   │  │ │
│  │   │ ☐ Rolling     │ │ ☐ Store      │ │                 │  │ │
│  │   │ ☐ Water       │ │ ☐ Other      │ │                 │  │ │
│  │   └───────────────┘ └──────────────┘ └─────────────────┘  │ │
│  └───────────────────────────────────────────────────────────┘ │
│      [  OK  ]    [ Reset ]    [ Cancel ]     [ Help ]          │
└──────────────────────────────────────────────────────────────┘
```

13

Color

Color can add a new dimension to graphical screen usability. Color draws attention because it attracts the user's eye. If used properly, it can emphasize the logical organization of a screen, facilitate the discrimination of screen components, accentuate differences, and make displays more interesting. If used improperly, color can be distracting and visually fatiguing, impairing the system's usability.

STEP 9

- Choose the proper colors for all screen elements.
  - Identify the advantages and uses of color.
  - Understand possible problems and cautions.
  - Understand color and human vision.
  - Identify effective foreground/background combinations.
  - Identify colors and color combinations to avoid.

The discussion to follow begins by defining color. Next is a review of how color may be used in screen design and some critical cautions in its use. Then, the human visual system and the implications for color are discussed. Finally, guidelines are presented for choosing and using colors.

COLOR—WHAT IS IT?

Wavelengths of light themselves are not colored. What is perceived as actual color results from the stimulation by a received light wave of the proper receptor in the eye. The "name" that a color is given is a learned phenomenon, based on previous experiences and associations of specific visual sensations with color names. Therefore, a color can only be described in terms of a person's report of his or her perceptions.

The visual spectrum of wavelengths to which the eye is sensitive ranges from about 400 to 700 millimicrons. Objects in the visual environment often emit or reflect light waves in a limited area of this visual spectrum, absorbing light waves in other areas of the spectrum. The dominant wavelength being "seen" is the one that we come to associate with a specific color name. The visible color spectrum and the names commonly associated with the various light wavelengths are shown in Figure 13.1.

To describe a color, it is useful to refer to the three properties it possesses: hue, chroma or saturation, and value or intensity, as illustrated in Figure 13.2. Hue is the spectral wavelength composition of a color. It is to this we attach a meaning such as green or red. Chroma or saturation is the purity of a color in a scale from gray to the most vivid version of the color. Value or intensity is the relative lightness or darkness of a color in a range from black to white. Lightness differences are usually described by two-word descriptors such as light red or dark blue.

Primary colors of illuminated light are red, green, and blue, whose wavelengths additively combine in pairs to produce magenta, cyan, and yellow. The three primary colors additively combine to produce white. The long-wavelength colors (red) are commonly referred to as "warm," and short-wavelength colors (blue) as "cool."

Color Uses

- Use color as a formatting aid to:
  - Relate or tie fields into groupings.
  - Differentiate groupings of information.
  - Associate information that is spatially separated.
  - Highlight or call attention to important information.
- Use color as a visual code to identify:
  - Screen components.
  - The logical structure of ideas, processes, or sequences.
  - Sources of information.
  - Status of information.
- Other color uses:
  - Realistically portray natural objects.
  - Increase screen appeal.

Color may be used as a formatting aid in structuring a screen, or it may be used as a visual code to categorize information or data.

As a formatting aid. As a formatting aid, color can provide better structure and meaning to a screen. It is especially useful when large amounts of data

Figure 13.1. The visible spectrum.

Color	Approximate Wavelengths in Millimicrons
Red	700
Orange	600
Yellow	570
Yellow-green	535
Green	500
Blue-green	493
Blue	470
Violet	400

Figure 13.2. The relationship of hue, chroma, and value.

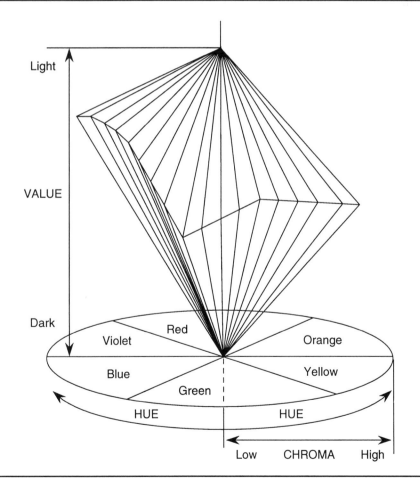

must be included on a screen and spacing to differentiate components is difficult to employ.

For example, differentiation of logical groupings of fields can be enhanced by displaying them in different colors. Spatially separated but related fields can also be tied together through a color scheme.

Color can also replace highlighting as a means of calling attention to a field or fields. Color is much more flexible than other techniques because of the number of colors that are available. Color as an attention-getting mechanism must, however, be chosen in light of the psychological and physiological considerations, to be described shortly.

As a visual code. A color code shows what category the data being displayed falls into. It has meaning to the screen's user. A properly selected color coding scheme permits a user to identify a relevant category quickly without having to read its contents first. This permits focusing concentration on this category while the remaining data is excluded from attention.

One common color-coding scheme to differentiate screen components is to display captions and data fields in different colors. Another is to identify data from different sources—data added to a transaction from different locations, or text added to a message from different departments, may be colored differently. Color coding to convey status might involve displaying, in a different color, data that passed or failed system edits. Color can also be used as a prompt, guiding a person through a complex transaction.

Color as a visual code must be relevant and known. Relevance is achieved when the code enables a user to attend only to the data that is needed. A relevant code, however, will be useless unless it is also understood by the persons who must use it. Not knowing a code's meaning will only distract and degrade performance.

Other color uses. Color can also be used more realistically to portray objects in the world around us that must be displayed on a screen. It is also thought that the addition of color increases a screen's appeal and makes display work more pleasant.

Possible Problems with Color

- Color's high attention-getting quality may be distracting if it causes a person to:
  - Notice differences in color, regardless of whether the differences have any real meaning.
  - Visually group items of the same color together, regardless of whether these grouped items are related.
- Indiscriminate or poor use of color on one screen may interfere with color's attention-getting capacity on another screen.
- The sensitivity of the eye to different colors and color combinations varies, some being visually fatiguing.

- Some people have color-viewing deficiencies.
- Some colors may exhibit confusing cross-disciplinary and cross-cultural connotations.

The simple addition of color to a screen will not guarantee improved performance. What may have been a poorly designed product will simply become a colorful poorly designed product. When used improperly, color may even impair performance by distracting the viewer and interfering with the handling of information. Possible problems may be caused by the perceptual system itself and/or the physiological characteristics of the human eye.

High attention-getting capacity. Color has an extremely high attention-getting capacity, which causes the screen viewer to associate or "tie together" screen elements of the same color, whether or not such an association should be made. The user thus might search for relationships and differences that do not exist or that are not valid. The result is often bewilderment, confusion, and slower reading. The effect achieved is often described as a "Christmas tree."

Interference with use of other screens. Indiscriminate or poor use of color on some screens will diminish the effectiveness of color on other screens. The rationale for color will be difficult to understand and its attention-getting capacity severely restricted.

Varying sensitivity of the eye to different colors. All colors, in the eye of the viewer, are not equal. The eye is more sensitive to those in the middle of the visual spectrum (yellow and green), which appear brighter than the extremes (blue and red). Thus, text comprised of colors at the extremes is thought to be more difficult to read. Research evidence on this topic is mixed. Watanabe et al. (1968), Pinkus (1982), Post (1985), and Matthews and Mertins (1987, 1988) found that acuity, contrast sensitivity, target recognition, legibility, or performance were not influenced by color. On the other hand, Haines et al. (1975), Pokorny et al. (1968), and Radl (1980, 1984) found advantages for spectral center colors in reaction times, resolution, and error rates.

Also, it is thought that some combinations of screen colors can strain the eye's accommodation mechanism. The wavelengths of light producing blue are normally focused in front of the eye's retina, the red wavelengths behind it. Simultaneous or sequential viewing of red and blue cause the eye to continually refocus to bring the image directly onto the retina, thereby increasing the potential for eye fatigue. Those expressing this view include Ostberg (1982), Sivak and Woo (1983), Murch (1983), and the Human Factors Society (1988). Again the research evidence is mixed. Donohoo and Snyder (1985) found refocusing problems with a relatively saturated blue phosphor. No refocusing problems were reported in studies addressing short-term display viewing by Matthews and Mertins (1987), Walraven (1984), and Matthews et al. (1989). Matthews does say that his test materials included relatively simple screens, and "Failure to find a large influence of display color on visual performance might be attributed to the moderate density of screen information." Thus the accommodation mechanism was not severely tested, and generalization to a more dense screen is not warranted.

What does one conclude after looking at the research addressing the above problems? The reasonable assumption is that they have neither been proved nor disproved. We have not properly defined all the terminal-based tasks being performed. The studies have used only a few of the many terminals in existence, and a firm definition of "visual fatigue" remains elusive. Finally, none of the studies have addressed extended terminal viewing. The prudent course is to be cautious and avoid using colors and combinations which color theory claims could create problems. As shall be seen, the color palette to be used in screen design will be small, so avoiding potential problem areas will not be terribly restrictive.

The perceived appearance of a color is also affected by a variety of other factors, including the size of the area of color, the ambient illumination level, and other colors in the viewing area. Failure to consider the eye and how it handles color, then, can also lead to mistakes in color identification, misinterpretations, slower reading, and, perhaps, visual fatigue.

Color viewing deficiencies. Another disadvantage of color is that about 8 percent of males and 0.4 percent of females have some form of color-perception deficiency—colorblindness. The most common form of colorblindness is red-green, which affects about 2.5 percent of the population. Red and orange is confused with green and yellow. The visual color spectrum in this form of colorblindness ranges from blue to white to yellow. Another common colorblindness exists for blue and yellow. For an individual with color-perception deficiency, all the normal colors may not be discernible, but often differences in lightness or intensity can be seen. A person experiencing any form of colorblindness must not be prohibited from effectively using a screen.

Cross-disciplinary and cross-cultural differences. Colors can have different meanings in different situations to different people. A color used in an unexpected way can cause confusion. An error signaled in green would contradict the expected association of red with stop or danger. The same color may also have a different connotation, depending upon its viewer. Marcus (1986) provides the following quite different meanings for the color blue:

> For American movie audiences—tenderness or pornography.
> For financial managers—corporate qualities or reliability.
> For health care professionals—death.
> For nuclear reactor monitors—coolness or water.

The proper use of color requires an analysis of the expectations and experiences of the screen viewer.

The use of color in screen design must always keep these possible problems clearly in focus. The designer must work to minimize their disruptive and destructive effects. Always keep in mind that poor use of color is worse than not using it at all.

COLOR AND SCREEN DESIGN—WHAT THE RESEARCH SHOWS

The effectiveness of color in improving the usability of a display has yielded mixed research results. On a positive note, color has been shown to improve performance (Kopala, 1981; Sidorsky, 1982), to improve visual search time (Christ, 1975; Carter, 1982), to be useful for organizing information (Engel, 1980), to aid memory (Marcus, 1986b), and to demarcate a portion of a screen (as opposed to lines or type font, Wopking et al., 1985). Color has also created positive user reactions (Tullis, 1981), was preferred to monochromatic screens for being less monotonous and reducing eye strain and fatigue (Christ, 1975), and is more enjoyable (Marcus, 1986b).

On the other hand, it has also been shown that color does not improve performance (Tullis, 1981), may impair performance (Christ and Teichner, 1973; Christ, 1975), and is less important than display spacing (Haubner and Benz, 1983). It has also been demonstrated that poor character-background color combinations lead to poorer performance (McTyre and Frommer, 1985). Finally, no evidence was produced that color, as compared to black and white, can significantly improve aesthetics or legibility or reduce eye strain (Pastoor, 1990).

Research has found, moreover, that as the number of colors on a display increases, the time to respond to a single color increases, and the probability of color confusion increases (Luria et al., 1986). Many studies have found that the maximum number of colors that a person can handle is in the range of four to 10, with emphasis on the lower numbers (for example, Brooks, 1965; Halsey and Chapanis, 1951; Luria et al., 1986).

The conclusion to be derived from these studies is that for simple displays, color may have no dramatic impact. Indeed, a monochromatic display may serve the purpose just as well. As display complexity increases, however, so does the value of color. A second conclusion is that people like using color and think it has a positive influence on their productivity, even though it may not.

To be effective color must be properly used. Poor use of color will actually impair performance, not help it.

When using color, keep in mind its value will be dependent upon the task being performed, the colors selected, how many are used, and the viewing environment.

COLOR AND HUMAN VISION

To understand how color should be used on a screen, it is helpful to know something of the physiology of the human eye. The reader requiring a detailed discussion of this subject is referred to Murch (1983, 1984).

The lens. The lens of the eye, controlled by muscles, focuses wavelengths of light on the retina. The lens itself is not color corrected. The wavelengths of light creating different colors are focused at different distances behind the lens, the longer wavelengths (red) being focused further back than the shorter wavelengths (blue). The result is that colors of a different wavelength than the color actually being focused by the lens appear out of focus. To create a sharp image of the out-of-focus colors requires a refocusing of the eye. Excessive refocusing (such as between red and blue) can lead to eye fatigue.

The effect of this focusing for most people is that blues appear more distant and blues appear closer. It can give a three-dimensional appearance to what is being viewed. A critical problem is that the wavelength of light creating reds can never be brought into focus on the retina but is always focused in front of it. A sharp blue image is impossible to obtain.

Very pure colors require more refocusing than less pure colors. Therefore, a color with a large "white" component will require less refocusing.

The lens does not transmit all light wavelengths equally. It absorbs more wavelengths in the blue region of the spectrum than those in the other regions. Additionally, as the lens ages, it tends to yellow, filtering out the shorter blue wavelengths. Thus, as people get older, their sensitivity to blue decreases.

The retina. The retina is the light-sensitive surface of the eye. It comprises two kinds of receptors, rods and cones, that translate the incoming light into nervous impulses. Rods are sensitive to lower light levels and function primarily at night. Cones are stimulated by higher light levels and react to color. The sensitivity of cones to colors varies, different cones possessing maximum sensitivity to different light wavelengths. About two-thirds (64 percent) of the cones are maximally sensitive to longer light wavelengths, showing a peak response at about 575 millimicrons. These cones have traditionally been referred to as "red" sensitive cones. In actuality, however, the peak sensitivity is in the yellow portion of the visual spectrum (see Figure 13.1). About one-third (32 percent) of the cones achieve maximum sensitivity at about 535 millimicrons and are commonly referred to as "green" sensitive cones. The remainder (2 percent) primarily react to short light wavelengths, achieving maximum sensitivity at about 445 millimicrons. These are known as "blue" sensitive cones. Any lightwave impinging on the retina evokes a response, to a greater or lesser degree, from most or all of these cones. A perceived "color" results from the proportion of "stimulation" of the various kinds.

Rods and cones vary in distribution across the retina. The center is tightly packed with cones and has no rods. Toward the periphery of the retina, rods increase and cones decrease. Thus, color sensitivity does not exist at the retina's outer edges, although yellows and blues can be detected further into the periphery than reds and greens. The very center of the retina is devoid of "blue" cones, creating a "blue-blindness" for small objects fixated upon.

The receptors in the eye also adjust, or adapt, their level of sensitivity to the overall light level and the color being viewed. Adaptation to increases in brightness improves color sensitivity. Color adaptation "softens" colors.

The brightness sensitivity of the eye to different colors also varies. It is governed by output from the "red" and "green" cones. The greater the output, the higher the brightness, which results in the eye being most sensitive to colors in the middle of the visual spectrum and less sensitive to colors at the extremes. A blue or red must be of a much greater intensity than a green or yellow even to be perceived.

The ability of the eye to detect a form is accomplished by focusing the viewed image on the body of receptors to establish "edges." Distinct edges yield distinct images. Edges formed by color differences alone cannot be accurately focused and thus create fuzzy and nondistinct images. A clear, sharp image requires a difference in brightness between adjacent objects, as well as differences in color.

The components of the eye—the lens and retina—govern the choices, and combinations, of colors to be displayed on a screen. The proper colors will enhance performance; improper colors will have the opposite effect, as well as greatly increase the probability of visual fatigue.

COLORS IN CONTEXT

Colors are subject to contextual effects. The size of a colored image, the color of images adjacent to it, and the ambient illumination all exert an influence on what is actually perceived. At the normal viewing distance for a screen, maximal color sensitivity is not reached until the size of a colored area exceeds about a three-inch square. Smaller size images become desaturated (having a greater white component) and change slightly in color. Also, small differences in actual color may not be discernible. Blues and yellows are particularly susceptible to difficulties in detecting slight changes. Finally, small adjacent colored images may appear to the eye to merge or mix. Red and green, for example, might appear as yellow.

Adjacent images can influence the perceived color. A color on a dark background, for example, will look lighter and brighter than the same color on a light background. A color can be *induced* into a neutral foreground area (gray) by the presence of a colored background. A red background can change a gray into a green. Induced colors are the complement of the inducing color. Complementary afterimages can also be induced by looking at a saturated color for a period of time.

Colors change as light levels change. Higher levels of ambient light tend to desaturate colors. Saturated colors will also appear larger than desaturated colors.

CHOOSING CATEGORIES OF INFORMATION FOR COLOR

- Choosing categories of information for color requires a clear understanding of how the information will be used.
- Some examples:
  - If different parts of the screen are attended to separately, color code the different parts to focus selective attention on each in turn.

—If decisions are made based on the status of certain types of information on the screen, color code the types of status the information may possess.

—If screen searching is performed to locate information of a particular kind or quality, color code these kinds or qualities for contrast.

—If the sequence of information use is constrained or ordered, use color to identify the sequence.

—If the information displayed on a screen is packed or crowded, use color to provide visual groupings.

Color chosen to classify data on a screen must aid the transfer of information from the display to the user. This requires a clear understanding of how the information is selected and used. The examples above describe some common ways of classifying information for color coding purposes.

It is important to remember, however, that data on one screen may be used in more than one way. What is useful in one context may not be in another and may only cause interference. Therefore, when developing a color strategy, consider how spatial formatting, highlighting, and messages may also be useful.

CHOOSING COLORS TO DISPLAY

General Considerations

Colors chosen for display on a screen must consider these factors: the human visual system, the possible problems that its use may cause, the contextual effects that may occur, the viewing environment in which the display is used, and the task of the user. The primary objective in using color is communication, to aid the transfer of information from the screen to the user.

Usage

- Design for monochrome first.
- Use colors conservatively.
  —Do not use color where other identification techniques such as location are available.

Design for monochrome first. A screen should be as capable of being effectively used as if it were in a monochrome environment. Spatial formatting, consistent locations, and display techniques such as highlighting, mixed- and upper-case characters should all be utilized to give it a structure independent of the color. This will permit the screen to be effectively used:

- By colorblind people.
- On monochrome displays.
- In conditions where ambient lighting distorts the perceived color.
- If the color ever fails.

Use colors conservatively. Only enough colors to achieve the design objective should be used. More colors increase response times, increase the chance of errors due to colors confusions, and increase the chance of the "Christmas tree" effect. If two colors serve the need, use two colors. If three colors are needed, by all means use three. A way to minimize the need for too many different colors is not to use it in situations where other identification methods are available. A menu bar, for example, will always be located at the top of the screen. Its position and structure will identify it as a menu bar. To color code it would be redundant.

Discrimination and Harmony

- For best absolute discrimination, select no more than four or five colors widely spaced on the color spectrum.
  — Good colors: red, yellow, green, blue, brown.
- For best comparative discrimination, select no more than six or seven colors widely spaced on the color spectrum.
  — Other acceptable colors: orange, yellow-green, cyan, violet, or magenta.
- Choose harmonious colors.
  — One color plus two colors on either side of its complement.
  — Three colors in equidistant points around the color circle.
- For older viewers or extended viewing, use brighter colors.

For best absolute discrimination, use four to five colors. The population of measurable colors is about 7.5 million (Geldard, 1953). From this vast number, the eye cannot effectively distinguish many more than a handful. If color memorization and absolute discrimination is necessary (a color must be correctly identified while no other color is in the field of vision), select no more than four to five colors widely spaced along the color spectrum (Smith, 1988; Marcus, 1986b). Selecting widely spaced colors will maximize the probability of their being correctly identified. Good choices are red, yellow, green, blue, and brown (Marcus, 1986b).

Two good color opponent pairs are red/green and yellow/blue. All of these colors except blue are easy to resolve visually. Again, be cautious in using blue for data, text, or small symbols on screens because it may not always be legible. If the meaning for each of more than five colors is absolutely necessary, a legend should be provided illustrating the colors and describing their associated meanings.

For best comparative discrimination, use six to seven colors. If comparative discrimination will be performed (a color must be correctly identified while other colors are in the field of vision), select no more than six or seven colors widely spaced along the visual spectrum. In addition to those above, other colors could be chosen from orange, yellow-green, cyan, and violet or magenta. Again, be cautious of using blue for data, text, or small symbols.

If the intent is to portray natural objects realistically, the use of more colors might be necessary.

Choose harmonious colors. Harmonious colors are those that work well together or meet without sharp contrast. Harmony is most easily achieved with a monochromatic palette. For each background color, different lightnesses or values are established through mixing it with black and white. Marcus (1986a) suggests a minimum of three values should be obtained.

Harmonious combinations in a multicolor environment are more difficult to obtain. Marcus recommends avoiding complementary colors—those at opposite sides of the circle of hues in the Munsell color system, a standard commercial color system. He suggests using split complements, one color plus two colors on either side of its complement, or choosing three colors at equidistant points around the color circle.

For older viewers or extended viewing, use bright colors. As eye capacity diminishes with age, data, text, and symbols in the less bright colors may be harder to read. Distinguishing colors may also be more difficult. For any viewer, long viewing periods result in the eye adapting to the brightness level. Brighter colors will be needed if either of these conditions exist.

Emphasis

- To draw attention or to emphasize, use bright or highlighted colors. To deemphasize, use less bright colors.
  - The perceived brightness of colors from most to least is white, yellow, green, blue, red.
- To emphasize separation, use contrasting colors.
  - Red and green, blue and yellow.
- To convey similarity, use similar colors.
  - Orange and yellow, blue and violet.

To draw attention or emphasize, use bright colors. The eye is drawn to brighter or highlighted colors, so use them for the more important screen components. The data or text is the most important component on most screens, so it is a good candidate for highlighting or the brightest color. Danger signals should also be brighter or highlighted. The perceived brightness of colors, from most to least, is white, yellow, green, blue, and red.

Keep in mind, however, that under levels of high ambient illumination, colors frequently appear washed out or unsaturated. If some means of light attenuation is not possible, or if colors chosen are not bright enough to counter the illumination, color should be used with caution.

Use contrasting colors to emphasize separation. To emphasize the separation of screen components, use contrasting colors. Possible pairs would be red/green and blue/yellow.

Use similar colors to convey similarity. Similar colors convey a similar meaning. Related elements can be brought together by displaying them in a similar color. Blue and green, for example, are more closely related than red and green.

Common Meanings

- To indicate that actions are necessary, use warm colors.
  — Red, orange, yellow.
- To provide status or background information, use cool colors.
  — Green, blue, violet, purple.
- Conform to human expectancies:
  — In the job.
  — In the world at large.

To indicate that actions are necessary, use warm colors. The warm colors, red, yellow, and orange, imply active situations or that actions are necessary. Warm colors advance, forcing attention.

To provide background or status, use cool colors. The cool colors, green, blue, violet, and purple, imply background or status information. Cool colors recede or draw away.

Conform to human expectancies. Use color meanings that already exist in a person's job or the world at large. They are ingrained in behavior and difficult to unlearn. Some common color associations, as described by Marcus (1986b) are the following:

- Red   — Stop, fire, hot, danger
- Yellow   — Caution, slow, test
- Green   — Go, OK, clear, vegetation, safety
- Blue   — Cold, water, calm, sky, neutrality
- Gray   — Neutrality
- White   — Neutrality
- Warm colors — Action, response required, spatial closeness
- Cool colors — Status, background information, spatial remoteness

Some typical implications of color with dramatic portrayal, also by Marcus, are the following:

- High illumination   — Hot, active, comic situations
- Low illumination   — Emotional, tense, tragic, melodramatic, romantic situations
- High saturation   — Emotional, tense, hot, melodramatic, comic situations
- Warm colors   — Active, leisure, recreation, comic situations
- Cool colors   — Efficiency, work, tragic and romantic situations

Proper use of color also requires consideration of the experiences and expectations of the screen viewers.

Location

- In the center of the visual field, use red and green.
- For peripheral viewing, use blue, yellow, black, and white.
- Use adjacent colors that differ by hue and value or lightness.

In the center of the visual field, use red and green. The eye is most sensitive to red and green in the center of the visual field. The edges of the retina are not sensitive to these colors. If used in the viewing periphery, some other attention-getting method such as blinking must also be used.

For peripheral viewing, use blue, yellow, black, or white. The retina is most sensitive to these colors at its periphery.

Use adjacent colors that differ by hue and value. Colors appearing adjacent to one another should differ in hue and lightness for a sharp "edge" and maximum differentiation. Also, adjacent colors differing only in their blue component should not be used so that differentiation is possible. The eye is poorly suited for dealing with blue.

Ordering

- Order colors by their spectral position.
  - Red, orange, yellow, green, blue, indigo, violet.

If an ordering of colors is needed, such as high to low, levels of depth, and so on, arrange colors by their spectral position. There is evidence that people see the spectral order as a natural one (Fromme, 1983). The spectral order is red, orange, yellow, green, blue, indigo, and violet, most easily remembered as "ROY G BIV."

Foregrounds and Backgrounds

Foregrounds

- Use colors as different as possible from background colors.
- Use warmer, more active colors.
- Use colors that possess the same saturation and lightness.
- For text or data, use desaturated or spectrum center colors.
  - White, yellow, green.

- To emphasize, highlight in a light value of the foreground color, pure white, or yellow.
- To deemphasize, lowlight in a dark value of the foreground color.

Backgrounds

- Use a background color to organize a group of elements into a unified whole.
- Use colors that do not compete with the foreground.
- Use cool, dark colors.
  — Blue, black.
- Use colors at the extreme end of the color spectrum.
  — Red, magenta.

Foregrounds

Use colors as different as possible from background colors. A widely different foreground will maximize legibility.

Use warmer, more active colors. Warmer colors advance, forcing attention.

Use colors that possess the same saturation and lightness. Exercise caution in using more fully saturated red and orange, however, as they may be difficult to distinguish from one another.

For text or data, use desaturated or spectrum center colors. Desaturated or spectrum center colors do not excessively stimulate the eye and appear brighter to the eye. Saturated colors excessively stimulate the eye. Marcus (1986a) recommends avoiding the use of pure white in text (except for some highlighting) because of the harsh contrast between the text and background. He suggests text should be off-white in a multicolor palette. The ISO Color Standard (Smith, 1988) suggests that for continuous reading tasks, desaturated, spectrally close colors (yellow, cyan, green) should be used to minimize disruptive eye problems.

Highlight in a light value of the foreground color, pure white, or yellow. Lowlight in a dark value of the foreground color. Marcus (1986a) suggests that to call attention to a screen element, it may be highlighted in a light value of the foreground color. If off-white is the foreground color, highlight in pure white. Yellow can also be used to highlight. To deemphasize an element, lowlight in a darker value of the foreground color. In lowlighting, a strong enough contrast with both the background and the non-lowlighted element must be maintained so that legibility and visual differentiation is possible.

The simultaneous use of highlighting and lowlighting should be avoided. Used together they may create confusion for the viewer. Also, as with other display techniques, be conservative in using highlighting and lowlighting so that simplicity and clarity are maintained.

Backgrounds

Use a background color to organize a group of elements into a unified whole. A background color should organize a group of elements into a unified whole, isolating them from the remainder of the screen.

Use colors that do not compete with the foreground. A background must be subtle and subservient to the data, text, or symbols on top of it.

Use cool, dark colors. Cool, dark colors visually recede, providing good contrast to the advancing lighter, foreground colors. Blue is especially good because of the eye's lack of sensitivity to it in the retina's central area and increased sensitivity to it in the periphery. Lalomia and Happ (1987) in a study addressing foreground and background color combinations, found the best background colors to be black and blue. In a similar study, Pastoor (1990) found that cool colors, blue and bluish cyan, were preferred for dark background screens.

Use colors at the extreme end of the color spectrum. Other spectrally extreme colors, such as red and magenta, also make better background colors. Marcus (1986a) recommends, in order of priority, the following background colors: blue, black, gray, brown, red, green, purple.

Color Palette and Default

- Provide a default set of colors for all screen components.
- Provide a palette of six or seven foreground colors.
    - Provide two to five values or lightness shades for each foreground color.
- Provide a palette of six or seven background colors.

Provide a default set of colors. Most people do not know how to apply color to create a clear and appealing screen. Others may have the talent and skills but not the time to select a proper combination. For these users, a preselected set of colors should be developed for all screen elements.

Provide a palette of six or seven foreground and background colors. To provide some flexibility, and to permit users the opportunity to change colors if they so desire, a palette of colors should be available. Marcus (1986a) suggests a maximum of six or seven foreground and background colors will provide the necessary variety. He also recommends that two to five values or lightnesses for each foreground color be developed.

With these palettes, however, some sort of guidance concerning maximum number of colors to use and what are good and poor combinations should be provided. This will make the color selection process more efficient and reduce the likelihood of visually straining conditions developing.

Gray Scale

- For fine discriminations use a black-gray-white scale.
  - Recommended values are white, light gray, medium gray, dark gray, black.

The perception of fine detail is poor with color. The eye resolves fine detail much better on a black-white scale. Marcus (1986b) recommends five tonal values for black and white, higher resolution screens: black, dark gray, medium gray, light gray, and white. He suggests the following general uses:

- White — Screen background
  Text located in any black area
- Light Gray — Pushbutton background area
- Medium Gray — Icon background area
  Menu dropshadow
  Window dropshadow
  Inside area of system icons
  Filename bar
- Dark gray — Window border
- Black — Text
  Window title bar
  Icon border
  Icon elements
  Ruled lines

Consistency

- Be consistent in color use.

Consistency in color usage should exist within a screen, a set of screens, and a system. A person can sense the relatedness of color in space and over time, thereby linking elements not immediately together. An identical background color in windows on different screens, for example, will be seen as related. Changing color meanings must be avoided. It will lead to difficulties in interpretation, confusion, and errors. In general, broadly defined meanings (such as red indicating a problem) permit more scope for variations without inconsistency.

ALPHANUMERIC AND GRAPHIC SCREENS

For displaying data, text, and symbols, colors selected should have adequate visibility, contrast, and harmony.

- Use effective foreground/background combinations.
- Use effective character combinations.
- Display no more than four colors at one time.
- Choose the background color first.

Use Effective Foreground/Background Combinations

Lalomia and Happ (1987) established effective foreground/background color combinations for the IBM 5153 Color Display. From a color set of 16 different foregrounds and 8 different backgrounds, 120 color combinations were evaluated for (1) response time to identify characters, and (2) subjective preferences of users. The results from each measure were ranked and combined to derive an overall measure of color combination effectiveness. The best and poorest color combinations are summarized in Table 13.1. In this table "Best" means the specified combination was in the top 20 percent for overall effectiveness; "Poor" means it was in the bottom 20 percent. Those combinations comprising the "middle" 60 percent are indicated by a dash (–).

The results yield some interesting conclusions.

- The majority of good combinations possess a bright or high-intensity color as the foreground color.
- The majority of poor combinations are those with low contrast.
- The best overall color is black.
- The poorest overall color is brown.
- Maximum flexibility and variety in choosing a foreground color exists with black or blue backgrounds (these backgrounds account for almost one-half of the good combinations).
- Brown and green are the poorest background choices.

Bailey and Bailey (1989), in their screen creation utility Protoscreens, have a table summarizing research-derived good foreground/background combinations. This table, which uses the results of the Lalomia and Happ study plus some others, is shown in modified form in Table 13.2.

The studies referenced above did not control character-background luminance-contrast ratios. Because of the characteristics of the eye, some colors appear brighter to it than others. A conclusion of the Lalomia and Happ study was that good combinations usually possessed a bright or high-intensity foreground color.

Pastoor (1990) equalized luminance-contrast ratios at preoptimized levels for about 800 foreground/background color combinations. For foregrounds brighter than backgrounds, the ratio was 10:1; for brighter backgrounds, 1:6.5. He then had the combinations rated with the following results:

- For dark on light polarity:
  - Any foreground color is acceptable if the background color is chosen properly.

Table 13.1. Effective foreground/background combinations. (From Lalomia and Happ, 1987)

Foreground	Background							
	Black	Blue	Green	Cyan	Red	Magenta	Brown	White
BLACK	x	–	–	Good	–	Good	–	Good
BLUE	–	x	–	–	Poor	–	–	Good
H.I. BLUE	–	–	Poor	Poor	–	–	Poor	Poor
CYAN	Good	–	Poor	x	–	–	Poor	–
H.I. CYAN	Good	Good	–	Good	Good	Good	–	–
GREEN	Good	Good	x	Poor	Good	–	Poor	Poor
H.I. GREEN	–	Good	–	–	–	–	–	–
YELLOW	Good	Good	–	Good	–	Good	–	–
RED	–	–	Poor	–	x	Poor	Poor	–
H.I. RED	–	–	Poor	–	–	–	–	–
MAGENTA	–	–	Poor	–	Poor	x	Poor	–
H.I. MAGENTA	Good	–	Good	–	–	Poor	–	–
BROWN	–	–	Poor	–	–	Poor	x	–
GRAY	–	Poor	–	–	Poor	–	Poor	–
WHITE	–	Good	–	Poor	–	–	–	x
H.I. WHITE	Good	–	Good	Good	–	–	–	–

(H.I. = High Intensity)

Table 13.2. Preferred foreground/background combinations from Protoscreens.

Backgrounds	Acceptable Foregrounds	
Black	Dark Cyan	Light Green
	Dark Yellow	Light Cyan
	Dark White	Light Magenta
		Light Yellow
		Light White
Blue	Dark Green	Light Green
	Dark Yellow	Light Cyan
	Dark White	Light Yellow
		Light White
Green	Black	Light Yellow
	Dark Blue	Light White
Cyan	Black	Light Yellow
	Dark Blue	Light White
Red	—	Light Green
		Light Cyan
		Light Yellow
		Light White
Magenta	Black	Light Cyan
		Light Yellow
		Light White
Yellow	Black	—
	Dark Blue	
	Dark Red	
White	Black	—
	Dark Blue	

- Increased saturation of the foreground only marginally affected ratings, implying that any dark, saturated, foreground color is satisfactory.
- Saturated backgrounds yield unsatisfactory ratings.
- Less saturated backgrounds generally receive high ratings with any foreground color.
- For light on dark polarity:
  - Combinations involving saturated colors tend to be unsatisfactory.
  - As foreground color saturation increases; the number of background colors yielding high ratings diminishes.
  - Generally, desaturated foreground/background color combinations yielded the best ratings.

Table 13.3. Effective two- and three-color combinations for dark background screens from Smith (1986).

Two-Color Combinations	
Good	*Poor*
White / Green	Red / Blue
Gold / Cyan	Red / Green
Gold / Green	Red / Purple
Green / Magenta	Red / Yellow
Green / Lavender	Red / Magenta
Cyan / Red	White / Cyan
	White / Yellow
	Blue / Green
	Blue / Purple
	Green / Cyan
	Cyan / Lavender

Three-Color Combinations	
Good	*Poor*
White / Gold / Green	Red / Yellow / Green
White / Gold / Blue	Red / Blue / Green
White / Gold / Magenta	Red / Magenta / Blue
White / Red / Cyan	White / Cyan / Yellow
Red / Cyan/ Gold	Green / Cyan / Blue
Cyan / Yellow / Lavender	
Gold / Magenta / Blue	
Gold / Magenta / Green	
Gold / Lavender / Green	

— Short wavelength, cool colors were preferred for backgrounds (blue, bluish cyan, cyan).

In general, Pastoor concluded that 1) there was no evidence suggesting a differential effect of color on subjective ratings or performance (except that for light on dark polarity, blue, bluish cyan, or cyan were preferred as backgrounds), and 2) overall, desaturated color combinations yielded the best results.

Use effective character combinations. Smith (1986) has recommended the two- and three-color combinations summarized at the left of Table 13.3 as being effective for dark background screens. She cautions against using the combinations described on the table's right side. She also suggests that light background screens should contain pastel colors with dark characters.

Display no more than four colors at one time. While not experimentally verified, experience indicates that more than four colors displayed at one time on a screen gives rise to a feeling of overkill. Marcus (1986a) suggests an even more conservative approach, a maximum of three foreground colors and, even better, only two. An application of good use of color can often be viewed in one's living room. Note the use of color by the television networks when textual or tabular information is presented (for example, sport scores, news highlights, and so on). The use of only two, or sometimes three, colors is most commonly seen.

So, while more than four colors may be displayed over a period of time or a series of screens, do not display more than four colors at one time on a single screen. For most cases, restrict the number of colors to two or three.

Choose the background color first. When choosing colors to display, it is best to select the background color first. Then choose acceptable foreground colors.

STATISTICAL GRAPHICS SCREENS

The visual, spatial, or physical representation of information—as opposed to numeric, alphanumeric, textual, or symbol representation—is known as statistical or data graphics. Common kinds of statistical graphics include bar graphs, line graphs, scatterplots, and pie charts. Color can also be used to render a statistical graphic screen more legible and meaningful.

Emphasis

- Emphasize the data display area.

The main emphasis of color in a statistical graphics screen should be in the data area. Brighter colors and highlighting should attract the eye to the presented data so that trends and conclusions can be quickly perceived. Supporting text, numbers, and legends should receive slightly less emphasis. Aids in data interpretation such as grids should receive the least emphasis.

Number of Colors

- Use no more than:
  - — Six colors at one time.
  - — Five values or lightnesses of one color.

Experience indicates that displaying more than six colors at one time on statistical graphics screens is "too much." Even five or six colors, however, may be distracting or confusing if they are not properly chosen or are not harmonious. Marcus (1986a) suggests a more pleasing arrangement can often be achieved for graphics with five or less segments by using one color and displaying each segment in a different value or lightness. (Five, as described earlier, is the maximum number for easy human differentiation.)

Backgrounds

- Surround images:
  - — In a neutral color.
  - — In a color complementary to the main image.

A neutral background will help set off a full color. A background in the complementary color of the main image will minimize visual afterimages.

Size

- Provide images of an adequate size for the task.
- If the image changes in size, use colors exhibiting a minimum shift in hue or lightness.
  - — White, yellow, and red on dark backgrounds.

As color areas decrease in size, they appear to change in lightness and saturation. Similar colors may look different and different colors may look similar. Interactions with the background color also increase. Thin gray images (lines or borders, for example) appear as a desaturated color complement of their background.

Provide adequate-size images. Where color identification is important, an image should be large enough to eliminate these distortions.

For images changing in size, use colors exhibiting minimum hue or lightness shifts. Marcus (1986b) recommends that white, yellow, and red be used for light text, thin lines, and small shapes on dark backgrounds (blue, green, red, light gray).

Status

- To indicate a status, use the following colors:
  - — Proper, normal, or OK   — Green, white, or blue
  - — Caution   — Yellow or gold
  - — Emergency or abnormal   — Red

The use of red, yellow, and green are well-learned color conventions.

Measurements and Area-Fill Patterns

- Display measurements in the following colors:
  - — Grids   — Gray
  - — Data points   — Yellow
  - — Variance or error bars   — Blue
  - — Out of specified range data   — Red
  - — Captions and labels   — Lavender, lime green, or cyan

- Display area-fill patterns in the following colors:
  - — Widely spaced dots   — Red
  - — Closely spaced dots   — Green
  - — Wide dashed lines   — Magenta
  - — Narrow dashed lines   — Cyan
  - — Wide crosshatch   — Blue
  - — Narrow crosshatch   — Yellow

Measurements. For measurements, Smith (1986) recommends the above. They balance emphasis considerations (gray for grids, yellow for data points, lavender, lime green, or cyan for labels) and human expectancies (red for out-of-specified range). Marcus (1986a) recommends that all text and the horizontal and vertical axis lines of a statistical graphic should be off-white. This will aid focusing main attention on the colored data.

Fill-in area patterns. To ensure that fill-in area patterns are identifiable, discriminable, and free from unintended brightness effects, the ISO Draft Color Standard (Smith, 1988) recommends the above.

Physical Impressions

Size

- To convey an impression of:
  - — Larger   — Use bright or saturated colors.
  - — Smaller   — Use dark or desaturated colors.
  - — Similar   — Use colors of equal lightness.

Weight

- To convey an impression of:
  - — Heavy   — Use dark, saturated colors.
  - — Light   — Use light, desaturated colors.

Distance

- To convey an impression of:
  - — Close   — Use saturated, bright, long-wavelength (red) colors.
  - — Far   — Use saturated, dark, short-wavelength (blue) colors.

Height

- To convey an impression of height, use desaturated, light colors.

Depth

- To convey an impression of depth, use saturated, dark colors.

Concentration Level

- To convey an impression of concentration level, use:
  - — High   — Saturated colors.
  - — Low   — Desaturated colors.

Magnitude of Change

- To convey an impression of magnitude of change, use:
  - — Lowest   — Short-wavelength (blue) colors.
  - — Highest   — Long-wavelength (red) colors.

Actions

- To convey an impression of action, use:
  - — Required   — Long-wavelength (red) colors.
  - — Not required   — Short-wavelength (blue) colors.

Order

- To convey an impression of order with color, use:
  - Low end of a continuum　　— Short-wavelength (blue) colors.
  - High end of a continuum　　— Long-wavelength (red) colors.
- When displaying an array of ordered colors, position:
  - Short-wavelength colors to the left side or at the bottom.
  - Long-wavelength colors to the right side or at the top.
- To convey an impression of order with value or lightness, use lightness order of a color (darkest to lightest or vice versa).

Neutrality

- To convey an impression of neutrality, use black, gray, and white.

Colors yield different physical impressions (Tedford et al. 1977; Smith, 1986; ISO Draft Color Standard; Smith, 1988). Bright, saturated colors convey a feeling of large and close. Dark, saturated colors mean heavy, far, and impression of depth. Desaturated, light colors indicate a light weight and height. Desaturated dark colors mean smaller. Long-wavelength (red) colors are associated with high rate of change, action required, and the high end of a continuum. Short-wavelength (blue) colors are associated with low rate of change, no actions required, and the low end of a continuum. Neutrality is best indicated by black, gray, or white.

COLORS TO AVOID

- Relying exclusively on color.
- Too many colors at one time.
- Highly saturated, spectrally extreme colors together:
  - Red and blue, yellow and purple.
- Low-brightness colors for extended viewing or older viewers.
- Colors of equal brightness.
- Colors lacking contrast:
  - For example, yellow and white, black and brown, reds, blues, and browns against a light background.
- Using colors in unexpected ways.
- Fully saturated colors for text or other frequently read screen components.
- Pure blue for text, thin lines, and small shapes.
- Colors in small areas.
- Color for fine details.
- Red and green in the periphery of large-scale displays.
- Adjacent colors only differing in the amount of blue they possess.
- Color to improve legibility of densely packed text.
- Too many colors at one time (again).

The proper use of color in screen design also suggests some things to avoid.

Relying exclusively on color. Consider the needs of colorblind viewers and the effects of ambient lighting on color perception. Do not underestimate the value and role of other techniques such as spatial formatting and component locations in good screen design.

Too many colors at one time. Using too many colors can increase response times, cause erroneous associations, interfere with the handling of information, and create confusion. The objective is a screen that communicates; a colorful screen is not the objective. Use just enough colors to create an effective communication. Again, consider the value of other techniques like spatial formatting and consistent component locations in good design.

Highly saturated, spectrally extreme colors together. Spectrally extreme combinations can create eye focus problems, vibrations, illusions of shadows, and afterimages. In addition to red/blue and yellow/purple, other combinations that might cause problems are yellow/blue, green/blue, and red/green (Marcus, 1985a).

Low-brightness colors for extended viewing or older viewers. The eye adapts to color during extended viewing. The eye's capacity also diminishes with age as the amount of light passing through the lens decreases. All colors will look less bright, and colors that are dim to begin with may not be legible. Brighter colors are needed to prevent reading problems.

Colors of equal brightness. Colors of equal brightness cannot be easily distinguished. A brightness difference must exist between adjacent colors.

Colors lacking contrast. Colors lacking contrast also cannot be easily distinguished.

Using colors in unexpected ways. Colors have become associated with certain meanings. Red, for example, is always associated with stop or danger. To display a critical or error message in green would violate an ingrained association and cause confusion.

Fully saturated colors for text and other frequently read screen components. Fully saturated colors excessively stimulate the eye, again possibly causing visual confusion.

Pure blue for text, thin lines, and small shapes. Due to its physical makeup, the eye has difficulty creating a clear and legible image for small blue shapes. They will look fuzzy.

Colors in small areas. Distortions in color, lightness, and saturation may occur.

Colors for fine details. Black, gray, and white will provide much better resolution.

Red and green in the periphery of large-scale displays. The edges of the retina are not particularly sensitive to red and green.

Adjacent colors only differing in the amount of blue they possess. Because of the eye's difficulty in dealing with blue, differences in color based upon varying amounts of blue in the color's mixture will not be noticed.

Color to improve legibility of densely packed text. Space lines between paragraphs of text or after about every five lines of data will work much better.

Too many colors at one time (again). Never overuse color (again). Too many colors at one time may make a screen confusing or unpleasant to look at. Use only enough color to fulfill the system's objectives.

14

Icons

The symbolic representation of objects, such as office tools or storage locations, and optional actions on a screen began with Xerox's Star, continued with Apple's Lisa and Macintosh, and has been building ever since. Indeed, the faces of many 1990s screens scarcely resemble their older siblings of the early 1980s.

STEP 10

- Choose window icons.
    - Determine what graphic images best represent the application.
    - Determine what relevant default icons are available and use them.
    - Create icons for images not represented by defaults through following established icon design guidelines.

To start, a definition of "icon," or more appropriately, "icons," is provided. Then, what influences an icon's usability is described as are a series of guidelines addressing the actual design of icons. Finally, several design guidelines for screens displaying icons are presented.

KINDS OF ICONS

Icons to reflect objects, ideas, and actions are not new to mankind. We've been there before. Early humans (100,000 years or so ago) used pictographs and then ideographs to communicate. Some of these early communications can be found on rock walls and in caves around the world. Until recently, this was also a way to communicate in some cultures (North American Indians, Australian Aborigines, for example). Again, traces can still be seen.

Word writing is traced back to Egyptian hieroglyphics from about 3000 B.C. This was followed by cuneiform (Babylonia and Assyria) from about 1900 B.C., and Chinese word signs (numbering about 50,000) around 1300 B.C. In 1000 B.C. the Phoenicians developed a 22-sign alphabet that the Greeks adopted about 800–600 B.C. The Greeks passed this alphabet on to the Romans about 400 B.C., who then developed a 23-character alphabet. It has been modified and embellished but has remained essentially the same for the last 2000 years.

Pictorial representations, then, have played a prominent role in mankind's history. Word writing, however, unleashed much more flexibility and richness in communication. This has caused some skeptics, such as Bigelow (1985), to wonder why, after taking 2500 years to get rid of iconic shapes, we are now reviving them on screens.

Whatever the past, today, objects or actions *are* depicted on screens by icons. The term icon by itself, however, is not very specific and can actually represent very different things. An attempt has been made by some to define the actual kinds of icons that do exist.

- Icon   — Something that looks like what it means.
- Index   — A sign that was caused by the thing to which it refers.
- Symbol   — A sign that may be completely arbitrary in appearance.

Marcus (1984) observes that what are commonly referred to as icons may really be indexes or symbols.

A true icon is something that looks like what it means. It is representational and easy to understand. A picture of a telephone or a clock on a screen is a true icon. An index is a sign caused by the thing to which it refers. An open door with a broken window indicates the possible presence of a burglar. The meaning of an index may or may not be clear, depending upon one's past experiences. A symbol is a sign that may be completely arbitrary in appearance and whose meaning must be learned. The menu and sizing icons on screens are examples of symbols. Strictly speaking, so-called icons on screens are probably a mixture of true icons, signs, and indexes.

- Resemblance   — An image that looks like what it means.
- Symbolic   — An abstract image representing something.
- Exemplar   — An image illustrating an example or characteristic of something.
- Arbitrary   — An image completely arbitrary in appearance whose meaning must be learned.
- Analogy   — An image physically or semantically associated with something.

Rogers (1989) notes that an icon is *used* in a number of different ways: for *objects* such as a document, *object attributes* such as a color or fill pattern, *actions* such as to paste, *system states* such as ready or busy, and *message types* like critical or warning.

The different ways icons are used may then be represented by different *design schemes*. A *resemblance* is an image that looks like what it means—a book, for example, to represent a dictionary. This is equivalent to Marcus's "icon." A *symbolic* is an abstract image that represents something. Fragile, for example, can be represented by a cracked glass. Marcus's "symbol" would be similar. An *exemplar* represents an example or characteristic of something. A sign at a freeway exit picturing a knife and fork has come to indicate a restaurant. An *arbitrary* image is not directly related in any way and must be learned. Marcus's "symbol" would be an equivalent. Finally, an *analogy* is an image physically or semantically associated with something—a wheelbarrow full of bricks for the move command, for example. Marcus's "symbol" would also be similar.

In a study looking at various kinds of icons, Rogers found that those depicting both an action and an object were quite effective. For example, a drawing of a page and an arrow pointing up means "go to the top of the page." She also found that arbitrary icons were only meaningful in very small sets, and that icons based on analogies were relatively ineffective.

CHARACTERISTICS OF ICONS

• Syntactics	— Their physical appearance.
• Semantics	— Their meaning.
• Pragmatics	— How they are produced or depicted.

An icon possesses the technical qualities of syntactics, semantics, and pragmatics (Marcus, 1984).

Syntactics refers to an icon's physical structure. Is it square, round, red, green, big, small? Are the similarities and differences obvious? Similar shapes and colors can classify a group of related icons, communicating a common relationship.

Semantics is the icon's meaning. To what does it refer—a file, a wastebasket, some other object? Is this clear?

Pragmatics are how the icons are physically produced and depicted. Is the screen resolution sufficient to illustrate the icon clearly?

Syntactics, semantics, and pragmatics determine an icon's effectiveness and usability.

USABILITY INFLUENCES

- Familiarity.
- Clarity.
- Simplicity.

- Consistency.
- Directness of "link."
- Context in which used.
- Complexity of task.
- Expectancies of users.
- Efficiency.
- Discriminability.

The usability of an icon or icons is dependent on the following factors.

Familiarity. How familiar is the object being depicted? Familiarity will reduce learning time (Carroll and White, 1973; Wingfield, 1968). How familiar are the commonly seen icons in Figure 14.1? Lack of familiarity requires learning the icons' meanings. Many unfamiliar icons require a great deal of learning.

Experience makes words and numbers often more familiar to a person than symbols. Confusion matrices have been developed through extensive research for alphanumeric data (0 versus O, 1 versus I). Graphic symbols may be more visually similar.

Clarity. Is the icon legible? Does the shape, structure, and formation technique on the screen permit a clear and unambiguous depiction of what it is? Screen resolution should be sufficiently fine to establish clear differences of form at the normal working distance. The resolution and pixel shapes for CGA, EGA, and VGA screens differ from one another. Icons must appear correctly and consistently no matter what kind of screen. If color is used, it should contrast well with the background. Poor clarity will lead to identification errors and slower performance.

Simplicity. Is the icon simple? Is the shape clean and devoid of unnecessary embellishments? Too many parts will only confuse the screen viewer.

Consistency. Are families of icons consistent in structure and shape? Are the same icons displayed in different sizes also consistent in structure and shape? Marcus (1984) says consistency is achieved through limiting the variations of angles, line thicknesses, shapes, and amount of empty space.

Directness of link. How "sign-like" is the icon; how well does it convey its intended meaning? For concrete objects and actions, direct links are more easily established. Adjectives, adverbs, conjunctions, and prepositions can cause problems, however. Also, how does one easily convey concepts like bigger, smaller, wider, or narrower?

Context. The context of a symbol may change its meaning. Does the "rabbit" symbol illustrated in Figure 14.1, if seen on a road sign in a national park, mean "go faster"?

Complexity of task. The more abstract or complex the symbol, the more difficult it is to extract or interpret its intended meaning. In the 1984 Stern study, the more concrete graphic messages were easier to comprehend than the more abstract. Icons, therefore, cannot completely replace words in some more complex situations.

Expectancies. The symbol may be comprehended, but a false conclusion may be reached about the desired action because of an incorrect expectancy. Bailey (1984) reported that a study of international road signs found that 8 percent of all drivers never saw the "slash" through the symbol on a road sign, which indicates "do not" do the pictured action. Their expectancy was that they could do it.

Efficiency. In some situations, a graphics screen may be less efficient, consuming more screen display space than a word or requiring more physical actions by the user. A telephone directory of 50 names and numbers listed on an alphanumeric screen may consume the same screen space required for 15 file cards. Raising an arm or moving a "mouse" may be slower than simply typing. In other situations icons can be more effective than words in communicating concepts in a smaller area of space. Their strength lies in situations where this occurs.

Discriminability. Symbols chosen must be visually distinguishable from other symbols. A person's powers of differentiation for shapes and other forms of codes have been experimentally determined over the years. The maximum number of

Figure 14.1.   Some common icons. What do they stand for? (From Micro Switch, 1984) See page 411 for the answers.

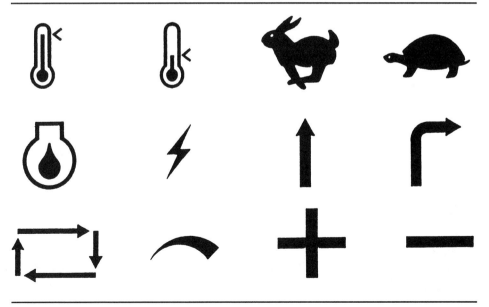

Figure 14.2 Maximum number of codes for effective human differentiation.

Encoding Method	Recommended Maximum	Comments
Alphanumerics	Unlimited	Highly versatile. Meaning usually self-evident. Location time may be longer than for graphic coding.
Geometric Shapes	10–20	High mnemonic value. Very effective if shape relates to object or operation being represented.
Size	3–5	Fair. Considerable space required. Location time longer than for colors and shapes.
Line Length	3–4	Will clutter the display if many are used.
Line Width	2–3	Good.
Line Style	5–9	Good.
Line Angle	8–11	Good in special cases (such as wind direction).
Solid and Broken Lines	3–4	Good.
Number of Dots or Marks	5	Minimize number for quick assimilation.
Brightness	2–3	Creates problems on screens with poor contrast.
Flashing/Blinking	2–3	Confusing for general encoding but the best way to attract attention. Interacts poorly with other codes. Annoying if overused. Limit to small fields.
Underlining	No data	Useful but can reduce text legibility.
Reverse Video	No data	Effective for making data stand out. Flicker easily perceived in large areas, however.
Orientation (location on display surface)	4–8	—
Color	6–8	Attractive and efficient. Short location time. Excessive use confusing. Poor for color blind.
Combinations of Codes	Unlimited	Can reinforce coding but complex combinations can be confusing.

Data derived from Martin, 1973; Barmack and Sinaiko, 1966; Mallory, et al., 1980; Damodaran, et al., 1980; and Maguire, 1985.

codes for effective human differentiation, including geometric shapes, are summarized in Figure 14.2. A person's ability to discriminate alphabetic or alphanumeric information is much more potent.

The icons depicted in Figure 14.1 have the following meanings (reading from left to right):

Hot
Cold
Fast
Slow
Engine Oil
Ammeter/Generator
Straight
Turn
Automatic
Variable Regulation (Increase/Decrease)
Plus/Positive
Minus/Negative

ICON DESIGN GUIDELINES

- Use existing icons when available.
- Create familiar and concrete shapes.
- Create visually and conceptually distinct shapes.
  - Incorporate unique features of an object.
  - Do not display within a border.
- Create shapes of the proper emotional tone.
- Clearly and simply reflect objects represented, avoiding excessive detail.
- Provide consistency in icon kind.
- When icon relationships exist, create shapes to communicate these relationships visually.
- When icons are used to reflect varying attributes, express these attributes as meaningfully as possible.
- Provide consistency in shape over varying sizes.
- Accompany icon with a label to assure intended meaning.
- Consider animating the icons.
- Test for:
  - Expectations.
  - Recognition.
  - Learning.

Icon design is an important process. Meaningful and recognizable icons will speed learning and yield a much more effective system. Poor design will lead to errors, delays, and confusion. While the art of icon design is still evolving, it is agreed that the usability of a system is aided by adhering to the following icon design guidelines.

Use existing icons. Many standard icons have already been developed for graphical systems. Use these standard icons where they are available. This will promote consistency across systems, yielding all the performance benefits that consistency provides. Where standard icons are not available, determine if any applicable icons have already been developed by trade or standards organizations. The International Standards Organization (ISO), for example, has developed standard shapes for a variety of purposes. Always consult all relevant reference books before inventing new symbols or modifying existing ones.

Create concrete and familiar shapes. Ideally, an icon's meaning should be self-evident. This is enhanced when concrete shapes are provided, those that look like what they are. An icon should also be intuitive or obvious, based upon a person's preexisting knowledge. Familiar shapes are those images that are well learned. Figure 14.3 illustrates concrete and familiar icons for a file folder, book, and telephone as well as images for the same objects that are more abstract and unfamiliar. Nolan (1989) found that concrete, familiar icons were preferred to abstract, unfamiliar ones.

Keep in mind, however, that familiarity is in the eye of the viewer. The concrete images pictured may be familiar to us, readers of this book, but not to a tribal chief living in a remote area of the world where these objects do not exist. Similarly, items familiar to those working on the factory floor may not be

Figure 14.3.   Concrete and familiar shapes.

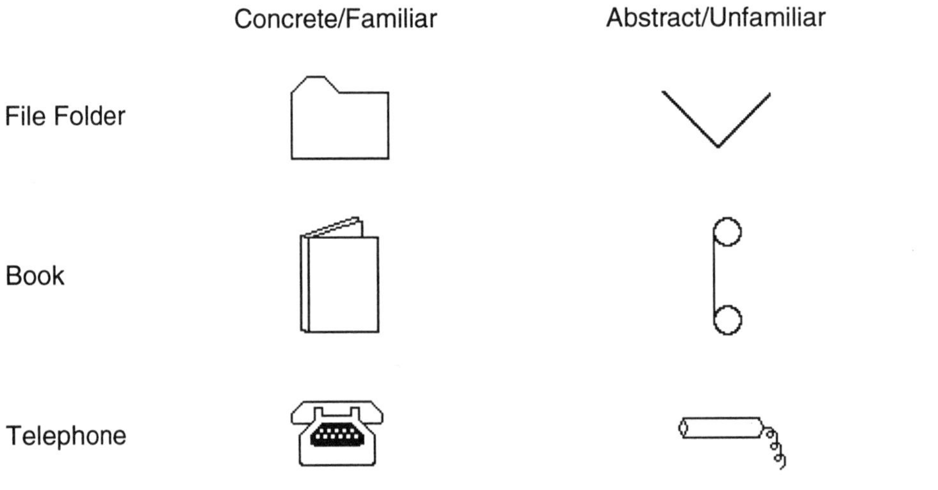

at all familiar in the office, and vice versa. Mayhew (1992) also cautions that some abstract images should not be discounted because they have become familiar, in spite of their being abstract. On a road sign, for example, an angled red bar inscribed over an object means do not do what is pictured beneath. While abstract, it is a very familiar shape today. If an abstract image must be used, it should be capable of being learned quickly and easily recalled. Familiarity can only be determined through knowing one's user.

Shneiderman (1987) suggests that simple metaphors, analogies, or models with a minimal set of concepts are the best places to start in developing icons.

Create visually and conceptually distinct shapes. It must be easy to tell icons apart so confusions between them are minimized. Differentiation is aided when icons look visually different from one another. It is also aided when icons are conceptually different—that is, they portray specific features of an object that are relatively unique within the entire set of objects to be displayed. Figure 14.4, based upon Mayhew (1992), illustrates how distinctiveness may be achieved for two similar items, a dictionary and a telephone book. Visual distinctiveness is achieved by incorporating unique features of each: for the dictionary, it is its content of letters and words, for the telephone book, numbers and the telephone bell.

Visual distinctiveness is degraded when borders are placed around icons, as illustrated in Figure 14.5. Borders tend to obscure the shape of the object being displayed.

Figure 14.4.   Visually and conceptually distinct shapes.

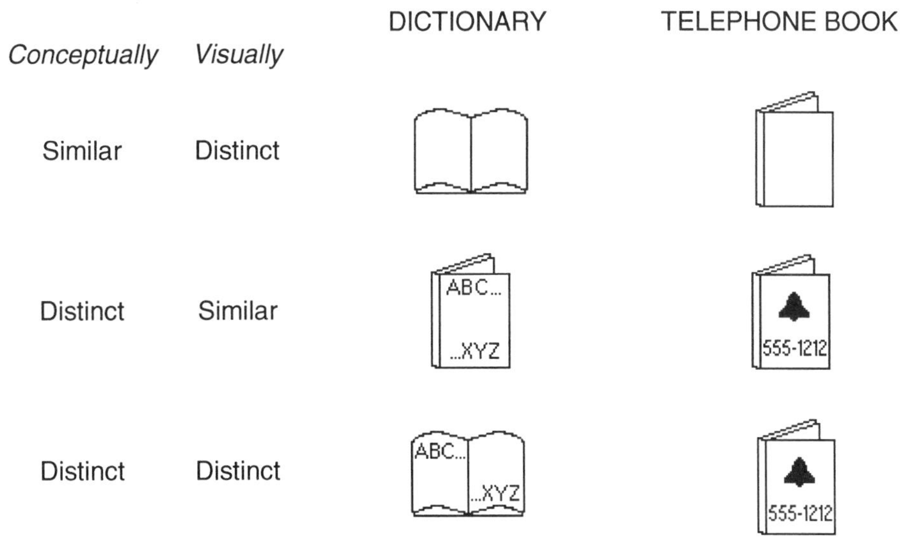

Figure 14.5. Borders degrading icon distinctiveness.

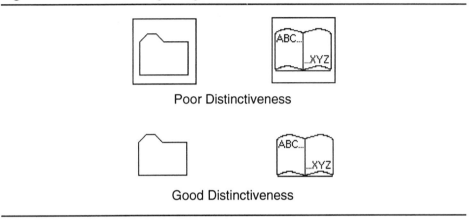

Poor Distinctiveness

Good Distinctiveness

Create shapes of the proper emotional tone. The icon should appropriately reflect the environment in which it is used. A sewage disposal system would be an inappropriate metaphor for an electronic mail system wastebasket.

Clearly and simply reflect objects represented. The characteristics of the display itself should permit drawings of adequate quality. Poorly formed or fuzzy shapes will inhibit recognition. Construct icons with as few graphical components as necessary, using no more than two or three, if possible. Also, use simple, clean lines, avoiding ornamentation. Too much detail inhibits rather than facilitates perception, as illustrated in Figure 14.6.

Provide consistency in icon kind. As previously noted, there are many different kinds of design schemes for icons (resemblance, symbolic, arbitrary, etc.) All these schemes might be used to create a meaningful family of icons for an application. Learning the meaning of icons and searching for the right icon, however, will be aided if the same design scheme is used for all icons within a family. In

Figure 14.6. Avoid excessive detail in icon design.

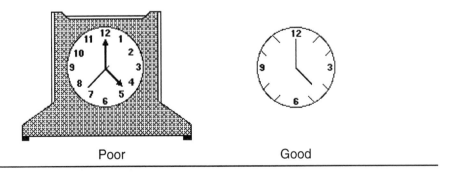

Poor   Good

presenting a series of icons for actions such as paint, cut, etc., one could, for example, (1) depict a before-after representation of the action, (2) depict the action itself being performed, or (3) picture the tool to perform the action. While a series of meaningful icons could be developed using each scheme, the best approach would be to use only one of these schemes to develop the entire family of icons.

Create shapes to communicate icon relationships visually. When icons are part of an overall related set, create shapes that visually communicate these relationships. Objects within a class, for example, may possess the same overall shape but vary in their other design details, as illustrated in Figure 14.7. Color may also be used to achieve this design goal.

Express attributes as meaningfully as possible. When an icon is also used to express an attribute of an object, do it as meaningfully as possible. The status of a document, for example, might be represented by displaying it in a different shade, but would be more effectively illustrated by filling it in, as illustrated in Figure 14.8. Shading requires remembering what each shading stands for, the proportion is more intuitively obvious.

Create consistent shapes. Create consistency in shapes of families of icons and in identical icons of differing sizing. Marcus (1984) says consistency is

Figure 14.7. Communication relationships in icons.

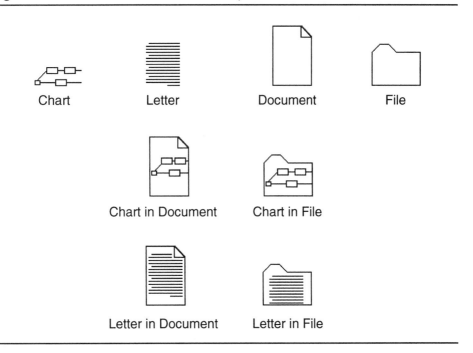

Figure 14.8. Expressing attributes in icon design.

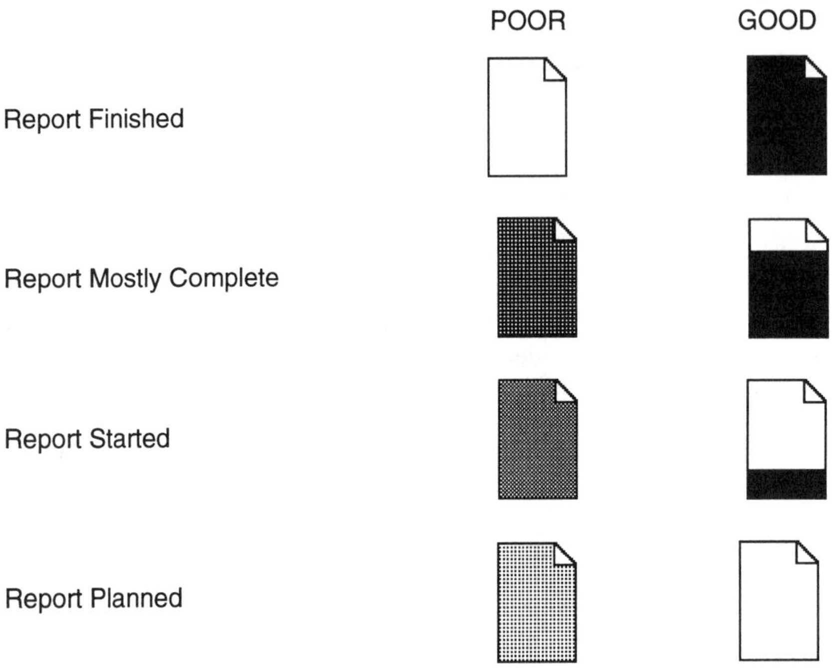

achieved through limiting the variations of angles, line thicknesses, shapes, and amount of empty space.

Attach a caption to assure intended meaning. The ability to comprehend and learn icons can be greatly improved by attaching textual captions or labels to the symbols. The preferred location is directly beneath the icon. Labels should always be positionally related to icons in a consistent way.

Consider animation. Recent research (Baecker et al., 1991) has explored the use of bringing to life on screens the icons representing the objects and actions. An animated icon appears to move instead of maintaining a static position on the screen. Existing examples of animated icons may be seen in the Sapphire windowing environment (Myers, 1984), and in the common "percent done progress indicators" (Myers, 1985).

Baecker et al. created a set of animated versions of the painting icons that appear in the HyperCard tool palette. Study participants found the animated icons useful and helpful in clarifying the purpose and functionality of the icons. These researchers caution, however, that there are many outstanding issues. Among them are that few animation creation rules exist, prototyping is difficult, a scheme for how they fit into a larger system is lacking, and whether they can be made useful for more complex and abstract concepts is not known. The reader interested in more information is referred to Baecker and Small (1990).

Test for expectation, recognition, and learning. Choosing the objects and actions, and the icons to represent them, will not be easy. So, as in any screen design activity, adequate testing and possible refinement of developed symbols must be built into the design process. Icon recognition and learning should both be measured.

SCREEN DESIGN GUIDELINES

- Follow all relevant general guidelines for screen design.
- Provide simple analogies and a minimal set of concepts to start.
- Limit the number of icon types to 12, if possible, and at most 20.
- Arrange icons:
    — In a meaningful way reflecting the organization of the real world.
    — To facilitate visual scanning.
    — Consistently.
- Place object and action icons in different groups.
- Permit arrangement of icons by the user.
- Permit the user to choose between iconic and text display of objects and actions.

In designing iconic screens, consider the following:

Follow relevant general guidelines. All general guidelines for screen design should be followed. Icons are but one part of a larger "picture."

Provide simple analogies. Shneiderman (1987) suggests that simple metaphors, analogies, or models with a minimal set of concepts are the best places to start in developing icons.

Keep the number of symbols under 20. A person's ability to identify shapes is limited (see Figure 14.2). Brems and Whitten (1987), based upon a literature review, suggest using no more than eight or so functions that require icons at one time. If labels are attached to icons, however, the meaning of the icon is greatly clarified. Too many icons on a screen, however, will greatly increase screen clutter and create confusion. In general, fewer is better.

Arrange icons in a meaningful way. Organize icons in a way that reflects the real-world organization of the user. Place object icons and action icons in different groups.

Arrange icons to facilitate visual scanning. Visual scanning studies, in a non-iconic world, universally find that a top-to-bottom scan of columnar-oriented information is fastest. Generalization of these findings to an icon screen may not necessarily be warranted if icons have attached labels. Columnar orientation icons (with labels below the icons) will separate the labels from one another by the icons themselves. The labels will be farther apart and fewer icons will fit in a column than in a horizontal or row orientation. A row orientation would seem to be more efficient in many cases, as adjacent icons will be in closer physical proximity. Until research evidence is established to the contrary, organizing icons either in a column or a row seems appropriate. In either case, a consistent straight eye movement must be maintained through the icons.

Place object and action icons in different groups. Conceptually similar items should always be arrayed together. Locating them will be easier.

Permit arrangement of icons by the user. Allow the user to arrange the icons in a manner that is meaningful for the task. A default arrangement should be provided, however.

Permit iconic or text display. In some situations, and for some users, pure text labels may be more meaningful than icons. The option to display text only should always be provided.

15

Other Screen Design Considerations

In addition to presenting menus and controls, screens are used for a variety of other purposes. Effective messages, feedback, and guidance and assistance are also necessary elements of good design.

STEP 11—PROVIDE THE PROPER MESSAGES, FEEDBACK, AND GUIDANCE.

- Provide the proper words, messages, and text.
  - Choosing words.
  - Establishing the proper message structure and tone.
  - Writing and presenting text.
  - Presenting sequence control guidance.
- Provide the proper feedback.
  - Dealing with time delays.
  - Flashing for attention.
  - Using sound.
- Provide guidance and assistance as needed.
  - Managing problems.
  - Presenting help.

CHOOSING THE PROPER WORDS AND TEXT

System communications to the user should simply, clearly, and politely provide the information one must have to work effectively with a system. Words, messages, and text must adhere to established design principles.

Words

- Do not use jargon, words, or terms:
  - — Unique to the computer profession.
  - — With different meanings outside of the computer profession.
  - — Made up to describe special functions or conditions.
- Use:
  - — Standard alphabetic characters to form words or captions.
  - — Short, familiar words.
  - — Complete words; avoid contractions, short forms, suffixes, and prefixes.
  - — Positive terms; avoid negative terms.
  - — Simple action words; avoid noun strings.
  - — The "more" dimension when comparing.
- Do not:
  - — Stack words.
  - — Hyphenate words.
  - — Include punctuation for abbreviations, mnemonics, and acronyms.

Words displayed on screens should be easily comprehended, with minimum ambiguity and confusion. Some ways to achieve this are given below.

Do not use jargon. Jargon consists of several forms. It may be words or terms that are unique to the computer profession such as Filespec or Abend; words with different meaning outside of data processing such as Boot or Abort; or made-up words to describe special functions or actions such as Ungroup or Dearchive.

Use standard alphabetic characters. Standard alphabetic characters are most familiar to screen viewers. Never use restricted alphabetic sets. Symbols should be used only if they are familiar to all who are using the screen. Common symbols that may be considered as substitutes for alphabetic characters are # for number, % for percent, and $ for dollar. Again, all potential screen users must be familiar with a symbol if it is used as a substitute for alphabet characters.

Use short, familiar words. Shorter words tend to be used more often in everyday conversation, and so they are more familiar and easier to understand (of course, there are exceptions). The most important factor is familiarization, not length. A longer but familiar word is better than a short, unfamiliar word.

Use complete words. A complete word is better understood than a contraction or short form. Thus, "will not" is better than "won't," "not valid" is better than "invalid."*

> *"Invalid" has come into such widespread usage in computer systems that one may ask whether this should be an exception to this rule. Maybe, but what happens in a medical system where screens are developed for use about, or by, invalids?

Words can also be more difficult to understand if they contain prefixes and suffixes, like "un-," or "-ness." Comprehension often involves decomposing such complex terms to establish their basic root meaning and then modifying the meaning to account for the various prefixes and suffixes (Wright, 1984). Structural complexity hinders comprehension.

Use positive terms. It is generally easier to understand positive, affirmative information than the same information expressed in a negative way. Therefore, avoid the prefixes "ir-," "in-," "dis-," and "un-." Implicitly negative terms, such as "decrease," should be replaced with positive terms, such as "increase."

Use simple action words. Substitute noun strings with simple action words. Instead of saying, for example, PROJECT STATUS LISTING, say LIST PROJECT STATUS.

Use the "more" dimension when comparing. When using comparative terms, the "more" dimension is easier to deal with. The opposite of the "more" is usually considered the "negative." So, use "longer" rather than "shorter," "bigger" rather than "smaller." (Wright and Barnard, 1975; Clark & Card, 1969.)

Do not stack words. Text is more readable if the entire statement is on one line.

Do not hyphenate words. Again, for better readability, never break a word between two lines.

Abbreviations, mnemonics, and acronyms should not include punctuation. This permits better readability and avoids confusion between the punctuation and data fields.

Messages

Messages are communications provided on the screen to the screen viewer. Several different types of messages exist and they may be displayed in different forms and places. A message should possess the proper tone and style and be consistent within itself and with other messages.

Types. Screen messages fall into two broad categories: system and prompting. System messages are generated by the system to keep the user informed of the system's activities. They reflect the state of the system as it exists at that moment in time. Prompting messages are instructional messages provided on a screen.

System messages are of several kinds. *Notification / status / informational* messages provide information about the state of the system when it is not immediately obvious to the user. They may confirm that nonobvious processing is taking place or is completed. They may also be used to provide intermediate feedback when normal feedback is delayed. No user actions are normally necessary with these kinds of messages, although confirmation that the message has been seen can be requested.

Warning messages call attention to a situation that may be undesirable to the user. The user must determine whether the situation is in fact a problem and may be asked to advise the system whether or not to proceed. A deletion request by a user is a common action that generates a warning message. When a user requests a deletion, a message asking for confirmation of the deletion is usually presented.

Action / critical messages call attention to conditions that do require a user action before the system can proceed. An error message is an action/critical message.

Question messages ask a question and offer a choice of options for selection. It is not a CUA SAA standard but may be used when there is a question to be asked and the message does not appear to be suited to the above described types.

The second category of messages, **prompting** messages, are instructional messages that tell the user how to work with, or complete, the screen displayed. They may be permanently affixed to a screen, or they may appear as the result of a help request. Prompting messages are of most benefit to the novice or casual system user.

Message Structure, Location and Layout

Structure

- Use mixed-case letters.
- Use contrasting background and foreground colors for each type of message.

Location

- Always use the message line for messages that must not interfere with screen information.
- Pop-up windows may be used for all kinds of messages, if available.
- Pop-up windows should be used for action/critical messages.

Layout

- In a message area:
  — Left-justify the message.
  — Allow space for the longest message.
- In a pop-up window:
  — Include an icon to the left of the text for each message type, if feasible.
    — Notification/Status/Informational—Lower-case *i* within a circle.
    — Warning—Exclamation point within a circle.
    — Action/Critical—Stop Sign (STOP within a hexagon).
    — Question—A question mark symbol within a circle.
    — Follow other relevant guidelines for window display.

Messages should consist of mixed-case letters following normal sentence-style capitalization. They may be displayed either in the message line or in pop-up windows. All action/critical messages should be displayed in a window if one is available. If windows are used, and the creation of an icon is possible, also include with the message text a unique icon for each type of message. This icon will immediately identify to the user the kind of message being presented.

Examples of the various system messages, derived from SAA CUA are illustrated in Figure 15.1. Included in each message window is the icon, the

Figure 15.1. Message pop-up windows with icon, text, and buttons

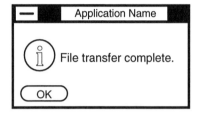

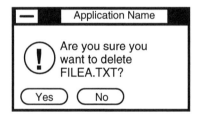

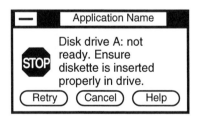

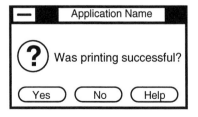

message text, and one or more pushbuttons for user acknowledgments and actions.

The notification/status/informational message window contains an OK pushbutton for confirmation that the message has been read. When OK is selected, the message is removed. SAA CUA also recommends a HELP button should be included in this window. The Warning message window provides OK and CANCEL, or YES and NO pushbuttons, depending on the message content. When an action is selected, the window is removed. A HELP button is again also recommended. The Action window includes RETRY, CANCEL, and HELP pushbuttons. RETRY assumes some action has been taken to correct the problem and directs the system to attempt to continue. With CANCEL the system does not take any further action. The HELP button is optional. The question window might include OK, CANCEL, and HELP pushbuttons.

Message Tone and Style

Sentences

- Sentences must be:
  - — Brief, simple, and clear.
  - — Directly and immediately usable.
  - — Affirmative.
  - — In an active voice.
  - — Nonauthoritarian.
  - — Nonthreatening.
  - — Nonanthropomorphic.
  - — Nonpatronizing.
  - — In the temporal sequence of events.
  - — Structured so that the main topic is near the beginning.
  - — Cautious in the use of humor.
  - — Nonpunishing.

Other Considerations

- Abbreviated, more concise versions of messages should be available.
- Something that must be remembered should be at the beginning of the text.

A message must minimize ambiguity and confusion, allowing easy, correct, and fast interpretation. It must also have the proper tone; threatening, rude, or impolite messages can evoke negative response.

The following guidelines will lead to easy, correct, and fast message interpretation and acceptance.

Shneiderman (1982B), in restructuring messages along such guidelines, found higher success rates in problem resolution, lower error rates, and improved user satisfaction.

Sentences

Use brief, simple sentences. A message that has to be explained does not communicate. It fails as a message. Brief, simple sentences are more readily understood than longer sentences containing multiple clauses. Break long sentences into two or more simple sentences if this can be done without changing the meaning.

Roemer and Chapanis (1982) created messages at three levels of reading ability (fifth, tenth, and fifteenth grade) and tested them on people of varying verbal abilities. The fifth-grade version was found to be best for all levels. People of high verbal ability did not perceive the fifth-grade version as insulting, as some had feared.

Provide directly and immediately usable sentences. Searching through reference material to translate a message is unacceptable, as are requirements for transposing, computing, interpolating, or mentally translating messages into other units.

Use affirmative statements. Affirmative statements are easier to understand than negative statements. For example, "Complete entry before returning to menu" is easier to grasp than "Do not return to menu before completing entry" (Herriot, 1970; Greene, 1972).

Use active voice. Active voice is usually easier to understand than passive voice. For example, "Send the message by depressing TRANSMIT" is more understandable than "The message is sent by depressing TRANSMIT" (Herriot, 1970; Greene, 1972; Barnard, 1974).

Be nonauthoritarian. Imply the system is awaiting the user's direction, not that the system is directing the user. For example, phrase a message "Ready for next command", not "Enter next command."

Nonthreatening. Negative tones or actions, or threats, are not very friendly. Since errors are often the result of a failure to understand, mistakes, or trial-and-error behavior, the user may feel confused, inadequate, or anxious (Shneiderman, 1987). Blaming the user for problems can heighten anxiety, making error correction more difficult and increasing the chance of more errors. Therefore, harsh words like "illegal," "bad," or "fatal" should be avoided.

It is also suggested to avoid the word "error" in messages when it implies a user error (Paradies, 1991). "Error" tends to focus the attention on the person involved rather than on the problem. For example, instead of saying "Error— Numbers are illegal," say, "Months must be entered by name." Since the computer does not have an ego to be bruised, an excellent design approach would be to have it assume the blame for all miscommunications.

Be nonanthropomorphic. Having the computer "talk" like a person should be avoided for several reasons. An attribution of knowledge or intelligence will, first, imply a much higher level of computer "knowledge" than actually exists, creating shattered user expectations. Second, this attribute eliminates the distinction that actually exists between people and computers. People "control" computers; they "respect the desires" of other human beings. Third, many people express anxiety about using computers by saying things like "they make you feel dumb." The feeling of interacting with another person who is evaluating your proficiency can heighten this anxiety (Shneiderman, 1987). There is some research evidence that a nonanthropomorphic approach is best, being seen as more honest (Quintanar et al., 1982), more preferred (Spiliotopoulos and Shackel, 1981), and easier to use (Gay and Lindward, in Shneiderman, 1987).

So, do not give a human personality to a machine. Imply that the system is awaiting the user's direction, not vice versa. Say, for example, "What do you need?", not "How can I help you?"

Be nonpatronizing. Patronizing messages can be embarrassing. "Very good; you did it right" may thrill a fourth-grader, but would be somewhat less than thrilling to an adult. Being told "You forgot again" once may be acceptable, but being told three or four times in one minute is another story. A commonly available video golf game, after a particularly bad hole, returns with the suggestion to "Try another sport." A golf professional who played this game took great offense to this advice and walked away. A person may disagree with patronizing conclusions, so why risk the offense?

Order words chronologically. If a sentence describes a temporal sequence of events, the order of words should correspond to this sequence. A prompt should say, "Complete address and page forward" rather than "Page forward after completing address" (Clark & Clark, 1968).

Messages that begin with a strange code number do not meet the user's needs. A code number, if needed at all, is only necessary after reading the message and should therefore be placed in parentheses at the end of the message.

Avoid humor and punishment. Until an optimal computer personality is designed, messages should remain factual and informative, and should not attempt humor or punishment. Humor is a transitory and changeable thing. What is funny today may not be funny tomorrow, and what is funny to some may not be to others. Punishment is not a desirable way to force a change in behavior, especially among adults.

Other Considerations

Display abbreviated versions of messages when requested. People are impatient with noninformative or redundant computer messages. A problem, however, is that the degree of computer-to-person message redundancy depends on the person's experience with the system. And it may vary with different parts of a system. So the availability of abbreviated or detailed messages allows tailoring of the system to the needs of each user. During system training and early implementation stages, detailed versions can be used. Individuals can switch to abbreviated versions as their familiarity increases, but they should always be able to receive detailed messages.

Place information that must be remembered at the beginning of text. One can remember something longer if it appears at the beginning of a message. Items in the middle of a message are hardest to remember.

Some words to forget. Words should be meaningful and common to all, not just to the designers. Language perceived as "computerese" may confuse or intimidate some users (Loftus et al., 1970; Wason and Johnson-Laird, 1972). The vocabulary of the designer often finds its way into messages or system documentation. While not always bad, some words have particularly harsh or vague meanings to many users. These words, which are summarized in Table 15.1, should be avoided whenever possible. Suggested alternative words are presented (derived from IBM, 1984).

Table 15.1   Some words to forget.

Avoid	Use
Abend	End, Cancel, Stop
Abort	End, Cancel, Stop
Access	Get, Ready, Display
Available	Ready
Boot	Start, Run
Execute	Complete
Hit	Press, Depress
Implement	Do, Use, Put Into
Invalid	Not Correct, Not Good, Not Valid
Key	Type, Enter
Kill	End, Cancel
Output	Report, List, Display
Return Key	Enter, Transmit
Terminate	End, Exit

Text

Presentation

- Include no more than 40–60 characters on each line.
  - —A double column of 30–35 characters separated by 5 spaces is also acceptable.
- Do not right-justify.
- Use headings to introduce a new topic.

- Separate paragraphs by at least one blank line.
- Start a fresh topic on a new page.
- Emphasize important things by:
  — Positioning.
  — Boxes.
  — Bold typefaces.
  — Indented margins.
- Use lists to present facts.
- Use paging (not scrolling).
- Provide a screen design philosophy consistent with other parts of the system.

The typical screen is a little too wide for comfortable reading of text. It is difficult for the eye to keep its place as it moves from the end of one line to the beginning of the next line. Rehe (1974) recommends that a text line should contain no more than 40–60 characters. Lichty (1989) suggests the line width should be even less, 1.5 lower-case alphabets or 39 characters. For greater screen efficiency, it may be desirable to consider two columns of text, each about 30–35 characters wide.

Rehe also found that non-right-justified (or ragged-right edge) text lines are just as legible as justified text lines. Large spaces in right-justified text interrupt eye movement and impede reading.

Another study found that the reading speed of right-justified text was 8 to 10 percent slower than non-right-justified text (Trollip and Sales, 1986). Lichty states that non-right-justified text has advantages in word hyphenation not being required and the visual interest it generates. It is best for very narrow columns of text. Full left and right justification, Lichty says, is familiar, predictable, and orderly. It is best for long works that require continuous reading and concentration, long text, newspapers, and novels.

Headings to introduce new topics provide breaks or pause points for the reader. They provide obvious closure points. Starting new topics on new pages reinforces the needed breaks. Separating paragraphs by a blank line will result in more cohesive groupings and alleviate the impression of a dense screen.

Emphasize important points by placing them in unusual places, drawing boxes around them, using bold typefaces, or providing indented left and right margins. In addition to their emphasizing capabilities, they make the screen more interesting.

Use lists to present facts. Lists are convenient, simple, and uncluttered. Designate items in a list with a "bullet," a lower-case letter *o*, or a dash (—).

Paging through screens, rather than scrolling, has been found to yield better performance and to be preferred by novice system users (Schwarz et al., 1983). Expert users were found to perform satisfactorily with either paging or scrolling. A severe disadvantage of scrolling for novices is loss of orientation. While experts can handle scrolling, the best choice if all users are considered is paging.

If scrolling is going to be used, the preferred approach is "telescoping", in which the window moves around the data. This method is more natural and causes fewer errors than the "microscope" approach, in which the data appears to move under a fixed viewing window (Bury et al., 1982).

Writing

- Use short sentences composed of familiar, personal words.
  - Cut the excess words.
  - Try to keep the number of words in a sentence under 30.
- Cut the number of sentences.
- Keep the paragraphs short.
- Use the active writing style.
- Use the personal writing style, if appropriate.
- Write as you talk.
- Use subjective opinion.
- Use specific examples.
- Read it out loud.

Simple words and short sentences are the cornerstone of good writing. Keeping sentences under 30 words can be achieved. Long sentences often result from trying to express more than one idea in the sentence. They also result from trying to give a list of items and from the use of unnecessary words. Use separate sentences for separate ideas. Put multiple items in a list format, and delete all unnecessary words. Short paragraphs provide breaking points and make the page look less threatening.

The active writing style is easier to read and understand. It almost always uses less words and leaves no unanswered questions (contrast the passive "The customer name should be typed" with the active "Type the customer name").

The personal style, the use of "you" and "I" ("Now you must press the Enter key"), keeps the writing active, makes writing directly relevant to the reader, and is more interesting. Materials read by a wide variety of people for informational purposes only should not use the personal style, however.

Write in the way you would say something to the reader. Also, use subjective opinion ("This screen is not used very often") to reinforce the users' understanding of what they are reading. It does not tell anything specific, but reinforces facts already read or about to be read. Do not overuse subjective opinion and make sure it is correct. Overuse makes facts harder to find, and an incorrect opinion casts suspicion on all the facts being presented.

The best way to explain a general rule is to show how it applies through examples. Examples should be short, relevant, and easy for the reader to relate to. They should also be visually different from the main text, either through indentation, boxing, or some other technique.

Finally, read what you have written out loud to yourself. If it sounds wordy, stilted, or difficult, it will to the reader, too. Rewrite it.

Conventions

- Establish conventions for referring to:
  — Individual keyboard keys.
  — Keys to be pressed at the same time.
  — Field captions.
  — Names supplied by users or defined by the system.
  — Commands and actions.

In messages and text it is often necessary to refer to keyboard keys, field captions, file names, commands, or actions. These components should be described in the same manner whenever referenced. Keyboard keys should always be referenced as they are inscribed on the keyboard. (They usually appear in a mixed-case text format.) A useful convention for referring to keys that should be pressed at the same time is a plus (+) sign between the key descriptions (Alt+F10). Names may be enclosed in quotes ("Pending").

Sequence Control Guidance

- Consider providing a guidance message telling how to continue at points in the dialogue where:
  — A decision must be made.
  — A response needs to be made to continue.
- Consider indicating what control options exist at points in the dialogue where several alternatives may be available.
- Permit these prompts to be turned on or off by the user.

Consider providing prompts telling the user how to continue when a decision, and response, must be made to continue. For example, it might be indicated that:

> Information is current through August 26, 1991.
> Press ENTER to continue.

Where several control options exist, consider providing a prompt such as:

> Press S to Save, D to Delete, or P to Print.
> Type C to create a new file, or E to edit a new file: _

For experienced users, these kinds of prompts can become noise. Allow users to turn them on or off as needed.

PROVIDING THE PROPER FEEDBACK

All user actions must be reacted to in some way. Feedback, as has been noted, shapes human performance. Without it, we cannot learn. To be effective, feedback to the user for an action must occur within certain time limits. Excessive delays can be annoying, interrupt concentration, cause the user concern, and impair productivity as one's memory limitations begin to be tested.

Response Time

- System responsiveness should match the speed and flow of human thought processes.
  - If continuity of thinking is required and information must be remembered throughout several responses, response time should be less than two seconds.
  - If human task closures exist, high levels of concentration are not necessary and moderate short-term memory requirements are imposed; response times of two to four seconds are acceptable.
  - If major task closures exist, minimal short-term memory requirements are imposed; responses within 4 to 15 seconds are acceptable.
  - When the user is free to do other things and return when convenient, response time can be greater than 15 seconds.
- Constant delays are preferable to variable delays.

What the ideal system response time is has been the subject of numerous studies. Unfortunately, there still does not exist definitive time or times that are acceptable under all conditions. What is clear is that dissatisfaction with response time is dependent on user expectations. It is also clear that expectations can vary, depending on the task as well as the situation. The ideal condition is one in which a person "perceives" no delays. A response time is too long when one "notices" that the system is taking too long. The following paragraphs summarize some study conclusions and some tentative findings.

The optimum response time is dependent upon the task. There is an optimum work pace that depends on the task being performed. Longer or shorter response times than the optimum lead to more errors (Barber and Lucas, 1983). In general, response times should be geared to the user's short-term memory load and to how he has grouped the activities being performed. Intense short-term memory loads necessitate short response times. While completing chunks of work at task closures, users can withstand longer response delays.

The human *now*, or psychological present, is two to three seconds. This is why continuity of thinking requires a response time within this limit. Recent research indicates that for creative tasks, response times in the range of four-tenths to nine-tenths of a second can yield dramatic increases in productivity, even greater in proportion to the increase in response time (Smith, 1983). The probable reason is the elimination of restrictions caused by short-term memory limitations.

As the response-time interval increases beyond 10 to 15 seconds, continuity of thought becomes increasingly difficult to maintain. Doherty (1979) suggests that this happens because the sequence of actions stored in short-term memory beyond that time is badly disrupted and must be reloaded.

The response time guidelines above, then, relate to the general tasks being performed. Their applicability to every situation is not guaranteed.

Satisfaction with response time is a function of expectations. Expectations are based, in part, on past experiences. These experiences may be derived from working with a computer, or from the world in general, and they vary enormously across individuals and tasks.

Dissatisfaction with response time is a function of one's uncertainty about delay. The degree of frustration with delay may depend on such psychological factors as a person's uncertainty concerning how long the delay will be, the extent to which the actual delay contradicts those expectations, and what the person thinks is causing the delay. Such uncertainty concerning how long a wait there will be for a computer's response may in some cases be a greater source of frustration than the delay itself (Nickerson, 1969).

People will change work habits to conform to response time. As response time increases, so does think time (Cotton, 1978; Boies, 1974; and Butler, 1983). People also work more carefully with longer response times (Bergman et al., 1981). In some cases, more errors have been found with very short response times. This may not necessarily be bad if the errors are the result of trial-and-error learning that is enhanced by very fast response times.

Constant delays are preferable to variable delays. Carbonell et al. (1969) point out that it is the variability of delays, not their length, that most frequently distresses people. From a consistency standpoint, a good rule of thumb is that response-time deviations should never exceed half the mean response time. For example, if the mean response time is four seconds, a two-second deviation is permissible. Variations should range from three to five seconds. Shneiderman (1987) suggests, however, that response time variation should not exceed 20 percent. Lower response time variability has been found to yield better performance (Miller, 1977), but small variations may be tolerated (Bergman et al., 1981; Weiss et al., 1982).

More experienced people prefer shorter response times. People work faster as they gain experience, a fact that leads Shneiderman (1987) to conclude that it may be useful to let people set their own pace of interaction. He also suggests that in the absence of cost or technical feasibility constraints, people will eventually force response time to well under one second.

Very fast or slow response times can lead to symptoms of stress. There is a point at which a person can be overwhelmed by information presented more quickly than it can be comprehended. There is also some evidence indicating that when a system responds too quickly, there is subconscious pressure on users to respond quickly also, possibly threatening their overall comfort (Elam, 1978), increasing their blood pressure, or causing them to exhibit other signs of anxious behavior (Brod, 1984). Symptoms of job burnout have been reported after substantial reductions in response time (Turner, 1984).

Slow and variable response times have also been shown to lead to a significant build-up of mood disturbances and somatic discomfort over time, culminating in symptoms of work stress, including frustration, impatience, and irritation (Schleifer, 1986).

DEALING WITH TIME DELAYS

General

- If an operation takes five seconds or less to complete, present a "busy" signal until the operation is complete.
  — For example, display an hourglass pointer.
- If an operation takes longer than five seconds to complete, display a progress indicator or message in addition to an hourglass pointer.
- If an operation is very time-consuming:
  — Consider breaking the operation into subtasks and providing progress indicators for each subtask.
  — Consider using a separate base window.
    — Users can close the window to an icon and start a new activity while waiting.
- When an operation not visible to the user is completed, present an acknowledgment message that it is completed.

Progress Indicators

- Provide a long rectangular bar that is initially empty but filled as the operation proceeds.
  — Dynamically fill the bar.
  — Fill with a color or shade of gray.
  — Fill from left to right or bottom to top.

Percent Complete Messages

- Provide a message that indicates the percent of the operation that is complete.
- Useful if a progress indicator takes too long to update.

Elapsed Time Messages

- Provide a message that shows the amount of elapsed time the operation is consuming.

- Useful if:
  — the length of the operation is not known in advance.
  — a particular part of the operation will take an unusually long time to complete.

The user should always be kept informed of a system's processing status through a message or graphics. A "Please wait . . ." message can be presented to indicate more complex processing has been delayed or is continuing. An indication of the percentage of processing that has been accomplished can be given through a message ("22 of 27 transactions have been processed"), or graphics such as an hourglass or rectangular processing bar, as illustrated in Figure 15.2. Processing being completed that is not visible to the user should also always be acknowledged ("Search complete, Jones not found").

Figure 15.2. Processing progress indicators.

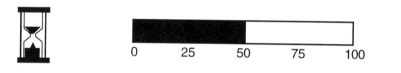

FLASHING FOR ATTENTION

- Attract attention by flashing when an application is inactive but must display a message to the user.
  — If a window, flash the title bar.
  — If minimized, flash its icon.
- To provide an additional message indication, also provide an auditory signal (one or two beeps).
  — Very useful if:
    — The window or icon is hidden.
    — The user's attention is frequently directed away from the screen.
- When the application is activated, display the message.
- Do not display the message until requested by the user.
  — Preserves the user's control over the work environment.
  — Ensures that the message is not accidentally closed through an inadvertent key press.

The attention of the user may be quickly captured by flashing an element on the screen. It is very useful if an application is inactive and a message exists for the user to read. Flashing is annoying to many people so it should not be overused on the screen.

USE OF SOUND

- Always use in conjunction with a visual indication.
- Use no more than six different tones.
  — Assure that people can discriminate among them.
- Do not use:
  — More than two notes in any given alert.
  — Jingles or tunes.
  — Loud signals.
- Use consistently.
  — Provide unique and similar tones for similar situations.
- Provide signal frequencies between 500 and 1,000 Hz.
- Allow the user to adjust the volume or turn the sound off altogether.
- Test the sounds with users over extended trial periods.
- Use sparingly because sounds:
  — Are annoying to many people, including users and nonusers in the vicinity.
  — Can easily be overused, increasing the possibility that they will be ignored.
  — Are not reliable because:
    — Some people are hard of hearing.
    — If they are not heard, they leave no permanent record of having occurred.
    — They can be turned off by the user.

Sound is useful for alerting the user:

- For minor and obvious mistakes.
- When something unexpected happens.
- Where visual attention is directed away from the screen and immediate attention is required.
- When a long process is finished.

Tones used must be discriminable, nonannoying, and consistently used. Therefore, they must be thoroughly tested for discrimination and effectiveness. Since sounds can be annoying to some people, they should be capable of being turned down or off by the user. More than two notes and jingles or tunes focus attention on the sound itself, which is distracting. Loud sounds can be irritating, especially to those with sensitive hearing.

Never consider sounds reliable because they can be turned off, they leave no permanent record of their existence, and not all users will be able to hear all tones because of hearing defects. Sounds should always be used in conjunction with a visual indication of some kind.

PREVENTING ERRORS AND PROVIDING GUIDANCE

In spite of our lofty design goals, people will make mistakes using our system. When they occur, they must be properly managed and relevant guidance provided.

PROBLEM MANAGEMENT

Prevention

- Accept common misspellings, whenever possible.
- Before an action is performed:
  — Permit it to be reviewed.
  — Permit it to be changed or undone.
- Provide a common action mechanism.
- Advise of irreversible changes.

Detection

- Immediately detect all errors.
- Maintain the item in error on the screen.
- Visually highlight the item in error.
- Display a corrective message on the screen with the error.
- Use auditory signals conservatively.

Correction

- Provide a constructive correction message saying:
  — What problem was found.
  — What corrective action is necessary.
- Initiate a clarification dialog if necessary.

The magnitude of errors in computer systems is astounding. Shneiderman (1987) describes studies reporting error rates in commands, tasks, or transactions as high as 46 percent. In addition to stranding the user and wasting time, mistakes and errors interrupt planning and cause deep frustrations.

Some experts have argued that there are no "errors" as such; they are simply "iterations" toward a goal. There is much truth to that statement. It is also often said that "to err is human." The corollary to that statement, at least in computer systems, might be, ". . . to forgive, good design."

Whatever we call them, errors will occur. People should be able to correct them as soon as they pop up, as simply and easily as they are made. One objective of this book is to reduce or eliminate errors in computer systems. The focus here is on the mechanics of error prevention, detection, and correction.

Prevention. Where possible, human misspellings of commands and requests should be accepted by the system. Person-to-person communication does not require perfection. Person-to-computer communication should impose no more rigor. Inappropriate use of shift keys should also be discouraged, where possible, since they are such a large cause of keying errors. Actions made should be reviewable and changed by the person who made them. Human memory is poor and keying or selection errors will occur.

A common *send* mechanism should be provided to transmit an action to the system. Two or more keys to accomplish the same purpose, especially if their use is mandated by different conditions, can be confusing and more prone to errors. If an action causes a nonreversible change, and the change is critical, the user should be requested to confirm the change. A separate key should be used for this purpose, not the send key.

Detection. All errors should be immediately detected and communicated to the user through a highlighting display technique (for example, high intensity or contrasting color). This does not mean the user should be interrupted for each error that occurs. It is preferable to wait for a closure point, such as the end of a screen.

The items in error, and error messages, should be displayed on the screen being viewed. If multiple error messages occur, and it is impossible to display all of them at one time, provide an indication that there are additional messages. Say, for example, "+ 2 other errors." Also, provide with a distinct difference the same error message displayed more than once, if the first attempt to correct failed.

Be cautious in using auditory signals to notify of an error. Many users, especially those with status or position, do not want their mistakes advertised.

Correction. Explicit and constructive error messages should be provided. These messages should describe what error occurred, and how it should be corrected. Corrective actions will be clearer if phrased with words like "must be" or "must have." Shneiderman (1982), in restructuring messages following guidelines such as this, and others previously described, found improved success rates in fixing errors, lower error rates, and improved user satisfaction.

All error ambiguities should be resolved by having the system query the user. Errors should be corrected with minimal typing.

Another important error control measure is to have the system identify and store errors. This will allow tracking of common errors so that appropriate prevention programs can be implemented.

Guidance and Assistance

A system should provide:

- Online documentation that supplements hard copy documentation.
- User-selectable prompting.
- A HELP facility.

New system users must go through a learning process that involves developing a conceptual or mental model to explain the system's behavior and the task being performed. Documentation, Help displays, and prompting serve as cognitive development tools to aid this process.

While it is desirable that the human-computer interface be so "self-evident" and "intelligent" that people never experience difficulties, this lofty goal will not be achieved in the foreseeable future (Quinn and Russell, 1986). So a great deal of emphasis should be placed on creating good documentation and managing the trouble that does occur. Indeed, a survey by Jereb (1986) found that documentation was the second most important factor influencing the decision to purchase something (quality was first).

Technical information, unlike works of fiction, is seldom read for pleasure. People turn to it only when a question has to be answered. Failure to provide the guidance and assistance needed in learning, answering questions, and problem solving makes it very difficult for the user to recover from trouble on his own and to avoid future trouble by learning from his mistakes. The result is most often more errors and great frustration.

Guidance and assistance is provided through documentation, both hard copy and online. Broadly speaking, online documentation is every communication provided online to help people to do their work effectively. Included are procedure manuals, computer-based training, tutorials, computer-generated messages, and a Help facility.

The focus of the next few pages will be on reference information, including prompting and online help. For more information on computer-based training and tutorials, see Charney and Reder (1986) and Dede (1986).

Current problems with documentation. Wright (1991) feels that poor manuals are usually not the result of stupid and careless writing. Most writers, professional or not, try to communicate their ideas as well as they can. Poor products, however, suggest that being a native speaker of the language is not a sufficient qualification to ensure communicative success. Rather, four other factors contribute to bad design.

First are organizational factors including management decisions concerning who does the writing, product developers, or specialist technical authors. Product developers, by their nature, are more interested in the technical aspects and seldom have time to focus on writing. Another organizational factor is the frequency and nature of the contact between writers and developers. Successful writing requires that frequent contact be maintained between writers and developers. If not, modifications may go undocumented, and functionality may occur that is difficult to explain.

Second is the time scale allocated for the writing process. Successful writing also involves detailed early planning, drafting, testing, and considerable revising. Without adequate time being made available for the writing process, the planning, testing, and revising processes are limited, thereby increasing the potential for a mismatch between the product and its documentation.

Third, there is not yet a clear theoretical rationale about what content should be included in documentation and how this information should be presented. Until this is developed, one cannot be sure that the documentation being developed is the most effective that it can be.

Finally, there are the resources. Adequate resources are needed to include people with different skills in the documentation development process. Required are people good at visual layout, writing, and test and evaluation. Rarely does the same person possess more than one of these skills. Without the proper expertise, documentation will also suffer.

How readers interact with documentation. Wright (1981, 1988) has suggested that there are three broad stages through which a reader interacts with documentation: finding information that is relevant, understanding what the documentation says, and applying that understanding to the current task in order to solve the problem that prompted him to turn to the documentation.

Finding information is enhanced through use of contents pages and index lists. It is also enhanced if browsing is made easy through clearly visible page headings and subheadings. Pictures and symbols can also be used to draw the reader's attention to particular kinds of information.

Understanding information is achieved through a variety of factors. Included are following good writing principles. Understanding can also be maximized through testing and revision of materials as necessary.

Applying information involves reducing the number of inferences that readers must draw. Make all procedures explicit, for example, 1. First, do this . . . , 2. Then, do that . . .

Hard copy versus online documentation. A question frequently asked is whether the system documentation should be hard copy, online, or both. Advantages exist for each. Online documentation is always there and available when needed, can be rapidly accessed, and is difficult to misplace. It is easy to update and guarantees that all users possess the same version. It also does not require workspace for storage.

Its disadvantages include a less familiar format than the traditional manual. It is not as "readable" and is less easy to "browse" in. Less information can be displayed on a "page" at one time. It is not portable and cannot be annotated, written on, or marked in any way. Illustrations may be difficult to include. If the screen is filled with other work, it may require erasing what is being questioned in order to find answers. Online documentation also requires learning additional commands in order to be effective.

Is online documentation or help better than a hard copy manual? The evidence does not always indicate that it is. Several studies have found manuals, or manuals in conjunction with online materials, superior to online help or documentation alone (Dunsmore, 1980; Watley and Mulford, 1983; and Cohill and Williges, 1985). Shneiderman (1986) reported that people took almost half as long again to use online documentation as they did to use the same information in hard-copy form. It appears that the advantages associated with a paper format outweigh those associated with an online format.

Is online documentation or help better than no hard copy manual? Yes, concluded Cohill and Williges (1985). Task time and errors were reduced when a system version with a help facility was compared to the same system without one.

Is a well-designed help facility better than a poorly designed one? Magers (1983) found that a well-designed one was better. Good writing, task orientation, context sensitivity, and good examples all contribute to good online help.

Does online help result in faster problem solving? No, found Czaja et al., (1986) and Elkerton and Williges (1984). Elkerton (1988) suggests that implementation of help or online documentation is made difficult by several factors. First, workers tend to be task or goal oriented. Detailed information on how to operate the system to perform a specific task is often lacking, documentation often only referencing commands and functions. Second, people tend to be active learners who learn best by doing rather than by passively reading documentation or training materials. Computer-presented material does not easily keep the user active and involved. Third, current practices in software design consist of iterative design with extensive user testing. Usability problems to be solved through online documentation or help cannot be finally resolved until after the user interface is fully implemented. Last, online documentation or help is not often viewed as an integral part of interface design. It is often thought of as a remedy for poor design.

In conclusion, the evidence indicates that some kind of online help or documentation is necessary. The style, structure, and writing of the materials are crucial to its effectiveness, it should be goal or task oriented, and it should keep the user active. Online and hard copy documentation should also supplement, not duplicate, each other.

Selective prompting. Prompting is instructional information. It takes the form of messages or other advice, such as the values to be keyed into a field. Prompting is also the system's way of requesting additional or corrected information, or of guiding users step by step through tasks.

Inexperienced users find prompting a valuable aid in learning a system. Experienced users, however, often find prompting undesirable. It slows them down, then adds "noise" to the screen, and reduces the amount of working information that can be displayed at one time.

Ideally, prompting should be available only as needed. People should be able to selectively or completely turn prompting on or off as needed. As an alternative, two separate sets of screens could be made available, one with prompts, the other without.

Help Facility

The most common form of online documentation is the help system. The overall objective of a help facility is to assist people in recalling what to do. Its benefits include improving the usability of a system, providing insurance against design flaws that may develop, and accommodating user differences that may exist (novice vs. expert). Typical methods of invoking help include: through a typed command, a Help key or pushbutton, or selecting a help option from a multiple-item menu.

Although some studies have found a help system can aid performance (Borenstein, 1985; Magers, 1983), the specific design characteristics that enhance an online help are still relatively unknown (Elkerton, 1988; Elkerton and Palmiter, 1991). Elkerton and Palmiter identify three broad areas of help that must be addressed in creating a help: its content, its presentation, and its access mechanisms. Of these, presentation and access are best understood (see Elkerton, 1988; Kearsley, 1988; Wright, 1988). Knowledge about help content, however, is meager.

Elkerton and Palmiter propose that the content (and structure) of an effective online help can be specified using the GOMS model (Card, et al., 1983). Using GOMS, information is provided to the user on GOALS for meaningful tasks, on OPERATORS for actions required to be performed, on METHODS for accomplishing the goals, and where multiple interface methods exist, and on SELECTION RULES for choosing a specific method. Elkerton (1988) presents a set of suggested principles for online assistance (which he calls Online Aiding). These principles are reproduced in Table 15.2.

Some general guidelines for help are as follows:

Kind

- Collect data to determine what helps are needed.

Training

- Inform users of availability and purpose of help.

Availability

- Provide availability throughout the dialogue.
- If no help is available for a specific situation, inform the user as such and provide directions to where relevant help may exist.

Structure

- Make as specific as possible.
- Provide a hierarchical framework.
  - Brief operational definitions and input rules.
  - Summary explanations in text.
  - Typical task-oriented examples.

Interaction

- Provide easy accessibility.

- Leave the Help displayed until:
  — The user exits.
  — The action eliminating the need for help is performed.
- Provide instructions for exiting.
- Return to original position in dialogue when help is completed.

Location

- Minimize obscuring screen content.
- If in a window, position priorities are: right, left, above, and below.

Content

- Minimize the help's length.
- Develop modular dialogues that can be used to describe similar and dissimilar procedural elements of the interface.
- Provide step-by-step interface procedures to assist the user with specific problems.
- Provide procedural demonstrations of interface procedures to aid quick learning of simple operations.
- Provide information to help users select between multiple interface methods.
- Provide users with an understanding of representative tasks to increase their knowledge of when to apply specific skills.

Style

- Provide easy browsing and a distinctive format.
  — Contents screens and indexes.
  — Screen headings and subheadings.
  — Location indicators.
  — Descriptive words in the margin.
  — Visual differentiation of screen components.
  — Emphasized critical information.
- Concise, familiar, action-oriented wording.
- Reference to other materials, when necessary.

Consistency

- Provide a design philosophy consistent with other parts of the system.

Title

- Place the word "Help" in all Help screen titles.

Table 15.2. Suggested design principles for providing online advice based on the GOMS model.

Use GOALS in online aiding to do the following:

1. Describe what can be done in task-oriented terms (interface actions and objects) for improved initial skill learning.
2. Provide an adjustable level of detail on interface procedures for accommodating the information needs of a wide range of users.
3. Provide procedurally incomplete advice so that users can actively learn for improved long-term performance and understanding with the interface.
4. Provide feedback to users that may help in reminding them of appropriate procedures to use, particularly when recovering from errors.
5. Develop modular assistance and instructional dialogues that can be used to describe similar and dissimilar procedural elements of the interface.

Use OPERATORS in online aiding to do the following:

1. Describe simple actions, such as pressing specific keys or finding specific objects on the display, that are common to many interface procedures to assist the user in current task performance.
2. Provide detailed knowledge of interface procedures that inexperienced users can actively learn and that more skilled users can combine with other procedural knowledge to improve long-term performance and understanding of the interface.
3. Monitor user actions to provide context sensitive help or to diagnose user problems actively.

Use METHODS in on-line aiding to do the following:

1. Present step-by-step interface procedures to assist the user with specific problems.
2. Improve user understanding and acceptance of on-line advice.
3. Decrease the cognitive load of users who are learning a new interface task by providing an explicit procedure for users to follow.
4. Provide procedural demonstrations of interface procedures so that users can quickly learn simple operations.
5. Map sequences of users' actions to a reduced set of interface goals to help provide context-sensitive advice to users.

Use SELECTION RULES in on-line aiding to do the following:

1. Help users select between multiple interface methods.
2. Provide users with an understanding of representative tasks to increase their knowledge of when to apply specific interface skills.

From Elkerton (1988)

Guidelines for online help include:

Kind. Usability problems that exist should be systematically identified through testing and evaluation. Monitoring user actions can be a useful tool in identifying user problems. Online help can then be developed to address these problems.

Training. Inform users of the availability and purpose of helps. Never assume that it will be obvious.

Availability. Make help available at all points in the dialogue. It is especially critical that help be available consistently in all similar situations. For example, if one particular system menu has help, assure all menus provide a help. If no help is available for a specific situation, inform the user as such and provide directions to where relevant help may exist, including hard-copy materials.

Structure. The help response should be as specific as possible, tailored to the task and the user's current position. When accessed, the Help facility should be aware of the kind of difficulties a person is having and respond with relevant information. Only the information necessary to solve the immediate problem or to answer the immediate question should be presented. If the Help facility is unsure of the request, it should work with the user through prompts and questions to resolve the problem.

A Help facility should be multilevel, proceeding from very general to successively more detailed and specific explanations to accommodate a wide range of users. The first level should provide brief definitions and rules, simple reminders, and memory joggers sufficient for skilled users. The second level should incorporate more detailed explanations in a textual format. The final, and deepest, level should provide guidance in the form of task-oriented examples.

Interaction. A Help facility should be retrievable simply, quickly, and consistently by either a key action, selection, or command. Leave the Help displayed until the user explicitly exits the Help, or performs the action eliminating the need for help. Instructions for exiting the Help should always be provided. These may take the form of displayed pushbuttons, function keys, or something similar.

Help should not disrupt processing. Easy return to the point of the problem should be permitted. Ideally, the problem or work should be retained on the screen when Help is accessed, but this will not always be possible unless the system provides a windowing capability.

One potential danger of the Help facility, as Barnard et al. (1982) found, is that a person's recall of command operations is related to frequency of Help facility access; fewer Help requests were associated with better command recall. The researchers speculate that the availability of Help may become a crutch and lead to less effective retention. People may implement a passive cognitive strategy. A Help facility may influence performance in systematic and subtle ways.

Location. When a Help is displayed, minimize relevant obscuring screen content. If Help is displayed within a window, position priorities are right, left, above, and below.

Content. Minimize the Help's length, whenever possible. Carroll et al., (1986) recommend the development of help text in the form of "minimal manuals." These manuals are explicit and focus on real tasks and activities, and they have been found to be significantly better than traditional help texts (Black et al., 1987; Carroll et al., 1986).

Elkerton (1988) suggests that few Help users want detailed, fact-oriented knowledge such as a hierarchical list showing the syntax of a command. Instead, they want to know the methods to complete a task. Without knowledge of how to do things, users are left to browse through a wealth of information with little understanding of what may be useful. Hence, he recommends, among other things, providing the following:

- Step-by-step interface procedures to assist the user with specific problems.
- Procedural demonstrations of interface procedures to aid quick learning of simple operations.
- Information to help users select between multiple interface methods.
- Users with an understanding of representative tasks to increase their knowledge of when to apply specific skills.

Wright (1984) recommends that when procedural steps are presented, consecutive numbering will make them easy to follow.

Style. Provide easy browsing and a distinctive format. Often the exact location of information needed to answer a question cannot be definitely established. Providing information in a format that can be easily skimmed aids the search process and also helps the user become familiar with the information being presented. The following techniques enhance the skimming process:

- Contents screens and indexes.
- Screen headings and subheadings.
- Location indicators.
- Descriptive words in the margin.
- Visual differentiation of screen components.
- Emphasized critical information.

Wording should also be concise, familiar, and action oriented. Reference to outside material may be included in the Help text, especially if the help information cannot be provided in a concise way.

Consistency. The Help design philosophy should be consistent with the philosophy used in other parts of the system. This includes presentation techniques, style, procedures, and all other aspects.

Title. For easy identification, place the word "Help" in all Help screen titles.

16

Testing

The design of graphical screens is a complicated process. A host of factors must be considered and numerous tradeoffs made. Indeed, the design of some screens may be based on skimpy data and reflect the most "educated guess" possible. Also, the implications for some design decisions may not be fully appreciated until the results can be seen. To wait until after a system has been implemented to uncover any deficiencies and make any design changes can be aggravating, costly, and time-consuming. To minimize these kinds of problems, screens must be tested and refined *before* they are implemented. This is accomplished through creation, evaluation, and modification of a prototype in an iterative manner.

STEP 12—TEST AND REFINE THE SCREENS AS NECESSARY.

- Develop a prototype.
- Test the prototype through:
  - Checklists.
  - Structured observation.
  - Classic experiments.
  - Usability testing.
- Modify the prototype as required.
- Test the system.
- Evaluate the working system.

DEVELOP A PROTOTYPE.

A prototype is a simulation of the actual system. It should be interactive, allowing the user to key or select data using controls, navigate through menus, retrieve displays of data, and perform basic system functions. A prototype, however, need not be functionally complete, possessing actual files or processing data. By nature, it cannot be used to exercise all of a system's functions, just those notable in one manner or another.

A prototype should be capable of being rapidly changed as testing is performed. Today, many software support tools for prototyping are available that permit the prototype to be integrated directly into the application code.

TEST THE PROTOTYPE.

Testing of a prototype is an iterative process and must be planned in advance. It involves the following steps:

- Define which usability issues are to be tested.
- Design a test that will yield data relevant to those issues.
- Solicit, select, and schedule users to participate in the test.
- Conduct the test and collect relevant data.
- Analyze the data and generate redesign recommendations.

The functions tested are usually those:

- Most important to the system.
- Most representative of the system.
- Most problematical, their design foundation being less firm.

Several testing techniques are available.

A *checklist* summarizing screen design and layout requirements imposed by a system's standard or guideline document may be prepared. Individual screens may be evaluated for compliance. Failure to comply indicates a design modification is necessary.

A *structured observation* of users performing the tasks can be accomplished. Errors, confusion, frustrations, and complaints can be noted and discussed with the user. It is also useful to have the user "think aloud" about what they are doing. Look for patterns of problems with particular operations or displays that indicate redesign may be necessary.

Where two or more design alternatives exist, either of which may appear acceptable, a *classic experiment* may be developed to compare them directly. Two or more prototypes may be constructed, identical in all aspects except for the design issue (type of control, wording of an instruction, etc.). Speed and accuracy measures can be collected and user preferences solicited. The result will be objective measures of performance and subjective measures of user satisfaction, thereby permitting a more well-informed selection of the best alternative.

A *usability test* can be conducted to compare user performance against the performance goals previously defined (see Chapter 7). Specific tasks are performed by users, measures of performance taken, and the results compared with the stated goals. Failure to meet these usability design objectives will indicate redesign is necessary.

MODIFY SCREENS AS REQUIRED.

Prototypes must, of course, be modified based on the design recommendations made during testing. The testing process continues in an iterative manner until all problems are solved and criteria are met.

TEST THE SYSTEM.

After the prototyping is complete and all code written, a final system test must be performed to assure no software bugs exist and performance meets all specifications. The screens and interface must also be again tested to assure all established usability criteria are being met. The design steps and methods are identical to those for prototype testing.

SCREEN EVALUATION.

Testing never stops with system implementation. Screens, like any part of a system, must be continually evaluated to assure that they are achieving their design objectives. Problems detected can be corrected in system enhancements and new releases. The testing techniques used in prototype evaluation can also be applied in this design phase.

References

Apple Computer, *Human Interface Guidelines: The Apple Desktop Interface*, Addison-Wesley Publishing Company, Inc., Reading, MA, 1987.

Backs, Richard W., Walrath, Larry C., and Hancock, Glenn A., Comparison of Horizontal and Vertical Menu Formats. *Proceedings of the Human Factors Society—31st Annual Meeting*, 1987, Santa Monica, CA.

Baecker, R., and Small, I., Animation at the Interface, Laurel, B. (Ed.). *The Art of Human-Computer Interface Design*, Addison-Wesley, 1990, pp. 251–267.

Baecker, Ronald; Small, Ian; and Mander, Richard, Bringing Icons to Life. In *Proceedings: Human Factors in Computing Systems*, CHI '91, pp. 1–6.

Bailey, R.W., Ph.D., Is Ergonomics Worth the Investment? *Proceedings: World Conference on Ergonomics in Computer Systems*, pp. 37–108, Los Angeles, CA; Chicago, IL.; New York, NY; Amsterdam, The Netherlands; Dusseldorf, West Germany; Helsinki, Finland. Sept. 24–Oct. 4, 1984.

Bailey and Bailey Software Corporation, Protoscreens, Ogden, Utah, 1989.

Baker, J.D., and Goldstein, I., Batch vs. Sequential Displays: Effects on Human Problem Solving. *Human Factors*, 1966, 8: pp. 225–235.

Barber, Raymond E., *Response Time, Operator Productivity and Job Satisfaction*. Ph.D. dissertation, NYU Graduate School of Business Administration, 1979.

Barber, Raymond E., and Lucas, H.C., System Response Time, Operator Productivity and Job Satisfaction. *Communications of the ACM 26*, Nov. 1983, 11: pp. 972–986.

Barmack, J.E., and Sinaiko, H.W., *Human Factors Problems in Computer-Generated Graphic Displays*. Inst. for Defense Analysis. AD-636170, 1966.

Barnard, P., *Presuppositions in Active and Passive Questions*. Paper read to the Experimental Psychology Society, 1974.

Barnard, P.; Hammond, N.; MacLean, A.; and Morton, J., Learning and Remembering Interactive Commands. In *Proceedings: Human Factors in Computer Systems*, pp. 2–7. Gaithersburg, MD., March 15–17, 1982.

Benest, I.D., and Dukic, D., High-Level User-Interface Objects. *Designing and Using Human-Computer Interfaces and Knowledge Based Systems*, G. Salvendy and M.J. Smith (eds.). Elsevier Science Publishers B.V., Amsterdam, 1989, pp. 597–604.

Bennett, J.L., The commercial impact of usability in interactive systems, B. Shackel (ed.). *Man-Computer Communication, Infotech State-of-the Art*, Vol. 2, Maidenhead: Infotech International, 1979, pp. 1–17.

Bennett, J.L., Managing to meet usability requirements, J.L. Bennett, D. Case, J. Sandelin, and M. Smith (eds.). *Visual Display Terminals: Usability Issues and Health Concerns*, Englewood Cliffs, NJ: Prentice-Hall, 1984, pp. 161–184.

Bergman, Hans; Brinkman, Albert; and Loelega, Harry S., System Response Time and Problem Solving Behavior. *Proceedings of the Human Factors Society–25th Annual Meeting*, 1981, pp. 749–753, Santa Monica, CA.

Bigelow, C., Proceedings of the Typography Interest Group ACM CHI '85. *SIGCHI Bulletin*, 17(1), 1985, pp. 10–11.

Billingsley, Patricia A., Navigation Through Hierarchical Menu Structures: Does It Help to Have a Map? In *Proceedings of the Human Factors Society– 26th Annual Meeting*, 1982, pp. 103–107. Santa Monica, CA.

Billingsley, Patricia A., Taking Panes: Issues in the Design of Windowing Systems. *Handbook of Human-Computer Interaction*, M. Helander (ed.). Elsevier Science Publishers B.V. (North-Holland), 1988, pp. 413–436.

Billingsley, Patricia A., The Standards Factor: Catching Up With Committees. *SIGCHI Bulletin*, Volume 23, Number 1, January 1991, pp. 6–10.

Black, J.B.; Carroll, J.M.; and McGuigan, S.M., What kind of minimal instruction manual is most effective? *Proceedings of CHI+GI 1987*, New York: ACM, pp. 159–162.

Bly, Sara A., and Rosenberg, Jarrett K., A Comparison of Tiled and Overlapping Windows. *Proceedings CHI '86 Human Factors in Computing Systems*, pp. 101–105.

Boies, S.J., User Behavior on an Interactive Computer System. *IBM Systems Journal 13*, 1, 1974, pp. 1–18.

Bonsiepe, G., A Method of Quantifying Order in Typographic Design. *Journal of typographic research*, 1968, 2, pp. 203–220.

Borenstein, N.S., The design and evaluation of on-line help systems. Unpublished doctoral dissertation, Department of Computer Science, Carnegie-Mellon University, Pittsburgh, PA, 1985.

Bouma, H., Interaction Effects in Parafoveal Letter Recognition. *Nature, 226*, 1970, pp. 177–178.

Bower, G.H.; Clark, M.C.; Lesgold, A.M.; and Winenz, D., Hierarchical Retrieval Schemes in Recall of Categorical Word Lists. *Journal of Verbal Learning and Verbal Behavior*, 1969, 8: pp. 323–343.

Brems, Douglas J., and Whitten, William B., II, Learning and Preference for

Icon-Based Interface. In *Proceedings of the Human Factors Society–31st Annual Meeting*, 1987, pp. 125–129.

Brod, Craig, *Technostress: The Human Cost of the Computer Revolution*. Addison-Wesley Publishing Company, Reading, MA, 1984.

Brooke, J.; Bevan, N.; Brigham, F.; Harker, S.; and Youmans, D., Usability assurance and standardization—work in progress in ISO. *Proceedings IFIP Interact '90*, Cambridge, UK, August 17–31, 1990, pp. 357–361.

Brooks, R., Search Time and Color Coding. *Psychonomic Science*, 1965, 2:281–282.

Brown, C. Marlin, *Human-Computer Interface Design Guidelines*. Norwood, NJ: Ablex Publishing Co., 1988.

Burns, Michael J. and Warren, Dianne L., Formatting Space-Related Displays to Optimize Expert and Nonexpert User Performance. *Proceedings CHI '86 Human Factors in Computing Systems*, April 1986, pp. 274–280.

Bury, K.F.; Boyle, J.M.; Evey, R.J.; and Neal, A.S., Windowing Versus Scrolling on a Visual Display Terminal. *Human Factors, 24*, pp. 385–394, 1982.

Butler, T.W., Computer Response Time and User Performance. *ACM SIGCHI '83 Proceedings: Human Factors in Computer Systems*, Dec. 1983, pp. 56–62.

Cairney, P. & Sless, D., Communication Effectiveness of Symbolic Safety Signs with Different User Groups. *Applied Ergonomics*, 13, 1982: pp. 91–97.

Callan, J.R., Curran, L.E.; and Lane, J.L., Visual Search Times for Navy Tactical Information Displays (Report # NPRDC-TR-77-32). San Diego, CA: Navy Personnel Research and Development Center, 1977. (NTIS No. AD A040543)

Carbonell, J.R.; Elkind, J.I.; and Nickerson, R.S., On the Psychological Importance of Time in a Time-Sharing System. *Human Factors* 10, 1969: pp. 135–142.

Card, S.K., User Perceptual Mechanisms in the Search of Computer Command Menus. In *Proceedings: Human Factors in Computer Systems*, pp. 190–196. Gaithersburg, MD., March 15–17, 1982.

Card, S.K.; Moran, T.P.; and Newell, A., *The Psychology of Human-Computer Interaction*, Hillsdale, NJ: Lawrence Erlbaum, 1983.

Card, S.K.; Pavel, M.; and Farrel, J.E., Window-Based Computer Dialogues. *Human Computer Interaction—INTERACT '84*/B. Shackel (ed.). Elsevier Science Publishers B.V. North Holland IFIP, 1985, pp. 239–243

Card, Stuart; Moran, Thomas P.; and Newell, Allen, The Keystroke-Level Model for User Performance with Interactive Systems. *Communications of the ACM 23*, 1980, pp. 396–410.

Carroll, J.B., and White, M.N., Word Frequency and Age of Acquisition as Determiners of Picture Naming Latency. *Quarterly Journal of Experimental Psychology, 25*, 1973, pp. 85–95.

Carroll, J.M.; Thomas, J.C.; and Malhotra, A., Presentation and representation in design problem-solving. *British Journal of Psychology*, 71, 1980, pp. 143–153.

Carroll, J.M.; Smith-Kerker, P.L.; Ford, J.R.; and Mazur, S.A., *The Minimal Manual* (Research Report RC 11637), Yorktown Heights, NY: IBM T.J. Watson Research Center, 1986.

Carroll, John M., and Carrithers, Caroline, Blocking Learner Error States in a Training-Wheels Systems. *Human Factors*, 26(4), 1984, pp. 377–389.

Carter, R.L., Visual search with color. *Journal of Experimental Psychology: Human Perception and Performance*, 8, 1982, pp. 127–136.

Charney, D.H., and Reder, L.M., Designing interactive tutorials for computer users. *Human-Computer Interaction*, 2, 1986, pp. 297–317.

Christ, R.E., Review and Analysis of Color Coding Research for Visual Displays. *Human Factors* 17, No. 6, 1975, pp. 542–570.

Christ, R.E., and Teichner, W.H., Color Research for Visual Displays. *JANAIR Report No. 730703*, Department of Psychology, New Mexico State University, 1973.

Citibank, reported in *USA Today*, Arlington, VA 1989.

Clark, H.H., and Clark, E.V., Semantic distinctions and memory for complex sentences. *Quarterly Journal of Experimental Psychology*, 20, 1968, pp. 56–72.

Clark, H.H., and Card, S.K., Role of semantics in remembering complex sentences. *Journal of Experimental Psychology*, 82, 1969, pp. 545–553.

Cohill, Andrew M., and Williges, Robert C., Retrieval of HELP Information for Novice Users of Interactive Computer Systems. *Human Factors 27(3)*, 1985, pp. 335–343.

Cooper, A., Remark: Window viper. *PC World*, August 1985, pp. 25–37.

Cotton, Ira W., Measurement of Interactive Computing: Methodology and Application. National Bureau of Standards Special Publication 500–548, 1978, 101 pages.

Cuff, R.N., On Casual Users. *International Journal of Man-Machine Studies* 12, 1980, pp. 163–187.

Cushman, William H., Reading for Microfiche, a VDT, and the Printed Page: Subjective Fatigue and Performance. *Human Factors, 28(1)*, 1986, pp. 63–73.

Czaja, S.J.; Hammond, K.; Blascovich, J.J.; and Swede, H., Learning to use a word-processing system as a function of training strategy. *Behavior and Information Technology*, 5, 1986, pp. 203–216.

Dainoff, M.J.; Happ, A.; and Crane, P., Visual fatigue and occupational stress in VDU operators. *Human Factors*, 23, 1986, pp. 421–438.

Damodaran, L.; Simpson, A.; and Wilson, P., Designing Systems for People. *NCC*, Manchester and Loughborough University of Technology, 1980.

Danchak, M.M., CRT Displays for Power Plants. *Instrumentation Technology* 23, No. 10, 1976, pp. 29–36.

Davies, Susan E.; Bury, Kevin F.; and Darnell, Michael J., An Experimental Comparison of a Windowed vs. a Non-Windowed Operating System Environment. *Proceedings of the Human Factors Society—29th Annual Meeting*, 1985, pp. 250–254, Santa Monica, CA.

Dede, C., A review and synthesis of recent research in intelligent computer-assisted instruction. *International Journal of Man-Machine Studies*, 24, 1986, pp. 329–353.

Desaulniers, David R., and Gillan, Douglas J., The Effects of Format in Computer-Based Procedure Displays. *Proceedings of the Human Factors Society—32nd Annual Meeting*, 1988, pp. 291–295.

de Souza, F., and Bevan, N., The use of guidelines in menu interface design. In *Proceedings IFIP Interact '90* (Cambridge, U.K., August 27–31, 1990) pp. 435–440.

Dickey, G.L., and Schneider, M.H., Multichannel Communication of an Industrial Task. *International Journal of Production Research, 9*, 1971, pp. 487–499.

Digital Equipment Corp. *XUI Style Guide*. Order No. AA-MG20A-TE, Maynard, MA, December, 1988.

Dodson, D.W., and Shields, N.J., Jr., Development of User Guidelines for ECAS Display Design. (Vol. 1) (Report No. NASA-CR-150877). Huntsville, AL: Essex Corp., 1978.

Doherty, W.J., The Commercial Significance of Man-Computer Interaction. In *Man/Computer Communication*. Vol. 2, pp. 81–94. Maidenhead, Berkshire, England: Infotech International, 1979.

Dondis, Donis A., *A Primer of Visual Literacy*, The MIT Press, Cambridge, MA, 1973.

Donohoo, D.T., and Snyder, H.L., Accommodation during color contrast. In *Society for Information Display Digest of Technical Papers*, New York Palisades Institute for Research Sciences, 1985, pp. 200–203.

Draper, Stephen W., The Nature of Expertise in Unix. *Human-Computer Interaction–INTERACT '84*/B. Shackel (ed.) Elsevier Science Publishers B.V. (North Holland) IFIP, 1985, pp. 465–471.

Dray, S.M.; Ogden, W.G.; and Vestewig, R.E., Measuring Performance with a Menu Selection Human-Computer Interface. In *Proceedings of the Human Factors Society–25th Annual Meeting, 1981*, pp. 746–748. Santa Monica, CA.

Dunsmore, H.E., Using Formal Grammars to Predict the Most Useful Characteristics of Interactive Systems. In *Office Automation Conference Digest*, pp. 53–56. San Francisco, April 5–7, 1982.

Dunsmore, H.E., Designing an Interactive Facility for Non-Programmers, *Proceedings ACM National Conference*, 1980, pp. 475–483.

Durding, B.M.; Becker, C.A.; and Gould, J.D., Data Organization. *Human Factors* 19, No. 1, 1977: pp. 1–14.

Eason, K., *Man-Computer Communication in Public and Private Computing*. HUSAT Memo 173. Loughborough, Leicester, England, 1979.

Ehrenreich, S.L., Computer Abbreviations: Evidence and Synthesis. *Human Factors 27(2)*, 1985, pp. 143–155.

Elam, P.G., Considering Human Needs Can Boost Network Efficiency. *Data Communications*, October 1978, pp. 50–60.

Elkerton, J., and Willeges, R.C., The effectiveness of a performance-based assistant in an information retrieval environment. In *Proceedings of the Human*

Factors Society—28th Annual Meeting, Santa Monica, CA: Human Factors Society, 1984, pp. 634–638.

Elkerton, Jay, Online Aiding for Human-Computer Interfaces. *Handbook of Human-Computer Interaction*, M. Helander (ed.). Elsevier Science Publishers B.V. (North-Holland), 1988, pp. 345–364.

Elkerton, Jay, and Palmiter, Susan L., Designing Help Using a GOMS Model: An Information Retrieval Evaluation. *Human Factors*, 33(2), 1991, pp. 185–204.

Ells, J.G., and Dewar, R.E., Rapid Comprehension of Verbal and Symbolic Traffic Sign Messages. *Human Factors*, 21, 1979, pp. 161–168.

Engel, F.L., Information Selection From Visual displays. In *Ergonomic Aspects of Visual display Terminals*, E. Grandjean and E. Vigliani (eds.). London: Taylor and Francis Ltd, 1980.

Engel, S.E., and Granda, R.E., *Guidelines for Man/Display Interfaces*. IBM Technical Report, 19 December 1975. TR 00.2720.

Foley, J., and Wallace, V., The Art of Natural Graphic Man-Machine Conversation. *Proceedings of the IEEE* 62, No. 4, April, 1974.

Francik, Ellen P., and Kane, Richard M., Optimizing Visual Search and Cursor Movement in Pull-Down Menus. *Proceedings of the Human Factors Society—31st Annual Meeting*, 1987, Santa Monica, CA.

Frankenhaeuser, M., Psychoneuroendocrine Approaches to the Study of Emotion as Related to Stress and Coping. In *Nebraska Symposium on Motivation* (1978), edited by H.E. Howe and R.A. Dienstabier, pp. 123–161. Lincoln: University of Nebraska Press, 1979.

Frese, M.; Schulte-Gocking, H.; and Altmann, A., Lernprozesse in Abhangigkeit von der Trainingsmethode, von Personenmerkmalen und von der Benutzeroberflache (Direkte Manipulation vs. konventionelle interaktion). In W. Schonpflu/M. Wittstock (eds.), *Software-Ergonomie '87*, Tagung 11/1987 des German Chapter of the ACM, Berlin: Teubner.

Fromme, F., Incorporating the Human Factor in Color CAD Systems. *IEEE Proceedings of the 20th Design Automation Conference*, 1983, pp. 189–195.

Furnas, G.W.; Gomez, L.M.; Landauer, T.K.; and Dumais, S.T., Statistical Semantics: How Can a Computer Use What People Name Things to Guess What Things People Mean When They Name Things? In *Proceedings: Human Factors in Computer Systems*. Gaithersburg, MD., March 15–17, 1982.

Galitz, Wilbert O., CRT Viewing and Visual Aftereffects. *UNIVAC Internal Report*. Roseville, MN, 1 August 1968.

Galitz, Wilbert O., *User-Interface Screen Design*, QED Publishing Group, Wellesley, MA, 1992.

Gardell, B., Tjanstemannens Arbetsmiljoer (Work Environment of White-collar Workers). Preliminary report. The research group for social psychology work. Department of Psychology, University of Stockholm, Report No. 24, 1979.

Gaylin, Kenneth B., How are Windows Used? Some Notes on Creating an Empirically-Based Windowing Benchmark Task. *Proceedings CHI '86 Human Factors in Computing Systems*, pp. 96–100.

Geldard, F.A., *The Human Senses*. New York: John Wiley, 1953.

Gittens, D., Icon-Based Human-Computer Interaction. *International Journal of Man-Machine Studies*, 24, 1986, pp. 519–543.

Gould, John D. and Grischkowsky, Nancy, Doing the Same Work with Hard Copy and with Cathode-Ray Tube (CRT) Computer Terminals. *Human Factors, 26(3)*, 1984, pp. 323–337.

Gould, John D., How to Design Usable Systems. *Handbook of Human-Computer Interaction*, M. Helander (ed.). Elsevier Science Publishers B.V. (North-Holland) 1988, pp. 757–789.

Gould, John D.; Boies, Stephen J.; Meluson, Mia; Rasamny, Marwan; and Vosburgh, Ann Marie, Empirical Evaluation of Entry and Selection Methods for Specifying Dates. In *Proceedings of the Human Factors Society—32nd Annual Meeting,* 1988, pp. 279–283.

Greene, J.M., *Psycholinguistics: Chomsky and Psychology.* Harmondsworth, Middlesex, U.K.: Penguin, 1972.

Greene, Sharon L.; Gould, John D.; Boies, Stephen J.; Meluson, Antonia; and Rasamny, Marwan, Entry-Based Versus Selection-Based Interaction Methods. In *Proceedings of the Human Factors Society—32nd Annual Meeting—1988*, pp. 284–287.

Greenstein, Joel S., and Arnaut, Lynn Y., Input Devices. *Handbook of Human-Computer Interaction*, M. Helander (ed.). Elsevier Science Publishers B.V. (North-Holland), 1988, pp. 495–519.

Grudin, Jonathan, and Barnard, Phil, When Does an Abbreviation Become a Word? and Related Questions. *CHI '85 Proceedings*, pp. 121–.

Guastello, S.J.; Traut, M.; and Korienek, G., Verbal versus pictorial representation of objects in a human-computer interface. *International Journal of Man-Machine Studies*, 31, 1989, pp. 99–120.

Haines, R.M.; Dawson, L.M.; Galvan, T.; and Reid, L.M., Response time to colored stimuli in the full visual field (NASA TN D-7927). Moffett Field, CA: NASA. 1975.

Hair, D. Charles, Legalese: A Legal Argumentation Tool. *SIGCHI Bulletin*, Vol. 23, No. 1, January 1991, pp. 71–74.

Hall, Edward T., The Hidden Dimension, Anchor Books, New York, 1982, 217pp.

Halsey, R.M., and Chapanis, A., On the Number Absolutely Identifiable Spectral Hues. *Journal of Optical Society of America*, 41, 1951, pp. 1057–1058.

Harpster, Jeffrey L.; Freivalds, Andris; Shulman, Gordon L., and Leibowitz, Herschel W., Visual Performance on CRT Screens and Hard-Copy Displays. *Human Factors, 31(3)*, 1989, pp. 247–257

Hatfield, Don, Lecture at Conference on Easier and More Productive Use of Computer systems, Ann Arbor, MI, 1981, (In Shneiderman, 1986).

Haubner, P., and Benz, C., Information Display on Monochrome and Colour Screens. *Abstracts: International Scientific Conference on Ergonomic and Health Aspects in Modern Offices*, Turin, Italy, November 7–9, 1983, p. 72.

Haubner, Peter, and Neumann, Frank, Structuring Alphanumerically Coded Information on Visual Display Units. *Proceedings: International Scientific Conference: Work With Display Units*, Stockholm, Sweden, May 12–15, 1986, pp. 606–609.

Heckel, Paul, The Elements of Friendly Software Design. Warner Books, New York, NY, 1984, 205 pages.

Hendrickson, Jeffrey J., Performance, Preference, and Visual Scan Patterns on a Menu-Based System: Implications for Interface Design. In *Proceedings Human Factors in Computing Systems*, CHI '89, May 1989, pp. 217–222.

Herriot, P., *An Introduction to the Psychology of Language*. London: Methuen, 1970.

Hiltz, S.R., *Online Communities: A Case Study of the Office of the Future*. Ablex Publishers, Norwood, NJ, 1984.

Hiltz, Starr Roxanne, and Kerr, Elaine B., Learning Modes and Subsequent Use of Computer-Mediated Communication Systems. *Proceedings CHI '86 Human Factors in Computing Systems*, pp. 149–155.

Hulteen, Eric, in Walker, 1989.

Human Factors Society, American national standard for human factors engineering of visual display terminal workstations. Santa Monica, CA: Author, 1988.

Hutchins, Edwin L.; Hollan, James D., and Norman, Don A., Direct manipulation interfaces. In Norman, Don A., and Draper, Stephen W. (eds.), *User Centered System Design: New Perspectives on Human-Computer Interaction*, Lawrence Erlbaum Associates, Hillsdale, NJ, 1986.

International Business Machines, Software Design Principles. *Proceedings: Software Ease of Use Workshop*, Boca Raton, FL, Oct. 22, 1984.

International Business Machines, Systems Application Architecture. *Common User Access, Panel Design and User Interaction*, SC26-4351-0, IBM, Boca Raton, FL 1987.

International Business Machines, System Application Architecture. *Common User Access, Advanced Interface Design Guide*, SC26-4582, IBM, Cary, NC, 1989a.

International Business Machines, Systems Application Architecture. *Common User Access, Basic Interface Design Guide*, SC26-4583, IBM, Cary, NC, 1989b.

International Business Machines Corporation, *Systems Application Architecture Common User Access Advanced Guide to User Interface Design* (SC34-4289), 1991.

Johansson, G.; Aronsson, G.; and Lindstrom, B., Social, Psychological and Neuroendocrine Stress Reactions in Highly Mechanized Work. *Ergonomics* 21, 1978, pp. 583–599.

Johnson-Laird, A., They look good in demos, but windows are a real pain. *Software News*, 42, April 1985, pp. 36–37.

Karasek, R.A., Job Demands, Decision Latitude, and Mental Strain: Implications for Job Redesign. *Administrative Science Quarterly* 24, 1979, pp. 285–311.

Karasek, R.A.; Baker, D.; Marxer, F.; Ahlbom, A.; and Theorell, T., Job Design Latitude, Job Demands, and Cardiovascular Disease: A Prospective Study of Swedish Men. *American Journal of Public Health* 71, 1981, pp. 694–705.

Karat, John, Transfer Between Word Processing Systems. *Proceedings: In-*

ternational Scientific Conference: Work With Display Units, pp. 745–748. Stockholm, Sweden, May 12–15, 1986.

Karat, John, Evaluating user interface complexity. *Proceedings of the Human Factors Society—31st Annual Meeting*, 1987, pp. 566–570.

Kaster, Jürgen, and Widdell, Heino, The Effect of Visual Presentation of Different Dialogue Structures on Ease of Human-Computer Interaction. *Proceedings: International Scientific Conference: Work With Display Units*, Stockholm, Sweden, May 12–15, 1986, pp. 772–776.

Kearsley, G., *On-Line Help: Design and Implementation*, Addison-Wesley, Menlo Park, CA, 1988.

Keister, R.S., and Gallaway, G.R., Making Software User Friendly: An Assessment of Data Entry Performance. In *Proceedings of the Human Factors Society—27th Annual Meeting*, 1983, Santa Monica, CA, pp. 1031–1034.

Kiger, J.I., The Depth/Breadth Tradeoff in the Design of Menu Driven User Interfaces. *International Journal of Man-Machine Studies*, 1984, 20, pp. 201–213.

Kintish, W., Comprehension and Memory of Text. In *Handbook of Learning and Cognitive Processes*, edited by W.K. Estes, vol. 6. Hillsdale, NJ, Lawrence Erlbaum Associates, 1978.

Kolers, P., Some Formal Characteristics of Pictograms. *American Scientist*, 57(3), 1969, pp. 348–363.

Kopala, C.J., The Use of Color Coded Symbols in a Highly Dense Situation Display. *Proceedings of the Human Factors Society—23rd Annual Meeting*, 1981, Santa Monica, CA, pp. 736–740.

Kruk, Richard S., and Muter, Paul, Reading of Continuous Text on Video Screens. *Human Factors, 26(3)*, 1984, pp. 339–345.

Kühne, Andreas; Krueger, Helmut; Graf, Werner; and Merz, Loretta, Positive Versus Negative Image Polarity. *Proceedings: International Scientific Conference: Work With Display Units*, Stockholm, Sweden, May 12–15, 1986, pp. 208–211.

Lalomia, Mary J., and Happ, Alan J., The Effective Use of Color for Text on the IBM 5153 Color Display. *Proceedings of the Human Factors Society—31st Annual Meeting*, 1987, Santa Monica, CA, pp. 1091–1095.

Landauer, T.K., and Nachbar, D.W., Selection from Alphabetic and Numeric Menu Trees Using A Touch Screen: Breadth, Depth, and Width. *Proceedings CHI '85 Human Factors in Computing Systems*, pp. 73–78.

Ledgard, H.; Whiteside, J.A.; Singer, A.; and Seymour, W., The Natural Language of Interactive Systems. *Communications of the ACM 23*, No. 10, Oct. 1980, pp. 556–563.

Lee, Eric, and MacGregor, James, Minimizing User Search Time in Menu Retrieval Systems. *Human Factors, 27(2)*, 1985, pp. 157–162.

Lichty, Tom, *Design Principles for Desktop Publishers*, Scott, Foresman and Company, Glenview, IL, 1989, 201 p.

Liebelt, L.S.; McDonald, J.E.; Stone, J.D.; and Karat, J., The Effect of Organization on Learning Menu Access. In *Proceedings of the Human Factors Society—26th Annual Meeting*, 1982, Santa Monica, CA, pp. 546–550.

Lodding, K., Iconic Interfacing. *IEEE Computer Graphics and Applications*, 3(2), March/April 1983, pp. 11–20.

Loftus, E. F.; Freedman, J.L.; and Loftus, G.R., Retrieval of Words from Subordinate and Supraordinate Categories in Semantic Hierarchies. *Psychonomic Science*, 1970, pp. 235–236.

Luria, S.M.; Neri, David F.; and Jacobsen, Alan R., The Effects of Set Size on Color Matching Using CRT Displays. *Proceedings of the Human Factors Society—30th Annual Meeting*, 1986, Santa Monica, CA, pp. 49–61.

MacKenzie, J. Scott; Sellen, Abigail; and Buxton, William, A Comparison of Input Devices in Elemental Pointing and Dragging Tasks. In *Proceedings Human Factors in Computing Systems, CHI '91*, 1991, pp. 161–166.

Magers, Celeste S., An Experimental Evaluation on On-Line HELP for Non-Programmers. *Proceedings CHI '83 Human Factors in Computing Systems*, pp. 277–281.

Maguire, M.C., A Review of Human Factors Guidelines and Techniques for the Design of Graphical Human-Computer Interfaces. *Comput & Graphics*, Vol. 9, No. 3, 1985, pp. 221–235.

Mayhew, Deborah J., *Principles and Guidelines in Software User Interface Design*, Prentice Hall, Englewood Cliffs, NJ, 1992.

Mallory, K., et al., Human engineering guide to control room evaluation. Essex Corporation. Technical Report NUREG/CR-1580, Alexandria, VA, July 1980.

Mann, T.L., and Schnetzler, L.A., Evaluation of formats for aircraft control/display units. *Applied Ergonomics*, 17.4, 1986, pp. 265–270.

Marcus, Aaron, Icon design requires clarity, consistency. *Computer Graphics Today*, November 1984.

Marcus, Aaron, Proper color, type use improve instruction. *Computer Graphics Today*, 1986A.

Marcus, Aaron, Ten Commandments of Color. *Computer Graphics Today*, 1986B.

Marcus, Aaron, *Graphic Design for Electronic Documents and User Interfaces*, ACM Press, New York, NY, 263 p., 1992.

Martin, J. *Design of Man-Computer Dialogues*. Englewood Cliffs, NJ: Prentice-Hall, 1973.

Matthews, M.L., and Mertins, K., The influence of color on visual search and subjective discomfort using CRT displays. In *Proceedings of the Human Factors Society—31st Annual Meeting*, 1987, Santa Monica, CA: Human Factors Society, pp. 1271–1275.

Matthews, M.L., and Mertins, K., Working with color CRTs: Pink eye, yellow fever, and feeling blue. In *Proceedings of the Ergonomics Society's 1988 Annual Conference*, E.D. Megaw (ed.). London: Taylor & Francis, pp. 228–233.

Matthews, Michael L.; Lovasik, John V.; and Mertins, Karen, Visual Performance and Subjective Discomfort in Prolonged Viewing of Chromatic Displays. *Human Factors*, 31(3), 1989, pp. 259–271.

Mayer, Richard E., From Novice to Expert. *Handbook of Human-Computer*

Interaction, M. Helander (ed.). Elsevier Science Publishers B.V. (North-Holland) 1988, pp. 569–580.

McDonald, J.E.; Stone, J.D.; and Liebelt, L.S., Searching for Items in Menus: The Effects of Organization and Type of Target. In *Proceedings of the Human Factors Society—27th Annual Meeting*, 1983, Santa Monica, CA, pp. 834–837.

McTyre, John H., and Frommer, W. David., Effects of Character/Background Color Combinations on CRT Character Legibility. *Proceedings of the Human Factors Society—29th Annual Meeting*, 1985, Santa Monica, CA, pp. 779–781.

Microsoft Corporation, *The Windows Interface: An Application Design Guide*, Microsoft Press, 1992.

Microswitch (A Honeywell Division), *Applying Manual Controls and Displays: A Practical Guide to Panel Design*, Freeport, IL, 1984.

Miller, D.P., The Depth/Breadth Tradeoff in Hierarchical Computer Menus. In *Proceedings of the Human Factors Society—25th Annual Meeting*, 1981, Santa Monica, CA.

Miller, G.A., The Magical Number Seven, Plus or Minus Two: Some Limits on our Capability for Processing Information. *Psychological Science 63*, 1956, pp. 81–97.

Miller, L.A., and Thomas, J.C., Behavioral Issues in the Use of Interactive Systems. *International Journal of Man-Machine Studies 9*, No. 5, Sept. 1977, pp. 509–536.

Miller, L.H., A Study in Man-Machine Interaction. *Proceedings of the National Computer Conference*, 46, AFIPS Press, Montvale, NJ, 1977, pp. 409–421.

Mitchell, Jeffrey, and Shneiderman, Ben, Dynamic Versus Static Menus: An Exploratory Comparison. *SIGCHI Bulletin*, Vol. 20, No. 4, April 1989, pp. 33–37.

Mosier, J.N., and Smith, S.L., Application of guidelines for designing user interface software. *Behaviour and Information Technology 5*, 1 (January–March 1986) pp. 39–46.

Moskel, Sonya; Erno, Judy; and Shneiderman, Ben, Proofreading and Comprehension of Text on Screens and Paper. *University of Maryland Computer Science Technical Report*, June 1984.

Murch, G., The Effective Use of Color: Physiological Principles. Tektronix, Inc. 4 p., 1983.

Murch, G., The Effective Use of Color: Perceptual Principles. Tektronix, Inc. 6 p., 1984.

Muter, Paul; Latremouille, S.A.; Treurniet, W.C.; and Beam, P., Extended Reading of Continuous Text on Television Screens. *Human Factors 24*, 1982, pp. 501–508.

Myers, B., The User Interface for Sapphire. *IEEE Computer Graphics and Applications*, 4(12), 1984, pp. 13–23.

Myers, B., The Importance of Percent-Done Progress Indicators for Computer-Human Interfaces. *Proceedings of CHI '85*, 1985, pp. 11–17.

Nelson, Ted, Interactive systems and the design of virtuality. *Creative Computing*, Vol. 6, No. 11 (November 1980), 56 ff., and Vol. 6, No. 12 (December 1980), 94 ff.

Nickerson, R.S., Man-Computer Interaction: A Challenge for Human Factors Research. In *IEEE Transactions of Man-Machine Systems*, MSS-10, No. 4, Dec. 1969.

Nielsen, Jakob; Mack, Robert L.; Bergendorff, Keith H.; and Grischkowsky, Nancy L., Integrated Software Usage in the Professional Work Environment: Evidence from Questionnaires and Interviews. *Proceedings CHI '86 Human Factors in Computing Systems*, pp. 162–167.

Nolan, Peter R., Designing Screen Icons: Ranking and Matching Studies. *Proceedings of the Human Factors Society 33rd Annual Meeting*, 1989, pp. 380–84.

Open Software Foundation, OSF/Motif Style Guide, Prentice Hall, Englewood Cliffs, New Jersey, 1991.

Ortega, Kerry A., Problem-Solving: Expert/Novice Differences, *Factors Society Bulletin*, Vol. 32, No. 3, March 1989.

Ostberg, O., Accommodation and visual fatigue in display work. In *Ergonomics Aspects of Video Display Terminals*, E. Grandjean and E. Vigliana (eds.). London: Taylor & Francis, 1982, pp. 41–52.

Paap, Kenneth R., and Roske-Hofstrand, Renate J., The Optimal Number of Menu Options per Panel. *Human Factors, 28(4)*, 1986, pp. 377–385.

Paap, Kenneth R., and Roske-Hofstrand, Renate J., Design of Menus. In *Handbook of Human-Computer Interaction*, M. Helander (ed.). Elsevier Science Publishers B.V. (North-Holland), 1988, pp. 205–235.

Paradies, Mark, Root Cause Analysis and Human Factors. *Human Factors Bulletin*, 34(8), August 1991, pp. 1–4.

Parton, Diana; Huffman, Keith; Pridgen, Patty; Norman, Kent; and Shneiderman, Ben, Learning a Menu Selection Tree: Training Methods Compared. *Behaviour and Information Technology 4*, 2, 1985, pp. 81–91.

Parkinson, Stanley R.; Sisson, Norwood; and Snowberry, Kathleen, Organization of Broad Computer Menu Displays. *International Journal Man-Machine Studies, 23*, 1985, pp. 689–697.

Pastoor, Siegmund, Legibility and Subjective Preference for Color Combinations in Text. *Human Factors*, 32, (2), 1990, pp. 157–171.

Perlman, Gary, Making the Right Choices with Menus. *Human Computer Interaction—INTERACT '84/B*. Shackel (ed.). Elsevier Science Publishers B.V. (North Holland) IFIP, 1985, pp. 317–321.

Pinkus, A.R., The effects of color and contrast on target recognition performance using monochromatic television displays (Report AFAMRL-TR-82-9). Wright-Patterson AFB, OH: AFAMRL, 1982.

Pokorny, J.; Graham, C.H.; and Lanson, R.N., Effects of wavelength on foveal grating acuity. *Journal of the Optical Society of America*, 58, 1410, 1968.

Polya, G., *How to Solve It*. Doubleday, New York, 1957.

Post, D.I., Effects of color on CRT symbol legibility. *SID Digest*, 16, 1985, pp. 196–199.

Pulat, B.M., and Nwankwo, H.H., Formatting alphanumeric CRT displays. *INT. J. Man-Machine Studies*, 26, 1987, pp. 567–580.

Quinn, Lisa, and Russell, Daniel M., Intelligent Interfaces: User Models and Planners. *Proceedings, CHI '86 Human Factors in Computing Systems*, pp. 314–318.

Quintanar, Leo R.; Crowell, Charles R.; and Pryor, John B., Human-Computer Interaction: A Preliminary Social Psychological Analysis. *Behavior Research Methods & Instrumentation 14,2*, 1982, pp. 210–220.

Radl, G.W., Experimental investigations for optimal presentation mode and colors of symbols on the CRT screen. *Ergonomics Aspects of Video Display Terminals*, E. Grandjean and E. Vigliana (eds.). London: Taylor & Francis, 1980, pp. 127–135.

Radl, G.W., Optimal presentation mode and colors of symbols on VDU's. *Health Hazards of VDT's?*, B.G. Pearce (ed.). Chichester, England: Wiley, 1984, pp. 157–168.

Reed, A.V., Error-Correcting Strategies and Human Interaction with Computer Systems. In *Proceedings: Human Factors in Computer Systems*, Gaithersburg, MD., March 15–17, 1982, pp. 236–238.

Rehe, R.F., *Typography: How to Make It More Legible*. Carmel, IN.: Design Research International, 1974.

Remington, Roger, and Williams, Douglas, On the Selection and Evaluation of Visual Display Symbology: Factors Influencing Search and Identification Times. *Human Factors, 28(4)*, 1986, pp. 407–420.

Robert, Jean-Marc, Some Highlights of Learning by Exploration. *Proceedings: International Scientific Conference: Work With Display Units*, Stockholm, Sweden, May 12–15, 1986, pp. 348–353.

Roemer, J., and Chapanis, A., Learning Performance and Attitudes as a Function of the Reading Grade Level of a Computer-presented Tutorial. In *Proceedings: Human Factors in Computer Systems*, Gaithersburg, MD., March 15–17, 1982, pp. 239–244.

Rogers, Y., Icons at the Interface: Their Usefulness. *Interacting with Computers: The Interdisciplinary Journal of Human-Computer Interaction*, 1, no. 1, April 1989, pp. 105–17.

Savage, R.E.; Habinek, J.K.; and Blackstad, N.J., An Experimental Evaluation of Input Field and Cursor Combinations. In *Proceedings of the Human Factors Society—26th Annual Meeting*, 1982, Santa Monica, CA, pp. 629–633.

Schleifer, Lawrence M., Effects of VDT/Computer System Response Delays and Incentive Pay on Mood Disturbances and Somatic Discomfort. *Proceedings: International Scientific Conference: Work With Display Units*, Stockholm, Sweden, May 12–15, 1986, pp. 447–451.

Schwarz, Elmar; Beldie, Ian P.; and Pastoor, Siegmund, A Comparison of Paging and Scrolling for Changing Screen Contents by Inexperienced Users. *Human Factors, 25(3)*, 1983, pp. 279–282.

Seppala, Pentti, and Salvendy, Gavriel, Impact of Depth of Menu Hierarchy on Performance Effectiveness in a Supervisory Task: Computerized Flexible Manufacturing System. *Human Factors, 27(6)*, 1985, pp. 713–722.

Shackel, B., The concept of usability. *Proceedings of IBM Software and Information Usability Symposium*, Poughkeepsie, NY, 15–18 September, 1981, pp. 1–30; and in J.L. Bennet, D. Case, J. Sandelin, and M. Smith (eds.). *Visual Display Terminals: Usability Issues and Health Concerns*. Engle wood Cliffs, NJ: Prentice-Hall, 1984, pp. 45–88.

Shackel, Brian, Usability—Context, Framework, Definition, Design and Evaluation. *Human Factors for Informatics Usability*, B. Shackel and S.J. Richardson (eds.). Cambridge University Press, 1991, pp. 21–37.

Shannon, C.E., and Weaver, W., *The Mathematical Theory of Communication*. Urbana, IL: The University of Illinois Press, 1949.

Shneiderman, B., The Future of Interactive Systems and the Emergence of Direct Manipulation. *Behaviour and Information Technology, I*, 1982, pp. 237–256.

Shneiderman, B., Human-computer interaction research at the University of Maryland. *SIGCHI Bulletin*, 17, 1986, pp. 27–32.

Shneiderman, B., and Margono, S., A study of File Manipulation by Novices Using Commands vs. Direct Manipulation. *Proceedings of 26th Annual Technical Symposium of the Washington, DC. Chapter of the ACM*. Gaithersburg, MD: National Bureau of Standards, 1987.

Shneiderman, Ben, Control Flow and Data Structure Documentation: Two Experiments. *Communications of the ACM*, Vol. 25, No. 1, Jan. 1982A, pp. 55–63.

Shneiderman, Ben, System Message Design: Guidelines and Experimental Results, in Badre, A. and Shneiderman, B. (Editors). *Directions in Human / Computer Interaction*, Ablex Publishers, Norwood, NJ, 1982B, pp. 55–78.

Shneiderman, Ben, *Designing the User Interface: Strategies for Effective Human- Computer Interaction*. Addison-Wesley Publishing Co., Reading, MA, 1987, pp. 448.

Shneiderman, Ben; Mayer, R.; McKay, D.; and Heller, P., Experimental Investigations of the Utility of Detailed Flowcharts in Programming. *Communications of the ACM*, Vol. 20, 1977, pp. 373–381.

Sidorsky, R.C., Color Coding in Tactical Displays: Help or Hindrance. *Army Research Institute Research Report*, 1982.

Sivak, J.G., and Woo, G.C., Color of visual display terminals and the eye: Green VDT's provoke the optimal stimulus to accommodation. *American Journal of Optometry and Physiological Optics*, 60, 1983, pp. 640–642.

Smith, D., Faster Is Better—A Business Case for Subsecond Response Time. *Computerworld*, 1983.

Smith, D.C., Harslem, E.F., Irby, C.H., Kimball, R.B., and Verplank, W.L., Designing the Star User Interface. *Byte,* April 1982.

Smith, R.B. (1987) Experiences with the Alternate Reality Kit. An example of the tension between literalism and magic. *Proceedings of the CHI'87 Human Factors in Computing Systems Conference*. New York: Association for Computing Machinery, pp. 61–67.

Smith, Wanda, Computer Color: Psychophysics, Task Application, and Aesthetics. *Proceedings: International Scientific Conference: Work With Display Units*, Stockholm, Sweden, May 12–15, 1986, pp. 561–564.

Smith, Wanda, Standardizing Colors for Computer Screens. *Proceedings of the Human Factors Society—32nd Annual Meeting,* 1988, pp. 1381–1385.

Snowberry, K.; Parkinson, S.R.; and Sisson, N., Computer Display Menus. *Ergonomics,* 26, 1983, pp. 699–712.

Spiliotopoulos, V., and Shackel, B., Towards a Computer Interview Acceptable to the Naive User. *International Journal of Man-Machine Studies 14,* 1981, pp. 77–90.

Stern, Kenneth R., An Evaluation of Written, Graphics, and Voice Messages in Proceduralized Instructions. *Proceedings of the Human Factors Society—28th Annual Meeting,* 1984, pp. 314–318, Santa Monica, CA.

Stewart, T.F.M., Displays and the Software Interface. *Applied Ergonomics,* Sept. 1976.

Streveler, D.J., and Wasserman, A.I. Quantitative measures of the spatial properties of screen designs. In *Proceedings of Interact '84 Conference on Human-Computer Interaction,* England, Sept. 1984.

Sun Microsystems, Inc., *Open Look™ Graphical User Interface Application Style Guidelines,* Addison-Wesley, Reading, MA, 1990.

Taylor, I.A., Perception and Design. *Research Principles and Practices in Visual Communication,* J. Ball and F.C. Pyres (eds.). Association for Educational Communication and Technology, 1960, pp. 51–70.

Tedford, W.H.; Berquist, S.L.; and Flynn, W.E., The Size-Color Illusion. *Journal of General Psychology 97,* No. 1, July 1977, pp. 145–149.

Teitelbaum, Richard C., and Granda, Richard, The Effects of Positional Constancy on Searching Menus for Information. *Proceedings CHI '83 Human Factors in Computer Systems.* pp. 150–153.

Tetzlaff, Linda, and Schwartz, David R., The Use of Guidelines in Interface Design. In *Conference Proceedings: Human Factors in Computing Systems,* CHI '91, 1991, pp. 329–334.

Thacker, Pratapray (Paul), Tabular Displays: A Human Factors Study. *CSTG Bulletin,* 14, (1) Human Factors Society, 1987, p. 13.

Thovtrup, Henrik, and Nielsen, Jakob, Assessing the Usability of a User Interface Standard. In *Conference Proceedings: Human Factors in Computing Systems,* CHI '91, 1991, pp. 335–342.

Tinker, M.A., Prolonged Reading Tasks in Visual Research. *Journal of Applied Psychology 39,* 1955, pp. 444–446.

Tombaugh, J.W.; Paynter, B.; Dillon, R.F., Command and Graphic Interfaces: User Performance and Satisfaction. *Designing and Using Human-Computer Interfaces and Knowledge Based Systems,* G. Salvendy and M.J. Smith (eds.). Elsevier Science Publishers B.V., Amsterdam, 1989, pp. 369–375.

Treisman, A., Perceptual Grouping and Attention in Visual Search for Features and for Objects. *Journal of Experimental Psychology: Human Perception and Performance, 8,* 1982, pp. 194–214.

Trollip, Stanley, and Sales, Gregory, Readability of Computer-Generated Fill-Justified Text. *Human Factors 28(2),* 1986, pp. 159–163.

Tufte, Edward R., *The Visual Display of Quantitative Information.* Graphics Press, Cheshire, CT, 1983, 197 pp.

Tullis, T.S., An Evaluation of Alphanumeric, Graphic and Color Information Displays. *Human Factors 23*, 1981, pp. 541–550.

Tullis, Thomas S., Designing a Menu-based Interface to an Operating System. *Proceedings CHI '85 Human Factors in Computing Systems*, pp. 79–84.

Tullis, Thomas Stuart, Predicting the Usability of Alphanumeric Displays. Ph.D. dissertation, Rice University, 1983, 172 p.

Turner, Jon A., Computer Mediated Work: The Interplay Between Technology and Structured Jobs. *Communications of the AACM 27*, 12, Dec. 1984, pp. 1210–1217.

Vartabedian, A.G., The Effects of Letter Size, Case and Generation Method on CRT Display Search Time. *Human Factors 13*, No. 4, 1971, pp. 363–368.

Verplank, Bill, Designing Graphical User Interfaces, *CHI'88 Conference on Human Factors in Computing Systems*, May 15, 1988.

Vitz, P.C., Preference for Different Amounts of Visual Complexity. *Behavioral Science 2*, 1966, pp. 105–114.

Walker, Marilyn A., Natural Language in a Desktop Environment. In *Designing and Using Human-Computer Interfaces and Knowledge Based Systems*, G. Salvendy and M.J. Smith (eds.). Elsevier Science Publishers B.V., Amsterdam, 1989, pp. 502–509.

Walker, R.E.; Nicolay, R.C.; and Stearns, C.R., Comparative Accuracy of Recognizing American and International Road Signs. *Journal of Applied Psychology 49*, 1965, pp. 322–325.

Wallace, Daniel, Time Stress Effects on Two Menu Selection Systems. *Proceedings of the Human Factors Society—31st Annual Meeting*, 1987.

Walraven, J., Perceptual artifacts that may interfere with color coding on visual displays. *Proceedings of NATO Workshop: Color Coded vs. Monochrome Electronic Displays*, C.P. Gibson (ed.). Farnborough, England: Royal Aircraft Establishment, 1984, pp. 13.1–13.11.

Wason, P.C., and Johnson-Laird, P.N., *Psychology of Reasoning: Structure and Content*. London: Batsford, 1972.

Watanabe, A.; Mori, T.; Nagata, S.; and Hiwatashi, K., Spatial sine wave response of the human visual system. *Vision Research*, 8, 1968, pp. 1245–1263.

Watley, Charles, and Mulford, Jay, A Comparison of Commands' Documentation: Online vs. Hardcopy. Unpublished student project, University of Maryland, Dec. 8, 1983, In Shneiderman, 1987.

Weiss, Stuart Martin; Boggs, George; Lehto, Mark; Shodja, Sogand; and Martin, David J., Computer System Response Time and Psychophysiological Stress II. *Proceedings of the Human Factors Society—26th Annual Meeting*, 1982, pp. 698–702.

Wertheimer, M., *Productive Thinking*, Harper and Row, New York, 1959.

Whiteside, John; Jones, Sandra; Levy, Paula S.; and Wixon, Dennis, User Performance with Command, Menu, and Iconic Interfaces. *Proceedings CHI '85 Human Factors in Computing Systems*, April 1985, pp. 185–191.

Wichansky, Anna M., Legibility and User Acceptance of Monochrome Display

Phospher Colors. *Proceedings: International Scientific Conference: Work With Display Units*, Stockholm, Sweden, May 12–15, 1986, pp. 216–219.

Williams, James R., The Effects of Case and Spacing on Menu Option Search Time. In *Proceedings of the Human Factors Society-32nd Annual Meeting,* 1988, pp. 341–343.

Wingfield, A., Effects of Frequency on Identification and Naming of Objects. *American Journal of Psychology, 81*, 1968, pp. 226–234.

Wopking, M., Pastoor, S., and Beldie, I.O., (1985) Design of user guidance in videotex systems. In *Proceedings of the 11th International Symposium on Human Factors in Telecommunications* (pp. 1/8–8/8). Cesson-Sevigne, France: Centre Commun d'Etudes de Television et Telecommunications/ Boston: Information Gatekeepers.

Wright, P., Problems to be solved when creating usable documents. Paper presented at IBM symposium on Software and Information Usability. Available as HF077 from IBM Hursley, Winchester, UK. 1981.

Wright, P., Issues of content and presentation in document design. *Handbook of Human-Computer Interaction*, M. Helander (ed.). Elsevier Science Publishers B.V. (North-Holland), 1988, pp. 629–652.

Wright, P., and Barnard, P., Just Fill in This Form: A Review for Designers. *Applied Ergonomics* 6, 1975, pp. 213–220.

Wright, P., and Lickorish, A., Proof-Reading Texts on Screen and Paper. *Behaviour and Information Technology 2, 3*, 1983, pp. 227–235.

Wright, Patricia, User Documentation. *Proceedings: World Conference on Ergonomics in Computer Systems*, 1984, pp. 110–126, Los Angeles, CA; Chicago, IL; New York, NY; Amsterdam, The Netherlands; Dusseldorf, West Germany; Helsinki, Finland, Sept. 24–Oct. 4, 1984.

Wright, Patricia, Designing and Evaluating Documentation for I.T. Users. *Human Factors for Informatics Usability*, B. Shackel and S.J. Richardson (eds.). Cambridge University Press, 1991, pp. 343–358.

Zahn, C.T., Graph-Theoretical Methods for Detecting and Describing Gestalt Clusters. *IEEE Transactions on Computers, X-20*, 1971, pp. 68–86.

Zwaga, H.J., and Boersema, T., Evaluation of a Set of Graphics Symbols. *Applied Ergonomics, 14*, 1983, pp. 43–54.

Zwahlen, Helmut T., and Kothari, Nimesh, The Effects of Dark and Light Character CRT Displays Upon VDT Operator Performance, Eye Scanning Behavior, Pupil Diameter and Subjective Comfort/Discomfort. *Proceedings: International Scientific Conference: Work With Display Units*, Stockholm, Sweden, May 12–15, 1986, pp. 220–222.

Index